Spirits of the Place

Spirits of the Place

Buddhism and Lao Religious Culture

John Clifford Holt

University of Hawai'i Press
Honolulu

© 2009 University of Hawai'i Press
All rights reserved
Printed in the United States of America
Paperback Edition 2011

16 15 14 13 12 11   6 5 4 3 2 1

Library of Congress Cataloging-in-Publication Data

Holt, John.
  Spirits of the place : Buddhism and Lao religious culture
/ John Clifford Holt.
      p.   cm.
  Includes bibliographical references and index.
  ISBN 978-0-8248-3657-3 (paperback : alk. paper)
  1. Laos—Religion.   2. Buddhism—Laos.
  3. Spirits—Laos.   4. Religion and sociology—Laos.
  I. Title.
  BL2067.H66 2009
  294.3'35—dc22
                                          2009014399

University of Hawai'i Press books are printed on acid-free
paper and meet the guidelines for permanence and
durability of the Council on Library Resources.

Designed by the University of Hawai'i Press production staff
Printed by The Maple-Vail Book Manufacturing Group

For My Teachers

Frank Reynolds

Joseph Kitagawa

Stanley Tambiah

Paul Claspers

Contents

(Plates follow page 194)

Preface

For thirty years my research and writing, as well as a good deal of my teaching, has focused on understanding Theravada Buddhists within the context of Sri Lanka's religious culture. For that reason many of my reflections throughout this study of Buddhism and religious culture in Laos are comparative.

Laos and Sri Lanka are important venues for Theravada's persistence in the contemporary world, but their historical experiences, of course, have been quite varied, and so the manner in which aspects of the *sasana* (Buddhist tradition) have been cultivated in each has varied significantly as well. Buddhism was first introduced to Sri Lanka from India in the third century BCE, more than a millennium before any form of Buddhism reached the geographic area in Southeast Asia that is now Laos and more than a millennium and a half before Sri Lanka's distinctive lineages of Theravada tradition were cultivated among the Lao. Moreover, the wider religious cultures within which Theravada has been domesticated in Laos and Sri Lanka respectively are also definitively unique when compared. Sri Lanka's proximity to India has resulted in more sustained Hindu influence. Though Hindu influence is notable in Laos, it is not nearly so emphatic, especially at the level of common lay religious culture. Instead, in Laos indigenous cults of *phi* (spirits) and *khwan* (vital essence) have predominated, while Hindu influence has been limited, though not exclusively, to royal elite circles. In any case the comparative comments interspersed throughout this book are aimed at determining what may be distinctive about Lao religious culture and its articulation of Buddhism, not to overly emphasize its historical dependence upon Sri Lanka, though Sri Lanka, while not very familiar to contemporary Lao people, has been sometimes lionized in Laos as the mother load of Theravada's origins and purity.

Over these past thirty years most of my travel itineraries to Sri Lanka, for extended or brief stays, were simply a combination of marathon flights between New England, where I make my home and teach, and South Asia, where I do my research and writing, without any stopovers in between. About ten years ago Sree Padma (my wife) and I decided that we no longer wanted to endure the travails of "airplane asceticism." We began to break our journeys in either Europe or

Southeast Asia. The Southeast Asian stopovers were very rewarding, especially in yielding perspectives on how Buddhism relates to various other religious cultures with which it has been long wedded. In December, 2004, we spent ten days in Luang Phrabang, Laos, where neither of us had ever traveled before. Our timing was fortuitous, for we avoided the catastrophic tsunami that ravaged the southeast coast of Sri Lanka (the very location where we had originally planned to stay with friends over that unforgettable Christmas holiday).

In anticipation of that first visit to Laos, I located relevant scholarly sources that could inform our impending visit. I easily discovered several helpful political histories and anthropological studies of Laotian society.[1] I already knew of detailed French scholarly studies of Lao culture published over many decades,[2] but I was surprised to discover, given the importance of Laos to the history of Theravada, that only a few specialized academic studies of recent origin focused on its religious culture per se. While Marcel Zago's masterful descriptive compendium of Lao religious ritual, written in French before the revolution of 1975, remains the standard reference work for Lao religious culture, it is, regrettably, not well distributed and now, inevitably, getting somewhat dated. Thus there is no single volume of an accessible sort that can introduce interested students of religion directly to Buddhist tradition within the social and historical contexts of Lao religious culture. That is one of the primary purposes of this book, although I am by no means an expert on the subject, and my work cannot begin to approximate the precision, intimacy, and scope of Zago's earlier work. Though I am on "temporary loan" from studies specific to Sri Lanka, my hope is that this book will be a gateway or introduction for some, a useful collation of knowledge for others, an interpretation that provokes further reflection for a few more, and a stimulus for future studies of Laos and its religious culture as the country becomes more accessible to outsiders and as its own intellectual resources develop further. I am under no illusions that this is a definitive work, but I do hope it will help more than it hinders.

While writing this book, I have tried not to overburden my reader with too much scholarly apparatus or specialized and esoteric discussions. As a consequence I am also quite sure that I have sometimes oversimplified, perhaps recapitulating some conventional views that to specialized scholars of Laos are, in fact, far more complex than I may have conveyed. I apologize in advance for my innocence. I have also resisted the temptation to organize my presentation exclusively from a historical perspective focused on the accomplishments or failures of Lao kingship and related colonial and postcolonial national politics. Other scholars who are far more competent in their knowledge of political history of Laos have written excellent historical overviews. Instead, this book, while broadly following a temporal outline from the second through the fourth chapters, is more topical and thematic in nature, taking up issues of some distinctive importance for understanding what is unique about Buddhism in its Lao milieu. So, the approach deployed throughout is not simply expository, but rather analytical and problem-oriented. In addition, I am not primarily interested in ascertaining a normative understanding of Theravada in Southeast Asia as it can be constructed from a study of its venerable textual traditions or from its leading monastic or royal apologists. Rather I am much more concerned with the manner in which Buddhist ideas and practices have been construed within more common and widespread circles.

While I have tried to write cautiously, I have also relied heavily upon many scholars who have preceded me. Consequently some of the book's sections are clearly synthetic. As early as the first several days of my extended stay in Luang Phrabang, I was acutely aware of my own limitations. In Sri Lanka, where I have spent many years living and conducting research, I studied and acquired Sinhala sufficiently to conduct fieldwork comfortably. I am also familiar with that country's scholarly resources (libraries, archives, and so forth) and count many people in its academic community among my close personal friends. Moreover, my knowledge of Sri Lanka's history is specific and extensive, generated from the research that made possible the writing of three substantial analytical books (1991, 1996, 2004) that cut across various historical eras. In Laos I was without any of these advantages; I have knowledge of Sanskrit, Pali, French, the general history and philosophy of Theravada Buddhism, and theory in relation to the history of religions, but only an extremely rudimentary (quite crude and circumscribed) understanding of spoken colloquial Lao. Indeed, after my first two weeks in Luang Phrabang, when it fully dawned on me how little I actually knew about Laos and its culture, how odd aspects of its Theravada Buddhism appeared to me, and when I simultaneously realized that finding people who could enter into intellectual discourses about Buddhism, culture, and society from an academic perspective would be extremely difficult, if not impossible, I was tempted to confess failure, pack up my stuff, and head for the familiar confines of Kandy to focus on a subject I could more confidently comprehend. But I did not. Following bouts of self-doubt, I finally came to the conclusion that being aware of what I did not or could not know could be advantageous. I subsequently set about reading many tracts of research in a number of areas of knowledge that I knew that I had no hope of learning firsthand by myself. I also came to know through this reading that there remain huge holes in what we know about Laos historically. I then redesigned and circumscribed my fieldwork into a program that I knew I could manage with a decent translator at my side. When I found that the senior monks of Luang Phrabang, those who have become ordained through undertaking the *upasampada* rite, were not especially forthcoming in my early conversations with them, for reasons I can now speculate about, I decided to concentrate on finding out what I could about Luang Phrabang's rather gregarious *samaneras* (monastic novices). Finally, I decided to write comparatively about what I saw in relation to what I already knew about Theravada and its religious culture in Sri Lanka. In the past the comparative method has been deployed often to ascertain commonalities between religious traditions. But I have made use of it here in order to determine differences. Thus I have done what I have done as a result of what I could do under the circumstances, given my various handicaps and given my past experiences as a scholar.

As the general scholarly situation now stands in relation to Laos, I do not think that it would be unfair to say, on the one hand, that many scholars working in the various subfields of the humanities and social sciences have a limited understanding of the Buddhist and Hindu religions, and, on the other hand, that many scholars of religion in Southeast Asia seem to have considered only very lightly the significance of the cultural and political history of the region. While what I offer in this book is certainly not a definitive study based on copious amounts of primary source analyses and original fieldwork research, it is written with a view of trying to bridge some of the existing (and in some cases yawning) gaps of understanding regarding the nature of Buddhism in Laos within the context of its religious and political cultures. At least this has been my aim.

Research and writing for this book were supported by a National Endowment of the Humanities Fellowship for College Teachers in 2006–2007, a Rockefeller Foundation Bellagio Study Center Residency in April and May, 2007, the Numata Chair of Buddhist Studies, which I held at the University of Calgary in the fall semester of 2006, and research funds made available by the Freeman Foundation allotted by the Faculty Resources Committee at Bowdoin College in 2004 and 2006–2007.

Acknowledgment of the many individuals who assisted me while I was living and working in Laos are omitted owing to the potentially sensitive nature of some information disclosed within this study. Exceptions to the anonymity of those who helped me in Laos are Joy and Jason Smith, who have since emigrated to Chiang Mai. They provided space, food, conversation, and encouragement during many hot days in Luang Phrabang. As for the many others who helped me, I wish to thank them all—translators, lay informants, *bhikkhus*, and *samaneras*—for their profound generosity of time and spirit. Here I also publicly assert that I am alone responsible for any and all information and interpretations given in this work.

Frank Reynolds, Justin McDaniel, Martin Stuart-Fox, and Grant Evans read through drafts of the manuscript. They should not be blamed for any errors I have committed or misconceptions I have stubbornly insisted on maintaining. Rather, their insights were extremely helpful in producing some of the virtues this book contains. I also wish to thank my longtime colleagues John Strong and Roger Jackson, who, along with Frank Reynolds and especially Sree Padma, supported and encouraged me to undertake this new direction in research and writing.

Finally, although he did not figure directly or recently in the formulation of this book, I wish to acknowledge and thank Stanley Tambiah, one of my teachers well over thirty years ago at the University of Chicago, who, in addition to Frank Reynolds, originally inspired me to consider the vast array of issues related to the study of Buddhist religious and political cultures in Southeast Asia.

Romanization and Diacritics

Romanization of the Lao language remains something of a scholarly adventure owing in part to attempts in the past by both French and English speakers to provide accurate phonetics. While quoting others in this book, I have retained their own romanization schemes. Thus, the reader is bound to encounter variable spellings for many Lao terms, such as in *muang, meuang,* or *muong.* In the end I decided to follow Grant Evans's example in transliteration. The Pali and Sanskrit transliterations herein are conventional, except that I have not used diacritics. (I wanted either to use diacritics in all of the languages or not at all and finally opted for the latter because of the hopeless condition in relation to Lao. My apologies for that too!)

All the photographs, both black and white and the color plates, were taken by me. The maps were created by Samuel Holt.

Introduction

Laos and Its Religious Culture

The political history and religious culture of Laos are exceedingly rich, a complex tapestry of interwoven strands. Culturally, bedrock "animistic" perceptions held by virtually all of its disparate peoples, including the majority Lao, have been layered over by Indic or Sinitic philosophical conceptions, social values, and political ideals. Other more specific and subtle religious, social, and cultural influences have come by way of the neighboring Khmer, Thai, Burmese, and Vietnamese, by the colonial French, and by the contemporary world of international tourism. Laos has never been easy to field conceptually. Thus, Goscha and Ivarsson introduced their superb collection of essays on how Lao political history has been constructed in this way:

> Many have seen Laos making a delicate "balancing act," an almost never-ending struggle between its two larger mainland Southeast Asian neighbors—Vietnam . . . and Thailand. . . . For some it is a Buddhist kingdom and a Marxist state. Others have analyzed it in terms of its position in Cold War Southeast Asian geopolitics and the seemingly endless wars occurring next door in Vietnam. It was the "next domino" to fall to communism, the "buffer" or the "linchpin" to holding the line for the "free world" against the "spread of communism" further into the region. Some writers continue to conceptualize Laos as a "special" part of larger French, Vietnamese, Indochinese or Thai worlds, with the Lao playing the role of "apprentices," if not "younger brothers." Others simply pass over Laos rapidly, a sideshow to seemingly more important histories. (2003: xi)

From considered comments like this, it seems as though Lao culture and society have not been often considered, especially by outsiders, as at the center of their own history. (Indeed, since some of what I say in this book about Lao religious culture arises out of comparison to what I know about Sri Lanka, I am not completely immune from this criticism either.)

That said, Goscha and Ivarsson also contend that although many Lao observers now regard the current political boundaries of Laos as unnatural, as a truncated by-product of French-Thai political machinations in the late nineteenth century, modern nationalist and Marxist historians have continued, nonetheless, to construct linear accounts of the "nation-state," accounts that attempt to take "Laos" far back into a hoary past. Some of these accounts of Lao history begin with considerations of mythic origins relevant only to the proto-formation of what later became the Kingdom of Lan Xang, which was centered first in Luang Phrabang and later in Vientiane. In the process of writing history in this manner, myth and tradition have been conflated to telescope a projected teleology, one firmly rooted in perspectives highly conditioned by interests vested in modern political history. The history of Laos, Goscha and Ivarsson aver, remains intensely contested, especially when the political present functions as a keen driver for an anachronistic reading of the Lao past. I have consciously tried to resist this.

While the past of Laos may be complex and contested, one of my primary methods for understanding Lao Buddhism and religious culture has been to situate my discussions within the vicissitudes of political history. I have done so because Lao religious culture cannot simply be equated with philosophical or cosmological abstractions, nor can it be understood only as an individual Lao's privately elected worldview or "belief system." On the other hand, religious culture need not be regarded cynically as only a disguised political ideology to legitimate claims to power. In the West our conceptions of religion often either overly emphasize doctrine, soteriology, or personal meaning or are aimed at asserting religion's functionality in relation to political process. Consequently, these conceptions of religion are frequently too restricted in scope to grasp the profundity of sociocultural dynamics in play, especially in a religious culture like the one that has unfolded in Laos.[1]

Mandalas

Out of this concern for fielding sociocultural dynamics, central to the first chapter of this study is a consideration of the mandala, known to most Western students of Buddhism for its significance in meditation practice and artistic expression. In those contexts mandalas are elaborate symbols that represent various spiritual realities of the cosmos to be internalized through concentrated meditative pursuit. The earliest Indian constructions are essentially "cosmograms," or spiritual maps of cosmic powers, for the mind to explore and penetrate. They function as didactic cues for processing phases of the enlightenment quest. The macrocosms of cosmic power that mandalas map, often portrayed as otherworldly "Buddha-fields" and their associated virtues, are meant to be realized microcosmically, or individually, within an increasingly clarified mind. The subjective conscious apprehension of what the mandala symbolizes eventually gives way to a direct perception of "objective reality" or "reality-as-it-is." The evolutionary development of mandalas as visual expressions of the Buddhist spiritual path can be observed in the increasing sophistication of Buddhist art in both northern and southern Indian traditions of material culture from the early centuries CE.[2]

There is also another dimension of the mandala's significance, however, that is less well known to most people, especially Western observers or practitioners of Buddhism and Hinduism. In early historic India, mandalas were also used as architectural and spatial designs for the construction of great Buddhist monuments built by pious Indian kings, laity, and monks, especially for the evolving forms of the Buddhist reliquary stupa. They were also used as blueprints for the great Hindu temples that accompanied the rise of *bhakti* devotional religion dedicated to the emergent great gods of Hindu tradition, Siva or Visnu (or less frequently, one of the forms of the goddess) from the middle of the first millennium CE onward. Conceived in mandalic form, these great Hindu temples were regarded by devotees as vibrant this-worldly seats of power for Siva or Visnu, places where their magnanimous powers of divine compassion could be petitioned. Moreover, they were comprehended as local reproductions of their deities' heavenly abodes (Mt. Kailasa and Mt. Vaikunta respectively). The central tower of the Hindu temple, containing in its base the *garbha grha* (sanctum sanctorum) of the deity, symbolized the center of the cosmos as well. Thus the power of the deity occupying this space was identified as the power within this world that sustains its vitality. The center of the cosmos, also symbolized by the central temple tower or the spire of the stupa, from both the Hindu but especially the Buddhist perspective, could also be regarded as a this-worldly Mt. Meru, the heavenly abode of Sakka (Sanskrit: Sakra; the Buddhist rendering of the Vedic deity Indra, the *devaraja* or "king of the gods").

Most of these great monumental constructions, at first Buddhist but then predominantly Hindu after the fifth century CE, were constructed by ambitious kings who had mustered the capacity to marshal the labor and material resources necessary for such elaborate constructions. Many of these kings, in turn, fashioned themselves as either *cakkavattins* (dharma-wielding kings descending from a lineage of the Buddha and destined eventually to become buddhas in their own right) or in the Hindu context as *devarajas* (this-worldly royal incarnations of the deities they worshipped). The temples that these Indian rulers constructed, often the palaces that they inhabited, and/or the royal cities that they built, were regarded as the pivots of a political mandala, the very center of the known, inhabited world, where power from the ultimate center of the cosmos flowed into and then throughout their realms, ritually orchestrated by a cadre of priests at their service. The Hindu king, then, was a this-worldly version of absolute cosmic power and the Buddhist king an embodiment of the dharma that the Buddha had perceived and then made known. Both represented themselves, through their regalia, temple projects, and ritual articulations, as consecrated vectors of supernatural force.

It is this last dimension of the mandala's significance that seems to have become politically normative in many of the overtly Hindu and Buddhist kingdoms of Southeast Asia, especially at Angkor, where the ideology flourished from at least the ninth (and probably earlier) through the thirteenth century CE. Power was conceived and then realized through a dynamic process of vertical and horizontal, centripetal and centrifugal flows, from the parallel otherworldly reality to this world, and from the center of the mandala to its peripheries, and from its peripheries to the center, channeled and directed in a pulsating fashion. Kingdoms, as well as their subrealms, were understood as mandalas, as mandalas within mandalas, and in many cases as overlapping mandalas.[3]

Discussions about mandala polity are a major focus of consideration in Chapter 1 when I discuss the religious elements of Lao political history from the fourteenth through the nineteenth centuries. But I will not argue that the political formations erected by the Lao were simply the result of imported notions of classical Indian statecraft. Indeed, the term mandala is not directly deployed in the Lao texts and inscriptions that refer to the political realms of Lao kingship. Rather, what I shall try to illustrate is that indigenous understandings of power incipient in the indigenous cults of "cadastral" deities, or "gods of the land" and ancestor veneration, provided the Lao with a conceptuality to field and then inflect Hindu and Buddhist principles of polity quite uniquely. That is, the perceived power attributed to Lao kingship was not simply a by-product of the mandala's transposition from Indian to Lao cultural regions. To understand power and its relation to "mandalic" space, I also discuss the indigenous conception of *muang* (a tributary political mode operating largely at the village level) and the various spiritual powers that attend to it.

One of the theoretical maxims often operating in my mind while I was researching this study was this: fundamental transformations in the political economy of a society are inevitably reflected in the dynamics of its associated religious culture. Chapter 1 begins with a focus on the construction of a religious polity among the Lao and ends with an account of its unraveling due to the competing political and military aspirations of the Burmese, Vietnamese, and Thai. The second chapter focuses on the transformations of religion in Laos that occurred with the impact of French colonialism and then with America's powerful military presence during the Vietnam War. These impacts may have been equally, if not more, traumatic than the disestablishment of the Lao Lan Xang kingdom. But what remains remarkable throughout all of these political changes is the persistence of the

Lao spirit cults, a fact that seems to challenge the verity of the maxim I have just articulated regarding how social, political, and economic change affects religious culture. Despite sweeping political paradigm shifts in Lao history, the spirits of the place have endured.

The arrival in Luang Phrabang of a new political regime in the fourteenth century is believed by many to have been accompanied by Sinhala (Sri Lankan) forms of Theravada Buddhism that eventually provided the ideological rationale for a consolidated and imperial Lao political mandala. But the consolidation of specifically *Buddhist* political power in Laos probably did not, in fact, occur before the sixteenth century, and only then as a consequence of heavy cultural influence emanating from the neighboring kingdom of Lan Na (the region surrounding contemporary Chiang Mai, Thailand). My basic point in this discussion, of course, is that political change in Laos was accompanied by challenges and transformations in religion as well. In Chapter 2 I shall also observe how the colonial presence of the French, replete with alternative ideological conceptions of "nation" and "religion," impacted some Lao religious sensibilities, not only in how religion would be regarded in relation to the state, but also in relation to the very notion of "religion" itself. An account of the effect of these French notions on some of the Lao elite, and the consequences of French colonial policies for rural highland "tribal" peoples,[4] provides background for one of the primary discussions in the third chapter of this study, which is concerned with how the Theravada Buddhist *sangha* has been impacted in the twentieth and twenty-first centuries by the rather spectacular political sea changes of the era.

Having commented on the influence of the French colonial presence, I then briefly discuss the American military intervention in Laos between the mid-1950s and 1975, when American forces were finally withdrawn from Southeast Asia, thereby signaling the U.S. defeat in the Second Indochina War. Laos was severely devastated by this war—some have said "bombed back into the stone age"—and became an unwitting casualty of what was, in hindsight, a seriously misguided American foreign policy in Southeast Asia. America's military intrusions into Laos, ostensibly in response to North Vietnamese incursions, contributed to a radical destabilization of the county that exacerbated deep political divisions within the Lao metropole, while at the same time further fostering a process of alienation within some of the highland "ethnic minority" communities of Laos, a process that had begun initially during the period of French colonialism. Both consequences, among the elites as well as among the people of the countryside, contributed significantly to the political chaos that ensued. The intensity of the American bombing of Laos, an effort intended to stymie the movements of North Vietnamese regiments into Laos and supplies into South Vietnam, was unprecedented in the history of warfare. American planes dropped more bombs on Laos than the combined total tonnage dropped on Germany and Japan in World War II, about two-thirds of a ton for every inhabitant in the country.[5] Moreover, the CIA's "secret war" against the North Vietnamese, in which predominately upland ethnic Hmong fighters, among other minorities and Thai mercenaries, abetted conditions that ultimately led to social and political disintegration on a national scale, radicalized many monks in the Buddhist *sangha*.

Addressing the situation in Laos during the contemporary postwar period in the third chapter, I attempt to answer the following questions. Was there a place for Buddhism within the emergent Marxist revolutionary state? What was the state's disposition toward indigenous religious culture?

In the fourth chapter I ask how the opening up of the country in the 1990s, signaled by Luang Phrabang's newly acclaimed status as a tourist-attracting UNESCO World Heritage Site, altered or began to affect the Buddhist monastic vocation and Lao religious culture in general. Thus throughout Chapters 2–4 I trace the contours of Lao political history to determine its significance for religious change.

Nevertheless, there is yet another set of questions that has preoccupied my attention: how is Buddhism related to Lao conceptions of spirits (*phi* and *khwan*)? How and why have these cults persisted? These questions have been answered in various ways over the centuries. Some, including various royalty and monks, have periodically declared that these two aspects of the religious culture should have nothing to do with one another or that when the two have been related, the result leads to distortions in Buddhist understanding. Indeed, one of the most powerful sixteenth-century Luang Phrabang kings, Phothisarat, attempted to eliminate the worship of *phi* at the great shrines and to replace these shrines with Buddhist temples. Some leading monastic intellectuals during the late French colonial period articulated a wholly rational form of "purified" Buddhist thought that also excluded the veneration of spirits. Finally, the leaders of the communist revolutionary Pathet Lao, who took over the country in late 1975, in following a line of Marxist-Leninist orthodoxy, also attempted to ban the veneration of *phi* by essentially criminalizing the practice and labeling it a matter of "superstition" that needed to be suppressed if the nation-state was to realize its destiny as a "scientifically based" socialist society. Some Western scholars, in addressing the question of how Buddhism has been related to spirit cults, have argued that they are two separate but coexisting religious systems. Others have averred that Buddhism historically encompassed, subordinated, and then accommodated the cults of the *phi* to form a unique "blend" of emergent religious culture.

This last view is similar to, though not exactly what I have advanced in two of my previous books on the topic of deity veneration and Buddhism in Sri Lanka's religious culture. In those studies I illustrated not only how deities of Hindu origin and a bodhisattva of Mahayana Buddhist origin were assimilated and then transformed within the dominant purview of Theravada tradition, but I also illuminated the manner in which the Sinhalese have interpreted the significance of such supernatural figures from a Buddhist perspective. That is, I tried to show how Buddhists have "read" or construed the significance of important elements of popular or folkloric religious culture, and how they have done so rather inclusively at that. Certainly that kind of task could also be appropriate in the Lao cultural milieu. But my sense is that this approach would leave our understanding still wanting in an important way. During my time in Laos I came to realize that many Lao have understood the Buddha, dharma, and *sangha* in their own particular ways because of assumptions imbedded in their indigenous cultic worship of *phi* (spirits). Instead of concentrating on how Buddhists have "read" aspects of popular religious culture that they have assimilated, including the veneration of *phi*, *khwan*, and ancestors, I have explored the matter from the other way around: how have important aspects of Buddhism been construed or "read" in light of persisting forms of understanding rooted in traditional Lao conceptions of "spiritual power"? I became especially interested in the significance of conceptions that have to do with understandings of "the power of a place." While this issue is addressed in a number of discussions throughout this study, I take it up directly in the concluding fifth chapter.

Laos: Some Basic Facts

Laos has the fewest number of people of any country in Southeast Asia. The 1995 census, the most recent reliable data available to me as I write, reported a population of 4,575,000. (In 2007 the population was approximately 6 million.) The 1995 population figure was less than half that of Cambodia, less than a tenth that of Burma, about 7 percent of Thailand's, and 6 percent of Vietnam's (Sisouphanthong and Taillard 2000: 12). When the total population of Laos's Southeast Asian neighbors (excluding China) is compiled, the population of Laos forms only about 2.5 percent of the total for the Indochina peninsula, or only one in forty people. Population density is less than nine per square km, making the country three times less densely populated than Cambodia, Burma, and Malaysia (Sisouphanthong and Taillard 2000: 28). The most significant reason that Laos is less densely populated than its Southeast Asian neighbors lies in the fact it is mostly mountainous. Spectacular ranges of granite lace its topography from north to south.

The Lao Loum people—those Lao citizens who speak the Lao language, traditionally have grown wet rice along the Mekong River and its many tributary basins, whose religious culture is dominated by Theravada Buddhism and spirit cults, and whose settlement patterns followed the *muang* configuration—account for little more than half the population. In popular parlance the Lao Loum are "the ethnic Lao." But if other ethnic groups in the Tai-Kadai ethnolinguistic family are included along with the Lao Loum, peoples such as the Putai and Leu, two-thirds of the population of Laos can be accounted for.[6] As Sisouphanthong and Taillard have noted in their *Atlas of Laos*: "This is far less, below the Tai-Kadai family in Thailand (estimated at 83%), the Mon-Khmer in Cambodia (87%), and the Vietnamese/Kinh in Vietnam (87%)" (12). Mon-Khmer peoples, of whom more than half are Khmu, make up 23 percent of the population while Tibeto-Burmans and Hmong (or Meo), who migrated into northern Laos from southern China in the nineteenth century, form between 7 and 8 percent. The population of contemporary Laos, therefore, is very heterogeneous. Indeed, forty-seven disparate ethnic groups are noted in the government's census.

The heterogeneity of the population makes the distribution and delivery of education and health services, let alone communication per se, extremely difficult for a country with such an undeveloped infrastructure. In areas where non-Lao Loum ethnic minorities dominate, the numbers of the school-age population in school is quite a bit less than in those regions where the "ethnic Lao" dominate. With a high rate of population growth (about 2 percent per year),[7] the expansion of quality education throughout the country will continue to be a major challenge for the nation in the foreseeable future.[8] In 1996 the opening of the National University of Laos signaled an important moment for a developing nation seeking to cultivate human resources necessary to provide the country with its long-term technical and educational requirements. Other regional universities offering limited curricula, chiefly in agriculture, information technology, and economics/business, have recently opened as well.

In 1995 the population of Vientiane, the capital, was 166,500 (Sisouphanthong and Taillard 2000: 32). It is now (in 2008) probably in the vicinity of 225,000–250,000. When Vientiane's population is combined with other small cities, including Luang Phrabang, Xam Neua, Phonsavan, Pakse, Oudomxay, Savannakhet, and so forth, the total urban population still amounts to less than 10 percent of the total population. Eighty-five percent of the population is still engaged in agriculture. Laos, consequently, is the least industrialized country in Southeast Asia (29). The country is also 85 percent forested naturally, but swidden ("slash-and-burn") cultivation,[9] as well as the deforestation that has resulted from extensive (much of it illegal) logging (instigated by Chinese business concerns), has reduced the actual forest cover to 42 percent, down from 70 percent in 1940 (20).

In spite of economic reforms introduced in the 1990s and a breathtaking rise in the number of tourists now visiting the country, Laos remains among the world's poorest and least developed countries. With an average annual per capita income of $320 according to 1995 data, Laos is economically more advanced than Cambodia ($240) and Vietnam ($190),[10] but Laos is three times poorer than the next richest countries, Indonesia and the Philippines. Nevertheless,

> the Lao PDR is also the biggest recipient of official development assistance in Southeast Asia ... 67% of this aid comes from international financial institutions and only 31% from bilateral aid with Japan and Sweden being the largest donors. (Sisouphanthong and Taillard 2000: 30–31).

According to statistics reported by the Lao Front for National Construction in 2005,[11] there are currently about 22,000 Buddhist monks at 4,937 Buddhist temples in Laos.[12] At the same time, there are 95 Roman Catholic churches serving 42,000 parishioners, chiefly in urban areas. The LFNC reports 221 evangelical Protestant Christian churches in no less than seventeen of the country's eighteen provinces, 9 Bahai spiritual halls, 8 Mahayana temples serving predominantly Vietnamese Buddhists in Vientiane, Champasak, Pakse, and Savannakhet, and 400 Muslims, the great majority of whom reside in Vientiane. In January 2007 a representative from the Council for America's First Freedom, an organization linked to Christian evangelicals seeking unfettered missionary access to Asian and other "third world" countries, hailed these figures[13] as an encouraging sign of the Lao PDR government's willingness to open up Laos to the rest of the world. If this is indeed the case, it would appear that the Department of Religious Affairs of the Lao PDR is now pursuing a contradictory policy (and perhaps unwittingly at that, since Christian missionary work remains officially banned): it makes continuous efforts to link Lao Theravada Buddhism to the national public culture on the one hand while simultaneously turning a blind eye to Christian missionary work among the country's minority hill tribe peoples on the other.[14] But what is actually happening is far from clear.

The foregoing figures provide a skeletal social profile of contemporary Laos. When writing about Lao culture, however, one also has to take into account that most of the "ethnic Lao" population, and therefore Lao Buddhism and religious culture, actually resides outside of the current political boundaries of Laos. Indeed, owing to the vicissitudes of political history, especially during the early nineteenth century but also due to the fallout of the Vietnam War, the "ethnic Lao" are actually nine times more numerous in northeast Thailand than they are within the contemporary political boundaries of Laos per se (Hayashi 2003: 9). This figure, however, can also be somewhat misleading if it is not properly contextualized. The Japanese anthropologist Yukio Hayashi notes:

> [The government of] Thailand has a history of encouraging the Lao [in northeast Thailand] to discard their identity and assimilate by establishing regional

identities within its own borders; [but] Laos . . . has actively promoted the application of that name to *all* its citizens and, by using it to establish the nation's international identity, is attempting to eliminate its use as an indicator for a specific ethnic group. (2003: 31; emphasis mine)

The strategy by the central Thai government to dilute Lao identity has been pursued chiefly through two means: one has been to reform Lao Buddhism in the image of a royally sponsored, Pali book-based, Bangkok-centered form of Buddhism, and the other has been to replace the Tai-Lao language of the northeast region with the Bangkok Thai dialect. It is noteworthy, as Hayashi points out, that the Lao of northeast Thailand call themselves "Isan" or "Thai" when speaking to Thai from other regions of Thailand, or to foreigners, or when dealing with the central government, while to their own non-Lao neighbors in the same region, they refer to themselves as "Lao." "When Lao from Northeast Thailand and from Laos meet in public, it is usual to pat each other on the back and call each other brother, expressing a consciousness of their 'genealogy'" (Hayashi 2003: 47).

As I noted above, the "ethnic Lao," known only since the 1950s as "Lao Loum" because of an attempt first initiated by the then Royal Lao Government to generate an inclusive nomenclature for its heterogeneous population, make up about half of the population in Laos, but they cover only about 20 percent of the land space that comprises contemporary Laos, for they are confined to the lowland river basins of the Mekong and its tributaries. In Thailand, where the Lao make up only 20 percent of the population, they actually inhabit 30 percent of the nation's landmass (Hayashi 2003: 35; also see Map 0.1).

The Lao Theung, the ethnic minorities who reside in the uplands or on the mountain slopes, and Lao Sung, the minorities who reside at or near the mountaintops, occupy the remaining 70 percent of the land. In the northern province of Luang Phrabang, the region where I conducted most of the research for this book, the Khmu people comprise the vast majority of Lao Theung, while the Hmong are the predominant Lao Sung.

This last discussion begs some comment about the historical use of the term "Lao." Indeed, its history has been quite varied. Hayashi and others point out that the earliest written use of the term is found in an inscription authored by a king of the Sukhothai mandala (in what is now north central Thailand) in the thirteenth century, about a century before the Lao kingdom of Lan Xang was allegedly established by its popularly acclaimed progenitor, Fa Ngum. We also know that it was also used in the sixteenth century by the Portuguese to denote a specific area as well as the inhabitants of that area.

Hayashi also cites the well-known mythic motif that when Tai-speaking people migrated down the Mekong from southern China to displace the people speaking

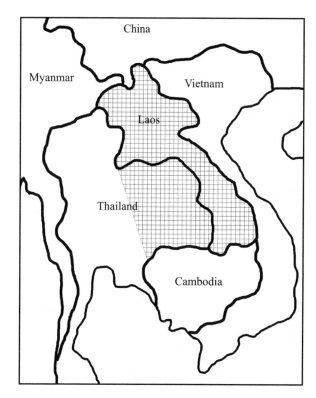

Map 0.1 Lao cultural areas in Laos and northeast Thailand (Isan)

the Mon-Khmer language, they gave the term *kha* (servant) to these people while referring to themselves as *thai* (free). As I shall show, this ancestral "theory" resides within a well-preserved "ethnic Lao" cosmogonic and migration myth. Regarding the specific social usage of the term "Lao," Hayashi writes that

> it was originally used as a term denoting the highest social rank. But later when the region became a vassal to Siam [in the eighteenth century], the Siamese rulers, in order to distinguish between [themselves] and others, applied the term Lao to those who had previously called themselves Thai, giving it the more contemptuous meaning [or] connotation that remains to this day [from the Thai perspective]. In this way, the term Lao came to denote a middle rank between the Thai and the Mon-Khmer. (2003: 35)

Adding to this discussion, Charles Keyes points out that

> until the end of the nineteenth century, the term "Lao" was used by the rulers, and even the ordinary people in Bangkok, in a rather vague way to refer to

peoples living to the North and Northeast of what had constituted the core of
old Siam (Ayudhya), who had followed cultural traditions and spoke languages
related to but clearly different from those of Siam. Under this rubric came not
only the peoples living in the principalities of Vientiane, Luang Prabang, and
Champasak that would later be included within French-controlled Laos, but
also those in the principalities of Chiang Mai, Nan, and others that would subsequently constitute Northern Thailand. In addition, most people living on the
Khorat Plateau in what is today Northeastern Thailand were also considered
Lao. (2002: 120)

What these comments by Hayashi and Keyes would seem to indicate, then, is that
the term "Lao" used to designate the Lao people and Lao language was originally
and consistently used by outsiders, rather than by the "ethnic Lao" themselves
until quite recently. Indeed, before the nineteenth century, the terms "Thai" and
"Lao" as ethnic terms were not in use at all, although "it is [now] common for
national histories to project such titles into the distant past" (Evans 2002b: 2).
Moreover, in the present Laotian nation-state, its meaning has been expanded
quite beyond reference to the ethnic "Lao Loum" people per se to include all contemporary citizens of the Lao Peoples Democratic Republic. Finally, the term is
also being used increasingly as an adjective (analogous to English "Laotian") for its
use in designating the language spoken and the culture practiced by the Lao Loum
people. In the first part of this study, which focuses upon the Lan Xang kingdom, I
have sometimes used the term Lao to refer to the interests of this kingdom, but it
should be understood that I have done so provisionally, in the absence of any other
better term I could consider.

Indeed, not only is the term "Lao" multifarious in its past and present designa-
tions, but the term "Laos" requires a deconstruction in its own right in order to
be properly contextualized. It is now quite clear that the introduction of the term
"Laos" designating a segment of French Indochina was meant by the French to
emphasize a cultural and political difference in relation to the Thai. The French
were quite conscious of the religious, cultural, and linguistic affinities that obtained between the Tai peoples under their own control and the Siamese, especially
after demarcation of the new territorial boundaries that they forced upon Siam
in 1893 through "gunboat" diplomacy. They continuously worried about Siamese
pretensions to lay claim over their former vassal states (Vientiane, Luang Phrabang, and Champasak) or the possibility that the Tai people under French control
would seek the patronage of the Siamese king. The French encouraged, directly
or inadvertently, the types of histories that would emphasized a narrow, vertical
genealogy of Laotian identity, one that articulated a trajectory of its nationhood
from the present back to the fourteenth-century figure of Fa Ngum. As will be

noted in later discussions, French policy was aimed at sharpening the distinction between "Thai" and "Lao" in whatever ways possible, while simultaneously building bridges to the Cambodian Khmer. Their efforts to engender an incipient Lao nationalism among the Lao elite, however, eventually undermined their own abilities to sustain their colonial interests.

Theravada Buddhism: A Brief Overview

Finally, a few words of introduction about Theravada Buddhism are needed. "Theravada" refers to the "way of the elders" and the manner in which this lineage of Buddhist monastic tradition chose to distinguish itself as a conservative and preserving force in maintaining the teachings of Gotama the Buddha, regarded as the latest in a series of twenty-four enlightened beings who, over many eons of time, have made known the truth of dharma to assuage the suffering condition of humanity, a suffering caused by ignorance and desire that can be overcome through the pursuit of wisdom, the practice of morality, and the cultivation of concentrated meditation. In its "canonical" scriptures (Tipitaka) written in the Pali language, a form of Prakrit derived from Sanskrit during the middle centuries of the first millennium BCE in Northern India, the subtle teachings of the Buddha about non-self (*anatta*), impermanence (*anicca* or *paticcasamuppada*), action (karma), and the disciplined life (*vinaya*) of the monk (*bhikkhu*) are presented in both sermonic and legalistic genres of literature. These texts were not committed to writing until the first century BCE in Sri Lanka, some four centuries or so after the life of the Buddha. Other Pali texts, such as the monastic noncanonical *Mahavamsa* written in Sri Lanka about 500 years later, trace the Theravada lineage of male and female monasticism back through the son (Mahinda) and daughter (Sanghamitta) of the great Indian Emperor Asoka. Asoka's children are thereby thought to have introduced the *bhikkhu* and *bhikkhunni sanghas* (monasticism) to Sri Lanka in the third century BCE. Through Asoka's children, Theravada is then traced back to the very time of the Buddha himself.

Within the monastic Mahavihara fraternity in Sri Lanka, the Theravada lineage thrived while the royal capital city Anuradhapura became a great cosmopolitan center of learning, thanks to the abilities of pious Buddhist kings who generously lavished their surplus wealth, a by-product of a sophisticatedly engineered, hydraulic-based agricultural system, upon the *sangha*. Here a Buddhist civilization took root and expressed itself through literary and artistic modes of culture for more than 1,300 years before it was sacked in the tenth century CE by an invading army of the imperial South Indian Cola empire, resulting in the destruction of the extensive infrastructure that had supported a "monastic landlord" social and political economy. But within a few generations, the Theravada male monastic lineage was revived and reestablished in a new capital city, Polonnaruva, and it is from Polonnaruva that the monastic and Pali literary traditions were exported first to Burma in the eleventh century,[15] and subsequently over the following two centuries into Sukhothai and Lan Na in what is now northern Thailand, and finally to Angkor in the early fourteenth century. From Lan Na especially, though Lao tradition avers Angkor, Theravada made its way definitively into the cultural regions of the Lao. Thus the Lao were probably the last "ethnic people" of Southeast Asia who adopted Theravada on a wholesale basis. Theravada now remains a vital religion in contemporary Sri Lanka, Burma, Thailand, Cambodia, and Laos. There are also pockets of Theravada in eastern Bangladesh and established Theravada communities in urban Malaysia and Singapore, not to mention in the major cities of the United States, Canada, Australia, and the United Kingdom.

CHAPTER I

Powers of the Place

Buddhism and the Spirit Cults of Muang Lao

Working at a great distance from the object of study, one
sometimes risks confusing a library with a country.
—Paul Mus, *India as Seen from the East*

If the spirit cults at the root of Southeast Asian religious cultures are not "time-
less" or "primordial" in nature, to use now controversial and frequently discredited terms, then surely, at least, they must be recognized as archaic and ruggedly
persistent. While it is not uncommon for many Lao, or outside observers of Lao
culture, to say "to be Lao is to be Buddhist,"[1] it is also true that Lao understandings of Buddhism have been conditioned by unique historical experiences and
interpreted through Lao cultural assumptions. Marcel Zago, the premier student
of Lao religion, has observed that

> the Buddhism practiced by the Lao has through time evolved a distinctive char-
> acter of its own with deep roots in the general culture and the native religious
> substratum. Most apparent at the ritual and administrative level, this Lao char-
> acter of Theravada Buddhism has also led to the evolution of a view of life and
> reality [that] is often in conflict with that of the Buddhist canon. (1976: 121)

Zago's comments about how Lao apprehensions of Theravada have been conditioned by "the native religious substratum" are salient for the direction of this
chapter, especially his subsequent comment (1976: 121) that the enduring notions
of *phi* (spirit) and *khwan* (vital essence or soul) are at variance with Buddhist cosmological perceptions and doctrinal assertions. So are comments by Ian Harris,
who shares a similar perspective of the religious and cultural context in neighboring Cambodia. He says that

recent Cambodian religious traditions contain much that is archaic . . . [t]he cult of the *neak ta* [spirits] may be regarded as a foundational layer upon which later traditions have been overlaid. Some of these tutelary spirits probably predate the arrival of Indic [Hindu and Buddhist] influences. (2005: 79)

Moreover, later in his account of the radical Khmer Rouge attempt to eradicate all forms of religious culture in Cambodia during the "Pol Pot period" of madness from 1975 to the Vietnamese intervention in 1979, Harris writes:

The terrible recent history of Cambodia demonstrates that Buddhism can survive even when its institutional forms have been destroyed. Its apotropaic rituals possess an enduring power for suffering humanity, while its symbolism and language have the protean ability to adapt in even the most extreme circumstances. (2005: 189)

By apotropaic, Harris is referring to those dimensions of religious culture that are more magical and esoteric in character: primarily private ritual appeals to tap various unseen spiritual powers by means of aural incantations, the manipulation of visual symbolism of the supernatural, and the veneration of localized deities or spirits, all of which are quite similar in nature to the spiritual world of the Lao. It seems ironic from what Harris has observed in modern Cambodia that those aspects of religious culture that have been the *least* publicly institutionalized or supported, those that are the least modern and rational, are those that seem most capable of surviving radical social and political change.

This has also been the case throughout the history of Lao religious culture. Indigenous roots of Lao religious culture are not only responsible for the manner in which many aspects of Buddhism have been understood conceptually and practically, but also for why Buddhism itself has been sustained (despite the fact that spirit cults are often seen to be in conflict with Theravada doctrinal tenets). In this chapter I will try to explain how and why this is the case by indicating how the ontology of the "native religious substratum" has continued to inform and condition what it has meant, and what it can still mean, to be religious within Lao Buddhist religious culture.

In comparison with the cults of deities in Sri Lanka's religious culture that I have previously studied in some depth (Holt 1991a, 2004), cults that are now very highly institutionalized in nature, what first impressed me most about the cults of the *phi* and *khwan* in Laos, in addition to their ubiquitous presence, was, paradoxically to me, their relatively and comparatively *non*institutionalized social presence. In Sri Lanka, elaborate shrines to *devatas*, from those on the one hand who are regarded as simply lower-level village deities (such as Huniyam or *gam-*

bara deviyo) and who are thought to act upon petitions of an often utterly mundane nature, to those high gods on the other hand, such as Visnu, Skanda, Natha, and Pattini (the four guardian deities—*satara varan devi*), whose identities are truly national in scope and who are thought to assist in very serious matters that require their powerful assistance, are part and parcel of the public religious landscape and frequently constitute an important presence within the very precincts of Theravada Buddhist *viharas* (temples). The cults of the *devatas* in Sri Lanka have been thoroughly integrated into what is quite self-consciously regarded as a Theravada Buddhist religious culture. Many of these deity shrines (*devalaya*), including those not found specifically within the precincts of Buddhist temples, are impressive autonomous institutions supervised by socially prestigious lay administrators (*basnayake nilames*), supported historically through royal endowments of land dedicated for the shrine's continuous physical and ritual maintenance, and operated by a cadre of full-time specialist priests (*kapuralas*), who regularly offer liturgical petitions on behalf of Buddhist laity to deities whose powerful and attractive anthropomorphic likenesses form the focus of devotional attention within highly symbolically decorated sanctum sanctora.

By contrast, in Laos the representation of the supernatural *thewada* and *phi* is much more subtle and is almost always aniconic;[2] that is, there are virtually no artistic traditions of sculpting anthropomorphic images of *phi* or portraying their mythic or supernatural exploits in temple mural paintings, and so forth. While diminutive spirit houses for *phi* are regularly positioned near the boundaries of premises for many commercial establishments (usually hotels and guesthouses in urban areas like Vientiane and Luang Phrabang), the shrines for village guardian *phi* are usually either very humble sheds or ramshackle canopies with little or no symbolic representation located in the forest outside of the boundaries of the inhabited village area, or their presence is indicated simply by a pole or pillar placed at a central location in the village, often in front of the house of the village headman. In either case, whether the *phi* shrine is located in the forest or in the center of the village, *phi ban* (village spirits), unlike the village *devata* of Sri Lanka, are rarely, if ever, anthropomorphized.[3] Some stupas (such as That Dam in central Vientiane) or sacred trees within *vats* (temples) are also regarded as the abode of *phi*. However, there are no freestanding buildings "housing" *phi* within which petitioners can enter to offer their invocations or petitions. Nor will we find full-time administrative or priestly specialists overseeing the well-being of a local village *phi* cult or orchestrating an open public ritual (*puja*) at regular times during the week, as in Sri Lanka.[4] There is usually an annual or semiannual public ritual in honor of the *phi ban*, but any other interaction with the village guardian spirit is totally dependent upon individual, private initiative and the availability of the part-time ritual specialist.

Photo 1.1 Signs of the times: spirit house (lower left) and satellite dish (upper right), Luang Phrabang

The relative lack of an iconic tradition for the representation of *phi*, the relative lack of social administration related to the cult, and the relative paucity of public ritual orchestration is, I think, a sure indication of a relative lack of institutionalization of the *phi* cults in general.[5] Yet there is no doubt that the various cults of *phi* are related intimately to a number of important social institutions beginning with the family household, then extending to private or commonly held village fields, the village *vat*, the village itself, collections of villages (*muang*), regional chiefdoms, kingdoms, and at times, as I shall show, even the institution of Theravada Buddhism itself.[6] But in Laos, *phi* seem to be significantly more nebulous in nature and function than the *devata*s of Sri Lanka, the *nat*s of Burma, and the *neak ta* in Cambodia's Khmer religious culture.[7]

The typical spirit house we find in Lao urban centers is an especially relevant example of what I mean by relative lack of institutionalization (see Photo 1.1). In contemporary Laos, spirit houses are often constructed so that they resemble miniature Buddhist *vat*s (temples). This style of spirit houses would, in itself, seem to indicate the domestication of the *phi* cult within a religious culture now dominated by Theravada Buddhism. Yet I want to emphasize that there is no image of any kind to be found within the Buddhist-*vat*-inspired-and-styled spirit house. The spirit house usually remains an empty dwelling, precisely because the spiritual force that it symbolically represents refuses, ultimately, to be permanently embodied, for in essence the *phi* are actually not embodied personages at all. Rather, they are fundamentally bodiless or "post-embodied" forces, wills, or powers. So it would appear that the *phi* of Lao religious culture, unlike the *devatas* in Sri Lanka, the *nats* in Burma, and the *neak ta* in Cambodia, have not been subjected to, at least not to the same extent, the powerful processes of "Hinduization" or "Buddhi-cization" that have contributed significantly to the anthropomorphizing of spirits or minor deities in those other nominally Buddhist religious cultures.[8] Although, we shall see, the epic *Ramayana* found a home and was transformed within Lao royal courts as the *Phra Lak Phra Lam* or *Rama Jataka* (see Appendix 1) and although some Lao literature entertained by the elites became coated with a Buddhist moralizing, the popular religious culture of the Lao was never subjected as intensively to the kind of matchmaking identification process between indigenous deities and Hindu gods or Buddhist bodhisattvas that occurred so extensively in Sri Lanka, Burma, and to some degree in Cambodia. Moreover, the *phi* cults have not been subjected to the process of karmic rationalization either, karma being the means of determining why hierarchy exists within divine pantheons in various Buddhist religious cultures, especially in Sri Lanka. My sense is that, historically, the *phi* cults of the Lao cultural regions of Laos and northeastern Thailand have remained relatively less encompassed or acculturated ("sanskritized" or "buddha-cized"), that is until recently in northeast Thailand.

Consequently, what we do not see in play within Lao religious culture, as we do see very clearly in the Sinhala Buddhist religious culture of Sri Lanka, is a thoroughly Buddhist rationalization that serves to interpret various aspects of popular religion, including the cult of *phi*. In Sri Lanka, we can expect to find a variety of ballads, poetry, and/or mythologies, in written or oral forms, explaining, from a Buddhist perspective, how it is that particular deities or spirits have risen to a current status of great power because of how, in the past, they have accumulated vast loads of merit by means of virtuous exploits, thereby earning a special warrant from the Buddha himself to dispense power on behalf of the dharma to deserving suffering people within a certain region or throughout the country as a whole. It is possible, through a study of this kind of episodic vernacular literature, to chart the "career" of a deity from his or her human origins as a prince, princess, or village or regional headman to his or her apotheosis finally as a Buddhist-sanctioned supernatural being enlisted to assist in the Buddha's bidding to assuage the experience of *dukkha* (suffering; unsatisfactoriness). In each instance, the trajectory of the deity is framed within an understanding that he or she is on a morally and karmicly empowered dharmic path that will eventually culminate in the experience of *nibbana* (nirvana). In Laos I have yet to run across any claim that any *phi* are regarded as advanced candidates for *nibbana*. Although *phi* are often protective in nature, their power, rather than being understood as unambiguously good

or morally based, is also understood to be potentially destructive, if not sometimes downright malevolent. For *phi* can be of many kinds. Rather than begging
a comparison to the *devata*s of Sri Lanka, the power of *phi* is more reminiscent
of the power of *yaksa*s, a power to be feared because it is ambivalent in nature,
and less morally informed or engendered. Yet even then, *yaksa*s are often anthropomorphized and karmicly accounted for in Sri Lanka. The power of *phi* seems less
domesticated, less morally guided, less buddhisticly channeled, more intrinsic
rather than cultivated, and hence more to be feared because of its ambiguity. In
any case it is certainly less institutionalized in Lao religious culture, especially in
relation to the Theravada Buddhist tradition per se.

It seems to be the case, therefore, that while Theravada Buddhism in Laos may
have become the accepted and authorizing religion of the Lao royal courts beginning in Luang Phrabang perhaps as early as the late fourteenth century CE,
and while the monastic *vat* (monastery) eventually became the veritable hub of
the *ban* (village) in ethnic Lao cultural areas, the popular religious culture of the
Lao in the form of *phi* cults was never subjected to the same degree of Buddhist
rationalization, or provided with a Buddhist ontology, as with the cults of *devata*s
and *yaksa*s in Sinhala Buddhist Sri Lanka. Within Lao cultural regions, Buddhist
conceptuality remained more confined and less pervasive in terms of its parameters of influence. Along with the related cult of the *khwan,* the cult of the *phi*
seems to have largely maintained its own basic conceptual ontology, which was
related to and sometimes informed Buddhist conceptuality, but at the same time
was understood apart from or in a complementary relation to it.[9] Other Western
scholars have characterized the relationship between the Buddhism and the spirit
cults in Lao religious culture as "blended"; still others have used terminology in
which Buddhism is seen as "encompassing" or "subordinating." Later I will try to
show, and this constitutes one of my major assertions, that rather than finding a
sustained interpretive Buddhist understanding of *phi* and *khwan* on the basis of
karma, which was clearly the bedrock principle and interpretive mechanism used
by the Sinhala Buddhists in Sri Lanka to explain the relative existences of supernatural beings, the converse is actually more likely to be found among the Lao:
Buddhist conceptuality, symbol, and ritual tends to be seen at the popular level of
Lao culture through the lenses of the indigenous religious substratum constituted
by the cults of *phi* and *khwan.* Following the French historian of religions Paul
Mus, I would also suggest that this archaic ontology reverberates or resonates with
the same kind of indigenous religious culture or substratum out of which Buddhism itself originally emerged.[10]

By making this assertion I have entered the territory of a long-standing debate
that needs to be outlined, at least briefly, before I continue. Mabbett and Chandler
have framed it succinctly:

It is easy to find traces of profound Indian impact in [Southeast Asian] religion, in script and language, in architecture, in craft, in custom, in popular lore. It is also easy, by a change in focus, to find evidence that indigenous practices in all spheres of life persisted largely uninfluenced, and that apparently Indian forms were really local ones in disguise—local gods with Indian names, local architectural motifs or local legends with Indian top-dressing. (1975: viii)

It may seem that I have opened this discussion by siding with those who attempt to document aspects of indigenous religious culture that have been sustained despite centuries of Hindu or Buddhist cultural influence in Southeast Asia. This is *not* really my complete aim. Rather, what I also find fascinating are those salient instances in which one side of this cultural dynamic has read or interpreted the other side and how these instances of "reading the other" have been the impetus for yet further reactions articulated through efforts to reform, purify, transform or, as we shall see, even to eliminate. Thus when Buddhist ideas and practices have been perceived through lenses that also refract the influence of the *khwan* and *phi* cults, some Lao, in various historical epochs, have reacted with efforts to separate Buddhism completely from such (mis)understandings. In my reading of Lao cultural and political history, I have found at least three historical attempts by various Lao elite to clearly delineate between Buddhism and the *phi* cults. In each attempt an effort was made to discriminate between so-called "religion" or Buddhism and so-called "superstition" or *phi*. In contextualizing each of these instances, it seems apparent to me that the motivation for these delineations may have been more politically rather than religiously (or spiritually) motivated, given the political implications of the *phi* cults that I shall now proceed to map. But within other instances of this dynamic of "reading the other," especially among contemporary Lao of northeastern Thailand, where Buddhist ideas and practices have functionally displaced ideas and practices related to the worship of *phi*, the understanding and practice of Buddhism itself has been extended and transformed. I will discuss this in Chapter 5.

Paul Mus and His "Spiritual Land Survey"

When I was a graduate student many years ago, I read, though with great difficulty, Paul Mus's groundbreaking study (1935) about Borobudur, the great monumental Mahayana stupa erected in the eighth century CE near what is now modern Yogyakarta, Indonesia. Mus's theoretical reflections on the monument's semiotics was breathtaking, insofar as he managed to illustrate how a Buddhist pilgrim's reading or "processing" of Borobodur's symbolism was tantamount to a realization of normative religious experience. What Mus demonstrated was how

the symbolism of Borobudur, as a "mesocosmic" mediating device, could facilitate a bridging experience between the microcosmic subjective consciousness of
the individual devotee and the macrocosmic objective reality represented by the
monument's serial and sculpted presentation of Buddhist doctrine. According to
Mus, the great stupa at Borobudur was a didactic representation of the Buddhist
path culminating in nirvana. It was constructed as a giant mandala that visu-
ally illustrates scriptural truths of Buddhist dharma through its extensive galler-
ies of sculpture situated on various ascending levels of the monument, which in
turn represent the hierarchical planes of existence in the Buddhist cosmos. It was
through reading Mus's magnificent study that I first came to appreciate the power
of mandalas as symbolic and spiritual devices that facilitate Hindu or Buddhist
religious quests.

Some thirty years later, through a reading of yet another Mus essay, I came
to understand how the indigenous ontology of the Lao spirit cults, associated
with the territorial conception of the *muang*, had made possible the significance
of mandalas in relation to the organization of political space in precolonial
Southeast Asia. Tambiah's study *World Conqueror, World Renouncer* (1976) and
Clifford Geertz's classic *Negara* (1981) lay bare the structures of Buddhist and
Hindu ideological rationales for the mandalic organization of political space in
Southeast Asian kingdoms, but the essay by Mus, entitled "India as Seen from the
East" (1975), explains *why* this model of political mapping reverberated so powerfully throughout the religio-political cultures of Southeast Asia and became,
therefore, such an effective and enduring political device. Reading the Mus essay, it is possible to clearly understand the dynamic interplay between imported
Hindu and Buddhist conceptuality on the one hand and the indigenous cult of
the spirits on the other, and how the presence of the latter rendered the former
so powerful.

In their introduction to the translation into English of Mus's essay,[11] Mabbett and Chandler summarize what Mus accomplished:

His [Mus's] achievement was to show how indigenous tradition, itself subtle,
abstract and complex, was married to the motifs of Indian lore, themselves dynamic and fertile, to make a vital whole. What he says is that, long before the
Aryans came to India, there was a network of cults throughout monsoon Asia,
Indian and Indo-China alike, in which the cult of the earth god was prominent.
The earth god, tutelary spirit of the community, was an abstract and highly
developed idea. It was not so much an anthropomorphic spirit inhabiting the
earth as the earth itself. As such, it was amorphous and inaccessible; but by a
subtle relationship of bi-presence it could be both amorphous as the earth and
embodied in a sacred site or object. (1975: x)[12]

What Mus presented was a daring grand-master theory, a type rarely advanced in contemporary scholarship owing to our predilections to contextualize our findings in historically specific moments. While Mus's perspective certainly does not transcend history, he does cross over serious cultural boundaries (between India, China, and Southeast Asia) that since his day have become, perhaps, overly reified in scholarly circles and, as such, resistant to the type of grand theoretical explanation that he envisaged. In his own words:

> The inhabitants of ancient India, Indo-China and southern China believed in spirits, present in all things and in all places—disembodied human souls, spirits of waters and woods, etc. . . . and . . . they also credited certain men with the magic power of conjuring them up or warding them off. . . .
>
> The two aspects [spirits and their conjuring] go together, and I believe that it is the activity of the sorcerers—their techniques of conjuring them up— which, more than anything else, has peopled the sphere of human life with various spirits: in fact the spirits are seen not at all in isolation but always in relationship with man, embodying in some fashion something that he desires if not something that he fears. Everywhere they are conceived in terms of humanity. The same is also the case with the most important among these spirits . . . , the lord of the soil, who deserves a special place. His cult, and the particular relationship he has with the collectivity which offers him the cult, would characterize, better perhaps than anything else, the form of religion which I believe to have been common at one time to the various parts of monsoon Asia. (1975: 9–10).[13]

When I first read these words, I actually dismissed his claim as the by-product of an earlier idealistic academic generation, a romantic European penchant for ascertaining the presence of universal patterns of religion at the expense of the rich textures of cultural specificity grounded in historical experience. The very notion of "monsoon Asia" struck me as quite overblown, a grand oversimplification, perhaps even similar to the invention of "Asia" in the proverbial Orientalist imagination. However, try as I might (and I tried very hard indeed) to think of specific contexts of religious cultures on the ground in village South India and Sri Lanka (specific locales with which I am quite familiar) that did *not* contain the element of a territorial spirituality embodied in the cults of village deities or "gods of the soil," I could not, for the life of me, think of an exception! While I do not claim omniscience in these matters, my own experiences in this regard are somewhat extensive. Certainly, the ubiquitous village goddesses, especially in Hindu South India, match up closely to Mus's "god of the soil," deities whose powers are conjured for reasons of fertility in and protection of the village. In both

mythic and ritual vicissitudes, the goddess represents both the protected boundaries and the continuing well-being of the South Indian village. Moreover, almost
every predominantly Sinhala village I have visited in rural Sri Lanka over the years,
at least every village that has not been whitewashed by Christianity or become
overly affected by "Buddhist modernism," "middle-class Buddhism," or so-called
"Protestant Buddhism,"[14] contains a shrine for either the village deity or a regional
bandara (region-specific "chief" deity). In the locales of Sinhala Sri Lanka, there
always seems to be a deity who is referred to as "the god who is in charge of this
place." Finally, from what I had been reading in the anthropological ethnographies
of Tai religious culture[15] (or of Khmer and Burmese religious cultures in their own
ways as well[16]), there could be no gainsaying the fact that the cult of *phi*, or spirits,
is largely centered on a concept of power that is regarded as intrinsic to a specific
territory, usually the village, but also relevant to a family's cultivated rice paddy
field, a family compound, or to the very sense of a social collectivity, insofar as the
deity in question frequently symbolizes the interests of the village or the family. On
this, Mus had further written:

> We are dealing with an entity endowed in some respects with a profoundly im-
> personal character. Not quite a genie: it is not a superhuman being, but a being
> to be abstracted from man; invisible, but made in his image, if we could see it.
> Its basis is rather in *events* than in a human person. At a later stage, the thought
> came to be endued with anthropomorphism and there was a god [or goddess]
> of a locality; but at the level we are trying to visualize, the *locality itself is a god.*
> An impersonal god, defined above all by a localization: *we shall continue to come
> across vestiges of these conceptions even in the most learned religions.* (1975: 11;
> emphasis mine)

What Mus was arguing for in this passage, then, was a notion of power found within or attributed to a given, specific place, a power that accounts for the dynamism
of life associated with that locality: its energy or its ethos, depending on either the
topographical or social nature of its associated territoriality. While this power is
fundamentally impersonal in nature, it is later personalized through the social and
psychological experience of *events*; that is, through its existential realization, it is
given a conscious social recognition through embodiment.[17] While many others
after Mus, including my teacher Mircea Eliade, would write copiously about how
"sacred space" is the venue for "hierophany" (the place where the sacred reveals itself),[18] Mus had actually gone beyond (or *before*) this kind of interpretation in trying to account for the nature of "the Sacred," or better, the *power* of place. Rather
than attributing sacred power to "the Sacred's" own manifestation, what he argued
for is a process by which the "power of place" is transformed into an identification

of the "power of the group," as a result of the group's experience of the place, of the *events* that have occurred for the group in relation to it. The power of the place is not, therefore, transcendentally endowed, but rather is brought to fruition by its subjective social apprehension by the group.

I also want to underline Mus's comment that "vestiges of these conceptions" are to be found "in even the most learned religions" by noting that it is precisely this sense of territorial sacred power that is attached by the Lao to the Phra Bang (Buddha image) that became the palladium of their Lan Xang kingdom and from which the city of Luang Phrabang, Lan Xang's capital and ritual center for two centuries, takes its name. How the power of the Phra Bang was conceived as such, then, is a key example of how the conceptuality of spirit cults contributed to a uniquely Lao reading of the Buddha and Buddhism. But I will write more on this later.

Mus was not content with this identification of the religious construction of localized power, however. In a remarkable passage, which I cite below, he first distinguishes between the religious dynamic he has identified and how Levy-Bruhl's theoretically dedicated followers might construe it: as a "child-like primitive mentality" that arises from mistaking the difference between dream and reality. Moreover, and crucial for this discussion, Mus also asserts that the cult of spiritual power associated with locality is actually intrinsic to the manner in which land would later be politically organized and its legal status thereby authorized. And finally in this same passage he speculates on how, in some instances, recognition of the "power of place" eventually evolves into an anthropomorphic cult. This passage, therefore, is at the heart of his argument:

> It is not a "primitive mentality" that is reflected by this religious mode. The divinity, collective and without individual personality, seems to me to be implied by the chthonic cults.... As we shall see, it is connected with the way in which land is organized and doubtless with something like territorial law; perhaps indeed, impersonal though it is, it is never conceived of except as embodied by the materializations that gave it shape, even those which endow it with a personal form.... It is clear that for cults of this type, once they are established, the first problem is to reach the formless deity to make him aware of the needs and desires of the collectivity grouped around him. On the one hand, a god, impalpable by his own nature; on the other, a human group by reference to which he assumes his position as a god.... There arises ... a necessity to endow a local entity that is incorporeal and impalpable ... with eyes that can see the faithful, ears that can hear their prayers. (1975: 11–12)

Elaborating further on the emergence of this territorial spirit, its relation to community, and its eventual personification, Mus adds:

It is important to stress that this [place/soil/stone] is not the lodging, the "seat" of the god, but the god himself, consubstantially. Not the stone of the genie, but the stone-genie. In this religious scheme, one must distinguish three terms: the divine position, the human position, and the ritual position, which mediates between the two others. The stone corresponds to the divinization of the energies of the soil. Over against it stands a human group. Between the two is to be interposed a link in touch with man on the one hand and the god on the other. This link is the temporary personification of the divinity. (1975: 14)

Mus was also not satisfied to describe the metaphysical only in relation to its symbolic ritual embodiment. Perhaps he was too good a student of Indian and Chinese thought, and too influenced by Durkheim in his assumptions, to rest content without parsing out the sociological and political dimension of the religious dynamic that he had uncovered. In yet another pregnant passage I cite below, Mus moves to identify the social and political expression of the religious ontology of the "god of the soil." Specifically, the identification of the "god of the soil" is here modified to include not only the "energy of the soil" (as above), but also what constitutes the "union of the group" (see below), and finally, those who have previously invested their own energies in the soil: the ancestors of the group.

> The prestige attributed to the chief certainly did not begin purely with the institution of the chthonic ritual: but all that concerns us is that . . . this prestige is regarded theoretically as *a reflection of the local god in the chief.*
>
> In this way we can see how the human group finds itself obliged to secure an intermediary, who is its delegate, between the amorphous divinity of its soil and itself. [Through t]he person of the delegate, the earth-god and men commune. But *what better intermediaries could there be to define the union of the group and its soil than the ancestors* of the group, buried in the soil and thus restorers to it? Were not the dead chiefs formerly, in the rites, the land itself made man before their subjects? Now they are linked even more intimately to this land. (Mus 1975: 15–16; emphasis mine)

From these rich statements, I will try sum up the direction in which Mus's argument is headed: (1) the village chief, as the intermediary between the divine and the human, is also regarded as endowed with the power of the "god of the soil"; (2) thus, the village chief ("the delegate"), as the human social counterpart invested with the power of the "god of the soil," is the means through which the god and the community "commune," or through which power is distributed; the chief is the spiritual pivot; (3) moreover, like the village chief, the ancestors of the village also embody the power or energy of the soil;[19] (4) the village chief, therefore, stands in a relationship of "lineage" to the social past (ancestors) of the given place. What Mus has perceived, therefore, is not only a synchronic linkage between the power of the soil and the socially realized power of the chief, but also a parallel diachronic linkage between the power of the contemporary chief and past ancestors of the village. That is, the linkages are made not only between spiritual and human realms, but also through time's past and present. This is Mus's understanding of the spatial structure and temporal dynamic of the "spiritual" in his "religion of monsoon Asia."

In two subsequent passages Mus not only clarifies the relationships that he sees between the spiritual power of the land and its social realization, but also asserts that this pattern eventually evolved into the worship of dynastic, regional, national, or royal gods:

> We are concerned not with any stone but with one that is made the center of a clearly defined territory and it is almost a sociological tautology to say that the definition of this territory is at the same time that of a collectivity. So, taken together, these religious conventions would be equivalent to a *spiritual land survey*, the centre of each district being marked by one of the sacred stones. ... It may be added that the cult of the genie of the soil is associated with that of ancestors, and that the stone which embodies it has already been presented to us as a dynastic or familial contract. (1975: 20; emphasis mine)

Furthermore,

> to the *genius loci*, the personification of the energies of the earth, was owed the prosperity of the territory occupied by those who united to worship it, and who were defined as a group by this unity. The *yaksa* is everywhere a god of the soil, a cadastral god, a national or at least dynastic god in the city of the king, a community god at the level of village life. (1975: 29)

But this is not all. After establishing how divinity was linked to political territoriality, Mus argues that the principles he has identified were not only also present in the "religious substratum" of southwestern China and India, but that in both instances they were further organized into hierarchy. The result of this hierarchical stratification of power created not only the layers and levels of deities who came to populate supernatural pantheons, but also the hierarchical structure of the sociopolitical order as well. The divine pantheon of the supernatural order was none other than the "double" of the social and political order, each a mirror image of the other.[20]

Soon, we shall see the ramifications of Mus's argument for an understanding of the Lao *muang* and the Buddhist political mandala. But first, it is important to distinguish exactly what Mus has argued from what others have asserted about the parallelism or "doubling" that exists in Chinese and Indian constructions of the "sociocosmos." On the one hand, there are more theologically oriented scholars, many of whom were students of the phenomenology of religion, such as Eliade and van der Leeuw, who wrote at great length about the "reality of the sacred" and its proclivity to manifest itself within "hierophanies" or revelations. Essentially, this school argues for a "top-down" approach to understanding the nature of religion in its institutionalized, ritualized context. The world's religions as they have developed historically are understood as responses to the presence of a revelatory transcendental reality. It may be that the subjects of Mus's cult of the "god of the soil" would have understood their own experiences precisely in this way as well; for them, their cultic behavior was simply a response to their experiences of the life-giving force. But in his interpretation of the parallelism between the supernatural and the human social worlds, Mus is not simply recapitulating what the folk know, nor is he following the principle that Jonathan Smith (2005) has described as the method of tracking ontologies that proclaim: "as above, so below." What Mus's interpretation represents, instead, is a more Durkheimian-oriented theory that argues: "as below, so above." In the first place the "energy of the soil" was experienced within the social context of *events*. Its value was then valorized within ritual. In that sense, then, the subsequent constructions of hierarchy, in both supernatural and social forms, are not simply understood as calculated political machinations designed to legitimate the establishment of hierarchically imposed power, but rather as indices to those values that have been deemed worthy of consecration by the community. This interpretive understanding is what separates Mus's reading from the theological view or the phenomenology-of-religions view (for example, Eliade and van der Leeuw) on the one hand and a reductionistic Marxist reading of religion on the other. I have quoted and discussed Mus's theory at length because it is his theoretical perspective that I will use as a provisional template in what follows.

Ban and *Muang*

In Lao culture and society, beyond the nucleus of the family, the *ban* or the village is the basic social unit. While the constituency of the *ban* is made up of both nuclear and semi-extended families, it also the case that many smaller *ban* consist of one large pervasive set of kinship relations. "New blood" is imported into the village primarily through new husbands and sons-in-law, as it was (and still is) the custom that after marriage, a Lao groom will join his bride's family.[21]

Each *ban* has its authority vested in a headman, just as each village has its counterpart supernatural *phi ban* (village deity). At the same time the town or village is regarded as the locus of beauty, virtue, and prestige in contrast to the forest (Davis 1984: 82).

Transcending the individual *ban* is the *muang*, a nearly untranslatable term, but essentially a cluster of *ban* related to each other not only because of geographic proximity, but also for politically defensive reasons as well, with the *ban* that has the most economic means and most politically powerful family (usually meaning the greatest ability to produce rice) serving as its hub in hierarchical relation to the other *ban*.[22] At the hub of the *ban* at the center of the *muang* is the *chao muang*, or *muang* chieftain, whose own position of power, like the village headman who is empowered by the *phi ban*, is endowed by the power of the *phi muang*. The power of the *chao muang* is symbolized by a pole or pillar (*lak muang*) located just outside of his house that functions as an *axis mundi* or vector for the supernatural power that the *chao muang* claims and then distributes throughout the *muang* by his ritually efficacious actions. Aside from its "ritualization,"[23] the power of the *chao muang*[24] was used to muster surplus human resources from the *muang*'s various *ban* whenever needed and to coordinate any limited bit of trade or political undertakings between his *muang* and other *muang*. In exchange for his mobilizing role, the *chao muang* was owed a measure of tribute. That tribute, in addition to labor, might take the form of surplus food or handcrafts. The *chao muang* might, in turn, be subordinate to yet another more powerful *chao muang* and pay tribute to his superior by channeling a part of his surplus resources to him.

> The degree to which a settlement [*ban* or *muang*] is considered beautiful and civilized corresponds to the level it occupies in the *muang* hierarchy. All beauty and civilization flow from the upper-level *muang* and percolate down into the villages. At each stage in this downward flow, civilization loses some of its luster. (Davis 1984: 83)

While the directional flow of power or "civilization" is quite apparent here, the important point to grasp is that at each level, from family to village, to "district" *muang* (*tasseng*), to larger "regional" *muang*, these concentric and hierarchically related social units were the basic "political structure characteristic of all Tai peoples, who were remarkably free to conduct their own local affairs in return for allegiance, tribute and manpower in the event of war, contributions sustaining respectively the religio-symbolic, economic military bases of the central power of the mandala of which they formed a part" (Stuart-Fox 2003: 3).

I am unsure, at this point, how far retrospectively into Tai-Lao history the larger concept of mandala can be projected with any degree of certainty, though the dynamics of mandala polity seem remarkably anticipated by relations between *ban* and *muang*. Mandala conceptuality has been invoked, at least retrospectively, in relation to the specifically Buddhist legitimation of power relative to the founding of the Lao Lan Xang kingdom. The mandalic political structure of Angkor seems to have served as Lan Xang's model, as it did for other emergent Tai states, especially Ayutthaya (in what is now modern Thailand to the south and west).[25] Early sixteenth-century accounts of the fourteenth-century founding of the kingdom frame a story that casts Lan Xang in the lineage, if not the image, of Angkor. While these accounts are clearly written with a motive to legitimate Lan Xang in this particular light, they may also represent a reading of the present (sixteenth-century) ideology into the (fourteenth-century) past. While some scholars have been inclined to believe that the expanding organization of a mandala was already in the process of formation with Muang Sua[26] serving as its hub, possibly with the assistance of Mongol support, before the alleged founding declaration of the kingdom of Lan Xang by Fa Ngum in the mid-fourteenth century (Stuart-Fox 1998: 37), it is difficult to discuss Lao mandala political dynamics and structures before entering an historical period when we are more certain that its overtly Indic religious elements (for example, Buddhist and Hindu conceptions of polity) were actually in play; that is, probably not before the late fifteenth century, and more likely the early sixteenth century in northern Laos. It may indeed be the case that prior to the establishment of the Lan Xang kingdom by Fa Ngum in the mid-fourteenth century an emerging confederation of *muang* was in the process of being established, a process that would have made Fa Ngum's accomplishment, if indeed it occurred in the manner reported by mythically laced texts a century and a half later, that much more feasible.

All of this is historically murky, but my point here is that the *muang* seems to be a very archaic social conception intrinsic to the Tai people who emigrated out of southwestern China in the latter stages of the second half of the first millennium. While *muang* later became the constituent elements of a fully fledged, royally centered mandala, and while the *ban* is also a microcosm of the *muang*, and eventually the *muang* a microcosm of the mandala, *muang* as localized social structures definitely antedate the emergence of a fully fledged mandala polity that later characterized Buddhist-legitimated Lao kingship. What makes the mandala distinctive from the *muang* as a means of social and political organization is the fact that the principles of power have been recast through the religious language and hierarchical conceptuality of Hinduism and Buddhism. Moreover, at least in the Theravada Buddhist context, the rationale for the political legitimation of mandalas was *ethicized*.[27]

Since *ban* were miniature *muangs*, and *muangs* were miniature mandalas, the political mandala was the most highly evolved but also the most dependent of the three. In Lao culture, *muang* can be *muang* without mandalas, but mandalas cannot be mandalas without constituent *muangs*. Not only do *muangs* make mandalas possible, but it is quite evident that *muang*s precede fully fledged Buddhist kingships. Indeed, the relationship between *ban* and *muang* was

> the basis for the continuity that carries through those periods when central political authority disappeared.... The discontinuity of central political structures [mandalas] was overcome by the continuity of political culture based firmly at the village level, anchored in the socio-religious Lao worldview. (Stuart-Fox 2003: 10–11)

In my earlier discussion of Mus's "religion of monsoon Asia," I noted the hierarchical parallelism or mirror imaging that exists between this-worldly social structures of authority and otherworldly supernatural pantheons of divine power. I have also noted how the element of ancestor veneration came into play in that context. These same principles can be seen in relation to "proto-Lao" sociopolitical organization and the degree to which a *muang* could retain its ultimate autonomy in relation to other *muang*. In other words,

> *mueang* identity rested on mythic-historical descent and the marking out of the territory, initially perhaps through the force of arms, but subsequently justified as divinely determined. But relations between *mueang* rested on at least potentially equal claims to autonomy and inclusion, to legitimation through descent and to the potency of regional spirits. Small, less powerful *mueang* still reserved for themselves the right to autonomy, not just in their internal affairs, a right jealously guarded, but in relation to other *mueang* through tribute paid to more than one powerful *mueang*. All Tai were free men: all *mueang* were autonomous polities—at least in theory. (Stuart-Fox 2003: 74)

So despite the fact that most political history focuses almost exclusively upon the expansion and contraction of competing grand mandalas, the actual locus of power for most people remained quite localized in relation to *muang*s. Moreover, it was possible for a single *muang* to have cultivated multiple allegiances or to pay tribute to more than one mandala. The powers of mandalas could sometimes overlap.

Grant Evans points out that "besides labor the other major source of surplus in tributary systems is state control of trade. In precolonial Laos it was slave trading and control of land routes to southern China that provided vital revenue. ... [But m]arket transactions were peripheral to the peasant economy" (1990: 11). What this means is that the economies of the emergent grand *mandala*s, including Lan Xang, were essentially decentralized and therefore that these economies were almost wholly subsistence in nature rather than market-oriented. What little marketing existed was the province of royal centers that engaged in trade with other royal centers. Tribute that the center of the mandala demanded became, if not consumed, surplus exchanged in trade. "International relations" were of little interest to the local *muang*, unless the mandala of which it was a part decided to engage in war or needed to defend itself against the aggression of another mandala, in which case a *muang* would need to decide on its allegiance in relation to its own best interests.

From *Muang* to Mandala?

It is not until the early sixteenth century, some 150 years after the purported establishment of Lan Xang by Fa Ngum, that a written source, the *Nithan Khun Borom*, weaves together a myth of the creation of the world and the foundation of Lan Xang in Luang Phrabang within the context of a distinctive Buddhist worldview. The major accomplishment of this text, more in terms of ideology than in historical fact, is that it consolidates two rationales for the legitimacy of the emergent Lao central polity: one that emphasizes rule of its territory by divine descent and the other by royal Buddhist meritocracy, the former rooted in the indigenous ontology of the *phi muang* and a related ancestral cult and the latter ultimately coming from the Theravada Buddhist traditions of Sri Lanka, perhaps by way of Burma, northern Thailand, and possibly Angkor, the exact route not being clear. The *Nithan Khun Borom* avers that the Buddhist ideology, along with relics, scriptures, and monks, accompanied Fa Ngum in his triumphal return from Angkor. But some scholars find it more probable that Buddhist ideology actually reached Lan Xang through neighboring Lan Na (northern Thailand) in diffusive disseminating waves.[28]

Before turning attention to these two religious valorizations of political authority in Luang Phrabang, I will first sketch, however briefly, what little we know about the prehistory of the Lan Xang kingdom. "Tai people are believed to have originated in the region of southern Kwangsi, China and under pressure from an expanding Chinese empire began migrating southwest sometime in the first millennium CE" (Evans 2002b: 2). While this is undoubtedly so, details about the earliest principalities of northern Laos remain obscure. There is some evidence of material culture to indicate that both major forms of Buddhism, the Theravada and the Mahayana, were practiced in the nearby southern Chinese region of Nanzhao, a fact that may help to explain the characteristics of Buddha images found in Luang Phrabang dating to the eleventh and twelfth centuries, images that constitute the earliest vestiges of iconic material culture from the immediate urban vicinity (Stuart-Fox 1998: 31). However, aside from the apparent burial sites in modern Xieng Khuang Province known presently as the Plain of Jars, another megalithic site, Xuan Hin, located about fifty km southwest of Xam Neua in Huaphan Province, and settlement sites at Pak Ou recently discovered and identified by a University of Uppsala team in cooperation with the Lao National Museum, there is very little in the way of first millennium material culture remaining in modern northern Laos upon which to base historical conjecture. Yet it is possible, in order to contextualize the historical background of the origins of Lan Xang, to appeal to what is known about the macro political history of the general region in that era.

The earliest Tai states were able to surface within the region owing to Angkor's receding power to the east and the Mongol devastations of other kingdoms to the north and west, a combination that created, in effect, a political vacuum in

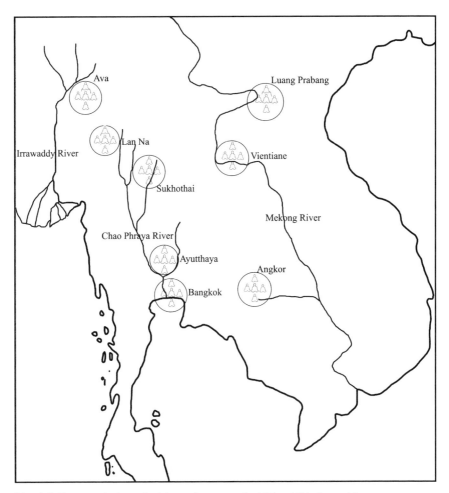

Map 1.1 Fourteenth through eighteenth-century Buddhist political mandalas

between. There were also significant political stirrings further south: military pre-occupations between Ayutthaya and Sukhothai in the 1350s provided an opportunity for Lan Xang to emerge from its status as a tributary vassal on the peripheries of the Lan Na and Sukhothai mandalas (Evans 2002b: 9).[29] After Lan Xang had emerged, it would seem as if its political consciousness was bifocal in nature. Like the other emergent contemporary Tai mandalas at Lan Na, Sukhothai, and Ayut-thaya (see Map 1.1), Lan Xang eventually adopted a political conceptuality laced with Buddhist and Hindu conceptions of kingship, ones seen to have long been in play at Angkor, whether or not these came directly to Lan Xang from Angkor or through Lan Na.

Yet, as Evans has pointed out:

> While Lan Xang was a Buddhist kingdom like Ayudhya and Sukhotai, its cul-tural roots lay closer to tribal Tai than did theirs. This is most apparent in the centrality of ritual sacrifices made to the territorial spirits of *muang* Lan Xang, in which the *phi* and *chao* of subordinate *muang* would gather in the capital for grand sacrifices. Furthermore, the laws associated with this state, the *kot-mai thammasat Kun Bulom*, are unsystematic and show little influence of Bud-dhism. (2002b: 10)

This brings us finally to a discussion of the relation between the two previously noted ontologies of power (the indigenous and the Buddhist), both of which are valorized in the Luang Phrabhang chronicles.

Myth and Legitimation of the Lan Xang Mandala

The *Nitham Khun Borom*, a chronicle written in the early sixteenth century under the sponsorship of Luang Phrabang Lao royalty, is ontologically bifocal. It con-tains two narrative cycles that account for Lan Xang's origins: the first is a Tai cre-ation myth still brought to life each year within the context of Luang Phrabang's annual New Year (Pi Mai) rites held every April; the second is a quasi-historical account of the kingdom's first ruler, Fa Ngum, which links his power directly to Angkor and to Sri Lanka's Sinhala Theravada Buddhism. The former is a cosmo-gonic myth clearly designed to link Luang Phrabang's royalty to the cult of the *phi muang*; that is, to explain the "divine right" of kings to rule by placing them within a lineage of ancestors traced back to the world's creation by supernatural power. The latter attempts to forge a link between Lan Xang's kingship and the lineage of the Buddha; that is, it ties Lan Xang to the wider, universal religious history and cosmology of Theravada tradition. While a century and half may have lapsed fol-lowing the founding of Lan Xang purportedly by Fa Ngum in 1353 CE before these two accounts of origins were knit together within the *Nithan Khun Borom* (1503 CE), and while their simultaneous presence in the text may reflect a compromise between competing loyalties in the royal court, both conceptual orientations represent shafts of legitimation that have remained vital throughout the subsequent history of Lao cultural history.

Goran Aijmer has created an excellent detailed summary of Lao creation myths as contained within the *Nithan Khun Borom* and other versions of the *Chronicle of Luang Phrabang*. It reads:

At the dawn of history earth, the planets, heaven, and the supreme deities, *then*,[30] were in existence. Deities and men paid constant visits to each other. There were also three *khun*—"elders"—who reigned over the lower world; they were called Pu Lang S-oegn, Khun K'an, and Khun Ket. The *then* issued orders that at each meal mankind should give an offering to them, but men disobeyed. The *then* caused a great inundation which submerged the entire world, and all men were drowned.

The three *khun* saved themselves on a raft together with their wives and children. Riding on the waters they arrived in the celestial kingdom. After some time the waters sank back again and the *khun* were returned to earth by the king of the *then*.[31] As they departed he presented them with a buffalo, and after their arrival in the earthly regions they started cultivation of rice with the help of their heavenly beast. Three years later the buffalo died, and they left the hide where the animal had fallen. A liane [vine] grew up from the nostrils of the dead buffalo. It grew high and from it emerged three enormous pumpkins. Pu Lang pierced the fruits with a glowing hot drill and Khun K'an made a second hole using a chisel, and through the holes mankind came out into the world. Pu Lang S'oeng gave instructions to the new inhabitants of the earth how to cultivate and build houses; the *khun* informed them of the institution of marriage and preached morals. Those who had come out through the hole made of the drill were Kha, while those who came out through the chisel hole were Lao.

Mankind was proliferating and the multitude did not obey the advice of the *khun*. The *then* appointed Khun K'lu and Khun K'ong kings, but the new monarchs failed to bring order because of their addictions to alcohol. The king of the *then* then appointed as king his own son Khun Bulom. Khun Bulom descended to earth riding on an elephant and bringing his two queens Nang Et Kheng and Nyommap'ala. He was followed by numerous *khun* carrying insignia of rank. The world once again was organized, agriculture and other techniques were introduced together with offerings, taboos and music. After this event the rattan bridge which spanned heaven and earth was cut and the two worlds were separated forever.

Soon a liane, named Khao Kat, emerged from a pool called Kuwa, and grew into the sky. Its foliage covered the earth, and shade and chill dominated the world. Rice production could not be maintained. An old couple, Thao Nyoeu and Thaon Ya, went out to cut the liane. Before setting out on this expedition they were promised that if they perished, they would receive offerings. They traveled for three months and three days. They cut the stem but in achieving their goal they were killed by the falling liane.

Again the kingdom became prosperous—the Lao worked the paddy fields while the Kha made swiddens in the mountains. Khun Bulom was blessed with seven sons. When they grew up he distributed elephants and parts of a heavenly treasure to each of them, just as his old father had provided for him. The seven sons were given domains by their father. Khun Lo, his eldest son born by Queen Nang Et Kheng, was given the *muang* of S'va, a founder of a dynasty which gave name to the domain. Khun Lo drove away the Kha ruler and installed himself on the throne.[32] (1979: 735–736)

A myth as rich as this is filled with many valorizations, but four related principles seem to stand out especially: (1) an original primordial unity between the world of the gods and the world of humanity was ruptured through humanity's refusal to recognize the hierarchy that exists between the power of the gods and the works of men; (2) the "elders" or ancestors, with the divinely given blessing of the buffalo, were responsible for the establishment of the economy (cultivation) and society (marriage and morality); (3) the repeated misbehavior of humanity engendered a need for further divine agency in the world, which took the form of divinely descended kingship, to sustain order in the economy and society; related to this is the claim that Muang Sua's (Luang Phrabang's) first ruler is none other than the grandson of the supreme deity; (4) the division of labor (wet and dry rice cultivation) and hierarchical (tributary) relationship between the lowland, river-basin-based Lao and the upland Kha is established. The message of the narrative is clear: the powers of the land and therefore power of the people who live on it are realized by respecting divine agency and design. Respecting this agency in its tangible form of kingship (Mus's "god of the soil" or "lord of the land") sustains prosperity.

Aijmer's own reading of this myth, one that also emphasizes its significance for the legitimacy of kingship in Luang Phrabang, is as follows:

The ruler of Luang Phrabang was descendant of the grandson of the highest divinities. All of the descendants of this apical ancestor were potentially divine rulers, capable at death of becoming guardian spirits entitled to altars and custodial personnel. Thus the royal lineage was of an origin entirely different from that of ordinary men who came into this world from pumpkins; going with this particular divine descent was a quality which not only justified the exercise of total power of the king, but also gave him the ability to establish kinship links with ogres and water spirits. (1979: 737)[33]

Another scholar of Lao religious culture, Charles Archaimbault, has a somewhat different emphasis in his reading of this myth. Though he risks extrapolating history from the myth, he makes the astute point that while the Kha are clearly subordinated to the Lao,[34] the myth implicitly recognizes their rights to land:

Whereas within the pumpkins, discriminating social distinctions were non-existent, once out of the pumpkins, . . . rigid social distinctions were established between the Laotians and the aborigines, as well as between different clans. The Kha . . . were installed in the mountains where they cultivated dry rice, while the Laotians became the people of the plains cultivating wet rice. This distinction in the way of life and this social stature could not have been established without violence. Thus when the Laotian chief, according to divine plan, came to set up the Kingdom of Luang Phrabang, he came into conflict with the Kha who already occupied the land. These he had to evict. Recognising their anterior right to the land—and here is an important fact that the [New Year] ritual emphasizes, he gave to his oldest son the name of the Kha chieftain whom he had just dispossessed. (1964: 59)

There are more versions of this myth of origins still extant. From an oral variant recovered by Archaimbault (1959), Aijmer has also provided a summary of an important complementary version that adds new elements and emphases to the first account I have provided above:

Pu Nyoeu (paternal grandfather Nyoeu=Thao Nyoeu) and Nya Nyoeu (paternal grandmother Myoeu=Thaon Ya) lived in heaven, but their ugly appearance scared the children of the *then* [Paya Thaen]. For this reason they were expelled from the celestial kingdom by the king of the *then*. At this time, the earth did not exist, but water was everywhere. The old couple, charged with the task by the celestial king, created the world by stamping on the water. But dwelling on newly created earth they felt lonely and they returned to heaven to ask for company. They once more scared the children and were, therefore, returned to earth; but before leaving heaven they were presented with three pumpkin seeds.

    Later these three seeds yielded three huge pumpkins. When they were ripe the old couple heard a noise from the inside, and they returned to heaven to ask advice. The children of the *then* [Paya Thaen] were scared again and the king infuriated. The couple were told that the pumpkins contained men, and they were given a drill, a chisel and an axe to open them. Out of the first pumpkin came the Kha, from the second the Lao, and from the third the "mandarins". The *then* [Paya Thaen] gave clothes, implements and three couples of animals modeled out of clay—buffalos, tigers and toads.

Pu Nyoeu and Nya Nyoeu had seven sons, and they divided the earth between them. They went to walk in the forest of the Himalayas where they captured a small lion which they called Sing Keo Sing Kham—Crystal Lion, Gold Lion. They tamed it and brought it along. Returning home they conquered a dangerous beast—a lion—[which they put] in an iron cage which they placed in their paddy field by the pond of S'va—the dwelling place of the King *Naga* (dragon) Thao K'am Leng. Suffering from injuries caused by the wild lion of Sangk'alok, the old couple died shortly afterwards. Before passing away they told men to make masks to represent them and their adopted son, Sing Keo Sing Kham. After their death, they became the tutelary deities of the kingdom and [were] called *devata* Luang. On the spot of their rice field where the lion was encaged, the pagoda Vat Visoun was constructed, and a reliquary—the T'at of the Watermelon—was built to cover the pond of the *naga*. (1979: 736–737)

While many substantive and structural similarities in this second version can be recognized, this version emphasizes that: (1) the world as we know it was created by the actions of a primordial ancestral couple, not by the gods, as in the first version; (2) the rupture of unity between the divine and human world is not seen as a consequence of humanity's refusal to acknowledge the fundamental hierarchical and divinely sanctioned order of the cosmos, but was a division based more on aesthetics (the ancestors were "ugly" and so frightened the children of the gods!); (3) there was a third class of human beings created, in addition to the Lao and the Kha who emerged from the pumpkin—these are the "mandarins" or aristocratic/bureaucratic administrators; (4) instead of an emphasis on the domestication of the buffalo, wild animals are introduced as dangerous powers that have to be controlled—the powers of nature that have to be "civilized," a motif that seems re-emphasized by the construction of the "Watermelon Stupa" at Vat Vixun on the pond of the local Naga king; and (5) this primordial ancestral couple who become the tutelary deities (*phi*) of Luang Phrabang are heroic and are succeeded in power and authority not only by their royal descendents, but by Buddhism itself (to wit Vat Vixun's eventual location). Thus, in comparison to the first version of the myth, which seems like an earlier invention, a further localization of principles has occurred. The primordial ancestors represent a more human or this-world-oriented articulation of agency. This move to the human orientation is also seen in the legitimacy given for the place of "mandarins," whose function is the administration of social order, and by recognition of the eventual civilizing triumph of Buddhism. It is this second version that continues to be rehearsed in the New Year Pi Mai rites of Luang Phrabang today.

In the mythic narratives just presented, we can see quite clearly how the ontology of the religious substratum articulated and valorized the power of place through the principle of this-worldly/otherworldly parallelism ("doubling" or "mirroring"). Moreover, it is also clear how ancestor veneration comes into play in relation to kingship and social hierarchy. These, of course, are two crucial ingredients described by Mus as constitutive of the "religion of monsoon Asia."

The Ideology of Royal Buddhist Legitimacy

What Theravada Buddhism added to the ideology of the power of place in Luang Phrabang seems almost negligible in structural terms, given the nature of "*muang* metaphysics" (Davis's phrase) already in place before its arrival. But what it did provide in terms of substance was a complementary *ethics of power*. That is, concomitant to the rationalization of divinely derived kingship, Lao kingship also became heir to specifically Buddhist conceptions of kingship that date back to the third century BCE reign of the Emperor Asoka in India, conceptions that were further nurtured and refined for a millennium and a half in Buddhist Sri Lanka before they were imported into Southeast Asia. This specifically Buddhist model of righteous rule had been wedded explicitly to overarching organizational principles of the Indic political mandala in Angkor before Fa Ngum happened on the scene. But before I address Fa Ngum's saga and its relevance to Luang Phrabang, I will ferret out briefly the ingredients of ideology that supported the rule of Buddhist kings, at least from the perspective of the monastic *sangha*.

In brief, this model of righteous rule was embodied in the mythic figure of the *cakkavattin*, a future universal royal power portrayed in detail in the *Cakkavatti-sihanada-suttanta* of the *Digha Nikaya* in the *Suttapitaka*, a text of eschatological, apocalyptic, and even millennial significance throughout Theravadan history. The *cakkavattin*, because of the vast sums of merit he has generated through his virtuous acts over many lifetimes, not entirely dissimilar from the career of a future Buddha per se, is a universal king who conquers the four quarters of Jambudvipa ("Rose-apple Island"; the human abode of men) on a nonviolent pilgrimage throughout the regions of his mandala. He succeeds by means of moral conquest, making present wherever he goes the virtues of the *pancasila* ("five-fold morality": observing the sanctity of life, truth, honesty, sexual propriety, and purity of mind [abstaining from intoxicants]). Moreover, the *cakkavattin* lays down the foundation of *dhamma*, preparing the world order morally for the appearance of the future buddha, Metteya (Maitreya), whose enlightenment and teaching of the *dhamma* will make possible not only untold prosperity for all, but the consummate experience of *nibbana* as well. The appearance of a *cakkavattin*, therefore, is a harbinger of a wonderful consummating collective future for all who have taken refuge in the Buddha, *dhamma*, and *sangha*. In various biographies of the Buddha, at Gotama's birth, the auspicious signs of his body are interpreted to mean that he will eventually become either a *cakkavattin* or a buddha. Thus, the image of the *cakkavattin* was a compelling ideal model for Buddhist kings to emulate, if not propagate.

There was, however, another important dimension to the ideal model of Buddhist kingship that contributes to the power of the Theravada royal legitimation scenario. According to the *jatakas* (the over 500 "birth stories" of the Buddha that recount his various spiritual perfections [*paramitas*] over many lifetimes), the Buddha (or more properly "the *bodhisatta*") was a royal prince not only in his final rebirth before he renounced the world in search of enlightenment, but in his penultimate rebirth as well. The *jataka* recounting this penultimate birth, the *Vessantara Jataka*, is easily the most popular *jataka* of all among the Lao, and apparently for Lao kingship as well, as we shall see. The substantive details of this *jataka* will be given in Chapter 4 within the context of an account of its ritual articulation in contemporary Luang Phrabang; for now it is enough to indicate that the *bodhisatta*-prince who serves as its protagonist, perfects the virtue of selfless giving by unconditionally giving away all of his great possessions, including even his loving children and virtuous wife. His actions are so prodigious that they produce unimaginable loads of merit, bringing him to the very threshold of buddhahood. This ideal model of virtuous kingship, with the implication that a king will eventually become a future buddha, is added to the *cakkavattin* profile, in addition to a specific ten-fold dharma for royalty to observe, to produce a compelling composite image of what a true Buddhist political leader can or should be. The preponderance of moral emphases found within these elements of kingship is why I have referred to the Theravada legitimation scenario as an *ethics of power*.

The Fa Ngum Saga and the Emergence of Lan Xang

While the figure of Fa Ngum in the fourteenth century has come to constitute the moment of political origins for the emergent Lao nation, at least from the perspective of indigenous, colonialist, nationalist, and Marxist historians, the traditional memories of this seminal figure are certainly not drawn from a history written without motives.[35] As Tambiah has noted with reference to the account of Fa Ngum in versions of the *Luang Phrabang Chronicle*: "Three essential features may be inferred from this [account]: the Laotian kingdom ... was a power in its own right; it was culturally influenced by Khmer civilization;[36] it also, like other Thai polities, espoused the cause of Sinhalese Buddhism" (1970: 29). Indeed, Tambiah has identified, in broad strokes, the major aims to which the saga of Fa Ngum has been enlisted. Fa Ngum's story of grand conquest to unite all Lao *muang* within one mandala is no doubt, as we might expect given the genre of literature within which it is presented, unabashedly embellished.[37] Be that as it may, it is still worth examining the Fa Ngum saga in detail, for it reveals much about how the past was ideally constructed for religious and political purposes.

Most sources[38] allege that Fa Ngum's birth took place in 1316 but differ on the reasons about why he was sent into exile by Phraya Khamphong,[39] his grandfather and the contemporary ruler of Muang Sua (Luang Phrabang). One account contends that Fa Ngum was sent away "because of the sexual peccadilloes of his father," Phi Fa, who allegedly had seduced one of the women of Khamphong's harem. Another version asserts that "because [Fa Ngum] was miraculously born with thirty-three teeth," omens were rife that his inauspicious presence threatened the well-being of the kingdom. Whatever the reason for exile, each account reports that Fa Ngum was placed on a raft and set adrift on the currents of the Mekong River accompanied by a cadre of thirty-three attendants.[40] In each version of his "exile" Fa Ngum winds up far downstream, where he is discovered and taken to Angkor, there to be given an education befitting a prince (Stuart-Fox 1998: 37). Commenting on the various versions accounting for Fa Ngum's exile, Stuart-Fox adds:

> More likely still, however, is that, as often happened, Fa Ngum and/or his father were actually banished either because an unsuccessful attempt had been made to seize the throne, or because Khamphong feared that one or the other harboured such ambitions. Alternatively, it is possible that Fa Ngum was not banished at all, but sent to Cambodia to study the arts of war and administration. (1998: 38)

Stuart-Fox's surmises contain a plausible scenario worth considering, especially since they represent his seasoned commentary on a story still taken literally by so many:

> The various versions of what happened thereafter differ in detail but broadly all agree that Fa Ngum was given a Khmer princess by the name of Kaeo Keng Nya in marriage, and that at the head of what was at first a predominantly Khmer army, he marched north, defeated his enemies and claimed the throne of Meuang Sua. . . . Fa Ngum's [subsequent] campaign on the southern Khorat

plateau can thus be seen as the first stage in a counter-attack that was almost certainly undertaken to re-impose Khmer, rather than assert Lao, control. (1998: 38)

In a world of realpolitik, it would seem clear that Fa Ngum is the symbolic focal point representing a change of regime taking place among the Lao at their most politically significant *muang* in a time of signal political transitions. His education in Angkor, his marriage to a Khmer princess, coupled with the fact that all versions agree that he was accompanied by Theravada Buddhist monks on his triumphal return, symbolize the establishment of a new political basis with grand ramifications: that his new regime was empowered by the most significant religious and political forces of the day (Khmer Angkor legitimated by Theravada Buddhism). While the legitimation scenario in this reconstruction is undoubtedly Khmer and Buddhist in substance, Fa Ngum is not quite seen simply as a vassal of Angkor either, but rather styled as Angkor's successor in the regions that came under his dominance. As Evans (2002b: 10) points out: "Angkor could not rein in this rogue vassal, challenged as the kingdom was by forces of Ayutthaya and Sukhothai." Moreover, according to one version of the saga, Fa Ngum acted with complete independence in forging an understanding with the other major political player (Vietnam) of the day.[41]

    With Angkor, Sukhothai, and Ayutthaya all politically or militarily preoccupied with each other at this time, and with the Vietnamese satisfied with negotiations about who was to pay what tribute to whom, Fa Ngum moved to consolidate his authority among the *muang* within his "Lao" orbit by appointing *chao muang* whose loyalty was beyond question. Holding a victory rite in Vientiane, he returned to Xieng Dong Xieng Thong (Muang Sua) and formally declared his kingdom Lan Xang Hom Khao, meaning "The Million Elephants and the White Parasol."

    In his concluding comments on the Fa Ngum saga, Stuart-Fox writes:

The story of Fa Ngum's conquests recalls an earlier paradigm provided by the great Indian Buddhist king Asoka. The conquest had been righteous, for wherever possible bloodshed had been minimized, through recognition of common ancestry. But ultimate justification for establishment of the kingdom had to lie in the conditions it created for the propagation of Buddhism. This may be why Fa Ngum was also credited with the introduction of Buddhism to Lan Xang. (1998: 44)

Lao retrospective readings of the establishment of Fa Ngum's new kingdom emphasize how it paved the way for the fruition of Buddhism, and thus connected the new kingdom with the broad universal history of Theravada Buddhism. But about a century and a half passed before the Phra Bang image was actually installed in Luang Phrabang, an event signaling formally the ascendance of Buddhism as the recognized power and primary ideology of the state. In addition, though the ideal image of the Buddhist *cakkavattin* would indeed eventually come to inform the profile of kingship in Luang Phrabang, this does not seem to have occurred before the reign of Chakkaphat Phaen Phaeo (1438–1479), "the first Laotian monarch to take a Buddhist name. The term *chakkaphat* is a modified Thai/Lao version of the Pali word *cakkavattin*" (Lorrillard 2003: 189). Moreover, the royal construction of Buddhist monasteries, according to Lorrillard's assessment of material cultural remains, did not begin in earnest until "the second half of the fifteenth century [when] . . . Chakkaphat Phaen Phaeo received aid from the kingdom of Lan Na—where Buddhism was flourishing—to repel a Vietnamese invasion" (2003: 189). Lorrillard has concluded that much of the substance, especially the styles of material culture that became dominant in Luang Phrabang, owe their origins to Lan Na's influence, rather than to Angkor's. Furthermore, when Stuart-Fox's later surmise regarding the currency of political legitimation scenarios in play during the actual time of Fa Ngum's establishment of the kingdom is considered, the situation at the time of the kingdom's establishment appears much more complex than the traditional sources would have it:

> At the time of Fa Ngum, however, the legend of Khun Borom establishing the right of royal descent and possession of territory, together with communal worship of powerful spirits associated with natural forces and the land itself probably counted for more than Buddhist conceptions of kingship. (1998: 50)

Eventually, the ideal Buddhist image of the *cakkavattin* became undeniably attractive to the Lao royal profile, along with the image of the ideal ruler of dharma articulated in a revamped Lao Buddhist version of the Hindu epic *Ramayana*. At the beginning, however, at least during the time dominated by Fa Ngum in the fourteenth century, it was probably not the substance of Buddhist and Hindu royal ideal images in play that bolstered his rule, but rather instead the principles of *muang* polity, those previously articulated in the ontology of the indigenous Lao religious substratum. For this is how the administration of power in the Lan Xang kingdom functioned in its early days:

> The kingdom was thus constituted on the *mandala* model, decentralized and segmentary in its political organization. Four principal *meuang*—Xiang Dong Xiang Thong, Xiang Khuang, Viang Chan Viang Kham, and Sikhottabong—formed the core, each with its own dependent, secondary *meuang*. From these

the greater part of the army was raised. The frontier *meuang* were responsible for immediately reporting any security threat directly to the capital. What held the kingdom together were the personal loyalties that existed between the king and his *chau meuang*. . . . Every two months, closer *meuang* had to dispatch a messenger to Xiang Dong Xiang Thong to report to the king. All tributary rulers (*chau meuang*) had also to submit a written annual report on their *meuang* (none of which have survived) and to present their tribute in person every third year. This required them to leave their *meuang* in the first month of the year in what was for many a long and arduous journey by elephant along narrow jungle paths and across swift-flowing rivers in order to arrive at the capital by the third month. There each paid homage to the king, renewed his oath of obedience, drank the sacred water of allegiance, and offered tribute. Any ruler not so doing would be considered lacking in loyalty, and could be deposed by an armed force sent to exact punishment. A principal requirement was for each *chau meuang* to participate in blood sacrifices to the powerful guardian deities of Xiang Dong Xiang Thong, in accordance with rules laid down by Fa Ngum's forebears. Their presence at these ceremonies presided over by the king symbolically recognized the superiority of the *Phi Thaen*, the ancestral spirits worshipped in the capital over the *phi seua* of regional *meuang*. Such rituals not only established a symbolic unity; they were believed to be essential for the preservation of the power and prosperity of the *mandala*, for only such powerful spirits could prevent malign *phi* from destroying Meuang Lao. (Stuart-Fox 1998: 45)

If this depiction is reasonably accurate, then it confirms the fact that the political and magical ontology of the spirit cults had come to be writ large with the establishment of a grand Lao mandala. This portrayal describes quite clearly how Lan Xang's public ritual cult expressed the spiritual principles of "doubling" (this-worldly and otherworldly parallelism), territoriality, ancestral lineage, and hierarchy.[42] We can also see clearly how the centripetal and centrifugal forces between the center and peripheries, what Tambiah has referred to as the "pulsating" affects of "galactic polity," came into play through the ritual comings and goings of the *chao muang* who came to the capital to pay tribute and to participate in renewing the excellence of the center. While we have no records of what transpired exactly in terms of the relations at the *ban* and *muang* levels of the mandala, or between lesser *muang* and regional *muang*, we are probably not far wrong in assuming that this same administrative and ritual pattern was replicated at those levels too. That is, the renewal of power experienced at the center was ritually confirmed and distributed throughout to the other *muang* subspaces of the mandala.

What followed over the next century and a half, however, was the increasing adoption of specifically Theravada Buddhist semiotics of power, not at all different in terms of the dynamics of interplay between the center and periphery, nor in terms of the basic Lao assumptions about the power of place, but different in terms of how power was mythically imagined and ideally acquired. Yet these Buddhist and Hindu concepts were probably interpreted and understood, at least in part, through the conceptual categories of the Lao indigenous religious substratum.

> Local *phi* were *subordinated* not to the higher truth of Buddhism so much as to the superior magical powers of its images and rituals. In its higher mystery, more potent magic, and the authority of its monks, gained through alliance with secular power, lay the appeal of Buddhism for the Lao peasantry. (Stuart-Fox 1998: 54; my emphasis)

While I think it is correct to say that the magical power of Buddhism eventually proved a potent attraction to the lay Lao peasantry, there is also an element of half-truth in this statement. On the one hand, it is doubtlessly true that the local *phi* were "*subordinated* not to higher truth of Buddhism," but rather to "superior magical powers of its [Buddhism's] images and rituals." But the other half of the issue, the part that I want to question, is whether Buddhism's "higher truths," as well as its own symbols and rites constitutive of magical power, were not themselves actually *subordinated* to or interpreted by means of the idiom of Tai-Lao magical power. Indeed, this is where I must part company with how the relationship between Buddhism and the spirit cults is presented by Stuart-Fox and Evans. Stuart-Fox consistently uses the language of "subsumed" (1998: 50), "incorporated" (53), and "subordinated" (54–55) to refer to the manner in which Buddhism established superiority. Evans uses the language of "encompassing" (2002b: 9, 11). Consequently, both, perhaps inadvertently, regard the spirit cults as passive agents in the relation between the two; that is, the indigenous religious substratum gets somehow uprooted and then recast within the new increasingly pervasive Buddhist worldview. My position is that the indigenous religious substratum was not passive at all; rather, it provided the categories and conceptuality of power that were used on the popular level to construe Buddhist "higher truths" in a manner understandable to the many.[43] Here, I am deliberately inverting the conventional understanding of the relationship between Buddhism and spirit cults in order to more accurately ascertain why it is that Lao Buddhism is understood in its uniquely Lao manner. I would also suggest that nowhere is this Lao understanding more evident than in the manner in which the Buddha himself was understood within Lan Xang. This brings me to an extended personal digression, the relevance of which will be seen shortly.

On a day-long field trip to Ayutthaya (Thailand) organized by the International Association of Buddhist Studies (IABS) in conjunction with its conference held in Bangkok in December 2002, I was taken, along with busloads of other conference participants, to four different temples of noted import. I had spent a week in Ayutthaya a few years earlier on one of those stopovers between New England and Sri Lanka that I mention in the preface, and I had spent that time visiting as many of its archaeological sites as possible. At the time of our IABS field trip in 2002, I was surprised at the choice of venues that had been selected for us to visit. All of the places we visited were temples housing Buddha images considered to be invested with great magical power. It was not so much the symbolic architecture of these temples that we were told to contemplate, nor their importance to the historical unfolding of the Buddhasasana in Thailand, but rather the potency of the images they contained. At that time my reaction of surprise was due to the fact that the notion of magically powerful Buddha images within the nominal Theravada religious culture of Sri Lanka, the one with which I am most familiar, is almost nonexistent, if not dramatically underplayed in comparison.[44] Any idea of an active presence of images to intervene in the affairs of humankind, that is, images attributed agency in this world of *samsara*, is almost exclusively restricted to images of the *devata*s, and not the Buddha. The iconic images of the gods in Sri Lanka are always regarded as consecrated embodiments or divine presences, and their ritual care and public access within their sanctum sanctora is very carefully attended to through properly observed liturgical rubrics. Although there may be some Sinhala Buddhists who might think of the Buddha, or buddha images, as constituting an active force within the world, this particular magical conception is limited to the manner in which the power of the Dalada, or "tooth-relic of the Buddha," is understood instead.

Over the centuries the Dalada, like the Phra Bang image for Lao kingship and Lao people, became the palladium for Sri Lankan kingship and the Sinhala people, from at least, if not earlier, the twelfth- and thirteenth-century CE Polonnaruva period. Over time, many Sinhalas came to believe in the Dalada's magical power, a power not only to protect and energize the power of kings (or even today's contemporary politicos), but also a power to cause rain in times of draught.[45] But in his definitive study of the cult of the Dalada, H. L. Seneviratne (1978) makes the salient point that the Dalada's sustained power and its traditional ritual care is a consequence of the fact that it is treated *as if it were a Hindu deity*. That is, it is treated as an object of power in a manner not all that different from the manner in which the sacred and powerful images of the *devata*s, especially the *satara varan devi* I mentioned earlier, are regarded. Indeed, the Dalada is often regarded in Sri Lanka as *devatidevata* or "the god beyond the gods," the pinnacle and basis of support in the conditioned world of *samsara*. This hierarchy of divine power is symbolically articulated in the annual ritual procession of the *asala perahara* in Kandy.

Moreover, the centrality of the Dalada as the pivot of the Sinhala mandala is apparent in the spatial layout and seasonal ritual proceedings of the capital city.[46] However, and this is the point that I want to stress, there are no anthropomorphic images of the Buddha per se in Sri Lanka that are so regarded as great repositories of power to be tapped for this-worldly reasons. They are categorically different in kind as representations of the Buddha: the Dalada is a *relic* of the Buddha;[47] Buddha images are not. While the Dalada as a relic retains active potency, Buddha images do not. The Dalada is identified physically with the actual historical Buddha of our era, Buddha images are not, except perhaps symbolically. When images are ritually consecrated in Sri Lanka, they are, indeed, sanctified, but not for the purpose of imbuing them with a sacred power to be tapped by those who will venerate them.[48]

These comparisons between the Sri Lankan and Thai-Lao contexts assisted me as I tried to make sense out of the cult of the Phra Bang image in Lan Xang, especially in terms of its significance for the Buddhist political mandala that was eventually established, since the Phra Bang came to represent the powerful center or *axis mundi* of this mandala kingdom. It has seemed to me that the key to understanding the significance of the Phra Bang in Lang Xang lies in the fact that it, too, had been probably regarded analogically *as if it were a Hindu deity*, at least in terms of the context of its Indic origins at Angkor. But more, in Luang Phrabang the analogy seems to have been further extended, so that it was also regarded analogically *as if it were the "phi mandala,"* maybe not so much considered as such among the learned monks of the monasteries that were eventually established by royalty in Luang Phrabang and elsewhere in Lan Xang, but rather functionally and structurally in the mind-sets of its many lay devotees, including its chief patron, the king.

I now want to return to Stuart-Fox's account of the foundation of Lan Xang to develop further the point I have just made in my extended digression. In describing the central significance of the Phra Bang, Stuart-Fox has this to say:

> Though the *Phra Bang* itself may be a fine example of Khmer sculpture, the *Pheun Phra Bang* (Story of the *Phra Bang*) tells how the image was miraculously cast in Sri Lanka, and from there transported to Cambodia before being brought to Laos. Many such popular stories of revered Buddha images were invented to assist in spreading belief in Buddhism through awe of the magical powers these images were believed to possess and their ability to "save humankind from sin."[49] But the association of great Buddhist kings with such images also fulfilled a powerful legitimizing function, for the stories of their miraculous provenance served . . . to anchor Lao culture firmly to its religious and intellectual roots in India and Sri Lanka. Lao history was thus universalized by becoming part of the universal history of Buddhist redemption.[50] (1998: 52)

While I would quibble with some of Stuart-Fox's overly Christian and theologically saturated language,[51] he is quite right in his general assessment of the significance of the Phra Bang image. It is definitely *not* an image of Sinhala origins. That
much can be established easily on stylistic grounds, quite apart from the fact that
no such conceptuality regarding the Buddha image exists in Sinhala religious culture (see Plate 1). We can, however, follow Stuart-Fox's lead by inquiring into how
images of the same genre were regarded within the Khmer Angkorian mandalic
milieu, since the possibility of Sri Lanka being its source is absolutely a dead end.
Harris's description in this regard is quite helpful:

> The various capitals of the Angkorian kings may be read symbolically as minia-
> ture images of the universe. The rivers and the *baraya*s represented the cosmic
> ocean; the enclosing walls, the iron-mountain chain (*cakravala*) at the limit of
> the world's golden disk; and the temples, the central world mountain, Mount
> Meru.
>
> . . . .
>
> Through their construction and accompanying rites, the kingdom was trans-
> formed into an ideal realm. At the center of the great city Angkor Thom [City
> of Dhamma] stands Jayavarman's pantheon, the Bayon, representing Mount
> Meru; the nearby royal palace is homologized to the residence of Indra; and
> Neak Pean, to the sacred Lake Anavatapta. We do know that the Siem Reap Riv-
> er, which flows through the city, had been identified with the Ganges sometime
> previously.... Symbolically then, the Angkorian state has become co-extensive
> with the entire world. (2005: 19, 22)

It would seem, then, that the eventual Buddhacization of the Lan Xang mandala
not only linked the history of the kingdom to the universal history of the Theravada Buddhist tradition, but it also contained within it the possibility that Lan
Xang would be regarded as a microcosm of the universe that was "co-extensive
with the entire world." Thus the new significance of Lan Xang was not only that
it was historically situated within the larger scope of the Buddhasasana, but that
it was now situated in an Indic Buddhist cosmos: that is, it had become a this-
worldly center of the mandalic cosmos, the linked counterpart to Indra's *devaloka*.
(Indeed, Phou Si, the scenic hill dominating the Luang Phrabang peninsula, is
still identified precisely with Mount Meru, the pivot of the mandala and the *axis
mundi* connecting the world of the gods and the world of men.) But to return to
the issue at hand, what can we make of the significance of Buddha images within
the context of this cosmic symbolism?

Within Angkorian cosmology for centuries, until the Mahayana orientation
of Jayavarman VII's thirteenth-century reign, the king had projected himself as

a *devaraja* ("god-king") or as the *devaraja*'s surrogate.[52] The great Khmer temples of the Angkor region built between the ninth and thirteenth centuries were constructed by kings who believed that they were providing "residences" for their deceased parents. While consecrating (or "promoting") their royal parents as the divine primordial cosmic couple of Hindu Purana cosmology, Siva and Uma (or Parvati), they achieved a Khmer synthesis of indigenous religious practices (the cults of ancestor veneration and territorial spiritual power) with the cosmology of Saivite Hinduism. The practice of promoting one's parents was based upon the following formula: just as the king's parents are equated with the ultimate generative powers of the cosmos, so the king and queen are regarded as their parents' this-worldly counterparts; thus the contemporary royal realm is a "double" of the ultimate heavenly realm where the promoted parents as Siva and Uma now dwell. As the this-worldly embodiment of this "doubling" phenomenon, the king is therefore *devaraja*, the "god-king" or the "god who is king." Significantly, *devaraja* is also the epithet most commonly ascribed to Sakka (Sanskrit: Sakra; Indra) in Pali Buddhist literature. Its use as an appellation for the king, therefore, in later Theravada Angkorian times, signals the "doubling" effect as well.

The cult of the *devaraja* has been the subject of much scholarly attention over the past century, and we need not rehearse much of that discussion here. Harris, however, has made an intriguing point, one that may impinge directly upon the manner in which the power of the Phra Bang image was eventually construed in Lan Xang:

> Earlier scholars, such as Coedes and Dupont, understood the *devaraja* to be either the deified king himself or a singular image of Siva standing in the king's stead. The matter has not been adequately solved, but it now seems likely that the *devaraja* was a special mobile image (*calanti pratima*) of a protective deity. (2005: 12)

Harris has presented this finding cautiously, but I want to reflect a little further on its possible ramifications for understanding how Lan Xang's Phra Bang, and other Buddha images in the Thai-Lao culture area (a culture area that was so profoundly impacted by the religious and political legacy of Angkor) came to be so highly valorized, and thus why the possession of these images became such vital matters for political and military contestation.

In his discussion of the "god of the soil," Mus points out that the spirit is intrinsically the place itself, "god-soil," or ultimately the "energies of the place" encountered in human *events*. If we apply this understanding in relation to Buddha images such as the Phra Bang, we are then left with the understanding that the image itself is not to be divorced from the reality that it is thought to represent.

That is, the Phra Bang *is* the presence of Buddha as it has been experienced in the *events* of the place it inhabits. The image is a form of the deity; therefore, it *is* the deity. I think that this is precisely the combination of issues that we meet in the figure of the Phra Bang in early sixteenth-century Lan Xang after the image was brought to the newly consecrated Vat Vixun in Luang Phrabang by King Vixun. Indeed, "Phra Bang" literally means "an embodiment (Bang) of the Buddha" (Phra). Thus the Phra Bang is not regarded simply as a symbol, the possession of which was a marker of the king's legitimacy, though of course it did function as that kind of signifier too. But within this context of cosmology, the Phra Bang constituted the veritable presence of the Buddha. It became the anchoring, centering power of the mandala, and the king was its primary caretaker and dispenser of its power. Therefore, just as the images of Siva and Uma within consecrated "ancestral" temples were to the kings and queens of Angkor, so the Phra Bang was to Lan Xang kings.

The Phra Bang, however, was not in Luang Phrabang during Fa Ngum's purported reign. Evans notes (2002b: 16) a legend about how the Phra Bang refused to go to Luang Phrabang because of premonitions about the moral future of Fa Ngum. This may be related to the tradition that Fa Ngum was deposed in 1374 because of his insistence that he exercise unfettered sexual rights over the women of the capital.

The Fa Ngum saga also presents a narrative in which factions of two kinds developed within his court: first, there was a tension between those who represented a "Khmer orientation" and those who sided with the "old aristocracy"; and second, there was factionalism between those who supported one form of Theravada monasticism over another. The first type of factionalism, ultimately rooted in the politics of power succession, would be enduring and of paramount significance.[53] Implicit in the split between the "Khmer-oriented" faction (symbolized by Fa Ngum himself) and the "old aristocracy" was a philosophical divide between the ideology of Theravada Buddhism and the ontology of the spirit cults. The initial impetus for the tension or split was probably occasioned by the growing cultic and social presence of the Buddhist *sangha*, especially in the royal capital but increasingly throughout the river basins and tributaries of the Mekong River.

On the basis of reading the most ancient versions of chronicles written at the end of the fifteenth and beginning of the sixteenth century, Lorrillard (2003: 188) notes that in addition to the Fa Ngum story, there are references to various Theravada monks who came to Luang Phrabang early on to establish the first monastery, named after Pasaman, a leading monk from Angkor. These were Sinhalese monks from Sri Lanka, apparently, whose first act was to plant a *bodhi* tree (*Ficus religiosus*) from a cutting that originated in Sri Lanka (likely from Sri Mahabodhi in Anuradhapura).[54] Lorrillard further notes that subsequently monasteries were built during virtually every royal reign "in order to preserve the ashes of a deceased member of the royal family. The constructions of stupas are sometimes mentioned. These appear to be funeral monuments." Noting the steady growth and spread of monastic institutions abetted by the support of royalty in the capital and in many important villages, Lorrillard writes in conclusion: "We can however establish with certitude, at a time between the second half of the fourteenth century and the second half of the fifteenth century, the emergence [throughout Lan Xang] of a new religious phenomenon" (2003: 196).

These findings by Lorrillard are quite suggestive. Given the eventual valorization of the Phra Bang image, and given that it seems to have been left behind in Vieng Kham rather than ritually established in the center of the new Lan Xang kingdom when the kingdom was being formally declared by Fa Ngum, it is interesting to observe that what the Sinhala monks did bring with them as a marker to indicate the spread of the Buddha's *dhamma* was not a magically empowered Buddha image, but rather a sapling of the *bodhi* tree, the aniconic symbol par excellence in Sri Lanka signaling the presence of the teaching of the Buddha. These Sinhala monks from Sri Lanka, as orthodox Theravadins, were apparently not participants in the cult of the Buddha image. Instead, they appear to have been learned scholars whose monastic legacy would eventually establish Lan Xang as a center of Theravada in the sixteenth century. Second, the rationale given for the establishment of royal monasteries as venues to "preserve the ashes of deceased members of the royal family" seems especially reminiscent of royal Khmer motivations for building temples on behalf of deceased parents. The royal proclivity for making merit, for being the primary patron of the Buddhist monastic community, has been merged here with the tradition of royal ancestor veneration. In these two cultic instances then, we see a combination of Sinhala Buddhist Theravada orthopraxy represented by conservative monks and a Khmer-influenced royal court motivated to support the growth and spread of Theravada monasticism through motivations rooted not only in Buddhist-inspired merit-making consciousness, but also through the persistent indigenous practice of ancestor veneration.

Royal support of the Buddhist *sangha* in these early years of Lan Xang would have created tension in the court among the spirit-cult-oriented "old aristocracy," as well as among those ritual practitioners, including *chao muang*, who might perceive the spread of monasticism as a rival to the conceptual, ritual, and political bases of their own powers. Indeed, the

establishment of a powerful and unified monastic order in close reciprocal relationship with monarchical authority came to provide additional weighty legitimation for Lao kings—but powerful social forces had first to be overcome. Opposition was not to Buddhism *per se*, for its beliefs were known and practised

already. Rather it was to the establishment of a Sangha under royal patronage displacing existing animist cults and their powerful priesthoods that was so
strongly resisted. (Stuart-Fox 1998: 51–52)

If this was indeed the case, then what caused the tensions between the two factions
of the court was not simply a matter of philosophical disagreement, but about
vested interests in political power structures. With the eventual relative triumph of
the *sangha*, signaled by the construction of *vat*s in the center of virtually every significant *muang* throughout the mandala, a rapprochement between the two rival
orientations was eventually forged, though periodically contested.

A second type of factionalism also seems to have existed within the Buddhist
side of this divide, a subfactionalism within the ranks of *sangha* supporters.

Once Xiang Dong Xiang Thong [Luang Phrabang] became the capital of an
imperial *mandala*, separate schools of Theravada Buddhism may have been encouraged and patronized by different factions at court for their own political
ends. Two new schools may well have been in competition: a Khmer school
introduced from Cambodia by Kaeo Keng Nya [Fa Ngum's queen] and her pro-
Khmer party (possibly led by the Cambodian/Sri Lankan monk Phra Thepha-
langka); and a "forest monastery" school from the middle Mekong in the figure
of Phra Pasman. Both would have encountered opposition not only from any
already established form of Buddhism, but more importantly from practitioners of the *phi* cults. Competition between opposing schools was probably behind the calling of a monastic council in 1359. But not until the death of Kaeo
Keng Nya in 1368, and the arrival at court of Princess Kaeo Lot Fa, daughter of
the King of Ayutthaya, does it seem likely that adherents of an invigorated Sri
Lankan school of Theravada Buddhism then dominant in Sukhothai and Ayutthaya finally gained the upper hand. (Stuart-Fox 1998: 53)

Thus the court of the early Lan Xang mandala was not only quickly internation-
alized, with royalty from Angkor and Ayutthaya who supported the Sri Lankan
Sinhala Buddhist orientation of the *sangha*, but Lan Xang also became a venue for
a debate about the manner in which the Buddhist monastic vocation should be
best realized.

Assuming that the debate was not driven by questions of ethnicity (a Khmer/
Sinhala/Thai faction on the one hand versus a middle-Mekong "Lao" faction on
the other), we can write with some confidence about its substance, for it is familiar terrain. From at least the first century BCE in Sri Lanka, there have been re-
current arguments between the so-called *granthadhura* and so-called *vipassanadhura* monks: the former arguing for a monastic lifestyle based on scholasticism

and service to the community while the latter maintain that the contemplative life of a monk is best realized beyond urban institutions or villages, in the forest where the discipline of meditation can be best pursued. In terms of *dhamma*, the primary issue between the two understandings has to do with whether the path of the Buddha culminating in enlightenment is best accomplished through compassionate and selfless service rendered "for the welfare of many" who suffer in *samsara*, or whether the path to *nibbana* is best realized through solitary meditation on the impermanence of existence, a phenomenal existence that is in a continuous process of change. That this debate would erupt in Lan Xang and involve factions of the court is not at all surprising,[55] owing to the fact that the introduction of this new way of being religious would beg for very basic definitions of what constitutes a Buddhist holy man. Moreover, one side, the *granthadhura*, would require a considerable material support to maintain its institutionalization (the *ban* and *muang vat*s), in return for offering the possibility of providing a "field of merit."

There were, then, economic, as well as political, ramifications to the debate. Forest monks, after all, do not require elaborate temples, so they are not expensive subjects who require much material support. Inevitably, the question would arise within the court: should so much in the way of material resources and labor be expended on the building of monasteries and the ritual maintenance of a new class of elite religious holy men? The first Buddhist holy men in the Lao Lan Xang capital were also, after all, "non Lao," or more accurately, from beyond *muang Lao*. Though most historians discount the presence or awareness of ethnic identity until the late nineteenth century, some degree of acknowledgement delineating differences between those who speak different languages (Khmer and Sinhala) and who are geographically "from away" cannot be entirely discounted either.

The Unfolding of the Buddhist Mandala

Following the deposition of Fa Ngum in 1374 and the reign of Chakkaphat (*cakkavattin*) Phaen Phaeo about seventy years later, little is known for certain,[56] except that perhaps the tensions we have noted above persisted. Despite the fact that Fa Ngum's eldest son succeeded him, a kind of father-son transition rarely effected seamlessly in Lan Xang history,[57] this succession "signaled a victory for the old aristocracy of Xiang Dong Xiang Thong over the 'Khmer faction' composed of Fa Ngum's former comrades-in-arms" (Stuart-Fox 1998: 63). Evans (2002b: 13–14) surmises that perhaps because Samsaenthai (Fa Ngum's eldest son) "had grown up in a Tai milieu and was perhaps better attuned to the cultural ways of the emerging mandala [and had taken] wives from the kingdoms of Ayudhya, Lan Na and Xiang Hung," his reign was not only acceptable to the "old aristocracy," but assured the kingdom of a "peaceful consolidation" as a result of alliances cement-ed through the diplomacy of marriage. Thus a new political balance was struck, one that rested on assuring the old aristocracy of their continued vested interests, while seeking recognition and cooperation from other Tai mandalas, rather than with the Khmer orientation. This balance remained intact until the reign of Chak-khapat Phaen Phaeo, who seems to have set into motion a pattern of increasing Buddhacization.

Lan Xang had plunged into a crises mode following the death of Lan Kham Deng, Samsaenthai's son (Fa Ngum's grandson) for a period of at least twenty years, a period that Evans (2002b: 14) says witnessed "the rapid ascent and over-throw of several claimants to the throne" until "Xainya Chakkhapat (r. 1442–1479) imposed his will and secured the kingdom by appointing his six sons and other close relatives to key administrative positions in the realm." Since "key adminis-trative positions in the realm" means positions held by *chao muang*, Chakkhapat Phaen Phaeo's reign constituted a thoroughgoing housecleaning. The "old aris-tocracy" was removed in favor of the king's relatives and the rule of the various regional *muang* became synonymous with "family rule." Few structural changes were effected in the mandala at this time, but the personal or familial nature of political rule, based upon the perceived charisma and power of the king, intensi-fied greatly. While stamping his family rule on to the Lan Xang mandala, Xainya Chakkhapat Phaen Phaeo strengthened the *sangha* in return for what appears to have been a quid pro quo agreement with powerful monks who had maintained close ties to the Ayutthaya *sangha*:

> The religious legitimation of his rule was reinforced by his first act upon be-coming king, the appointment of new abbots in two important monasteries. The move was designed to unify the Sangha after political turmoil of the previ-ous decade, and to reward his own monastic supporters. The increased influ-ence of the Sangha during the reign of Xainya Chakkaphat is evident. Senior abbots were given exalted titles (such as *Raxakhru* [*rajaguru*—"teacher of the king"] and *Maha Sami* [*maha svami*—"great sage"]) and invited to serve on the Royal Council, and all monks thereafter were addressed as *chau*, a title of nobility. (Stuart-Fox 1998: 64)

Indeed, Xainya Chakkhapat's reign was fortuitous for the *sangha*. The fact that monks were invited to serve on the Royal Council and that all monks henceforth were addressed as *chau* (*chao*), a term previously reserved for those individuals at the hub or administrative center of a *ban* or *muang*, clearly indicates an unprec-edented recognition of prestige. At the same time, because important positions of political administration were assigned to trusted members of the royalty, the *sangha* became the one social institution in the mandala that aristocrats not of the royal family, or other aspiring leaders from outside the center of the mandala, could hope to benefit from personally. In addition to the educational possibilities (of learning to read and write) that the *sangha* now afforded,

> the Sangha . . . provided the only means of social mobility in a highly hierarchical society. For the brilliant and ambitious who came to the attention of a powerful patron, transferal to a *vat* in the capital, perhaps even a place as a page at court, offered a rare opportunity for advancement. For those not so endowed, life as a monk at least ensured social respect and status. Even the lowliest village monk received the veneration of the highest member of the local nobility. (Stuart-Fox 1998: 56)

Xainya Chakkhapat's reign and his program of support for the Buddhist *sangha*, however, was eventually seriously threatened by the aggression of the powerful Le dynasty from Vietnam which, when it encountered resistance from Lan Xang forces in taking over the Plain of Jars, proceeded to invade Xieng Dong Xieng Thong and laid the center of the kingdom to waste. The impact of this invasion was traumatic.[58] Perhaps because the traditional *muang* political infrastructure of the mandala had been shattered and because the invading Vietnamese seem to have avoided destroying important *vats* of the *sangha*, especially

> in Xiang Dong Xiang Thong, monks from five major monasteries that the Vietnamese had spared took the lead in organizing the returning population to reconstruct the city. When the old king refused to return, however, Prince Thaen Kham was invited to ascend the throne, taking the name of Suvanna Banlang. . . . The Buddhist Sangha seems to have gained in influence in the years following the Vietnamese invasion. The abbots of three major monasteries—Vat Kaeo, Vat Manoram and Vat Pasman—were given judicial powers, and these three vats were declared sanctuaries where those accused of wrongdoing could undergo rehabilitation free from the threat of arrest. (Stuart-Fox 1998: 67–68)

If the *sangha* played an important role in reestablishing order and normality in Lan Xang following the Vietnamese assault, its own strong ties to the *sangha* in neighboring Tai mandalas proved especially significant in decades that followed not only in terms of enriching the Lan Xang *sangha* religiously, but politically as well. Trade and political connections to Lan Na and Ayutthaya were intensified.

The sculpture of Buddha images from this period reflect a concerted influence from Chiang Mai (Lan Na) and Ayutthaya. Veidlinger (2007: 101) makes the related points that within the contemporary Lan Na Tai context written scriptures "are not nearly given the position of prominence that is accorded to Buddha images or *tipitakadhara* monks" and that "while written copies of Pali texts were available to some extent, many were kept in libraries largely as symbols of royal power rather than as scholarly tool." Although there is no corroborating evidence for Lan Xang, it is likely that Pali texts transmitted in Luang Phrabang's *vats* at this time were prized as much for their cultic significance as they were for their discursive.

It is possible that in wake of the destructive war with the Vietnamese Le dynasty the ontology of the indigenous religious substratum was discredited, at least among the aristocracy. Or perhaps the increasing contact with the other Tai mandalas, abetted by the *sangha*'s inter-mandala relations, reinforced the social, political, and cultural fact that the aristocracies of these mandalas had by now thoroughly embraced Buddhism as the normative ideology. What was occurring in Lan Xang, then, was but a reflection of a wider pattern that was also occurring in Lan Na and Ayutthaya in terms of an ideological and intellectual triumph rooted in the conceptuality of Buddhist literary culture.

However, Harris has expressed some skepticism about the degree to which this ideological hegemony of Theravada Buddhism penetrated beyond the central aristocratic circle of the neighboring Khmer mandala during this very same time frame. Specifically he questions the theory advanced by some that in the fifteenth-century post-Angkorian period, Theravada Buddhism became a grassroots movement responsible for the eradication of the Angkor caste system, a theory he suggests the available evidence does not warrant. He also points out "it is not at all clear that Buddhism in Sri Lanka around the same period [fifteenth century] successfully operated beyond aristocratic control and the same holds good for Thailand, although admittedly somewhat later. It is probable that Cambodian Buddhism operated in much the same pattern" (2005: 27).

The issue Harris has raised in the Khmer context is important to consider in the Lao context as well. In fact, we know that the popular religion of the agricultural peasantry in the fourteenth and fifteenth centuries in Sri Lanka, as well as in the nominally Buddhist aristocratic court, was quite eclectic at this very time. Indeed, at both levels of society, religious and political culture was subjected to a rising tide of Hindu influence for a variety of reasons, including changing population demographics.[59] Within the political mandalas of Southeast Asia, there is no doubt that Buddhism was predominantly an urban phenomenon as it became the religion of the aristocratic elite. Moreover, the establishment of *vats* during this time was limited to those major *ban* or *muang* contexts in which adequate resources could support the ritual and fiscal life of a *vat*. We can also be sure that the non-Tai peoples of the countryside outside of the Lao-settled regions of the Mekong River basin and its tributaries, the Khmu in particular in northern Laos, remained quite outside the orbit of Buddhist institutional life.[60] The point I am making indirectly here by referring to the "non-Lao" population who lived within the orbit of the Lan Xang kingdom, but outside of the center's Buddhist ideological persuasion, is that these peoples retained their full embrace of the spirit cults. Insofar as they continued to live so intimately with the "ethnic Lao" and remained "animistic" means that the religious culture of the countryside remained predominantly spirit-cult-oriented. It is likely that the religion of the rustic Lao did so as well, and the extent to which any "rural Lao" would have become Buddhist exclusively seems quite remote, especially when "the continued worship at *ho phi* (spirit shrines) [even] by aristocratic families well into the twentieth century shows that these practices were never obliterated (Evans 2002b: 16). If the aristocrats at the center of the mandala persisted in the worship of spirits, there is even a better reason to assume that the veneration of *phi* remained the rule, rather than the exception, in the rural villages of the Lao. While the religion at the center of the mandala became increasingly Buddhist during the reigns of Vixun, Phothisarat, and Xetthathirat, those decades during the sixteenth century that constituted the halcyon days politically for the Lan Xang kingdom, the spirit cults were sustained, even though directly attacked at the center and in the regional *muang* of the mandala.

Buddhist-Mindedness in Sixteenth-Century Lan Xang

Some historians have speculated that the establishment of the *Buddhist* kingdom of Lan Xang rightly owes its origins to King Vixun, rather than to Fa Ngum. While Fa Ngum may have orchestrated a tribute-based unification of *muang Lao* and endeavored, apparently, to establish a Buddhist monastic presence in Xieng Dong Xieng Thong to legitimate his rule, it was not until the early sixteenth-century reign of Vixun (1501–1520), followed immediately by the reign of his son Phothisarat, that the symbolism of the royal regalia and the ritual life of a royal mandala center became unambiguously Buddhist in symbolic and institutional terms. No new political structures per se were initiated that would alter the pulsating or tributary dynamic constitutive of the mandala (Evans 2002b: 16), but the discourses of virtually all political and cultural life, at least at the center, were now articulated through thoroughly Indic forms, primarily the Theravada idioms. Vixun's reign marks the ritual establishment of the Phra Bang image in Vat Vixun, a monastery the monarch built especially for that very purpose. "Before it the lords [of the *muang*] would swear loyalty to their king, and hereafter the capital would be recognised as Luang Phrabang, 'the place of the Buddha Phra Bang'" (Evans 2002b: 16).

Vixun's patronage of the *sangha* was not limited to ritual and symbolic material expression, for he seems to have been to be a patron of the literary arts as well:

Vixun's twenty-year reign also saw a remarkable flowering of Buddhist studies in Lan Xang. Learned monks were invited to take up residence in Xiang
Dong Xiang Thong; sacred texts were copied and studied; and the monasteries became centers of literary culture. Most popular were still the *Jatakas*, to
which Lao monks added their own stories of former lives of the Buddha. A
Lao collection of fifty of these called the *Ha Sip Xat* contains twenty-seven that
are entirely unknown elsewhere.[61] A Lao version of the *Panchatantra* was produced, and the Lao version of the *Ramayana*, known as the *Phra Lak Phra Lam*
may also have been given its Lao literary form around this time. (Stuart-Fox
1998: 74)[62]

The *Vessantara Jataka* and the *Phra Lak Phra Lam* became centerpieces of royal
attention for Luang Phrabang kings throughout the remainder of their dynasty.
    The ritual recitation of the *Vessantara Jataka* eventually evolved into the most
significant occasion for merit-making (Boun Phravet) in the annual liturgical calendar of Buddhist *vats* throughout all Lao cultural areas (a subject explored in
detail in Chapter 4). It also became a most popular object for temple wall paintings or gilded wall sculptures, especially in royally sponsored/constructed *vats* (see
Photos 1.2 and 1.3).

Photo 1.2 Wall painting of scenes from the *Vessantara Jataka*, Vat Xieng Thong, Luang
Phrabang

Photo 1.3 Gilded wall molding of scenes from *Vessantara Jataka*, Vat Mai, Luang Phrabang

The *Phra Lak Phra Lam*, the Lao rendition of the Hindu *Ramayana* epic, given this title after the protagonists Lakshmana and Rama, was transformed into literature of the *jataka* genre. That is, the epic was recast as Buddhavacana, words originally uttered from the veritable mouth of the Buddha, and thus provided with sacred authority. This one important transformation itself tells us much about the degrees to which aspects of expressive culture in Lan Xang were subjected to a Buddhacization process. Moreover, the episodic content of the *Ramayana* was also retrofitted into Lao contexts so that the dharma articulated therein is actually focused more on proper modes of observing and sustaining familial relations, especially how marriage proposals should be conducted and arranged, than on the cosmic underpinnings of royal dharma that characterize earlier Indian versions, especially Valmiki's classical Sanskrit version. This shift in focus may be attributed to the grand importance that the Lan Xang political world at the time placed on "diplomatic marriages" with other important Tai mandalas. In the *Phra Lak Phra Lam*, Rama is none other than heir to the throne of Lan Xang, a proper prince who embodies meticulously the finer points of royal etiquette and Buddhist morality. Sita, the heroine, is Rama's niece on both his matrilinear and patrilinear sides. In the *Phra Lak Phra Lam*, Sita is still abducted by Ravana, but he is not a ten-headed, morally dubious *raksasa* (demonic) figure. Instead he is a handsome Khmer prince of Indraprasthanagara (literally "the city of Indra's dwelling place," but figuratively referring to Khmer Angkor[63]) and a cousin of Rama as well. There are many other fascinating transformations of the epic *Ramayana* into what becomes a Lao Buddhist "Rama Jataka" (so I have formulated Appendix 1 to summarize the nature and significance of some of them.) The *Phra Lak Phra Lam* not only became a dominant subject for evolving forms of ritual dance and theatrical puppetry supported by the royal court, but it also came to consist of a normative royal Lao commentary on the subjects of sibling rivalry and the proper nature of conducting sibling marriages, both modeled on the supposed behavior of the Buddha in one of his previous rebirths.[64]

As much as Vixun may have further enhanced his capital as a pivot of the mandala and inaugurated a trajectory leading to the development of Luang Phrabang as a seat of learning and flourishing high culture, his son, Phothisarat, who assumed the throne at the young age of nineteen and ruled for twenty-seven years, extended and further intensified the efforts initiated by his father. From a gleaning of the *Luang Phrabang Chronicle*, Stuart-Fox provides this summary of Phothisarat's religious dispositions and policies:

> The young king was nineteen and a devout Buddhist, and his first act was to build and dedicate a magnificent monastery to the memory of his father. In 1523, a mission was dispatched to Chiang Mai, capital of Lan Na, to bring back copies of the entire Buddhist Tipitaka and other texts, and to invite learned monks to a great monastic council.[65] Two years later the king himself was inducted into the Sangha by its Supreme Patriarch, Maha Sichantho, abbot of Vat Vixun, who personally presided over the king's religious education during his traditional three-month retreat. The king's devoted orthodoxy made him intolerant of the widespread popular worship of spirits, or *phi*, some associated with ancestral cults, others with significant natural phenomena, and others still believed responsible for causing all kinds of accidents and sickness. In 1527 Phothisarat issued a famous decree proscribing the worship of *phi* as groundless superstition, and ordering their shrines to be destroyed and their altars thrown into the river. . . . [Moreover] Phothisarat was so far as we know the

first Lao king to record his gifts to the Sangha in stone in his own lifetime, such meritorious deeds were proof of his divine status as a *bodhisattva*, or Buddha-to-be. (1998: 74–75)

Phothisarat was the first Lao king to record his pious actions in support of the *sangha* within inscriptions and, according to the Lan Na *Jinakalamali*, received a full set of the Pali texts composing the canonical Tipitaka from the king of Chiang Mai in 1523. Grant Evans adds these significant details:

> King Phothisarat ... erected new monastic buildings around That Phanom at the southern limits of Lan Xang and provided slaves for its upkeep. ... He issued a decree in 1527 that appears to have been primarily directed against the worship associated with *lak muang* and other regional spirits, which was controlled by local lords, and led to the destruction of major shrines. (2002b: 16)

We also know that in his zeal to suppress the veneration of *phi*, Phothisarat specifically ordered that the old shrine of the ancestral guardian deities of Luang Phrabang, the former *axis mundi* of the pre-Buddhist *muang*, should be destroyed. On the very same site of the old guardian *phi* shrine, next to the *vat* his father had constructed for the enshrinement of the Phra Bang, Phothisarat constructed Vat Aham, another temple of continuing historical importance. On this site the oldest stele inscription surviving in Luang Phrabang refers to the Phothisarat's acts of establishing this *vat*, the purification of its boundaries, and proclaims a litany of prescriptions incumbent on monks to follow, similar in kind to the royal *katikavata*s issued by Sri Lankan kings to ensure discipline within the *sangha*.[66] That the efforts of Phothisarat to establish Luang Phrabang as a seat of orthodoxy had gained some international renown is noted by Harris (2005: 33) who mentions that "signs of Buddhist regeneration [in Cambodia] are ... shown by the significant numbers of Cambodian monks who traveled to Luang Prabang to study Theravada Buddhism, particularly during the reigns of King Phothisarat and his son Setthatirath."

In terms of setting forth a diplomacy designed to secure Lan Xang and to expand its influence throughout the region geopolitically, Phothisarat was married strategically to a princess from Lan Na (Lorrillard 2003: 190) and, for several compelling reasons,[67] shifted his capital from Luang Phrabang to Vientiane. Several important thresholds were crossed during Phothisarat's reign. His religious proclivities were harbingers reflective of important issues that have persisted throughout the history of religions in Lao culture areas.

One of the major aims of this study is to ascertain the manner in which Buddhist thought and practice have been construed in Lao religious culture through the prisms of the indigenous ontology of the spirit cults. Even though Phothisarat embodies a religious profile that is unabashedly orthodox Theravadin and inimical to the indigenous religious substratum, the litany of actions attributed to this pious king contain at least two important traces, or the latent presence, of spirit-cult persistence. The first trace is evident in Phothisarat's enshrinement of his royal father's cremated remains within the consecrated grounds of a Buddhist monastery. Vat Aham was built precisely to honor and venerate his deceased royal parent: recapitulating the practice of royal Khmer to promote, in a cosmic and soteriological fashion, the ultimate identity/destiny of royal parents. Phothisarat's cultic actions to enshrine his father's remains (and memory) are clearly a Buddhist transformation of ancestor veneration and thus echoes of the residual principle of the "god of the soil" or the "spiritual power of the place." As we will see later, votive stupas used to enshrine the remains of important monastic abbots were understood as venues for worshipping a transformed presence as a "*phi vat*." In both of these examples, there is evidence of an enduring belief that a powerful person, seen as responsible for founding, structuring, or ordering a particular space, whether kingdom or *vat*, persists as a type of spiritual presence within that space.

Phothisarat's zealous enthusiasm to continue his father's promotion of Buddhist learning on the one hand and his campaign to eradicate the cult of *phi* on the other may have been a by-product of several factors. No doubt Phothisarat personally benefited a great deal from Vixun's efforts to create a powerful Buddhist *sangha* and monastic literary culture: he was raised and educated in a very sophisticated, if religiously conservative environment. Only a teenager when he ascended the throne, Phothisarat relied heavily upon his trusted monastic teachers for advice and counsel, and it is abundantly clear that the *sangha* was one of the chief beneficiaries of his reign. His exposure to the Buddhist literary world was not limited to the three months he spent in rain-retreat (*vassa*), the annual three-month period of reflection when the recitation and study of texts traditionally intensified within the monastic routine. Rather, literary learning comprised a central focus of his entire education. What seems apparent is that his "Buddhist-mindedness"[68] was not only of learned origins but also a by-product of the relative simplemindedness present in an overly guided or manipulated youth filled with pietistic passion. Whether Phothisarath's piety was the result of his own independent motivation or instilled by others, it was shrewdly political as well.

There are, at least, two ways in which to understand the rationale for Phothisarath's anti-spirit-cult campaign. The first involves situating it within the context of Theravada debates about what it means to be Buddhist religiously. A substantially similar argument took place in Sri Lanka, perhaps a century earlier, between two eminent monks who had both won enthusiastic support from the same king (Parakramabahu VI of Kotte). Sri Rahula, an eminently learned Theravada monk who had mastered at least six languages, had established a monastic academy (Totagamuwa) where not only were several languages taught, but the literatures and philosophies of Hindu and Mahayana traditions formed part of the academic curriculum as well. Deities of Hindu origin, gods of obscure indigenous origin, and bodhisattvas of the Mahayana tradition (including Avalokitesvara, who seems to have been Sri Rahula's own *ishta devata* or personal deity) were objects of cultic veneration. The academy's students hailed from various parts of Sri Lanka and India too. In addition to presiding over this rather inclusive, philosophically eclectic, and religiously pragmatic milieu, Sri Rahula also espoused the practice of various forms of ritual "white magic." Rahula's defense of his wide-ranging religiosity was grounded in the assumption that the central aim of the Buddha's teachings was to assuage the condition of suffering (*dukkha*), the problematic nature of human existence in *samsara*. Therefore, any action understood as conducive to alleviating suffering could be enlisted in support of the Buddha's "mission," including the array of "unorthodox" practices that Sri Rahula had endorsed. On the other side of the debate was Vidagama Maitreya, a forest-oriented monk who condemned the worship of virtually all forms of supernatural deities on orthodox doctrinal grounds. He argued that the Theravada path, as realized primarily through moral and meditative pursuit, is essentially a religion of self-effort, a religious vocation that, apart from the Buddhavacana ("teaching [literally "words"] of the Buddha"], requires no external assistance from deities.[69] That is, magical practices are unnecessary to make progress on the path to *nibbana*. Vidagama Maitreya stopped short of denying the existence of the supernatural (as did the Buddha himself well before him), but his main point was that they are of absolutely no help when it comes down to the matter of experiencing the final religious attainment. Indeed, the veneration of deities and the performance of magical rituals form something of a lower level of religious activity and are concerned more with mundane matters (*lokiya*) than ultimate (*lokuttara*) ones. Or, to use the terminology invoked by Stuart-Fox, it would be "groundless superstition" to regard such beliefs and practices as efficacious in relation to the soteriological truth of the Buddha.

From this brief summary of the debate, we can see the merits of both positions in play: Sri Rahula saw the fundamental aim of the Buddhist religious quest as the alleviation of suffering, even if that means appealing to the compassion of external spiritual powers, while Vidagama Maitreya emphasized an interiorized self-reliant quest for the realization of the solitary and sublime experience of *nibbana*.

What is very interesting and quite distinctive when comparing the dispositions of Parakramabahu VI of Kotte and Phothisarat of Lan Xang, is that Parakramabahu did not take decisive action for or against either of the positions represented by Sri Rahula or Vidagama Maitreya. In the inclusive religious culture of his kingdom,[70] just as in the ethnic composition of his royal court, there was space provided for *difference.* The realities of political culture in Parakramabahu's kingdom were thus reflected in the realities of its religious culture. Pluralism was a fact of life. But in Phothisarat's kingdom, or at least in his capital, apparently a decision was made that there was no space or territory to be left for the provenance of the spirit cults. Since Veidlinger (2007) has spotlighted the role that forest-dwelling monks from Sri Lanka played in establishing the elite and royally supported literary culture of Lan Na, and since we know that Photisarat, with his close ties to Lan Na, also received an edition of the Tipitaka from Lan Na, it is not altogether surprising that his disposition was heavily swayed against propitiation of the spirit cults. While it is quite possible that Phothisarat was genuinely convinced, on grounds of the Theravada orthodoxy espoused by his *sangha* teachers, that the Buddha's path demanded an exclusion of the spirit cults (similar in substance to the position advanced by Vidagama Maitreya regarding the assistance of the gods), it would also not be irrelevant to consider the political dimensions of his campaign as well; for, insofar as kingship is inherently a political institution, it is never not far off base to attribute political motives to major royal policy formulations. And this suggests the second possible way of understanding Phothisarat's anti-*phi* campaign.

I would like to suggest that Phothisarath's campaign to eradicate spirit cults reflected the tension between two recognized theories of power. During his father's reign, Phothisarat had witnessed a veritable "changing of the guard" with respect to the manner in which the fundamental power at the center of the Lan Xang mandala was constituted, represented, and regarded. That "change of guard," as it were, refers to how the Phra Bang image had replaced the guardian *phi* of the city as the substance of power recognized at the pivot of the mandala. Indeed, the change in the city's name from Xieng Dong Xieng Thong to Luang Phrabang in the subsequent reign of Phothisarat's son, Xetthathirat, marks this replacement of identity rather ostensibly. As Evans has noted, Phothisarat had ordered the destruction of the poles or pillars containing or symbolizing the spirit-based (or *spiritual*) power of the regional *phi muang*, objects of cultic veneration symbolizing the ontological power replicated in politically this-worldly fashion by the *chao muang*. These destructive actions were then followed by the constructive emplacement of very strategic *vat*s, Theravada Buddhist monasteries that became, in the place of *lak muang*, new ritual centers of religious *and* political power.[71] Consequently, the power of the state became completely embedded in the structure of the *sangha*, and the *sangha*, in turn, vested completely in the state, a truly prodigious development with major historical ramifications for the remainder of Lao political and cultural history. Both state and *sangha* were related in a dynamic of mutual legitimation, now envisaged as excluding the *phi* cults. At the basis of the Buddhist ontology now royally enthroned was the authority attributed to the figure of the

Buddha, henceforth regarded as Lan Xang's unchallenged "culture hero." From this point in time forward, regional *chao muang* would also have to demonstrate their motivations and abilities to emulate the actions of the king in supporting the *sangha*. That is, they would also have to become chief patrons of the *vats*, in the same manner as the king, who as we know through the stone inscriptions he left behind, had postured as the *sasana*'s chief supporter and trumpeter of *dhamma*.

Yet this account of what amounts to a war of ontological displacement is too tidy. The rationale for the anti-spirit-cult campaign may have indeed been consciously forged and then rationalized on doctrinal grounds, grounds that conveniently abetted Phothisarat's political motivation to "clear the land" entirely, to abolish any grounds (spiritual-political) for any potential resistance to his power. Yet another process was also at work, I think, that may not have occurred consciously to the protagonists of this historical narrative, and this is the way that they understood the significance of the Buddha's presence embodied in the image of the Phra Bang. This is the second instance of latent traces of the *phi* cult that I want to note in relation to Phothisarat's actions. How was the power of the Phra Bang understood practically *and politically*? Was the Phra Bang simply understood as a symbol of the Buddha's *dhamma* or the monastic ideals of the *sangha*'s *vinaya*?[72] Or was it, as I have indicated earlier, an understanding of the Buddha's powerful presence embodied in an image; that is, an image-powerful presence of the Buddha?

If we return to the statements by Stuart-Fox and Evans that the powerful reigns of Vixun, Phothisarat, and Xetthathirat did not involve any *structural* changes to the Lan Xang mandala, and if we take seriously the Buddhist analysis about how the present is karmicly conditioned by the past, then another way of assessing how the power of the Phra Bang came to be understood surfaces. In the mandala structure of Lan Xang, consistent with the principles and dynamics rooted in the religious substratum and constitutive of *muang*-mandala polity, the Phra Bang functions analogically to the ontological power of a "mandala *phi*" or "*phi muang*." It is regarded as the originating and legitimating power of the past and present located at the pivotal center of political space. It is the "power in charge of this place," symbolic of the otherworldly parallel that infuses the power of the this-worldly king. It is also analogous in function to the *devaraja* image cult in Khmer Angkor. It is still possible, in this scenario, to say that the king is the *cakkavattin*, who righteously conquers and orders the world to prepare his realm for the presence of the Buddha without violating these principles of ontology operative in the indigenous religious substratum. Indeed, understood or read in this way, there is no inconsistency between the two.

What I have noted earlier, however, is that what Buddhism brings to the substance of power envisaged at the center is an *ethic*. The king and the "Buddha-

presence" of the Phra Bang may have been understood, although perhaps uncon-
sciously so, in terms of the "powers of the place," an understanding ultimately
to be found in the manner that Mus has described within the dynamics of the
"religion of monsoon Asia" and "the god of the soil." But, in addition, the Buddhist king must also rule by righteousness. While there may have been no structural changes to Lao *muang* polity when its center or pivot was buddhacized, its
quality was modified by a Buddhist ethical discourse. Just how ethically minded,
rather than simply Buddhist-minded, Phothisarat ruled Lan Xang is a question
that others may try to answer, but regardless of how that question is answered, it
is also clear that Phothisarat does not appear to have been a religiously tolerant or
inclusive king.

Phothisarat's son and successor, Xetthathirat, who reigned from 1548 until
1571, was also the son of Phothisarat's Lan Na queen, and he then married a Lan
Na princess. Indeed, he was living in Chiang Mai as its ruler after Lan Xang had
defended Lan Na from an Ayutthaya attack in 1546. Lan Xang had then annexed
Lan Na as a tributary to its mandala, when Phothisarat died prematurely at the
age of forty-seven (Evans 2002b: 16–18). At this, Xetthathirat quickly returned to
Xieng Dong Xieng Thong to consolidate his claim to the Lan Xang throne, in the
process temporarily uniting it with the rule of Lan Na. These developments began
a further intensification of Lan Na's cultural influence on Lan Xang.[73]

Xetthathirat's entire reign was plagued by war or its threat. With an invasion
looming out of the west from the Burmese kingdom of Pegu, Xetthathirat moved
the Lan Xang center from where it had been located for the past 200 years in Xieng
Dong Xieng Thong to Vientiane, where Phothisarat had actually spent much of
his own reign because Xieng Dong Xieng Thong appeared too vulnerable to possible Burmese attack. In his absence from Chiang Mai, even though he had left his
queen there to rule, Lan Na suffered from a dispute over succession that weakened
its defenses. Lan Na eventually fell to the invading Burmese. As a result,

> for the next two centuries, until 1776, Lan Na remained tributary to the Bur-
> mese. For Lan Na, this was a period of decline. Its immediate effect on Lan
> Xang, however, was to stimulate a cultural renaissance as families from Lan Na
> fled to Lan Xang and the center of northern Yuan/Lao literature and the arts
> moved east [to Vientiane]. (Stuart-Fox 1998: 78–79)

Since the center of gravity in relation to Lao demographics also had been moving
steadily south and east down the Mekong, the new location of the center of Lan
Xang in Vientiane was also better situated to administer "control over potentially
rebellious southern *meuang*" (Stuart-Fox 1998: 79).

The fall of Lan Na to the Burmese certainly intensified the cultural influence of Lan Na on Lan Xang. In particular, it seems to have increased the need for royal beliefs in the powers of its most prized Buddha images. Thus,

> religious politics and the importance of religious legitimation were reflected in Xetthathirat's decision to bring with him to his new capital [Vientiane] two of the three most revered Buddha images from Xiang Dong Xiang Thong. These were the *Phra Kaeo*, known as the Emerald Buddha, and the *Phra Xaek Kham*, both previously removed by Xetthathirat from Chiang Mai, not just to save them from the Burmese but to reinforce his own prestige and power. The *Phra Bang*, palladium of the former capital since the reign of Vixunnarat, remained in Xiang Dong Xiang Thong which was renamed Luang Phrabang in its honour. (Stuart-Fox 1998: 79)

Unlike his father, Xetthathirat was not left in peace to expend his energies on expanding the kingdom and promoting the interests of the *sangha*. However, when he was not preoccupied with war with the Burmese, he also proved to be a great benefactor of the *sangha*. He became, perhaps, the greatest builder of Buddhist monuments in Lao religious history.

> In fact we have more epigraphic records of his gifts to the Sangha (ten between the years 1551 and 1567) than for any other Lao king. Several new monasteries were founded during the reign, not only in the capital, but also in Luang Phrabang (Vat That) [as well as Vat Xieng Thong] and provincial centres. Royal *stupas* were built in several key *meuang*, and the That Phanom shrine was remodeled and repaired. The extensive building programme undertaken to embellish Viang Chan culminated in the construction of two great monuments. One was the Vat Phra Kaeo (1566) with its elaborate stairways and towering columns to house the Emerald Buddha, the new and powerful palladium of the Lao kings: the other was the That Luang *stupa* (1566–1567) situated in broad grounds one kilometer (less than a mile) east of the city walls, on the site of a former shrine reputed to contain a bone of the Buddha. (Stuart-Fox 1998: 80)

The That Luang was a massive stupa that served as the symbolic center of Lan Xang in Vientiane. Indeed, by now it should be clear that the Tai Buddhist communities, including those in Luang Phrabang and Vientiane, seemed to have made no discrimination between the powers attributed to a Buddha-relic housed in a stupa, on the one hand, and a duly consecrated Buddha image on the other.

But it should also be noted that Xetthathirat built the marvelous Vat Xieng Thong in Luang Phrabang as well, which is widely regarded as the crowning masterpiece of Lao Buddhist (or northern Tai) monastic architecture (as shown on the jacket). That Xetthathirat, in circumstances of grave military threat, was able to marshal the resources required to engage in such an energetic campaign for the construction of religious edifices, marks the impressive extent to which he was able to mobilize his power and the considerable degree to which the Lao *muang* were loyal to his rule. At the same time, from the religious worldview held by Xetthathirat, the construction of so many impressive *vats*, and the care that he lavished on Buddha images, must also be seen as politically strategic, insofar as his Burmese enemies were also Theravada Buddhists exercising similar scenarios of legitimation. That is, Xetthathirat not only sought the merit he acquired from his impressive construction of Buddhist stupas and his veneration of holy Buddha images, but he also sought to realize the presence of the powers that they were thought to contain. By defending these Buddha images as their rightful custodian, he continued to proclaim that his rule was sanctified. To the Burmese, he was in a sense saying: "My Buddha-presence is holier than yours; resistance to your power proves it."

Impressive as Xetthathirat's power was, and despite an alliance that he forged in the late 1560s with a harried Ayutthaya mandala to the south, the Burmese thoroughly sacked Ayutthaya in 1569. The Burmese "then turned . . . [their] attention to Lan Xang, the last remaining Tai state to hold out against [them]. On the advice of his general Saen Surin, Xetthathirat again resorted to guerrilla warfare" (Stuart-Fox 1998: 82). This successful defensive strategy provided, however, only a temporary reprieve. "Xetthathirat never returned from his ill-fated southern expedition" in 1571 (Stuart-Fox 1998: 83) to restore order in remote parts of Lan Xang. The circumstances of his death have remained something of a historical "mystery" (Evans 2002b: 19), but the subsequent succession crises that raged among the faction-riven Lao nobility that Xetthathirat's death engendered have not. The Burmese proceeded to take advantage of the internal political disarray to intervene and install their chosen vassal. Lan Xang lost its autonomy for about thirty years. It was not until 1638, when the military power of Pegu eventually atrophied, and another series of internal succession disputes had been endured in Vientiane, that King Surinyavongsa, whose fifty-seven-year rule constitutes the longest royal reign in all of Lao political history, brought stability and a renewed measure of autonomy to Lan Xang.

An Enduring Muang Lao

In retrospect, Surinyavongsa's period of rule can be understood, ironically, as a victim of its own success. Because Lan Xang, throughout much of the seventeenth century, enjoyed peace and prosperity, basically free from the need to defend itself against aggression, it continued to develop along traditional Buddhist political lines in relative isolation. The continued Buddhacization of its public culture only intensified.

> It was a time of prosperity and internal order, after the devastation of the previous years, when the wealth of the kingdom was poured into Buddhist endowments and embellishment of the capital. Famous for its architecture and its monasteries, Viang Chan [Vientiane] gained further renown as a center of religious learning, attracting monastic scholars from throughout the Tai world, and from as far afield as Cambodia and Burma. . . . Music, dance, theatre and the recitation of epic poetry all flourished in the cosmopolitan Lao capital. . . . Literature too experienced a second golden age. (Stuart-Fox 1998: 88)

With further regard to the literature of Suriyavongsa's time,

> much of the oral folk literature that was the common heritage of the northern Tai world—Yuan, Leu, Lao, Shan—had been given literary form in prose or verse. In the process these stories, copied and recopied by Buddhist monks, were imbued with Buddhist values. Heroes who fought with demons were *bodhisattvas* on the path to Buddhahood, their valiant deeds making spiritual merit. Even those stories which embroidered the historical exploits of kings and warriors, or recounted imaginary episodes in the life of some divine being or royal hero, inculcated Buddhist cautionary morality. Yet the spirit world which played so prominent a part in all these stories was still identifiably Lao, complete with *phi* both malignant and benign. (Stuart-Fox 1998: 97)

This portrait stresses a consolidation process at work, a process that emphasized the further valorization of Theravada institutions and ideals and the further infusion of Buddhism into the expressive culture of the Lao *muang*. But from this portrait the converse effect taking place in the dynamic relationship existing between Buddhism and the spirit cults cannot be seen: how Buddhism, rather than being the only active agent in the relation, was also transformed in the process. Because it is now impossible to recover the voices of the common folk, that particular consideration must be postponed to a consideration of the contemporary historical period. For now, the final sentence in the passage just quoted can be underscored: not only is there a return of the presence of the *phi*, but they have not been entirely transformed into Buddhist forces either.

Surinyavongsa's long seventeenth-century reign may be viewed as a triumphal recovery of the Vixun-Phothisarast-Xetthathirat paradigm. Though Lan Xang could celebrate itself as a prosperous and renowned Buddhist culture in this era, on the other hand

as an inland kingdom, Lan Xang was prevented from entering into direct relations with Western merchants. But for trade with Yunnan, exchange was indirect via neighbouring kingdoms. Among other disadvantages, these circumstances made it difficult to keep abreast of changing military technology and
tactics. More powerful and more accurate European firearms reduced the value
of elephants in warfare, while the availability of European mercenaries and purchase of European weapons (especially artillery) meant that advantage lay ever
more decisively with those kingdoms which had the means to pay for them.
What wealth Lan Xang did possess seems to have been expended primarily on
the monastic order and the court, rather than on equipping its army. By the
late seventeenth century, the power of Lan Xang, despite the magnificence of
it capital and the pomp and pageantry of its ceremonial, was already in relative decline *vis-à-vis* its more powerful neighbours. The dynastic collapse of the
early eighteenth century merely exacerbated an already deteriorating situation.
. . . Apart from its exclusion from international trade, what finally led to disintegration of the *mandala* of Lan Xang, was the destructive series of succession
disputes that followed the death of Surinyavongsa. (Stuart-Fox 1998: 98–100)

Indeed, the end of Surinyavongsa's long rule marks the end of Lan Xang as
we have known it. The inability of his nephews and grandsons to agree on succession resulted in the parceling out of the kingdom into three much weaker, yet
still, for the time being, autonomous *muang*: Luang Phrabang, Vientiane, and
Champasak.

The ruling family in each regional kingdom legitimized its succession through
traditional means: descent from Khun Borom via the ruling dynasty of Lan
Xang, reinforced by the magical power of a Buddhist image venerated with the
assistance of the local Sangha as the palladium of the kingdom. . . . [But] [l]ess
than two decades later, all three had been forced to acknowledge Siamese suzerainty. (Stuart-Fox 1998: 103)

Thus the unitary structure of the Lao Lan Xang mandala was fragmented, never
to be assembled again.

Before the segmentation of Lan Xang, the Phra Bang image had been removed
from Luang Phrabang to Vientiane in 1705 to shore up the legitimacy of the *muang*
amidst royal internecine disputes. After the fragmentation, which Evans (2002b:
24) notes was also partly the result of pressure from the Ayutthaya mandala to
alienate Luang Phrabang from Vientiane, both the Phra Keo (Emerald Buddha)
and the Phra Bang ensconced in Vientiane eventually became enticing targets of
legitimation to be seized by the rising power of Siam. And that is exactly what oc-

curred after the Thai threw off their Burmese shackles. The Burmese had reduced all Tai mandalas, including Luang Phrabang and Vientiane to vassal status in the 1760s. Evans describes succinctly what then transpired:

> Through factional alliances, Champasak was brought firmly within the Siamese mandala in 1778; [the Ayutthaya] army then marched on Vientiane and easily conquered it the following year with the assistance of its vassal state, Luang Phrabang. Members of the royal family were taken as hostages, along with their palladiums the Phra Keo and the Phra Bang . . . , while thousands of families were relocated to Saraburi, 120 kilometers northeast of Bangkok, as royal *kha* [slaves]. By the time of the establishment of the Chakri dynasty in Bangkok in 1782, the Siamese kingdom was the undisputed power in the region and Lan Xang had disappeared. (2002b: 25)

Indeed, the first Chakri dynasty king, Rama I, greatly expanded his mandala so that it included not only Lan Na, Luang Phrabang, Vientiane, and Champasak, but also most of what is now Cambodia, the northern Malay Muslim states, and the eastern Shan plateau (now mostly part of Burma). Significantly, the prized Phra Keo, or Emerald Buddha, originally from Chiang Mai in Lan Na but which had been installed during the time of Lan Xang's suzerainty in Vientiane by Xetthathirat, became the new image of Buddhist power, or the palladium of the Bangkok dynasty, where it remains to this day.

Eventually the son of the former Vientiane king was allowed to return from Bangkok with the Phra Bang image,[74] but there were no pretenses of granting autonomy in that gesture. Meanwhile,

> Bangkok, strategically better situated than Ayutthaya, rapidly developed into a busy cosmopolitan trading center, able to take advantage of increased trade not only with China, but also with the major European powers as trade picked up following the end of the Napoleonic wars. By contrast, the isolated Lao capitals were reduced to regional centers with limited wealth and resources, unable to maintain even comparably lavish courts. This did not, however, reduce the pride of their rulers in their ancient lineages, nor diminish the memories of past glories. The Lao kingdoms stubbornly resisted Siamese inroads in areas they considered theirs. (Stuart-Fox 1998: 115)

Given the Lao *muangs'* reduced status to vassalage and yet their "pride" in an "ancient lineage," expressions of periodic administrative resistance may be read as portents of what inevitably followed.

The Last Gasp: Chao Anouvong and the
Dispersal of the Vientiane Lao

The Lao revolt against Siamese hegemony led by Chao Anouvong in the early nineteenth century continues even today to spark political and nationalist emotion on both sides of the Mekong River: in modern Laos where Chao Anou is still regarded by some as a proto-revolutionary warrior who challenged Thai imperialist and feudalist rule,[75] in the Khorat plateau of northeast Thailand where the Isan people understand the centrality of Chao Anou's role in the memory of their migration, and among the central Thai where Chao Anou is regarded as a traitor whose forces were thwarted due to the intervention of patriotic loyalty and heroic resistance to unwarranted rebellion.[76]

Grant Evans, who has written a detailed account of the Chao Anou revolt (2002b: 25–32), refers to Chao Anou as "the last of the warrior kings" and to his revolt as "the last gasp of a dying premodern mandala state system" (25). Indeed, his revolt against the Bangkok mandala marked the final occasion in which the Lao attempted to free themselves from Siamese hegemony. The history of the event is rich indeed, but suffice to say that it took place within the early nineteenth-century era when Bangkok, intensely worried about Vietnamese military designs from the east, was simultaneously becoming increasingly wary of European colonial designs on Southeast Asia. Only two years earlier, the British had succeeded in wresting southern Burma from its king. Even before then, the Chakri dynasty had engaged in various policies designed to centralize direct power and further limit the power of its periphery vassals. As Evans notes:

> The mandala of Siam thus combined, uneasily, elements of a newly emerging absolutist state system and an older system in which power had been more dispersed and had allowed for the emergence of new men of prowess. Clearly this diverse dynamic was at work in Chao Anou. (2002b: 27)

Once he assumed the "kingship" of Vientiane from his older brother who had been "appointed" by Bangkok in 1782 (and who had returned with the Phra Bang image because King Rama I had determined that it had brought him "bad luck"), Anou began to test the continued viability of the "older system [that] had allowed for the emergence of men of prowess."[77] He developed a robust agenda to articulate power. The idioms that he chose were unabashedly those of a powerful Buddhist *cakkavattin* king

> by building a new palace, and then demonstrating his exalted *kamma* by constructing monasteries and Buddhist monuments and presiding over elaborate

religious ceremonies, both in Viang Chan [Vientiane] and at such major regional centers as Nakhon Phanom. In 1813, the king summoned a great monastic
council, only the third in Lao history. Instructions were given to carve a new jade
Buddha image to replace the *Phra Kaeo*, then in Bangkok. In 1816, this image
was ceremoniously installed in the refurbished Vat Phra Kaeo in Viang Chan.
An outer cloister was added to the That Luang *stupa*, and Anuvong ordered
work begun on Vat Sisaket [see Photo 1.4], a gem of Lao architecture and the
only building of this period to escape the destruction of 1827–1828. (Stuart-
Fox 1998: 117–118)

Such grandiose undertakings were not lost on Bangkok, especially the pro-
vocative acts of convening a grand monastic council, which implied that Anou's
kingdom would arbitrate Theravada orthodoxy, at least in the Lao cultural areas
over which the Siamese claimed hegemony, and the carving of a new jade (or "emerald") Buddha, which was placed in the *vat* that formerly housed the original
image, the very one now in Bangkok functioning as the palladium of the Bangkok mandala. Clearly, Anou had designs on reestablishing the autonomy of Lan
Xang.[78] In this he had hoped for external support not only from Luang Phrabang
and Champasak, but possibly from Vietnam, Burma, and even the British.

Photo 1.4 Vat Sisaket, sixteenth century, Vientiane

In 1826 Anouvong made his military move, entering the Khorat plateau under the pretext of assisting Bangkok in resisting a possible British incursion.[79] But his forces were soon engaged by a Bangkok army and forced into a northern retreat, during which they encouraged many people in the region to join them and attacked those who would not. "The uprising . . . ended in a fiasco. His son [Chao Anou's] was soon captured, and Anou himself forced to flee to Hue in Vietnam" (Evans 2002b: 28). The fury of Bangkok, ever more insecure, was unprecedented.

The devastation of the Lao areas was horrendous. Apart from the dead, thousands fled into the jungle to escape the fighting. According to Siamese reports, only about nine able-bodied men were taken prisoner for every 200 to 300 women and children. Food stocks had been destroyed and no new crops planted. By mid-year, disease and malnutrition had taken a dreadful toll. Tens of thousands of families were forcibly resettled closer to Bangkok, most in the central Chao Phraya basin. After months of mopping up, tracking down families who had fled Viang Chan [Vientiane], ordering the exemplary execution of those who had given them refuge, and organizing the administration of the region, the Siamese general, Chao Phraya Bodin, returned to Bangkok in February 1828 to find Rama III still far from satisfied. Anouvong had not been captured; Viang Chan had not been razed. The Siamese feared Vietnamese intervention. Bodin was ordered to return and complete his task of destruction. . . . This time the city of Viang Chan was totally destroyed and its entire population deported. Nothing remained but huts among the ruins when Doudart de Lagree and Francis Garnier visited the site almost forty years later. It was to be another thirty years before a new city began to be constructed from its ashes to serve as the administrative capital of French Laos. (Stuart-Fox 1998: 125)

The so-called "Lao-ization" of northeast Thailand dates back to this monumental moment of total and final devastation of the Vientiane mandala. Tens of thousands of Lao families were forcibly evacuated and deported across the Mekong River into a new region where the absolute political power of Bangkok was assured.[80] "The ensuing political stability [of northeast Thailand] provided by an ever more powerful Bangkok ensured rapid population growth, and over the coming centuries more ethnic Lao come to be found on the Khorat plateau than in Laos itself" (Evans 2002b: 31).

There were no more vestiges of the Lan Xang mandala remaining in Vientiane in the aftermath of the Chao Anou revolt, for there was nothing left of Vientiane at all. The Siamese strategy had been this: there will be no competitive "power of place" in Vientiane if there is no place of power in which it can be realized.[81] Before the Chao Anou revolt, Luang Phrabang had remained loyal to Bangkok as its vassal. Siamese soldiers would remain stationed in Luang Phrabang throughout the remainder of the nineteenth century, until Luang Phrabang became, through a series of unlikely events, a French protectorate. Meanwhile, in an act of apparent charity, the Siamese King Mongkut, in 1867, allowed the Phra Bang image, recaptured during the 1827 sacking of Vientiane, to be returned to Luang Phrabang, after an absence of 162 years.

CHAPTER 2

Interventions from Afar

Nonspiritual Powers in Place

In this chapter my primary aim is to ascertain the impact that accompanied Thai, French, and then American interventions not only politically but in terms of transformations of the religious culture beginning in the early decades of nineteenth century and continuing through to the end of the Second Indochina War in 1975. As before I will periodically include comparative observations with Sri Lanka.

Politics and Religion in Nineteenth-Century "Siamese Laos"

During the nineteenth century the powerful Bangkok-centered Chakri dynasty constrained any Lao aspirations for greater autonomy. Its control over remnants of the Lan Xang mandala was threatened on only two occasions. During the 1830s the Siamese counteracted Vietnamese influence and potential military incursions in the mountainous northeast Huaphan region and in the Xieng Khuang plateau, regions that had paid tribute traditionally to both Luang Phrabang and to Hue (Vietnam). In facing the Vietnamese challenge on Xieng Khuang's Plain of Jars, the Siamese resorted once again to their practice of enforced mass dispersal and relocation. Thousands of Phuan Buddhist[1] families were relocated to the Khorat plateau in northeast Thailand, there to join other Lao peoples from Vientiane regions who had been displaced there a few years earlier.[2] Then in the last two decades of the nineteenth century Chinese Haw marauders swept across much of northern Laos. Itinerant, militant, and greatly feared, the Haw were stubborn survivors of the failed millenarian Taiping rebellion in China.[3] Unable to control these intrusions and banditry, the Siamese failed to defend Luang Phrabang, which suffered a devastating sacking,[4] an event that proved to have prodigious political consequences.

While these two instances of political instability only partially mitigated Siamese hegemony in the northern areas formerly constitutive of Lan Xang, another important process was at work that indirectly worked against Siamese efforts to consolidate their influence. This was the process of modernization itself, so clearly apparent in Bangkok during the mid-century reign of King Mongkut and in the late-century rule of King Chulalongkorn. Modernization came to the Bangkok court as a result of increasing exposure to Western forms of knowledge, mounting international trade, the introduction of new forms of weaponry, and, perhaps most importantly, the concept of boundaried nation-states. These forces widened the social, economic, and cultural gaps between Bangkok and its peripheral vassals in Laos. Indeed, the political concept of mandala was jettisoned by the end of the century, with the ascendant concept of the boundaried nation-state taking its place. Though Siamese royalty publicly claimed that the Lao mandala were part of Siam (Ivarsson 2003: 242), Champasak and Luang Phrabang, the most peripheral of all, did not participate significantly in the processes producing the newly emergent modern national Thai identity.[5] As Evans (2002b: 37) puts the matter: "The collapse of Lan Xang exaggerated the difference between the increasingly worldly and sophisticated Siamese and the increasingly parochial Lao courts."

Nor does it seem that the Lao *sangha* was much affected by royal Siamese attempts to reform the Buddhist monastic system.[6] These reforms, designed to make the *sangha* more attuned to the modern world, were also influenced by Western conceptions of religion and scientific rationality. They were enacted to establish a monastic vocation that was more scholastically oriented, ethically rational, and consciously aware of discipline (for example, the *Vinaya*). A "new monk's" education in preparation for the full *upasampada* ordination included emphases on mastering Pali and systematically studying the Theravada *Tipitaka*. A rigorous academic examination system was put into place, designed to test the knowledge requisite of monks to be ordained. Subsequent advancement up the *sangha* hierarchy depended upon continuing demonstrations of academic knowledge. Ritual knowledge of the spirit world, and the ontological assumptions on which it is based, was ignored, if not discouraged. This was understood as a recovery of "true" or "original" Buddhism, of a purified monasticism uncontaminated by popular religious culture, and Bangkok's royalty institutionalized this reformed Buddhist *sangha* with the establishment of a new elite institution: the Thammayut Nikay. The influence of the Thammayut in nineteenth-century Laos, however, was minimal, though later in the twentieth century it had an important impact upon segments of the Lao *sangha*. For the time being, however, the Lao monastic vocation, as it had been long practiced in Luang Phrabang and in rural Lao villages, remained innocent of the grand new monastic paradigm being promulgated in Bangkok.

Thus most Lao within the nominal Bangkok mandala, especially outside of the courts of Luang Phrabang and Champasak, were not much aware of Bangkok's political claims over them or the new changes afoot in the Thai Buddhist *sangha*.

Except in those regions and during the two periods of instability noted above, the exercise of political power remained largely a *muang* matter. The powers of Lao mandala may have ebbed, but the Bangkok-based mandala that had replaced the center of Lan Xang remained a long and mediated distance away.

Enter the French

The presence of the French in Southeast Asia dates to seventeenth-century Roman Catholic missionaries who were initially successful in converting many Vietnamese, especially in and around Saigon, the hub of French Indochina. They were less successful, because they expended far less effort, when the French finally created French Laos two centuries later.

The geographical region that became French Laos in the late nineteenth century was rarely targeted in early colonial development schemes. In retrospect, French Laos owed its existence more to historical happenstance, a capital opportunity to expand their dominions that arose rather serendipitously, than to any well-laid plans that the French had designed for the area's economic exploitation.

When historians describe in general terms the area that later became French Laos, they often use such terms as "backwater," "remote," or "hinterland." For instance:

> French explorers in the 1860s found a country reduced to extremity. Only in Luang Phrabang were the vestiges of a great kingdom still evident.... The town itself was unpretentious, even if court ceremonial was not. Yet it remained a pale shadow of the pomp and circumstance of the court of Lan Xang at the time of Surinyavongsa.... For the next two decades Luang Phrabang remained a peaceful, rather depressed backwater. (Stuart-Fox 1998: 137–138)

These same French explorers were actually on their way to somewhere else. Pholsena points out that

> the French presence in the region of Southeast Asia became, from the mid-nineteenth century, motivated by economic interests and commercial competition with Britain. Indeed, the French hoped that their foothold in Indochina would allow the penetration of the Chinese market via a region from which the British were absent. (2006: 29)[7]

Thus many of the early French explorations were the result of trying to find a good route to southern China from Vietnam.

Meanwhile, from Bangkok's point of view,

the French expansion into Cambodia in 1863 and in Annam and Tonkin in 1883 and 1884 greatly worried the Siamese, who forced the court of Luang Phrabang to accept the presence of two Siamese commissioners. It was only a question of time before these new geo-strategic factors would bring to the fore-front the question of delimiting the western borders of a sought-after French protectorate over Laos. (Larcher-Goscha 2003: 218)

The actual catalysts for the establishment of a colonial protectorate over Lao cultural regions were French fears of economic and political competition from Britain (which had entirely disestablished Burmese kingship in the mid-1880s), the pillaging of Luang Phrabang by Chinese Haw cadres that destabilized local Siamese power, and the concomitant presence in Luang Phrabang of a politi-cally savvy and opportunistic civil servant, August Pavie, who seized the moment of Luang Phrabang's adversity and turned it into a pivotal advantage for the French.

Pavie's timely intervention during the Haw invasion on behalf of Ong Kham, then the Buddhist king of Luang Phrabang, became an auspicious, if not almost mythic event for later French legitimation scenarios of French Laos. Larcher-Goscha describes what transpired:

For several months, despite the fact that his every move and gesture were closely monitored by a Siamese commissioner, he [Pavie] struck up a friendship with the head monk at the Wat Mai temple and succeeded in meeting with King Ong Kham, when, in 1887, the principality was brutally sacked by Deo Van Tri. The latter, son of the Chief of the Tais of Lai Chau, had led this attack on Luang Phrabang in order to take revenge on the Siamese who had taken hostages, including his brothers, in the principality a few months earlier. In his diary, Pavie described in striking detail the real panic that had seized the inhabitants during the raid—the inhabitants fleeing the attackers from the one side of the Mekong to the other as if stricken with an inability to defend themselves. Now more than ever, Pavie made himself the bearer of the good French word to the Lao people, promising them a return to peace under French protection. . . . French colonial historiography accords an important place to this episode in so far as Pavie succeeded in saving Oun Kham who, thankful to his saviour, agreed to put his domain under French protection. Pavie's biographers would see in this event the founding act of French Laos. (2003: 219)

The actual founding of French Laos, however, did not formally occur until the bu-reaucratic implementation of the Franco-Siamese treaty of 1907. Initially, French claims rested on the degrees to which some of the Lao *muang* had formerly paid tribute to Annam (Hue), then under French control.[8] Indeed, the French regarded Laos as something of an extension of Vietnam, indicative of how they would rule Laos for the next fifty years.[9] At Pavie's urging in 1893,[10] the French ran gunships up the Chao Phraya River to the palace of the Siamese king in Bangkok to demand that: (1) *all lands* east of the Mekong River (not just those that had periodically paid tribute to Hue) be ceded to French control; (2) a 25 km "buffer zone" be established on the Mekong's west bank; and (3) extraterritorial claims be extended to "French subjects" in Siam (meaning all Lao, Phuan, or other peoples whose traditional origins were in what was now considered French Laos). In 1899 the area within the boundaries of French Laos was annexed to greater French Indochina. With this, the concept of a boundaried nation-state triumphed. Bangkok, in turn, also became preoccupied with fixing its own national boundaries and with establishing its own influence within.[11]

The Siamese realization of the boundaried nation-state was fraught with implications for Lao living on the Khorat plateau of northeast Thailand. Hayashi writes:

> When Laos was annexed to Indochina . . . , the word Lao was erased from the place names in the Khorat Plateau where the Lao lived and the use of Lao as a nationality forbidden in national censuses. [Before the French gunboat diplomacy with Bangkok, the Khorat plateau] was considered the home of the Lao . . . , there was only nominal rule by the central government. It was politically autonomous space, in reality closely related to the Lao kingdom located on the east bank of the Mekong. (2003: 49)

As early as 1885 the Siamese policy that *muang* could be freely established had been abolished by Bangkok, and a system of district and provincial administration under centralized control was instituted in 1893. Consequently, the mandala model of polity became politically moribund, for the most part only ceremonial when ritually articulated. This eventually was true for Luang Phrabang in French Laos too.

Auguste Pavie, as the first governor of "Le Laos Francais," formally kept his promise to the Luang Phrabang king that his mandala would retain its autonomy, but only as a French "protectorate."[12] What had formerly constituted the Vientiane and Champasak mandalas, however, would be administered directly by the French.

When the French seized control of the Lao cultural regions, they faced many challenges. For instance, the Lan Xang mandala, or "*muang* Lao," had fragmented nearly two centuries earlier, and because the surviving Lao mandala in Luang Phrabang and Champasak had atrophied, there was little in the way of "supra-

muang" Lao identity to build upon. Prince Phetsarath, the leader of the Lao Issara nationalists, the forerunners of the Lao struggle for independence,

> speaking in 1956, commented that during the early decades of French colonial rule: "The people of each *mueang* felt that their homeland was limited to that *mueang* and that other *mueang* were essentially other countries. This was because except for the province of Luang Phrabang, these other *mueang* did not have any king ruling over them, and so each *mueang* set itself up as independent." (Lockhart 2003: 131)

Phetisarath's comment signals an important issue germane to the new Franco-Lao political context: the absence of a powerful Buddhist kingship at the center of a Lao political mandala.

French colonial political developments in Laos were markedly different when compared with British rule in Burma and Sri Lanka, where Theravada Buddhist kingships had been disestablished, but there were, indeed, significant parallels in relation to the fate of the Lao *sangha*.[13] First, though the Lao were nominally subject to the Bangkok Buddhist king of the Chakri dynasty throughout the nineteenth century, the Lao *sangha*, as noted earlier, remained largely outside the orbit of concerted Siamese influence. Thus in those regions outside Luang Phrabang, during Siamese and then early French rule, the absence of royal initiatives (or a royally appointed *sangharaja*), led to a further decentralization and localization of the *sangha*. No efforts to instill a uniform monastic code of discipline through the reinforcement of the Vinaya or through issuing *katikavata*s (royal directives that functioned as addenda to the Vinaya) were forthcoming from powerful central authorities. In other words there was no Phothisarat or Chao Anou to take an active role in patronizing or purifying the *sangha*. The local village articulation of Buddhist thought and practice, therefore, became even more thoroughly wedded to the ritual and conceptual frameworks of the spirit cults. Second, without royal patronage, there were few initiatives for the support of monastic literary arts, though we know that vernacular texts continued to flourish.[14] A monk's knowledge of Pali texts tended to be construed more as a matter of magical prowess than as the result of linguistic and exegetical erudition.[15] Third, the *sangha*, in the absence of institutional centralization, lost any "supralocality" that it may have enjoyed earlier. It thereby ceased to function within Lao society as a means through which aspiring, talented individuals could transcend village or *muang* origins to begin a journey of upward social mobility. Buddhist monks were largely village monks who embodied the religio-cultural values of their immediate social environs. The French would try to change this, but with very limited success.

From my earlier account of Lan Xang in Chapter 1, it is clear that Buddhism exercised a profound influence upon Lao political culture from the fourteenth or fifteenth centuries forward. The Buddhist king often postured as a *cakkavattin,* the Phra Bang image was a palladium of the kingdom and its people, and the *sangha,* in exchange for royal patronage, functioned as an authorizing agent for the king's legitimacy.[16] All three of these cardinal elements of Lao Buddhist political culture were practically shorn of significance in French Laos, except symbolically in Luang Phrabang, where ritual articulation was at least ceremonially maintained. Moreover, because the Lao had been without a king within a unified Buddhist mandala for two hundred years, and because the Siamese king had been a distant force to most of the village Lao, and finally, because Lao polity had been so fragmented since the early eighteenth century, there was little if any political coherence to the Lao cultural regions.[17]

Indeed, the idea of a modern nation-state grew very slowly. Eventually cultivated by a few urban French-educated Lao elite, it never permeated much of the indigenous population.

The French did make administrative use of the old *ban/muang* administrative hierarchy, but only a few exceptional Frenchmen like Paul Mus, or perhaps other academic luminaries working for the Ecole Francais d'Extreme Orient (EFEO), understood traditional Lao conceptions of power. Few bridges were built to capitalize formally upon traditional Lao ontologies, because they were considered "irrational" and the product of debased superstitious beliefs. Not until the 1920s through the 1940s, when it more urgently served their own geopolitical purposes in sharpening Lao national identity over and against the Thai, did the French encourage a renewed vitality of Buddhism, and even then they sought to engineer Theravada according to an image of the religion quite foreign to its Lao context, though the claim was that Buddhism was being purified to reclaim its original rational bases.

French exploitation of Southeast Asia was rationalized by an idealistic commitment to a higher moral calling. As Evans notes,

The French had an additional burden, bequeathed to them by the 1789 Revolution, and that was their moral duty to spread the assumed universal values of the revolution—*liberte, egalite, fraternite*—around the globe. This unique *mission civilisatrice* bound together administration, adventurers, soldiers and sailors. . . . Republican ideals of equality and citizenship pitted the French colonizers against the old "feudal" classes and rationalized their overthrow. In its early days, French colonialism was committed to the idea of turning colonial peoples into "Frenchmen"—but they had to be "civilized" before they could reap republicanism's rewards. (2002b: 44)[18]

If these were the values of the *mission civilisatrice* during the early decades of French colonialism, then it is odd that the French did so little to instill them among the people they had subjugated in Laos. Indeed, there was an extraordinary lack of educational infrastructure put into place.

> State-sponsored education has always been a crucial vehicle for spreading the idea of nationhood, but in Laos French efforts in this respect were minimal. Reliance on the pagoda schools up until the 1930s [also] had the effect of largely excluding non-Buddhist minorities from education. (Evans 2002b: 71)

McCoy cites two statistics demonstrating the degree to which the French failed to impart the universal values that they cherished, underlining the paucity of effort that they put into educating the people of the country they had just mapped and claimed: "Because the French had little use for educated Laotians, by 1940 there were only 7,000 primary school students in a colony of one million people. *Not a single high school was constructed*" (1970: 82).

This negative legacy of the French stands in critical contrast to the British educational legacy in Sri Lanka. Not only were several fine institutions of higher education founded by British and American missionaries in cooperation with the colonial government, institutions still strongly in place in the present, but the Sinhalese, Muslim, and Tamil communities were also encouraged to establish their own schools as well. Before the British departed in the late 1940s, they left a fully established University of Ceylon, a flagship that eventually provided the professional and academic resources necessary for the further establishment of other universities and professional tertiary centers.[19]

Unfortunately the French did none of this in Laos, despite the fact that their efforts in Cambodia and especially Vietnam were much better. Consequently, the distribution and quality of education remains one of the country's greatest challenges today.[20] Yet because of their policy to leave traditional village *vat*s intact, they also guaranteed that the limited education of most Lao remained traditionally Buddhist in substance, without much relevance to the "higher ideals" of French colonial ideology, and without any relevance to the kinds of skills that might be needed for the economic development and administration of the country. For the highland tribal peoples in the mountainous zones, there were no educational provisions whatsoever.

Wherever it was established in Asia and Africa, European colonial rule was always administered in a "top-down" fashion. Indeed, the colonial experience of French Laos was a textbook example of how an administration by so few could be effected over so many. The actual presence of French personnel in Laos was so skeletal that it further guaranteed that French cultural impact on the common population was minimal, limited to a small urban elite, though that impact translated into great significance for the eventual political course of the colony.

Instead of educating and utilizing the skills of the people of Laos in the administration of their colony, what the French succeeded in achieving was the thorough infiltration of Vietnamese into the political and commercial matrix of the region, thereby minimizing the need for many of their own administrators.[21] McCoy notes just how small the actual numbers of French administrators were and why:

> After the dream of instant wealth faded, the French resigned themselves to maintaining order and managing their administration as inexpensively as possible. . . . Since one of the largest expenses of any colonial budget was maintaining the support of European officials at their normal standard of living, the French kept their colonial staff in Laos to such an absolute minimum that in 1904, the contingent of 72 officials was the smallest anywhere in the French empire. (1970: 77–78)[22]

Not only were the French few in numbers, but they remained aloof from the indigenous population as well: "Most subordinate positions in the provincial bureaucracies (translators, low-level clerks) were manned by the Gallicized Lao elite, the middle-level positions by French-educated Vietnamese, and the very highest positions were reserved for French officials" (McCoy 1970: 78). Commenting upon French racism as responsible for the tiered hierarchy of colonial administration, Stuart-Fox says:

> The colonial regime established a racial hierarchy with the French at the top, followed by the Vietnamese (dynamic, expansionist, industrious). Then the Lao (timid, lazy in decline), then the other ethnic groups whose chiefs were tributary to the Lao (such as the Lue and the Hmong, etc.) and finally the *kha* (the Lao Theung who had been slaves to the Lao).[23] (2003: 81)

These comments lead into two relevant discussions. The first is the short- and long-term consequences of importing so many Vietnamese to do much of the colonial French administrative bidding.[24] The second is more directly related to the colonial impact on religious culture, especially how French administrative rule impacted "highland" or "minority" non-Lao groups, in addition to the non-elite rural Buddhist Lao.

The degree to which the "ethnic Lao" lost political control is signaled by what happened in the newly rehabilitated city of Vientiane after the French decided to make it their administrative center. Both Vientiane and Luang Phrabang could lay relevant claims as the historic centers of the traditional Lao mandala. But Vientiane had been completely destroyed by Siam in the 1820s. It would have to be rebuilt entirely from scratch. Luang Phrabang had its own set of liabilities as a potential capital: it was not as centrally located as Vientiane, and its selection as the administrative center might send the wrong signal to the residual royalty of Luang Phrabang by inviting an overestimation of their importance in the new political scheme. In the end,

> Vientiane was rebuilt not as a symbolic center of a reunified Mueang Lao, but as a provincial French administrative town inhabited, it should be remembered, as much by Vietnamese representing French Indochina as by Lao.... Laos was seen as an extension of Vietnam, to be exploited by Vietnamese labor and French capital for the benefit of France. (Stuart-Fox 2003: 78)

Though Luang Phrabang was allowed to continue as a symbolic cultural center, the French made it clear that it was not the real political center of Laos. Not only would Vientiane become home to an increasing number of Vietnamese, far more than Lao in fact, but so too would the rest of the major Lao urban areas, with the exception of Luang Phrabang.[25] According to Lockhart:

> While the Vietnamese represented a relatively small percentage of the colony's total population—less than 3 per cent as late as 1936—they constituted the largest community in most towns except for Luang Phrabang. Moreover, the civil service and the educational system in Laos were dominated by Vietnamese, as were the colonial militia and the labor force in the tin mines. (2003: 131)

The legacy of the French policy to import Vietnamese as administrators and as the nonagricultural work force for the cities (who thereby became primary beneficiaries of the developing political economy), and to consciously attempt to forge the future destinies of both Vietnam and Laos into an economic togetherness, created enormous consequences in the near and long terms. In the near term, it was not surprising, given the level of Vietnamese immigration encouraged by the French, that "anti-Vietnamese sentiment was central to the Lao nationalism that stirred in the 1940s" (Evans 2002b: 70).

On the other hand, and in the long term, the Vietnamese were not resented by another group of politically aspirant Lao, but regarded instead as great allies in an anticolonial, anti-imperialistic struggle. During this same time when anti-Vietnamese sentiment was helping to fuel the birth of Lao nationalism under the leadership of the oldest royal prince (Phetisarath), political stirrings in Vietnam itself were being reflected simultaneously in the Vietnamese expatriate (Viet Kieu) community in Laos, a trajectory that proved attractive to major players in the future of

Laos: the younger royal prince Souphanouvong and Kaysone Phomvihane, both
of whom would later become the leaders of revolutionary socialist Laos. Lockhart
(2003: 131) observes that "it was this Viet Kieu (expatriate Vietnamese) community which served as the bridge for the penetration of Marxist ideology into Laos
and which became the locus for the limited activities of the ICP [Indochina Communist Party] in that colony."[26]

While much of the ideology of the communist Pathet Lao originated in the
socialist vision of Marx and Engels as further refined by Lenin, it was also filtered
through French-educated Vietnamese prisms as well. Ho Chi Minh was regarded
not only as the beloved dear old nationalist "Uncle Ho," but also as the heroic
revolutionary and ideological "godfather" of the entire Indochinese liberation
movement.[27]

Another specific legacy of French policies was their impact on the religio-
political cultures of rural highland "ethnic minorities" and non-elite Lao Buddhist peasants. To achieve their goal of linking Laos more thoroughly to Vietnam
through the building of roads, the French demanded corvee labor from various
highland peoples. This colonial practice of forced labor, along with the imposition
of heavy taxes, were sources of conflict between some of the highlanders and the
French. The political significance of this conflict has been explored in some depth
by other scholars, but the relevance of its religious dimension has not.

"Pacification" and Religion in the Highlands of French Laos

While village life in the nineteenth century remained largely unaffected by the
"modernization" occurring at the center of the Bangkok mandala, the establishment of French colonial power brought new demands to "peripheral people," especially the rural highland "ethnic minorities" of Laos.[28] From the perspective of
the French colonial government, a perspective shared by French entrepreneurs,

> Indochina had to become a self-supporting colony, and tax collection repre-
> sented the fundamental financial lever to facilitate the transformation of the
> colonies into profitable markets and producers. One of the impacts of the new
> system of taxation was to force the transformation of a predominantly subsis-
> tence economy into a monetary one, as money progressively replaced barter as
> means of exchange. (Pholsena 2006: 31)

The principle dynamic of power operating in the old Buddhist mandala system
had been its centripetal and centrifugal flows from the periphery to the center
and back to the periphery. The semiotics of the mandala, no matter at what level,
were always understood as articulating exchange. Within classical Pali Theravada

Buddhist political discourse, this exchange is most clearly articulated in the *Ag-ganna Sutta* of the *Digha Nikaya,* wherein the origins of Buddhist kingship are depicted in a mythic account of the first king, Mahasammata, elected by the people to provide protection and to uphold the general social moral order in exchange for a share of rice.[29] Therefore, in theory at least, royal power to uphold the moral order was understood as contractual. Within the context of Buddhist societies, this principle of reciprocity remains in play even on the basic personal levels of social exchange. For example, it operates in the simple interaction between a Buddhist laywoman (a symbol of the periphery) providing rice to a Buddhist monk (a symbol of the center). In exchange for food given to the monk, the laywoman gains merit. At every level of the mandala, there was a reciprocal process of giving and giving back, though at times the giving was coerced. Moreover, in the *Vessantara Jataka,* the most popular of all *jataka*s stories, celebrated in Laos as Boun Phravet, the ethic of giving is extolled as the ideal and ultimate way to perfect the religious life. Giving propels spiritual advancement. It is a spiritual and social ethic.

The hill tribes of French Laos, though not Buddhists, understood and partici-pated in the ethic of exchange. They were also participants in the Buddhist man-dala dynamic. As is evident in the Lao New Year myth that recounts the origins of Luang Phrabang, while the *Kha* were subordinated to the Lao king, their *place* was respected in exchange for tribute. For the tribute given to the Lao king, the *Kha* re-ceived their right to cultivate land and to subsist within a social context governed by moral order. They also earned the right, as was the case for Lao Buddhist *ban* and *muang,* to settle their collective affairs with a measure of autonomy. In Mus's terms, they could realize the powers of life intrinsic to the soil of the land that they cultivated.

This ethic of exchange, the centrifugal and centripetal flow of power between the periphery and center, was spoiled by the introduction of a new economic and political system. In the new colonial political economy, "the French demanded heavy taxes, opium, porters, and corvee road work from these tribes, *but gave them absolutely nothing in return*" (McCoy 1970: 79; emphasis mine). McCoy's statement may not hold in all instances, given the manner in which some high-land peoples, especially some sections of Hmong, benefited from their relations with the French, but it does, nonetheless, register how the old balance of give and take was disrupted. On their side of the relation, many highland tribes could not understand what benefit they might derive from heavy taxation or from doing the backbreaking work of building roads across the mountain ranges to link Viet-namese-dominated towns of the Mekong River basin to centers of commerce in Vietnam. (Indeed, construction of the roads to Vietnam made no practical sense to most other people living in Laos as well, since the traditional routes of travel and trade, in addition to cultural ties, were south to Siam and Cambodia and not east to Vietnam.) It is therefore quite unsurprising that "the imposition upon peasantry of systems of taxes and corvees as much as the introduction of commodity relations met with unpredictable results. Forms of resistance ran the gamut from tax evasions, to armed revolt, to intertribal warfare, to flight" (Gunn 2003: 141). Confrontations were not simply between indigenous people and Europeans either. What made them more complex is that both Vietnamese and Lao elite, the authoritative guarantors of the old mandala tributary dynamic, were also complicit in oppressing highland tribals and non-elite rural Buddhist Lao.[30] This came to haunt the Lao elite in the 1960s and 1970s.

What was at stake for some of the ethnic highlanders and the rural Buddhist Lao, or what led to their rebellions against the French (and against the complicit Vietnamese and Lao elites), was no less than the survival of their own morally based worldviews. As Gunn explains:

> The intrusion of the cash nexus destroys the peasants' moral community. The colonial state thus only increases social stratification at the expense of peasant welfare and generally destroys the peasant "little tradition" and the patron-client networks that anchor it to the wider the community. The violence that accompanies these structural dislocations is thus matched on the part of the peasantry by "defensive reactions" to maintain subsistence arrangements. (2003: 147)[31]

Indeed, there is much evidence that violent conflicts between highland peoples and the French were fundamentally generated by desperate attempts to reassert indigenous "subsistence arrangements." Yet what also came into play was an attempt to preserve bedrock religio-moral principles. The more than three decades long rural Lao rebellion led by Ong Keo and Ong Kommadan in the Bolovens plateau of southeast Laos is perhaps the most well-known example. For over a generation, not only was this resistance movement successful in avoiding taxation and corvee labor, and in the process rendering the entire region unsafe for the French, but in its final years it evolved into a "Maitreya cult," or a fully fledged Buddhist millenarian movement.

Maitreya, as I noted earlier, is the buddha of the future whose appearance heralds a new era of collective well-being: all material desires and spiritual aspirations will be fulfilled. The timing of Maitreya's appearance, like the timing of Gotama's (the Buddha of our era), is understood as the qualitative high-water mark of an eon, but one both preceded and followed by conditions of abject moral and material decline (the former reflected in the latter). Indeed, conditions of severe decline and the concomitant disestablishment of Buddhist political power have often been occasions for the resurgence of beliefs among Buddhist folk of Southeast Asia in the imminent appearance of Maitreya, whose presence, it is believed, will assuage conditions of human suffering. Maitreya thus embodies an eschatological hope for the future. This hope has often been expressed apocalyptically amidst social conditions brought about by economic hardship and political upheaval, conditions so stress-filled that Buddhists have equated their contemporary experiences of suffering as evidence of time's nadir, and they therefore expect time's subsequent rapid ascent to culminate in Maitreya's descent from Tusita Heaven.[32] Movements of this nature reflect a comprehensive social, economic, political, and religious rejection of the political powers and worldview that cause distress.

Leaders of Buddhist millenarian movements are usually understood as men of great magical or supernaturally endowed power who have the ability to facilitate the imminent arrival of the future ideal era. Whether Buddhist-inspired (as the movement led by Ong Keo) or not, all highland revolts in the early twentieth century were met by the French with "pacification" campaigns, a euphemism for violent repression. Violent responses, however, only further strengthened resistance. Noting how the French thought that the highland ethnic minorities were foolish for not knowing that it was in their best interests to submit, Pholsena (2006: 34–35) suggests that "the French policy of pacification heightened the highlanders' fierce sense of independence, and *indirectly* fostered ethnic-consciousness among some members of the highland population in southeastern 'Laos.'" I will pursue Pholsena's comment about "ethnic consciousness" shortly, but first I will indicate how highlander resistance to the French was co-opted anachronistically by later historians motivated by either nationalist or communist agendas.

In the mid-twentieth century, highlander revolts against the colonial system were "consistently reinterpreted by Lao Nationalist historians as the country's pioneering independence movements" (Pholsena 2006: 130), rather than as millennial movements or simply acts of resistance. In this way the chief aim of the emergent postcolonial modern nation-state was projected anachronistically into a context in which it never was consciously entertained. For Marxist-oriented historians writing at the service of the later socialist Lao Peoples Democratic Republic (PDR), highland movements were regarded analogously as antiforeign, anti-imperialist, and antifeudal stirrings igniting the revolutionary hopes that were finally realized in 1975.[33] Regarding these nationalist and revolutionary historiographies, Lockhart (2003: 152–153) says that both have de-emphasized ethnic diversity in favor of a constructed Lao people "and both have ignored the ethnic tensions and rivalries" between various highland groups. Making a similar point in the contemporary context, but framing it in a manner that indicates how it was probably much more true in the earlier part of the twentieth century than now, Ijima (2003: 165) says that "for Laos, the nationalist view of identity begins to blur if one leaves the cities to travel to remoter, hilly parts of the country, where the nation-building power of modern roads and communications have not yet penetrated deeply to

erase pre-existing identities and to transform the culturally diverse peoples living in the highlands into a larger Lao national family." When upland peoples are
encountered in their remote village contexts, they are still, even in the present day,
much more likely to refer to themselves as Khmu, Hmong, Phuan, and so forth,
rather than as Lao Theung or Lao Sung, and never as simply "Lao."

Gay has been especially critical of histories of colonial Laos that are pervaded
with a Pathet Lao motive. Though the Marxists are his targets, much of his criticism applies to the earlier nationalists too. I quote Gay at length because his comments are comprehensive and anticipate my conclusion.

> For ideological reasons, Lao historians have presented these [highland] move-
> ments as anti-colonial revolts and have refused to take into account their
> genesis. In this way, they avoid reference to irrational beliefs that Marxism
> condemns. . . . [B]y studying these movements only in their second phases,
> when transformed into armed struggles, Lao researchers are able to point to a
> national resistance against the colonial system in southern Laos.
>
> On the other hand, certain hesitations and variations are notable with-
> in the Marxist perception of these movements, especially with regard to the
> importance of religious and cultural factors in their emergence. . . . Archival
> and published documents demonstrate that none of these movements began
> as insurrections against the colonial system. Whether in the Bolawen plateau
> region or Savannakhet Province, a long period elapsed between the moment
> when a miracle worker initiated a movement and the moment when the move-
> ment was transformed into an insurrection against colonial power. Moreover,
> it was only when colonial administrators decided to arrest a miracle worker—
> and failed—that the movement became radicalized, bellicose and opposed to
> colonial power. . . .
>
> The gap that exists between the actual course of events earlier in this cen-
> tury and its representation in subsequent writings is created by the dogmatism
> of the authors and, in particular, by a materialist vision of reality *that minimizes
> and often ignores the psychological, religious and cultural variables influencing
> these movements.* These constraints permitted the authors to envisage only one
> aspect of the appearance and repression of these movements. This blinkered
> portrayal of events was reinforced by an ideological concept of what history
> *had* to be like, if it were to be shaped according to the desired tradition of the
> national struggle to safeguard (or recover) independence and of the march of
> societies towards socialism. These reductionist histories, mutilating reality, led
> to the creation of a gallery of heroes, who are more civic models than histori-
> cal persons, and to the perpetuation, against hard facts, of an illusion of ethnic
> cohesion and harmony. In re-appropriating these episodes of their national

past, contemporary Lao historians have tailored them to the dimensions of an official history. (2002: 294–295)[34]

Thus Pholsena and Gay provide important insights necessary to understand what happened between the French and highland peoples of Laos in the early twentieth century. Pholsena mentions an awakening of "ethnic identity," and Gay suggests that "psychological, religious and cultural variables influencing these movements" need to be recognized in accounting for their genesis. For the French, what was "madness," and for the later Marxists what was "irrational," was, for the affected highland peoples, nothing less than a defensive reformulation of their normative religious worldview and moral identity. It was certainly not a nationalist or socialist struggle. None of these movements became bellicose or "anticolonial" until after the French attempted forcibly to seize their leaders. Not until their moral identity (represented by their leader—in Mus's terms, the this-worldly counterpart of the "god of the soil") and modus vivendi (subsistence and exchange economy) were threatened, did these movements morph into armed insurrections. In more basic terms, these resistance movements were responses to threats about "what we do" and "who we are." They were initially about control of the indigenous political economy, about the power to live in one's own *place* in the conventional subsistence manner. Then, after serious confrontation, the movements elevated into questions of identity and questions of ontology. That is precisely why the idioms of resistance used to articulate power in these rebellious movements were often religious in nature, for religious thought and ritual expression were the traditional means through which power and identity were morally understood. Far from being patriotic struggles in the name of an independent or socialist Laos, these were movements mounted in defense, ultimately, of either the ontology of the indigenous religious substratum or the Buddhist political worldview.

Gunn (2003: 171) has argued that "the psychological dimension of shared oppression at the hands of the French by both the montagnard and lowland peasantry during the 1930s was an important factor in shaping the 'tactical' alliances between the communists and the minorities during the 1940s." Moreover, he has contended that "as premodern forms of protests, such 'millennial' outbursts seldom took on a national character but—arguably—assumed the form of protonationalist responses to the intervention of outsiders" (142). Thus Gunn seems to have recognized an intermediary phase that Gay points out is absent in both nationalist and Marxist historiographies.

As for the French, they came to fear the irruption of millenarian movements in Southeast Asia. Indeed, the modern, rational, "scientific," and demythologized Buddhism that they sought to encourage was aimed, in part, in providing an alternative to cosmological forms of the religion that were potentially politically threatening.[35] In their view Buddhism could be rehabilitated through purgation of its accretions and a re-emphasis of its canonical moral teachings, but the accretions per se (such as the spirit cults), along with other elements of cosmologically oriented folklore, had to be discouraged.

After the French left, nationalists and communists competed in trying to channel highlander disaffection into support for their respective causes. But before that later historical moment, as Pholsena (2006: 40) has described, "the highland populations in Laos were soon caught between the propaganda of the French, on the one hand, and that of the Vietnamese and Laos communist movements—the Viet Minh and the Pathet Lao—on the other, both sides being eager to gain their loyalty in the aftermath of the Second World War. The 'choice' between the two sides was contingent and, more often than not, guided by survival imperatives." That is, these revolts against the French were a matter of survival for both a material and a moral way of life. That the Vietnamese and Lao communists eventually were more successful than the nationalists in enlisting the support of the highlanders is not surprising in retrospect. Their success in the waning years of French colonial power was a harbinger of their later victories in mobilizing highland support against the nationalists who had formed the Royal Lao Government.[36]

A National Rational Buddhism

In the early decades of their colonial rule French policies generated a deleterious effect on the Buddhist *sangha*'s position within Lao society. Indeed the *sangha*'s traditional political function in relation to any ruling power was deemed irrelevant to the new colonial administrative scheme. While certainly in an enervated condition in the later nineteenth century, the reciprocal relation between Lao political power and the *sangha* was almost completely snapped by the French colonial intrusion.

Clearly and emphatically characterizing the deleterious nature of the French impact on the *sangha* in the first twenty years of colonial rule, Stuart-Fox asserts:

> French colonialism, though maintaining the courts of Luang Phrabang and Champasak intact, destroyed the legitimizing function of myth and religion because it usurped political authority. The king ruled only because the French permitted him to.
>
> The French pressure also threw into question the reciprocal relationship between the monarchy and the Sangha by relegating Buddhism to a marginal position in colonial society. The Sangha lost not only its *raison d'etre* as state religion in colonial Laos, but also its monopoly over education, at least in the centres of power. Only in the countryside did the Sangha retain its traditional

authority. In the towns, in line with their "*mission civilisatrice*", the French offered the Lao elite the benefit of French secular education, with its promise of access to the new power structure. The Lao elite eagerly accepted the new education and, with it, French philosophical tradition with its distinction between temporal and spiritual powers. As a result, the organic connection between the political and the religious order was destroyed for the Lao ruling class, and many lost faith in their own traditional form of government. (1996: 71–72)

Here it should be added that the higher education given to this elite took place not so much in the urban centers of Laos, but either in French academies located in Saigon or Hanoi, or in France itself. The Lao elite, including members of the extended royal family, were, in effect, culturally fused, in a fashion similar to the blend of French-Lao architecture that would be constructed in Luang Phrabang in the early decades of the twentieth century. This new Lao educated elite would regard the old religio-political culture as an archaic and premodern artifact. More importantly for the French, the "modernity" that they would engineer in Vientiane and Phnom Penh would necessarily have to mean something quite different from the modernization processes occurring in Bangkok. At least this was their primary aim, and a reconditioned Lao Buddhism, they thought, might abet its realization.

The initial French stance, a benign neglect of Buddhism, lasted until the 1920s, with the notable exception of the Ecole Francais d'Extreme Orient's attention to Pali canonical texts, epigraphy, and monuments. But EFEO's efforts, even then, were far more concentrated on Cambodia than Laos. While the nineteenth century did not witness a high degree of Siamese influence on the Lao in terms of the modernization programs unfolding in Bangkok, many Lao Buddhist monks, after the establishment of French control and the disestablishment of Buddhism as a political force in public life, began to seek their own higher forms of education in Siam, since monastic education languished in Laos under the French. This Buddhist education for the monastic elite was, therefore, substantively and philosophically quite different in orientation than what the French were providing for the Lao lay elite. Moreover, the recently established national boundaries between Siam and Laos were not a paramount barrier to most Lao Buddhists, especially in matters of pilgrimage, nor were they a barrier for the considerable numbers of *thudong* or ascetic wandering monks who regularly crossed the Mekong from one side to the other, from one boundaried country to the other. The French authorities soon began to worry about the potential political significance of these growing religious ties to Siam, especially in light of the fact that public Buddhism had been retained, even rejuvenated in terms of its political significance in contemporary Bangkok. That many Lao Buddhist monks were making their way to Bangkok for higher monastic education fueled this French worry. As Evans has noted:

> During the reign of Rama VI (1910–1925), a powerful ideology of royalist na-
> tionalism that would link the monarchy, Buddhism, and the state was elabo-
> rated in Siam, and this would reverberate in Laos. The need to nationalize Lao
> Buddhism received its first expression in the resurrection of Vat Sisaket [in
> Vientiane] as a center for Lao Buddhist ceremonial, or in the words of the Resi-
> dent Superieur, as "the Buddhist cathedral of Laos." (2002b: 71)

"Cathedral," of course, is not quite the correct translation of *vat*, but it does convey the French hope that they had provided for an important ceremonial space
of great religious significance to the Lao, but also a central space that was not of
a political nature.[37] Certainly the French did not have in mind the creation of a
mandalic center when they undertook the rehabilitation of Vat Sisaket (see Photo
1.4 in Chapter 1).

Around this very same time, in response to French concerns about growing
"pan-Thaiism," Albert Saurraut, the governor general of French Indochina, formally began the process of institutionalizing a secularized state educational system
modeled closely after the system in France, though "progress in establishing the
infrastructure was particularly slow outside Vietnam" (Harris 2005: 127).[38] The
first textbooks produced in Lao for secular education emphasized the historical
and cultural foundations of Champa (mostly Cambodia) and thus directed attention away from Lao roots in the Tai migration from southwestern China. A further
conscious effort was made to stress the cultural and historical links between Angkor and Luang Phrabang. Thus "the French turned the eyes of both their Theravada Buddhist colonies away from Siam and towards each other" (Evans 2002b:
72). A concerted effort was also initiated to emphasize the unique qualities and
legacies of the Lao language and its literature. One consequence of these efforts,
Chalong Soontravanich (2003: 119) asserts, is that "as early as 1918, a consciousness of a distinct Lao cultural identity, in this case the Lao writing system, language
and literature, was increasingly present among a handful of western educated Lao
elites." At work in this agenda was a deliberate effort to foster a specific "ethnic
Lao" identity upon which to build a strong national consciousness separate from,
and resistant to, the emerging Thai Buddhist identity that was then gaining momentum in Siam.

During this same year (1918), the famous French buddhologist Louis Finot
also completed his project of undertaking an inventory of extant Pali Buddhist
texts found in temple libraries throughout Laos.[39] Moreover, encouraged and
supervised by other scholars from the EFEO, the French also commenced a re-
building program of significant Buddhist "monuments," chief among them the
That Luang (see Plate 2) in Vientiane, as well as other important temples in Luang
Phrabang. These temples had, of course, been destroyed in Vientiane either by the

Siamese in the early nineteenth century or later in Luang Phrabang by the Haw invaders. What better ways to generate a sense of Lao Buddhist national identity distinct from the Buddhist-based nationalism now surfacing in Siam than to rehabilitate historically venerable centers of Buddhist rite and ceremony in Laos? In implementing this new strategy to counteract Thai influence, the French had completed something of a volte-face in their posture towards Buddhism, certainly a major adjustment to the posture they had deployed during the first two or three decades of their rule. Commenting on the political significance of this new French initiative, Evans writes:

> In this one could argue they [the French] were simply transposing the practices of French nationalism into the Lao context. The colonial state, of course, also transposed elements of the modern state into this context, which included an increasingly elaborate set of bureaucratic rules and regulations. Thus in 1927 a detailed code for the conduct of the Buddhist sangha (order of monks) was enacted. (1998: 50)

Each of these French undertakings in this multifaceted rehabilitation program was significant in regard to redefining, but also controlling and manipulating the importance of Buddhism within the evolving public culture of colonial Laos. By authorizing a code of conduct for the monks, the French established themselves as the ultimate regulators and definers of Buddhism. While the code of conduct also was a measure taken to prevent the potential politicization of the *sangha* by the Thai,[40] the dimensions of the Buddhism that the French sought to promulgate represent the European zeitgeist of the times, which emphasized rationality, morality, and a more secularized understanding of the role of religion.

Perhaps the single most important initiative in relation to religion undertaken by the French involved the establishment of Buddhist institutes of higher education for the *sangha*, one in Laos in Vientiane and one in Cambodia in Phnom Penh. The urgent priority of this undertaking is underscored by the fact that while the French may have been ultimately dedicated to the principle of the separation of religion from the state, and continued to have in mind a secular rule of law for its colonies, the Buddhist institute in Laos was the only institution of higher learning that they had established up to this point in time during their colonial administration of Laos. In establishing these Buddhist institutes, the French were not only trying to regulate monastic behavior (as when they issued the 1927 code of Buddhist monastic conduct), but they were determined to control the kinds of knowledge that would inform the modernization of the *sangha* as well. The French, therefore, and not the Thai, would be the conduits and arbitrators of modernity for the Lao. Religion would be understood as a cultural component that helps to construct a national identity, but Buddhism's institutionalization would be carefully monitored to ensure that it did not become a political force in its own right.

The Buddhist institute in Laos was established in 1931, shortly after the institute in Phnom Penh, which Harris has described as follows:

> On May 12, 1930, in the same year that Ho Chi Minh founded the Indochinese Communist Party, the colonial authorities established the Buddhist Institute in Phnom Penh, with King Monivong and King Sisavang of Laos attending its opening. Placed under the direction of Suzanne Karpeles, who had previously acted as head of the Royal Library, Institut Indigene d'Etude du Bouddhisme du Petit Vehicule[41]—its correct name—aimed to save Cambodian Buddhism from "degeneration" and to counteract Thai influence through the construction of a strong Indochinese sense of identity. . . . [T]he Buddhist Institute would eventually become closely linked with the modernist agenda of the Thommakay *sangha* faction. (2005: 137)

Virtually all scholars agree with Harris, Edwards (2007), and Evans (2002b: 72) that the establishment of these institutes was clearly politically motivated as "a deliberate attempt by the French to redirect Buddhist learning away from Siam."

From these accounts we can begin to tease out the kind of Buddhist religion that the French envisaged for the Lao. By Harris telling us that these institutes became linked to the "Thomakay faction," we know that the orientation to Buddhism was philosophically rationalistic, rigid in its adherence to the monastic code of the Vinaya, and opposed to the performance of apotropaic practices. "Village Buddhism" was seen as contaminated and degenerate, in need of a respectable rehabilitation. That, indeed, would be the mission of the institute's newly minted graduates. Saving Buddhism from its contemporary degenerated position was the goal also shared by EFEO's illustrious scholars, including Finot, Coedes, and Karpeles.

The thoroughly bookish orientation that the French scholars insisted upon in determining the curriculum and style of learning was mirrored in their own scholarly quests to create or recreate an accessible Pali canon. Karpeles's main task was to create a Khmer-Pali bilingual edition of the Tipitaka. (No similar French effort was launched among the Lao.) Learned study rested upon an almost biblical-studies method of rational exegesis of sacred texts. It stressed the authority of the Buddha's historical and more philosophically inclined teachings, chiefly those derived from sections of the *Suttapitaka* and *Vinayapitaka* that were not cosmologically oriented. There was little or no focus upon ritual knowledge or any kind of reference to supernatural agencies. Trappings of the "degenerate" indigenous religious culture still so vital to village Buddhism, such as the *Vessantara Jataka*, "which Karpeles classed as literature 'belonging to the domain of the profane' or as 'national folklore'" (Hansen 2007: 129) were regarded as puerile. It would seem as if Durkheim's celebrated view of the evolution of religion served a paradigm for what the French envisaged for the new Buddhism. In addition, Durkheim, as all good French students of religion would know, had written in his classic *Elementary Forms of Religious Life* that Theravada Buddhism had stretched attempts aimed at formulating definitions of religion away from the supernatural theological orientations because Theravada was basically atheistic in its doctrine and thus did not exert any supernatural claims to authority.[42] This particular interpretation of the Theravada, derived from a very narrow reading of *sutta*s and eagerly embraced by those who wanted to assert an affinity between Theravadin and modern scientific perspectives, was also basically congruent with the reformed Buddhist ideology being promulgated in Bangkok by the Siamese Thammayut Nikay. (This presented the French with a dilemma.) The Buddhist religious path to *nibbana* was understood exclusively as an anthropocentric spiritual exercise brought to fruition through assiduous self-effort. There was nothing supernatural in the progressive cultivation of *sila* (morality), *panna* (wisdom), and *samadhi* (concentrated meditation). The *devata*s, *yaksa*s, *peta*s, and other supernatural figures populating the traditionally envisaged Buddhist cosmos revealed in the Pali canonical texts became victims of a process of demythologization and were either totally erased or consigned to a premodern mentality.[43] Moreover, Buddhist thought was understood as either having anticipated, or was now regarded as completely congruent with scientific thought. Buddhist ideas such as *anicca* (impermanence), *paticcasamuppada* (dependent origination), and *bhavana* (the meditative practice of disciplining the mind to cultivate higher degrees of mental awareness) were emphasized. This wholly rational understanding of Buddhism could be regarded as a modern religion precisely because it was non-theological in orientation and because it did not assert the authoritative presence of the supernatural in the world. That is, Buddhism was conceived as a religion that was completely anthropocentric, ethical at its core, and rational in its method. It was, as the eminent Chuon Nath, speaking at the inauguration of the institute in Vientiane had put it, *scientific* in character.

Since it was provided by the French in Laos, there was no need to seek out a modern form of Buddhism in Bangkok.[44] In the selection of Pali texts now to be emphasized, monks would not spend their time memorizing the *jataka*s or chants to be recited on ritual occasions, but instead would encounter the towering figure of the philosophical Buddha, conceived as a human font of prosaic wisdom whose didactic tenets were to be translated into civilized modes of social conduct. As Durkheim had envisaged religion to be in its post-theological phase, Lao Buddhism was to be fundamentally moral in nature, reflecting the central values of the

Lao national community. Moreover, it would contribute to the cultivation of a Lao national character distinct from the Thai, in the same way that the Lao language would be understood as distinctive from the dialect of Bangkok Thai.

However, in providing these ingredients for the distillation of a nationalist Lao Buddhist identity, the French had unwittingly concocted a potage that would eventually overheat in a kettle of nationalism that by the 1940s proved too hot for them to handle. In an effort to make Buddhism respectable, the French abetted the process in which a national Lao consciousness would be nurtured and enriched.

Stirrings of Lao Nationalism

As early as 1931 harbingers of an incipient Lao nationalism among the French-educated Lao elite began to appear. Prince Phetsarath, who played a leading role in founding the Lao Issara movement for independence, "responded to an article in the *France-Indochine* [magazine] calling for closer integration of Laos into 'Indochina' by arguing vigorously for a separate Lao identity. He also actively promoted the appointment of Lao to replace Vietnamese in the colonial administration in Laos" (Stuart-Fox 2003: 82).

During the Second World War, the French in Laos, even under the Vichy government that had allied with the Japanese, remained wary of the other Japanese ally to the south, formerly Siam, but renamed "Thailand" in 1939. Plans were quickly designed for "the upgrading of the Ecole d'Administration" to be "a 'temple for the National Idea of Laos'" (Evans 2002b: 78).[45] The French government official placed in charge of implementing this plan was Charles Rochet, "head of the Educational Services of Laos," whose charge was "to awaken in Laotians a national spirit and to progressively achieve the moral unity of the country" (ibid.). McCoy describes what Rochet set out specifically to accomplish:

> Under [Charles] Rochet the Lao movement tried to arouse national sentiment among the younger Lao elite through a cultural renaissance of Lao literature, music and dance, creation of a national development program, and participation in patriotic gestures such as marches and rallies. . . . The movement's solid accomplishments included the construction of over 7,000 schools (more than had been built in the previous 47 years), significant expansion of a declining health system, and publication of the first Laotian newspaper. Rochet himself saw the movement as a last desperate attempt to save Laos from extinction. (1970: 94)

The earlier French effort to revivify Lao Buddhism was now part of a more ambitious attempt to affect a Lao "cultural renaissance." By 1942 the French also completed renovation of Vat Phra Keo in Vientiane, symbolically significant insofar as this temple had formerly housed the Emerald Buddha that had eventually become, after it had been removed from Vientiane, the symbolic palladium of Siamese kingship and the Thai people. Moreover, the French began to engage in very suggestive political conversations with the king of Luang Phrabang in which they promised an expansion of the Luang Phrabang protectorate over the southern regions of Laos as well, a move that could certainly elevate the Luang Phrabang royalty as a national symbol for all of French Laos.[46]

In March 1945, however, an unpredicted military and political event transpired that ushered in a plethora of major ramifications for this realpolitik. The Japanese rousted the French colonial Vichy government throughout Indochina and declared Laos, Cambodia, and Vietnam politically independent. Stuart-Fox succinctly describes this trajectory of events:

> French encouragement of the "renovation" of Lao culture and identity in the early 1940s was primarily in order to counter the appeal of the pan-Thaiism emanating from Bangkok. It was never intended to give rise to a nationalist movement for independence. The French authorities seemed unaware of the growth of national sentiment following the proclamation of the Lao independence under Japanese duress; or the urgency felt by many Lao in reclaiming their country from what they saw as the collusion of French and Vietnamese. The Japanese had set a precedent: Laos was a separate state in its own right. While the king in Luang Phrabang, out of touch with the political developments in the administrative capital of Viang Chan, was prepared to return his kingdom to France [after the defeat of the Japanese in August 1945], Prince Phetsarat took advantage of the political vacuum created by the Japanese surrender not only to reiterate Lao independence, but also to proclaim the unity of the Lao state. Only then were the provinces of southern Laos formally incorporated into the kingdom. Not since 1707 had the northern and southern *meuang* formed part of a unitary state. Phetsarat's proclamation of 15 September 1945, not the cobbling together of Lao territories as part of Indochina in 1893, marks the constitution of the modern Lao state. (1996: 35)

The fallout from this unilateral declaration of independence in September 1945 created confusion in the Lao political world between the king and crown prince in Luang Phrabang on the one hand and Prince Phetsarat in Vientiane on the other. Phetsarath had assumed the position of prime minister in the new government of independence, while the king of Luang Phrabang continued to favor the return of the French. Within a month of Phetsarath's declaration, the king had asked for Phetsarath's resignation (Lockhart 2003: 133). In response the new government's provisional assembly asked for the king to step aside and to await its decision on the fate of the Luang Phrabang monarchy.

Rivalry between branches of the royal family, seemingly a historical trademark of the Lao monarchy, continued to mark the national Lao political experience for the next thirty years. Within a matter of five months the fiscally impoverished and undermanned Lao Issara government, unable to resist French military forces that were moving up the Mekong in the spring of 1946, asked King Sisavangvong of Luang Phrabang to assume the throne as the country's constitutional monarch, reminiscent of the status given to the Bangkok Thai monarchy in the 1930s. By August an agreement was reached regarding a constitutional monarchy, but it was not an agreement forged between the Lao Issara government and the Luang Phrabang monarchy. Rather, it was forged between the Luang Phrabang king with the returning colonial French, who by this time had seized complete control of the towns along the Mekong, including Vientiane. In the meantime the Lao Issara government disintegrated, unable to find the means to defend itself militarily against the French and left to its fate by Luang Phrabang's royalty. Following Phetsarath's exile to Thailand which followed immediately upon the return of the French (Phetsarath did not return until 1957), his younger royal brothers, Souvanna Phouma and Souphanouvong, emerged as leaders respectively of those elite who either supported a neutralist political course in alliance with the Luang Phrabhang monarchy or those who "eventually allied with the traditional dissidents of the upland tribes to create a strong national revolutionary movement—the Pathet Lao" (McCoy 1970: 98).

Prince Souvanna Phouma, the often-beleaguered prime minister of successive Royal Lao governments, was ostensibly pro-Western in appealing for support to sustain Laos's neutrality within the context of an increasingly volatile Southeast Asian world. In the ensuing years he struggled to cobble together a succession of coalition governments. To his left, Prince Souphanouvong, who had fought on the side of the Lao Issara against the returning French, had already by the time the French returned met in Hanoi and consulted with a new political mentor, Ho Chi Minh. With the collapse of the Lao Issara, Souphanouvong's association with the Viet Minh deepened as he simultaneously sought to forge ties with disaffected tribal highlanders. He would eventually lead the "Issara faction" of the emergent Pathet Lao, though the real power of that movement would actually be vested in others working behind the scenes.[47] I shall briefly follow the course of both of these movements, the nationalist cause of the Royal Lao Government following the French departure in 1953 and the Pathet Lao revolutionary movement, but only for the purpose of ascertaining the manner in which Lao Buddhism fit into the ideological agendas of each. For after World War II "Buddhist monks were increasingly drawn into the ideological conflict that pitted generally conservative governments in Viang Chang against the revolutionary movement of the Pathet Lao. The Sangha became a target for political manipulation by both sides" (Stuart-Fox 1996: 87).

Buddhism to the Right and Center

The return of the French did not mean a return to the colonial days of old. Indeed, they never regained control over the highland regions of Laos. While the king of Luang Phrabang's cooperation with the French raised his profile among the "ethnic Lao" Mekong River basin communities and seemed to indicate a greater measure of Lao participation in national governance, the entire French colonial program in Southeast Asia was being called into question at this time not only from political movements within post–World War II France itself, but from the United States as well.[48] Meanwhile, remnants of the Lao Issara continued to mount propaganda pressures externally from Thailand and Vietnam, a harbinger of the future division of the group into two factions: a Thai-based one that accepted an amnesty in 1949 and returned to contest elections for the Royal Lao Government and a Vietnamese-based one that consolidated its influence in the highlands and formed the basis of the emergent Pathet Lao.

Elections for a Constituent Assembly were held in late 1946, and by 1949 the Royal Lao Government was delegated responsibility for the internal governance of the country under a new constitution. Only matters of foreign policy and security were left in the hands of the French. In 1953 the French granted full sovereignty to the Royal Lao Government. The French defeat by the Viet Minh at Dien Bien Phu in 1954 marked the final desultory end to French Indochina.

During the period between the French return and their final departure, some members of the Buddhist *sangha*, such as Mahaphan Anando, took up the public mantle as preservers and defenders of Lao culture and advocated political independence.[49] The *sangha*'s activism, especially in Vientiane, was viewed closely by every political faction in the country. The agitations led by the *sangha* for political independence signaled a Buddhist re-entry into the public political culture of the country, a re-entry that would be thoroughly justified in the eyes of nationalist-minded historians whose works sought to provide a linear historical foundation for the newly independent country. The political utility of the *sangha*, given its re-acquired supralocal significance, was also well understood by the fledgling Pathet Lao, perhaps even better than by the nationalist-dominated Royal Lao Governments. The *sangha* was not just a symbolic *bhumi putra*, but for the Pathet Lao one of the most promising means through which its political aspirations could be disseminated.

The general pattern of Buddhist public political activism was widespread throughout the Theravada world of the 1950s. Indeed, one could even argue that it was somewhat muted in Laos when compared with the dramatic political turn of events unfolding simultaneously in Sri Lanka and Burma. In Sri Lanka, politics entered a watershed, which the country has still not recovered from, in the national election of 1956 when the Oxford-educated and formerly Anglican S.W.R.D. Bandaranaike led his newly formed Sri Lanka Freedom Party to a resounding victory over the United National Party on a platform of "Sinhala only" as the national language and Buddhism as the state religion. In Burma, Prime Minister U Nu won election in which he gained broad grassroots support by using folk Buddhist idioms, including the concept of *loka nibbana* ("nirvana in this world") to articulate his roughly socialist vision for the Burmese. Historically, it does not seem out of place for the politicians and electorates of newly independent democratic countries to rekindle memories of an idealized political past and to emphasize language and religion as the definitive aspects of their cultures to reassert noncolonial identities and priorities. Indeed, the same forces were at work in the writings of Lao historians of the 1950s. Unfortunately, in all three of these national "renaissance" instances within the Theravada world, the ideological foundations of these post-independent political nationalisms (with their emphases on language and religion), while successful in appealing to an ethnically and demographically dominant group of the populace capable of swinging elections, have proven to be far too narrow in scope to hold together the disparate populations of the respective countries. Moreover, the passionate promulgation of narrowly based and ethnically driven ideologies has led to the exclusion, alienation, subordination, and disenfranchisement of minority populations. The minorities have, in turn, been driven into disillusionment that has fostered motivations for separatist or civil wars.

How was Buddhism situated within the constructed identities of Lao nationalism leading up to and following political independence from France? One way of answering this question is to consider the writings of Maha Sila Viravong, regarded by many as embodying the essence of modern Lao cultural identity[50] despite the fact that Maha Sila Viravong was deeply influenced by Thai nationalist scholars.[51] Highly educated as a young monk, having been mentored as well by Prince Phetsarath, he published the first grammar of the Lao language, which he modeled on Thai grammars, in 1935.[52] His very influential historical work, *Phongsawadan Lao*, reflects the definitive importance of Buddhism in the ideology of Lao nationalism. While it is no doubt similar in conception to Pali *vamsa* literature,[53] Keyes situates Sila's *Phongswadan Lao* in relation to the work of the earlier French historian Paul Le Boulanger.

Le Boulanger's work [*L'Histoire du Laos Francaise*] is the first to subsume the histories of Vientiane, Luang Prabang and Champasak as part of the national heritage of Laos. Although Le Boulanger's history was that of a French colony rather than a nation, it laid down the foundations for what would become the dominant narrative of a Lao nation. In the 1930s, this history was represented in the first Lao language textbooks. . . . [I]n the 1940s, Maha Sila Viravong, a learned ex-monk and active proponent of Lao nationalism, wrote a history that would become the most widely known history of Laos until the communist-led revolution of 1975. It remains to this day the basis for all national histories of Laos. (2002: 122)[54]

Like Le Boulanger's narrative, Maha Sila Viravong assumes a coherent linearity to Lao history, which he projects back through the fragmented *muang*s of Luang Phrabang, Vientiane, and Champasak to the Lan Xang mandala, but instead of specifying the basis of this unity in terms of geographical space (Le Boulanger mentions neither mandala or *muang*), Maha Sila Viravong bases his account on ethnicity, especially its constituent elements, namely, religion and language. The Lao language and Buddhist religion characterized the people of common ancestral descent within the political region formerly circumscribed by the old Lan Xang kingdom. In this regard Chalong Soontravanich provides an insightful elaboration:

It is quite clear that in his discussion of Lao history, Sila Viravong makes an attempt to define Laos as a nation, rightly or wrongly, in terms of people, that is all those who call themselves Lao and are descended from common ancestors, and in terms of territory, that is all the land under the rule of the Lan Xang Kingdom and its successors. *Phongsawadan Lao* is therefore the history of the Lao nation and not simply the royal chronicle of the old kingdom of Lan Xang. Laos is a nation with a common identity formed basically by a people of common stock who have settled on this land. . . . The Lan Xang Kingdom was also Laos' golden age in the sense that most of its kings were "ideal" Buddhist kings. Unlike most Lao kings after the kingdom disintegrated into the three principalities of Vientiane, Luang Phrabang and Champasak, the religious activities of Lan Xang kings in support of Buddhism and the sangha are well documented in the *Phongsawadan Lao*. This was a unified Laos and obviously a source of national pride. In addition, in Buddhist cultural terms, the disintegration of Laos after the reign of Souligna Vongsa was brought about by the mistreatment effected upon Phra Khru Yodkeo, one of the most respected senior monks of Vientiane, by Phya Chan the usurper, which caused mass emigration of Phra Khru's Yodkeo followers and eventually led to the founding of the principality of Champasak to the south. (2003: 115–116)

Chalong's commentary is quite revealing. First, Maha Sila Viravong has woven together deep-seated principles of Lao identity rooted in the indigenous religious substratum and skillfully combined them with a definitive role for Buddhism in Lao history. "Laos is a nation with a common identity formed basically by a people of common stock who have settled on this land" is a succinct attribution, pregnant with bedrock sociocultural and religious associations of ancestor veneration on the one hand, and the cultic celebration of the land, place, or soil experienced by a common community of descendants on the other. This is no doubt the reason why Sila Viravong found it necessary to historicize Lao mythic traditions of the founding of Luang Phrabang and then idealize the halcyon days of Lan Xang. Thus he defines Lao time (originating from the experience of the ancient ancestors) and Lao space (the geographical fruition of Lan Xang). For Maha Sila Viravong, Laos owes its primordial origins to how the land was experienced through paradigmatic *events* that engaged common ancestors. Moreover, he identifies the morality of this landed nation in terms of how Buddhist kings upheld the well-being of the *sangha* through their unstinting support, which he demonstrates by praising the building projects of Vixun, Phothisarat, and Xetthathirat in the sixteenth century and lavishly lauding the era of Pax Lao during Surinyavongsa's long seventeenth-century reign. In doing this, the very raison d'etre of the Lao nation is identified: it is the promotion of the Buddhasasana. The Lao nation is framed within the wider dispensation of Buddhism and derives its legitimacy in accordance with the degree to which it has contributed to Buddhism's sustenance. In Maha Sila Viravong's view, the cause of Buddhism remains the higher calling of the Lao. Indeed, the nation's disintegration is understood as having been brought about because of disrespect for the *sangha*, behavior that in turn makes subsequent claims to political rule by the abuser illegitimate.

Stuart-Fox has recently given an appraisal of *Phongsawadan Lao* in which he criticizes Maha Sila Viravong's work on historiographical grounds, but he also cites its crucial importance in providing an understanding of Lao history that had resisted earlier French interpretations.

> From this work, two broad categories are evident: to resuscitate the glories of earlier Lao mandala and to demonstrate the continuity of Lao history. Sila pushes the origins of the Lao people back more than 2,500 years to central China, and erroneously credits them with founding the kingdom of Nan Zhao. Moreover, he dates the arrival of Khun Lo, whom he accepts as an historical personage, in Mueang Sua precisely to the mid-eighth century. Twenty-two kings are said to have reigned from then until the advent of Fa Ngum, after which Sila is on firmer historical ground. But if the *Phongsawadan* is uncritical and methodologically unsatisfactory from a Western historiographical point

of view . . . , it provided for Lao readers a proud account of Lao history which
established Lan Xang as a powerful kingdom, able to hold its own against neighboring states. There was no suggestion here of national exhaustion, or any need
for France to "save" the Lao from racial extinction. (2003: 83)

In *Phongsawadan Lao* there is not only an attempt to define the history of the
Lao political and cultural experience in terms of common ancestral descent and
fidelity to Buddhism, but also an implicit program projected for the nation's continuing healthy existence.

This paradigm for the future of the Lao nation is substantively similar to the
kinds of nationalist histories inspired in Sri Lanka by the monastic chronicles,
the *Mahavamsa* and *Culavamsa* respectively, and the *Jinakalamalipakaranam*,
which functions analogously for Lan Na. In those venerable texts the relative value
assigned to kings of the past is measured in relation to what they have done to
promote the Buddhasasana. Conversely, their failures to do so are judged as the
moral liabilities that lead to their country's misfortunes. Historical studies abetting the rise of Sinhala nationalism in the 1950s stressed the current need of the
new nation-state to rehabilitate and to sustain Buddhism. *Phongsawadan Lao*, in
that same way, participates in the ethic of Buddhist *vamsa* literature, but also has
pretensions to be a work of modern historiography as well. In either case it is
clearly a history written with a nationalist motive, one that identifies Buddhism
with the moral quality of the state, and the sine qua non of Lao ethnic and cultural
sensibilities.

While certainly not as enduring or as influential as the work of Maha Sila Viravong, the writings of Katay Don Sasorith (who held the position of prime minister
of Laos briefly in 1953–1954), especially those contributions that he made to Rene
de Berval's well-known anthology of essays, *Le Royaume du Laos*,[55] are also indicative of the kinds of nationalist sentiments associated with Buddhism in the 1950s.
In Katay's perspective, Buddhism is the ideological substance holding together the
Lao mandala from the level of *ban* (village) to the royal center. Like Maha Sila
Viravong, his work is completely Lao-centered and ignores the historical experiences of other ethnic communities. Commenting on Katay's historiography,
Stuart-Fox (2003: 83) writes that his work illustrates very clearly "the Lao proclivity to slide easily from recounting early myth and legend to accepting their histo-
ricity."[56] More importantly, however, is the fact that Katay emphasized the enduring persistence of the *muang* as the essential feature of Lao culture and polity. For
Katay, without Buddhism and Lao kingship, the *muang* structure had unraveled
under French colonialism.[57]

Like the ethnic-based political ideologies that enjoyed electoral success because of their widespread popular appeal in Theravada-dominated Sri Lanka

and Burma in the 1950s, the nationalist histories written in Laos were effective in facilitating an elite articulation of the nation that empowered the leadership of the dominant ethnic group to grasp ownership of the country. But equating Lao ethnicity to a particular religion and language produced an exclusive concept of nationhood.

> What Katay's historiography did, therefore, was to justify a social and political order that reinforced elite domination and did nothing to bridge an ethnic divide that, in a state where ethnic minorities constituted almost half the population, had already taken on vital political dimensions. But leave them out was exactly what the French-educated aristocratic Lao political elite that inherited power in 1953 proceeded to do—with disastrous results, for it permitted the Pathet Lao to gain power through the loyalty of just those excluded groups by making room for them in a radically different political order legitimated by a radically different historiography (Stuart-Fox 2003: 84–85).

Pholsena has argued that emphasis placed on this conception of the "nation" was actually the "logic of race" inherited by the Lao elite from the French. That is, the structure of this nationalism was French, while its substance was Lao Buddhist. By comparison, earlier ideologies of Theravada Buddhist kingship in Sri Lanka, if not in Lan Xang itself, reflect a much more elastic conception of the state as responsible to a variegated population.[58] Modern democratic renditions of Buddhist-associated nationalisms seem less pluralistic in ethos. The prevailing ideology of Lan Xang as articulated mythically also seems more pragmatic insofar as space is recognized, albeit subordinated, for a reciprocating "other." Lockhart has commented on the ideological exclusivity of the early Royal Lao Government's national perspective: "It can be argued that education under the RLG never succeeded in broadening its vision to build a Lao nation because it failed to incorporate the various ethnic groups whose position—though strategically important— was psychologically and culturally peripheral from the perspective of the ruling elite in Vientiane and Luang Prabang" (cited in Pholsena 2006: 88). Pholsena then adds this: "It is reasonable to presume that the majority of the lowland Lao leaders in the mid-twentieth century were still guided by the traditional Buddhist concept and taxonomy that defined the relationships between rulers and ruled in terms of centre and periphery, on the one hand, and class and status (as well as race), at least as far as the ethnic groups encompassed under the 'Kha' category were concerned, on the other" (2006: 89).

Yet the difference between the "traditional Buddhist concept and taxonomy" and the one deployed by the Lao nationalists of the 1950s, at least as reflected in the writings of Maha Sila Viravong and Katay Don Sasorith, is that the old Buddhist taxonomy, which has a modicum of inclusivity, a sense of place provided for the subordinated "other," had been inserted into a French reading of what constitutes the nation-state, an ideology which by its very definition tends to be exclusive. That is, there is no sense of place or psychological space provided for the "other" (those who do not speak Lao and those who do not practice Buddhism) in the newly French-influenced Lao nationalist agenda. Rather, it is a hegemonic ideology without any dynamic of reciprocity, including precisely the type of manipulation of religion that is quite vulnerable to a Marxist critique. The new Buddhist-associated nationalism therefore recapitulated the nonreciprocal character of earlier French relations with many of the rural highlanders.

Elements of the Royal Lao Government in the 1950s must have recognized the possible implications of this Lao nationalist ideology. Indeed, the RLG formulated a new demographic taxonomy that would prove pragmatically more inclusive and enduring.

> In the 1950s, the use of the seminal terms "Lao Lum" or valley Lao, "Lao Theung" or Lao of the mountain slopes and "Lao Sung" or Lao of mountaintops, was initiated under the RLG. It was a stroke of genius. That classification is still being used in present-day Laos and is widely applied, even among academic works and in spite of the authorities officially forbidding its use. (Pholsena 2006: 134)

An inclusive taxonomy aimed at abetting an agenda of assimilation, this encompassing schematization has the effect of erasing some ethnic and cultural differences, in a way similar to how the identities of highland peoples who rebelled against the French were folded into nationalist or Marxist readings of recent history as "patriots" or "revolutionaries." Here the assumption in this taxonomy is that all disparate peoples within the nation are at least hybrid.[59]

While nationalist historians fronted Buddhism as a key ingredient constituting the new nation's identity, and while it was true that Buddhism was identified as an "official religion" in the first constitution, successive Royal Lao Governments from the mid-1950s until 1975 were commanded by French-educated Lao elite who had been secularized.[60] They were certainly not populists. In relation to Buddhism, however, they wanted to have it both ways: while they continued to believe that Buddhism was certainly a key ingredient in Lao national identity, they also believed that the *sangha* should remain apolitical.[61] Consequently the *sangha* was not only kept at a distance from the decision-making processes of the state, but also placed under direct government administrative control, where it was overseen by a succession of ministries. The ramifications were significant. "One important result of this exclusion of the Sangha from all political influence in Laos was that the higher clergy tended to withdraw into lives of seclusion, some even refusing to preach publicly at all . . . thereby leaving the way open for young, more radical monks to exercise undue influence over the lay population, an influence that could easily be directed, for example, towards the need for social reform or more democratic government" (Stuart-Fox 1996: 90–91).

By distancing themselves from the *sangha* in the world of realpolitik, these governments unwittingly contributed to the perception that they were increasingly removed from the common social and cultural pulses of the rest of the country. The consequence of American interventions in Laos beginning shortly after independence in 1954 would also widen spectacularly the gap between the French-educated elite in control of the government on the one hand and the highlanders and rural non-elite Buddhist Lao on the other. What would increasingly separate the rural agricultural populations of the country from the urban-based government was a dramatic infusion of foreign-derived material wealth into Vientiane. The *sangha* would respond critically to this development. This is hardly surprising owing to the fact recruits to the *sangha* were (and continue to be today), overwhelmingly from the countryside.

American Largesse

After sixty-three years of French colonialism, Laos remained, indeed, a supremely "low tech" environment.[62] Political independence by no means changed the basic conditions of a country dominated by subsistence agriculture. Despite its "backwater" condition, it was almost immediately thrust into the forefront of American foreign policy concerns following independence.

At the international Geneva conference convened in 1954 to settle French affairs in Indochina, Laos was declared a neutral country. The proximity of Laos to China, which had become communist under Mao in 1949, and to North Vietnam, which had just become communist in 1954 under the leadership of Ho Chi Minh, made Laos as well as Cambodia and South Vietnam the next "dominos" that could not be allowed to fall to the encroaching "Red Tide" so fearfully perceived by the West during the post–World War II era of the Cold War. From the American geopolitical perspective, Laos needed copious amounts of external assistance to defend itself from becoming the next domino. At the 1954 Geneva conference and afterward,

broadly stated, American foreign policy . . . was to see that Laos was "not allowed to go behind the Iron Curtain," in the words penned by Secretary of State John Foster Dulles during the Geneva Conference. . . . [But] first and most costly in its consequences, the American disregard for China as a major actor in Indochina was a mistake. Chou En-lai had approached Foreign Secretary Anthony Eden of Britain at Geneva to tell him, in terms that strongly suggested China was prepared to act as a guarantor of the settlement, that China would recognize the kingdoms of Laos and Cambodia so long as they did not allow military bases on their soil. (Dommen 1964: 245)

Agreeing in 1954 to Chou's overture might have changed the course of political history for Southeast Asia. For

eventually, the American purpose of securing the survival of an independent non-communist Laos failed. With the admitted benefit of hindsight, it seems clear that the reasons have much to do with ideology and mistaken analogies with European situations. American policy became ensnared in a web of contradictions. Instead of taking a forthright stand in support of Lao nationalism, the United States succeeded only in weakening the very leaders in Vientiane who offered what was perhaps the most feasible course, politically, militarily, for eliminating the threat posed by the PL-North Vietnamese alliance. (Dommen 1964: 246)

The eventual failure of American foreign policy took two decades to play out and, though that history is rich in detail and irony, I shall only briefly outline its course in order to determine its impact on Lao religious culture, especially the Buddhist *sangha*.[63]

Between 1955 and 1975 the key political figure in Laos attempting to steer the course of geopolitical neutrality internationally and a middle course between the forces of the right and left internally (in a manner often deemed too inclusive from the American perspective)[64] was Prince Souvanna Phouma, a suave cosmopolitan, French-educated and sophisticated, political master tactician who had outmaneuvered Katay to become the country's prime minister in 1954. For two reasons, the dire financial condition of Laos and the fact that the government was severely undermanned,[65] Souvanna Phouma continued Katay's earlier policy of wooing aid from the "free world." In the beginning, the United States agreed to pay the salaries of the national army (approximately 15,000 men), a force that the French had earlier assembled (Evans 2002b: 101). But soon American aid to Laos, in the hopes of stemming communist influence, mushroomed wildly. Not only did the Americans provide salaries for the military, but they tried to stimulate more broadly the Lao national economy as well.

The social, economic, and political consequences of this policy were prodigious. It produced dramatic distortions in the Lao political economy that became a catalyst for trenchant criticism of the government by the Buddhist *sangha* and the Pathet Lao. Roger Warner, emphasizing both the political and economic corruption that the policy invited, writes that by

> 1957 the U.S. had spent more on foreign aid to Laos per capita than it had on any other nation. That worked out to $150 per Laotian, twice the average person's annual income, though the average Laotian didn't get a penny of the aid. Some of the money went to support pro-American candidates in an election. They won by lopsided victories in balloting that was obviously, and embarrassingly, rigged. Other money went to a program to support the local currency, the kip. The Americans bought truckfuls of kip above the black-market rate, burned the banknotes, and gave the Laotian government dollars in exchange. Quickly realizing that bags of nearly worthless kip could be traded for dollars, Laotian [actually mostly Vientiane Chinese] merchants imported Mercedes and other luxury goods with their cheaply obtained American money, and then exported them to Thailand at a profit. The tiny class of rich elite got richer, and the poor were no better off than before.
>
> The Royal Lao Army's entire budget was paid by the U.S. government,[66] with much of the payroll going to nonexistent units. Graft was everywhere. (1996: 17)

In quite another vein Evans notes how the "irresponsible US aid" program inevitably led to internal political rifts among the Lao and considerable degrees of anti-American sentiment as well.

> In a few short years millions of dollars had rained down like manna from heaven on the cities of Laos, making some Lao wealthy, while many in political positions could at least afford a car or a new house. The bulk of the profits, however, melted into Chinese business networks. This fool's paradise came to an abrupt halt in 1958 when the Americans insisted on a devaluation of the kip against strong opposition from many of the Lao elite who had become intoxicated by this fabulous infusion of wealth. The corruption and wealth disparities created by the careless dispensation of American aid caused serious political rifts in Laos. What was for the USA a relatively small aid programme amounted to the difference between economic life or death for the RLG and its dependence on US aid created resentment towards the Americans. (2002b: 98–103)[67]

In his assessment on this same developing situation in the country, Geoffrey Gunn (2003: 264–265), whose observations complement Evans's, has pointed out how the American aid program aimed at creating a capitalist economy actually depressed the existing local Laotian economy, made the ruling elite entirely dependent on (or addicted to) foreign assistance, and spectacularly exacerbated the economic gap between the urban elite and the rural poor. Perhaps the most apt public commentary made by an important Lao politico on the effectiveness of the American aid program was offered by the Lao Issara leader, Prince Phetsarath, when he finally returned to Vientiane from exile in 1957 and had been appointed by King Sisavangvong of Luang Phrabang as his *ouparat* (viceroy): "Our greatest danger of Communist subversion arises from the bad use of foreign aid we receive. ... It enriches a minority outrageously while the mass of the population remains as poor as ever." (Evans 2002b: 109).

The Sangha as Protector of Traditional Culture

Created by American largesse, the party of conspicuous consumption being celebrated in Vientiane drew mounting criticism from elements of the *sangha*, especially in rural areas of the country, and from the emerging Pathet Lao as well. "The RLG elite ... found it increasingly difficult to even promote themselves as the protectors of the faith [Buddhism] and of 'Lao tradition,' given their dependence on U.S. support and adopted Western lifestyles. This was exploited by Pathet Lao propaganda" (Evans 1990: 186). Little, if any, of the foreign aid ever made its way beyond the vested interests of the urban elite and the immediate government circles in Vientiane (Dommen 1964: 259).

The Pathet Lao began in the early 1950s as a small force "estimated at only 5,000 men all concentrated in Sam Neua and Phongsaly" (Dommen 1964: 248)—the extreme northeast and north respectively on the borders abutting China and North Vietnam. But it increasingly won sympathy from Lao non-elites and highlanders throughout the rural regions of the country.[68] Pathet Lao rhetoric about "equality," combined with strident critiques focused on "the sharp decline of public morality" (Dommen 1964: 260–261), resonated with many who came to know about the bizarre situation unfolding in Vientiane. A common cause formed between elements of the *sangha* and the Pathet Lao, both critical of the bourgeois behavior seen in Vientiane and the government's increasing collusion with the American *falang* (foreigners). If the aim of the nationalist government had been to distance itself from the *sangha*, then it certainly did succeed in this instance, but not for the reasons it had avowed.

Prime Minister Souvanna Phouma often walked a political tightrope: his attempts aimed at forming national governments through coalitions that included Pathet Lao representation engendered strong American objections about the presence of possible communist subversives. Though Souvanna Phouma often argued that the best way to neutralize the threat of communism was to include its sympathizers within a larger representative whole, American ambassadors threatened to withdraw foreign aid between the late 1950s and the mid-1960s when coalition governments including Pathet Lao representation were formed. This happened initially in 1957, when Souvanna Phouma managed to bring the Pathet Lao into the government for the first time.[69]

In the new National Union coalition government, the Pathet Lao negotiated its interests so that Prince Souphanouvong was given the portfolio of the Ministry of Plan, Reconstruction and Urbanism, while his PL colleague, Phoumi Vongvichit, was appointed Minister of Cults and Fine Arts. In this new government, therefore, the Buddhist *sangha* was administered directly by an important political leader of the Pathet Lao. This might seem an odd or unlikely combination of bedfellows, especially in hindsight when it is now known fully that the Pathet Lao, even by this early time, was seriously committed to Marxist ideology.[70] But this negotiation to put the Buddhist *sangha* under Phoumi Vongvichit's administration was actually part of a carefully executed Pathet Lao plan to exploit the prestige and respect traditionally owed to the *sangha* in Lao society.[71] A year earlier, in 1956, the Lao Patriotic Front (LPF, the political front of the Pathet Lao) had organized its first association of Buddhist monks from northeastern Xam Neua province, where their armed cadres were already stationed following the 1954 Geneva Agreements when Xam Neua and Phongsaly had been turned over to the Pathet Lao. Subsequently, in other highland regions of the country brought progressively bring under their control, the Pathet Lao formed similar organizations until, in 1963, all these regional associations were amalgamated into the leftist-oriented National Association of Lao Buddhists.[72] Thus almost from the beginning of their organization, the Pathet Lao had a plan in mind for the *sangha*.

The *sangha* was probably the only social organization in the country with a supralocal presence at the time. Openly aligning Pathet Lao interests with the *sangha* in its traditional role of being the "protector of traditional culture" made shrewd political sense. Stuart-Fox has explained the Pathet Lao strategy in the following way:

> The incongruity of a communist minister Phumi Vongvichit, holding the religious affairs portfolio should not obscure the rationale behind the PL choice. The Ministry of Religious Affairs was responsible for supervision of the Sangha, a function it had inherited from the colonial administration. Instructions from the ministry could be passed down the Sangha hierarchy independently of civil administration. Control of this ministry thus provided the PL with a ready-made communication network from the administrative capital, Viang Chan, spreading out to the remotest villages. The ministry could also arrange, at government expense, discussion meetings for monks during which social criticism could be introduced. This technique was so effective that, even though the

Coalition government collapsed within months, Phumi Vongvichit reportedly succeeded in convincing a number of young bonzes of the justness of the communist cause. (1996: 88)

With knowledge of how the *sangha* was being manipulated by the Pathet Lao, a center-right non-coalition government (that excluded the Pathet Lao) under Prime Minister Phui Sananikone passed Royal Ordinance No. 160 in 1959,[73] a new law that gave the government authority to approve all senior appointments within the administrative hierarchy of the *sangha*. At the same time the government began to arrange for the arrival of elite Buddhist monks from the Thammayut Nikay in Thailand in a bid to re-emphasize the spiritual orientation of the *sangha* and in the process to stem the tide of the *sangha*'s politicization and its increasing sympathy for the Pathet Lao.[74] This move, in turn, spawned two opposition monastic organizations: the Movement of Young Monks against the Thai *dhammayut* and the Movement of Novices Claiming Their Rights. Each moved out of the government zones into Pathet Lao mountainous areas after the rightist takeover following the Kong Le neutralist coup in 1960 (Lafont 1982: 148). The government also attempted to enlist the *sangha* in economic development programs to capitalize on its traditional standing at the village level. Thus the government's posture towards the *sangha* was conflicted.

> During this period, the traditional world view was further weakened as a result of the ambivalent status of the Buddhist Sangha. Buddhism was left with no clear political or ideological role to play in the new Lao state. Crude attempts to involve the Sangha in the cause of anti-communism only further undermined its standing. Rather than strengthening Buddhism as an independent source of legitimation of government—its traditional role—government policy had the effect of compromising the independence of the Sangha. Reluctantly, the Buddhist hierarchy permitted monks to become involved in government-sponsored economic development programmes—a move which only led to intense debate within the Sangha, and a corresponding increase in divisive political activism on the part of young monks on both the political right and left. The authority and prestige of the Sangha suffered from this compromising descent from its traditional position of religious detachment. (Stuart-Fox 1996: 72)

Recognition of the *sangha*'s potential leadership in local economic development schemes is the theme argued in a report about *sangha*-based development programs launched in the 1960s, a scheme that operated into the early 1970s through an arrangement made between a United Nations advisor for community development and a Royal Lao Government commissioner for rural affairs. In a perspective reminiscent of the Pathet Lao's when Phoumi Vongvichit assumed governmental administrative control over the *sangha* in 1957, Boutsavath and Chapelier (1973: 2) premised the viability of their UN/RLG community development scheme in the following way: "As far as Lao society is concerned one of the main obstacles to Community Development activities is the relative absence of clans, age groups, work associations, village councils, or any structures which could permit the active expression of solidarity beyond the village limits. There is one exception, however: the Buddhist monastic body." The organizers of this development scheme not only recognized the potential of the *sangha* as a supralocal conduit for efforts aimed at improving the lives of rural villagers (which would therefore short-circuit potential appeals to Lao Buddhists by the rival Pathet Lao), but they were also buoyed by statistics from the government's Department of Religious Affairs that showed about a 10 percent increase in the number of ordained Buddhist monks from 1961–1968, at least in those areas still under the control of the Royal Lao Government of the time.[75] The Buddhist *sangha*, despite the great social and political turbulence of these years, remained the most robust social institution in the country. During these same years the *sangha* also became increasingly vocal in its criticism of the continuously widening gap between the urban and rural regions of the country socially, culturally, and economically.[76] In part it was recognition of this monastic criticism that led to the UN/RLG development effort in rural Lao villages, for the program challenged the monks to further develop their own village contexts in ways beneficial to traditional culture.

The rationale for cultivating *sangha* leadership in village-based development was predicated on a recognition of the this-worldly social orientations of village monks. Indeed, Boutsavath and Chapelier (1973: 19) recognized a possible theoretical objection in the beginning of their project, acknowledged it squarely in their report written for outside observers, and proceeded to explain quite clearly why their program for development was congruent with the social functions of Buddhist monasticism: "It must be noted that the ascetic ideal of the begging monk, living outside villages, is in contradiction with this image of the monk-advisor which gradually manifests itself to us. The monk is consulted by the villagers and, in return, his concerns may be extremely pragmatic, dictated by the care to assure, at one and the same time, a moral and secular leadership" (Boutsavath and Chapelier 1973: 3). In another section of their report, they construct in some detail a more accurate profile of the social significance and leadership qualities indicative of the monastic vocation in the typical Lao village context.

They [Theravada Buddhist monks] are invited to celebrate important events of family life such as the construction of a house, a birth, a death, the undertaking of a new activity or the celebration of a village festival. For example, for the *boun bangfai* (rocket festival), it is the monk who prepares the rocket and determines the explosive charge. And he is the one from whom the villagers seek advice, apply to for a horoscope, or simply visit for the pleasure of discussing something with an eminent and respected man. (1973: 11)

Boutsavath and Chapelier report that their program initially encountered skepticism from some villagers who regarded it as an American project with political implications, especially when it was known that the funding for the project came from the outside.

One of the major aims of the project was to encourage villagers to construct roads to facilitate the introduction of a local market economy. In the conclusion to their study Boutsavath and Chapelier point out how villagers finally were motivated to engage in the hard work of building roads, once they were convinced by Buddhist monks that their work would be regarded as a merit-making exercise: new roads would make it possible for more people to attend *bouns* (merit-making rites) at the *vats* of nearby villages. Once a Buddhist religious rationale (merit-making) was provided for the development project, villagers were willing to contribute the effort necessary to bring it to fruition.[77]

While the program reported upon by Boutsavath and Chapelier met with a modicum of success in some regions of Laos, the political and security situation of the country as a whole experienced repeated convulsions from the early 1960s until 1975. During this time as conditions deteriorated, and despite the fact that the *sangha* was still split politically between those sympathetic to the government and those who were opposed, it is clear that the Pathet Lao were gaining more and more support from many sections of the *sangha*, allied as they were in a deep criticism of a government that was seen to be in collusion with forces responsible for massive destruction and deteriorating conditions. But even before the war greatly intensified after 1964, the Pathet Lao had gained considerable sympathy.

A number of factors were important in this regard, not the least of which was the Sangha's "inverse class structure," in large part as a result of the two-tiered system of education that came into the existence under the French. While the children of the Lao elite attended secular schools established by the colonial authorities, children from the poorer sections of the population had to make do with the traditional education provided in the *vat* (Buddhist temple). Many boys from poor families joined the Sangha temporarily for this reason: by becoming novices they could obtain free board and lodging while pursuing their studies. The irrelevance of the largely religious education they received, however, meant that many youths were later disappointed when they went in search of employment: positions in government service went to the French-educated elite.... The PL were able to play on resentment within the Sangha against government recruitment policies to win over monks to their own cause. (Stuart-Fox 1996: 90)

What then occurred in Laos between 1964 and 1973, while the American CIA and military prosecuted a "secret war" against the Pathet Lao and the North Vietnamese without the knowledge of the American Congress, is one of the most tragic courses of events in twentieth-century history. Though catastrophic to Laos, even now the story is not well known abroad, especially in America.

The Impact of the American Military Campaign on the Buddhist Sangha

On the eve of his departure from office in 1961, President Dwight Eisenhower delivered his most memorable address when he warned the American public about the growing power of the nation's "military-industrial complex." At the same time, however, Eisenhower told President-elect John Kennedy, "If Laos is lost to the Free World, in the long run we will lose all of Southeast Asia" (Warner 1996: 35). The implication of these two statements, if Eisenhower was consistent, was that the United States should do whatever possible, short of a protracted war, to assure that Laos remained "free" or neutral.

In the fall of 1960, just before Kennedy assumed office, Vientiane suffered a series of political convulsions initiated by a neutralist military coup d'etat led by a morally indignant army captain, Kong Le, against the corrupt anti-communist rightist regime then fronted by Prime Minister Prince Somsanith and backed by the notorious military strongman Phoumi Nosovan. Gunn cites a Pathet Lao insider describing how this coup affected the *sangha*:

Monks ... were organized into clandestine movements in opposition to American involvement.... [B]efore the Kong Le *coup d'etat* in 1960, monks and novices were oppressed; however, the importance of the coup for the clergy was that it opened up the right of freedom of speech, which monks immediately took advantage of. Subsequently, some hundreds of monks rallied around the National League of Lao Buddhists, implying the active participation of the clergy in the political domain in a manner supportive of the "patriotic" [Pathet Lao] cause. (1982: 91)

Following the coup, Souvanna Phouma re-emerged briefly as prime minister only to find Phoumi Nosovan mounting a successful countercoup that sent Souvanna Phouma into exile and brought the rightist Champasak prince, Boun Oum, into power as Phoumi's new political front man. Kong Le's loyal army faction then joined forces with the Vietnamese-supported Pathet Lao cadres on the Plain of Jars in Xieng Khuang Province and mounted continuing pressure on Phoumi's troops. Now aware of how the actions of rightist governments in Laos since 1958 had only succeeded in stimulating greater communist influence throughout the country, "President Kennedy threw his weight behind a neutralized Laos, and U.S. support fell behind Souvanna Phouma."[78] This bold political move galvanized the Soviet Union and Britain, co-chairs of the 1954 Geneva conference on Laos, to summon a second Geneva conference in January 1962 (amidst continuing intense fighting). The second Geneva conference produced an agreement for a provisional coalition government composed of the three Lao political factions who were represented at the conference by the three political princes—the rightist Boun Oum, the neutralist Souvanna Phouma, and the leftist Souphanouvang. However, not before the United States withdrew all aid from Phoumi's government was the resolution for a coalition government realized. This resolution, however, only set the stage for the series of unfortunate events that led Laos into a spiral of chaos beyond its internal control.

Evans supplies a detailed description of the crucial events that plunged Laos into a full-scale war:

Many of the conditions from the original [1954] Geneva Conference were stipulated, including no foreign bases and a timetable for the withdrawal of foreign troops. The [provisional] government would exist only until a permanent government could be properly established through elections. The two sides would continue to administer their respective zones [see Map 2.1], although this meant, among other things, that the withdrawal of 10,000 Vietnamese troops from PL zones could never be verified. American and Thai military personnel left under international scrutiny, although the CIA continued to supply clandestine support to a burgeoning irregular army around the Plain of Jars, under the command of the Hmong, Colonel Vang Pao. While Souvanna Phouma hoped to build a strong centrist party, constructed partly out of defectors from the left and right, this plan foundered when his military power base, Kong Le's neutralist army, split over the acceptance of US military aid. The Soviet airlift to the Plain of Jars [in support of Kong Le] had ended, Kong Le's forces needed re-supplying, and Souvanna agreed to have Air America, a CIA-funded airline, ferry in US supplies. The Pathet Lao objected, and when in November a plane was shot down by a neutralist faction under Colonel Deuane Sunnarat, who had grown close to the PL, Kong Le's closest comrade Colonel Ketsana tried to arrest those responsible. He was prevented from doing so by the PL, and two months later was assassinated. In retaliation, the leftist-neutralist Minister

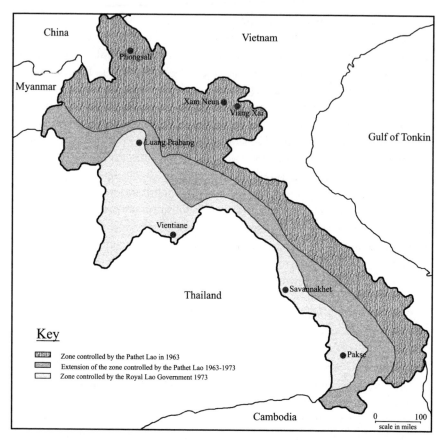

Map 2.1 Regions of Laos controlled by the Royal Lao Government and the Pathet Lao respectively

of Foreign Affairs, Quinim Pholsena, was assassinated in Vientiane. . . . Other scores were settled, and in fear of their lives, [Prince] Souphanouvong and Phoumi Vongvichit left the capital. On the Plain of Jars, the PL and Deuane's troops launched a major assault on Kong Le's soldiers who were driven to the western margin of the plain and to the margin of Lao politics. The neutralist armed forces role had effectively ended, and with it the prospects of a neutralist government as envisaged by Prince Souvanna Phouma. (2002b: 124–125)

In the years that followed, a weakened Royal Lao Government was unable to effectively coordinate its now increasingly decentralized and politicized military, and the United States, more worried about the course of events unfolding in neighboring Vietnam, began to take matters into its own hands, such that the American ambassador to Laos would be cynically referred to by some as "the second prime minister."

As the gravity of the situation in neighboring Vietnam worsened following the assassination of President Kennedy in November 1963:

> President [Lyndon] Johnson refused to believe that aid to the South Vietnamese regime caused as many problems as it solved. As far as he was concerned, he was trying to fix the mess he had inherited from his predecessor, John Kennedy, and from Eisenhower before that; and he didn't want to become known as the American president who had "lost" Vietnam. Few of the people advising him on Vietnam understood Asia in depth, and most of them favored further U.S. investment. Among them a feeling arose that South Vietnam was a test case of U.S. resolve against communist "wars of liberation" around the world. (Warner 1996: 130)

Thus on August 7, 1964, Democratic Party congressional supporters of the Johnson administration engineered the Gulf of Tonkin Resolution through the American Congress, a pretext based on "strategic lies" regarding alleged North Vietnamese attacks on the American Navy. The Gulf of Tonkin Resolution eventually became the U.S. government's "justification" for entering militarily into the Second Indochina War. What occurred militarily in neighboring Laos was then done in light of how it might contribute to the American war effort in Vietnam. Between 1964 and 1975, "more than US$500,000,000 flowed into the country" (Pholsena 2006: 17) and a relentless bombing campaign commenced. But just as the Americans saw Laos henceforth almost exclusively in relation to the intensifying conflict in Vietnam,[79] it was equally the case that "the DRV [Democratic Republic of Vietnam] would not allow Laos to separate its internal problems from the dynamics of the Vietnam War (Evans 2002b: 121). As the war intensified, both the Royal Lao Government and the Pathet Lao were increasingly marginalized in its prosecution as the U.S. military and the North Vietnamese executed their strategies independently. Thus the fate of Laos was not determined internally by Laotians.

After the collapse of the Lao coalition government in 1964, at least four "theaters of war" opened up in Laos. The first theater was the so-called Ho Chi Minh Trail, an arms supply route that began in North Vietnam and then snaked inside the eastern borders of Laos and Cambodia into South Vietnam where it finally reached Viet Minh cadres. Between 1964 and 1973 this route became the most heavily bombed region of Laos, receiving perhaps as much as 75 percent of all ordnances dropped from American war planes: "Interdiction of the Trail began in 1964, peaking with an average of 200 fighter-bomber sorties a day in mid-1967 to mid-1969. In calendar year 1971, the rate was 250 sorties per day all over Laos with

70–80 per cent directed against the Trail. In that year alone, 296,000 tons of bombs were dropped over the Trail, making it the most heavily bombed zone of the entire Indochina War theater" (Gunn 2003: 243).

The second theater focused mostly on the Plain of Jars in Xieng Khuang Province (see Map 2.2) in support of a "secret army" supplied by the CIA and directed by General Vang Pao of the Royal Lao Army, at least half of whose fighting force consisted of Hmong highlanders.[80] The deployment of this force was intended to either counter or bait the presence of three North Vietnamese army divisions, a tactic meant to divert pressure away from American forces fighting in South Vietnam.[81] Consequently during the years of battle between 1964 and 1975, "25% of Xieng Khuang Province was contaminated with bombs, including 85% of its villages destroyed" (see Photos 2.1 and 2.2).[82]

The third theater consisted of other regions of Laos unquestionably under Pathet Lao control, but especially Huaphan Province in the extreme northeast bordering North Vietnam, where the leadership of the Pathet Lao and many Pathet Lao cadres had retreated into caves in the vicinity of Vieng Xai. Roughly all of the populated mountainous regions of the country, holding a quarter to a third

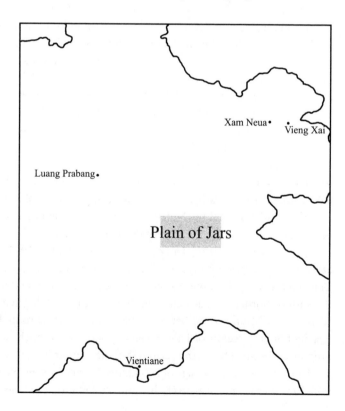

Map 2.2 Plain of Jars, Xieng Khuang Province

Photo 2.1 American bomb casings lining the entrance to the Luang Phrabang office of a German-funded program for finding and exploding unexploded ordnance in the Luang Phrabang region

Photo 2.2 Forty-year-old bomb crater in the Plain of Jars

of the entire population, also came under periodic bombardment. Hundreds of mountain villages were completely destroyed, and thousands of innocent people lost their lives or livelihoods.

The fourth theater was almost anywhere in the country. All but three provinces of Laos were bombed as a result of a U.S. military policy that required all bombers to return to aircraft carriers or airfields in Thailand with their ordnances discharged. If the weather over targets in Vietnam or the Ho Chi Minh Trail was inclement, or if American aircraft encountered severe antiaircraft artillery fire, the bombers were ordered to simply discharge their payloads over Laos. Thousands of bombs were randomly dropped on innocent people below.[83] In the end "Laos was subject to the heaviest bombing in the history of warfare" (Stuart-Fox 1996: 47). More precisely, it was "the most heavily bombed country on a per capita basis in history" (Pholsena 2006: 17), as "over two million tons of bombs were dropped . . . , more than on the operational fields of Europe during the Second World War" (Sisouphanthong and Taillard 2000: 59), "which worked out to two thirds of a ton for every man, woman, and child" (Warner 1996: 352).[84]

Not only was the American Congress duped into approving of the Gulf of Tonkin Resolution, but it was also not informed, and of course neither was the American public, about what the CIA, the U.S. Navy, and the U.S. Air Force did in Laos for the better part of a decade. To be sure, on the other side of the conflict, the North Vietnamese never publicly owned up to their machinations in Laos either.[85]

How, then, did the war and the internal political stalemates in Laos impact the Buddhist *sangha*? In short, it radicalized a significant segment of it. After the collapse of the second coalition government in 1964, Laos was effectively engaged in a civil war until 1974, when a third coalition was finally formed once the American bombing had halted. In the intervening decade the Pathet Lao had effectively controlled the mountainous areas of the country, while the Royal Lao Government controlled the lowland Mekong River basin and its tributaries (see Map 2.2). These regions roughly correspond to those dominated by the "ethnic minorities" on the one hand, and the "ethnic Lao" or Lao Loum on the other. Commenting upon this political and demographic bifurcation, Stuart-Fox has argued:

> The division of territory between the royal Lao government and the Pathet Lao had a double effect. For the royal Lao government it obviated the need to develop and carry through "ethnic policy", since in areas under government control Lao Theung constituted a negligible minority. As for the Lao Sung, they gained their own de facto autonomy. Thus for the royal Lao government the modern kingdom could be conceived as the traditional *mandala* reborn: politics in Laos could be equated with Lao political culture, and little needed changing. For

the Pathet Lao, by contrast, their ethnic Lao supporters constituted a minority. New political structures were essential to incorporate the majority comprising Lao Theung and Lao Sung—not in the form of autonomous regions, but to enable minority participation in a national political culture. Pathet Lao commitment to this end during the "thirty year struggle" was as commendable as it was necessary—not only for the Pathet Lao movement and its victory, but in laying the foundation for a new pluri-ethnic nationalism. (2002: 13)

This description could be parsed in several ways to gain a deeper understanding of the dynamics of the situation then in play, but I will constrain the parameters of discussion to highlight its relevance for the Buddhist *sangha*.

I am not sure that characterizing the policies of the Royal Lao Government during these years as "the traditional *mandala* reborn" completely captures the dynamics then in play, for Souvanna Phouma and other leading Lao politicos were secular nationalists, having been schooled in French social and political thought. It may be possible to assert that the increasing decentralization of the Lao military during these years might be compared to a reassertion of the *phu nyai* (regional chief) pattern, but the old ontologies of indigenous and Buddhist origins were simply not in play during these years of instability. Buddhism was trumpeted by nationalist historians as a force intrinsic to Lao Loum identity, but the *sangha*, as noted earlier, was distanced from any political influence in the government. Yet Stuart-Fox's larger point, pertaining to the irrelevance of the highland "ethnic minorities" for the government, stands well. The Lao Theung were basically left out of the government's concerns, their loyalty essentially conceded to the Pathet Lao.

Meanwhile, there can be no doubt that during these years the Buddhist *sangha* was increasingly politicized and polarized (Stuart-Fox 1996: 93). Since the 1950s, with its increasing alienation from the nationalist political elite and the emergent Westernization of Vientiane's culture fostered by the largesse of the American foreign aid program, elements of the *sangha* and the Pathet Lao had formed a concerted alliance of critical dissent. Both postured as the defenders of tradition in juxtaposition to the economic and political developments then occurring in the capital. The Pathet Lao, of course, had, since 1957, been seeking to cultivate the *sangha* in its cause on higher moral grounds and had designed practical ways to benefit from its support. Thus

the PL call for social, economic and moral reform struck a responsive chord in many young monks. . . . Throughout the period from 1962 until the ceasefire of 1973, the PL continued to infiltrate the Sangha in government-controlled areas. The benefits to be derived from this policy were obvious. Since the village *vat* was the center of gossip, monks were ideally placed to gather information, ranging from assessments of the political mood of the people—how they viewed the government on the one hand and the Pathet Lao on the other—to intelligence on government troop movements and weaponry. The traditional high status of the Sangha in Lao society meant that anything monks said carried special weight, particularly in rural areas. This made the Sangha a potentially valuable tool in furthering the PL's immediate aim of getting its message to the people. . . . A captured PL document dated January 1968 illustrates the way in which the PL were using the Sangha in their zone. It mentions the dispatch of thirty-three monks to various districts "to preach revolutionary ethics . . . to protect Buddhism, to revive real morality, to explain the revolutionary tasks to the people and to resist the psychological warfare of the American imperialists and their reactionary lackeys. (Stuart-Fox 1996: 92–93)

The Pathet Lao were manipulating the *sangha,* yet a very significant number of monks, perhaps the majority (Lafont 1982: 151), supported the growing revolutionary movement. In October1968 the Lao Patriotic Front, the public political face of the Pathet Lao, held a congress and issued the following statement as the third point of its platform.

To respect and preserve the Buddhist religion and to unify the various religions in order to contribute to the unity of the whole people and to strengthen the national anti-American resistance movement for national salvation.

To oppose all destructive activities carried out by the American imperialists and their valets [lackeys] against the Buddhist religion, particularly their distortion of Buddhist principles; their control over monks who are obliged to serve their criminal activities; their profanation of pagodas by using them for spreading a depraving culture; and their dividing of different Buddhist sects. To oppose the activities of the American imperialists and their valets aimed at sowing discord between different religions.

To respect and preserve the Buddhist religion, the purity and freedom of public worship and preaching by monks, to maintain pagodas, to promote unity and mutual assistance between monks and lay followers of different Buddhist sects. To promote solidarity between the priests and followers of other religions. (cited in Lafont 1982: 149)[86]

While we can infer from this statement a congenial relation between a significant section of the *sangha* and the Pathet Lao, attempting to ascertain exactly what happened within the Buddhist *sangha* in Pathet Lao–controlled areas during the war is quite difficult. From what I have been able to determine in interviews with individuals who spent the war years in Pathet Lao areas, the Pathet Lao remained very pragmatic in its approach to Buddhism. On the one hand, as Stuart-Fox indicates above, there was in play a strategy to win the *sangha* over to its side whenever possible, but in the process transforming it for the purpose of legitimating the Pathet Lao cause. In the next chapter, I shall explore the vicissitudes of this effort. On the other hand, some traditional Buddhist practices, especially the holding of *boun*s, were discouraged. On the basis of what he has surmised about Pathet Lao strategy in village regions they controlled, Evans has written:

> The communists set up "mass" organizations in the villages of women and youth, and committees for seemingly everything.... Youth organizations were especially important, as young people were seen as seeds of the "new society"; many were sent to Vietnam for further education. The PL efforts at education were appreciated, as was the suppression of even petty corruption. As everything was subordinate to the "higher aims" of the struggle, however, any "surplus wealth" had to be redirected to supporting the PL army. Thus the PL frowned upon "wasteful" expenditures on such things as ritual and the support of the Buddhist monkhood.... In older PL areas individuals carried work result books in which were recorded taxes paid, voluntary contributions made, celebrations and rallies attended, labour contributed to the revolution—in short a catalogue of their assets as a PL citizen. (2002b: 130)

What Evans describes squares generally with the portrait of life under the Pathet Lao that I was able to elicit from those individuals whom I interviewed at length. I can add some comments to Evans's description.

First, between 1964 and 1975, reliable informants who lived in extreme northeast Laos told me that there was no Buddhist *vat* in Vieng Xai, the "capital" of the Pathet Lao. They also reported that while Pathet Lao Army personnel did not worship *phi* or support Buddhist monks with alms, villagers were usually left alone to carry on with their religious lives. Few Buddhist monks could be found in the remote Pathet Lao–controlled areas because most of these areas were dominated by the non-Buddhist Lao Theung and Lao Sung. But in remote Mekong tributary areas where the Lao Loum predominated, their *vat*s were left untouched by the Pathet Lao, and monks were allowed to go about their normal lives. However, in no instance could any of my informants remember villagers being encouraged to practice Buddhism either. Certainly no *vat*s were built at the behest of the Pathet Lao, and male youth were not encouraged to join the *sangha* either. The Pathet Lao regulars did not practice any form of religion that these informants would recognize. Thus from this information it would seem that the Pathet Lao sought to make use of the *sangha* in government-controlled areas but basically conducted a hands-off policy regarding the *sangha* in the Lao Loum areas that they controlled.

Some informants explained to me that in the early 1960s, local bureaucrats of the Royal Lao Government had attempted to paint the communist insurgents as demons, replete with fangs and red tongues. But when Pathet Lao army regulars came into their village areas after they had been severely bombed, in order to assist the people affected, they began to win more sympathizers and were welcomed for their commitment to the villagers' well-being. What was demonic, instead, according to them, had appeared overhead in the skies. Many of the Pathet Lao regulars were women, a fact that also left a deeply positive impression on villagers. Indeed, what the Pathet Lao was most successful in doing within their regions was seizing the moral high ground in the conflict. According to the same informants, during the 1960s, as the war began to intensify, most village people living near the Ho Chi Minh Trail in the eastern mountain highlands were completely unaware of why the Americans were bombing. Many were forced to dig shelters in the ground for protection, while many others sought refuge in caves where they lived for as long as seven years. As Hayashi pointed out earlier, this experience of struggling together for survival produced comradeship.

In retrospect, when the last coalition government was formed in 1974, after a cease-fire had been finally arranged, the Pathet Lao adopted the same strategy towards the new government that they had adopted in relation to the Buddhist *sangha* in government-controlled areas during the war years: to subvert the Royal Lao Government from within. Evans (2002b: 170) notes: "Most significantly, PL troops would move into Luang Phrabang and Vientiane to form a joint police force, but there was no reciprocal movement of RLA troops into the other side's territory." When the coalition was formed, Prince Souphanouvong had come to Vientiane from Vieng Xai in a triumphal return, and some Lao saw this as a reuniting of brothers Souphanouvong and Souvanna Phouma. But Souvanna Phouma was now seventy-two years old and had been physically weakened by twenty years of intense political and personal stress. He suffered a heart attack two months after the coalition was formed and was flown to France for treatment, leaving the Vientiane side of the coalition in a very weak leadership position. He was replaced by Sisouk Na Champasak, an archenemy of the Pathet Lao. In the next seven months, with the withdrawal of American air support and Thai mercenaries, plus the fact that the North Vietnamese had not left their positions but instead had pressed forward with supplies down the Ho Chi Minh Trail into South Vietnam, and with a new offensive launched against Vang Pao's troops, the return of a weakened Souvanna Phouma could not counter the reality that Prince Souphanouvong had emerged as the country's leader (Evans 2002b: 170–172). Vang Pao then lost a crucial battle at a strategic intersection just north of Vientiane that left the road wide open for Pathet Lao troops to march into the capital in April 1975, the same month that Saigon in Vietnam and Phnom Penh in Cambodia fell as well.

In May, demonstrations demanded the removal of rightist ministers, and Sisouk Na Champasak fled into exile, quickly followed by Vang Pao. The Pathet Lao general, Khamouan Boupha, quickly dismantled the Royal Lao Government armed forces, Pathet Lao forces entered Savannakhet, Pakse, and other major towns, and demonstrations against the remaining government "rightists" began in Vientiane (Evans 2002b: 173).

Stuart-Fox summarizes how these dramatic political developments were fielded positively and publicly by many monks of the Buddhist *sangha*:

During the twelve months from April 1974, when the third Coalition government at last took office, to the fall of Saigon in April 1975, many monks readily accepted the eighteen point political programme adopted by the National Political Consultative Council at PL urging. The fifth point contained the usual call "to respect Buddhism and other religions; preserve pagodas and temples and other historic sites; defend the right to worship of Buddhist priests and other religious believers." It was not these guarantees alone, but the liberal democratic tone of the entire document, that caught the imagination of so many Lao monks and appealed to all but the most committed anti-communists. Unity and equality of all Lao nationals of all ethnic groups, free elections, freedom of speech, assembly and residence, the right to free enterprise and property ownership, development of the country's natural resources, and improvement of education and health services—all these were goals to which no one could take exception.

Little wonder then, that the Sangha contributed enthusiastically to popularizing the eighteen points of the programme of the PL. The role monks played in generating support for the PL position contributed materially to the PL victory in Laos. At a time when the civil service remained predominantly under rightist control, PL use of the communication network provided by the Sangha was facilitated by the fact that the minister of religious affairs was a member of the PL—a former monk named Suvannamethi. The way was thus prepared for the popular acclaim that greeted the guerillas of the Lao People's Liberation Army when they entered former rightist-held areas during the take-over of power between May and August 1975. . . .

Monks took a conspicuous part in the mass celebrations of welcome organized to greet the victorious Liberation Army; and an edict from the *Sangharaja* called on all monks and novices to work together with the revolutionaries for the good of the nation. For their part, the PL made a point of visiting pagodas to explain their intentions and distributed a booklet entitled *Action Plan for the Lao Sangha.* (1996: 94–95)

Conclusion

While the colonial policies of the French had alienated a significant percentage of the rural highland peoples and had created a Lao elite alienated in turn from its traditional religious culture, three observations can be made regarding the impact of post-independent national politics and the war upon the Buddhist *sangha*. All three indicate the degree to which considerable elements of the *sangha* had been radicalized to support the cause of the Pathet Lao. First, while nationalist ideologies fronted Buddhism as an important ingredient of national identity (which had the concomitant effect of excluding ethnic minorities), governments in Vientiane, influenced by the principled separation of religion and the state introduced by the French, chose to keep the *sangha* at a distance with regard to policy formulation. This contributed to a sense of alienation in the *sangha*, given the historic role that Buddhism had played in Lao public political culture. Only in a belated effort did the government involve monks in community development projects, seeking to capitalize on the potential support that the *sangha* could offer. Second, intoxication with American-derived wealth and power among the French-educated elite who ran the government and the military, along with Vientiane's avaricious business community, fostered a marked degree of alienation from the rural segments of the country and a heavy dose of criticism from the *sangha*, whose constituency was overwhelmingly of rural and agricultural origins. This provided the Pathet Lao with an opening to claim the moral high ground in representing themselves, along with members of the *sangha*, as the true defenders of the traditional way of life. Third, the government's identification with the American intensification of the war that brought about unprecedented loss of life and property destruction made the Pathet Lao's seemingly humanitarian agenda appeal to a significantly radicalized segment of the *sangha*, particularly after the Pathet Lao had successfully infiltrated its ranks.

CHAPTER 3

Questions of Place

Religious Culture in a Post-revolutionary Space

I n this chapter I bring the narrative about how changes in the political order in
Laos have impacted religious culture to the threshold of the contemporary scene
by examining how the Buddhist *sangha* and the spirit cults were affected by and
adjusted to the establishment and policies of the Marxist revolutionary Lao Peoples Democratic Republic (Lao PDR). This sets the stage for Chapters 4 and 5,
which give a synchronic account of contemporary religion in Lao cultural areas.

Changing of the Political Guard

Unlike the sudden, dramatic changes of power that occurred in Vietnam and
Cambodia in April 1975, which were accomplished by conclusive military routs
of government forces, the transition orchestrated by the Pathet Lao in Vientiane
was gradual and very shrewdly calculated. Because the Pathet Lao agreed to the "18
point program" when it joined Prince Souvanna Phouma in forming the coalition
government in 1974, its public political posture, at least until the spring of 1975,
appeared moderate. A change in that posture, however, was evident from May onward, as vitriolic demonstrations demanding the departure of all Americans were
organized outside of the U.S. embassy in Vientiane. By June, the offices of the U.S.
Agency for International Development (AID), ostensibly the development arm of
American foreign diplomacy, but in this instance also the organization coordinating on-the-ground support for military assistance, were closed indefinitely.[1]

Before the Pathet Lao gained enough confidence to organize its series of mass
demonstrations, however, it chose to subvert the Royal Lao Government from
within and to avoid major military assaults on Vientiane or other government-
controlled towns. Evans explains why the Pathet Lao chose this strategy.

> This [a military assault] could only have been done with the help of Vietnamese
> troops, an option unacceptable as it could have provoked reaction by the Thais.

The slowness of the [government] takeover was also partly due to the fact that
the PL's support was weak among the two-thirds of the people living in the
RLG-controlled zone. To grab for power too early and abolish the monarchy
risked an anti-PL uprising. Thus, using the legitimacy of the coalition government and proclaiming their desire for reconciliation and their support of the
monarchy, they slowly whittled away the opposition's power base. [Prince]
Souphanouvong's role in this process was absolutely crucial—his support for
the monarchy convinced many doubters, especially in the army, that the PL
desired peace and reconciliation. Only this explains the meekness and willingness with which generals and hundreds of other army officers [and government
servants] went off to the interior for "re-education." (2002b: 174)[2]

In September an ominous announcement was made. A "people's court" found
that "rightist" government ministers who had just fled the country faced the death
penalty if they returned to Laos, while twenty-five other important government
officials were sentenced to twenty-five-year prison terms in absentia (Evans 2002b:
174). Day by day, numbers of government officials either fled the country or were
replaced and then sent off to "seminar." In all, the Pathet Lao "seminar" camps
of internment eventually held more than 30,000 Royal Lao Government workers, army personnel, and others deemed sympathetic to the neutralist or rightist
sides. These included many schoolteachers and provincial bureaucrats. From August through October 1975 the Pathet Lao methodically cleaned out the coalition
government. Some people spent only a year in "seminar," others up to seventeen,
and still others never returned.[3] Matters took a an even more decisive turn when

> in November, demonstrations in Vientiane demanded the ousting of the coali-
> tion government. Souvanna Phouma and Souphanouvong extracted a letter of
> abdication from the king and the establishment of the LPDR was gazetted with
> Souphanouvong as President and Kaysone Phomvihan as Prime Minister. All
> other members elected to the new government were members of the NLHX
> ["Lao Patriotic Front"—Pathet Lao]. The one party state had arrived in Laos.
> (Evans 2002b: 175)

But these changes were only harbingers of more far-reaching developments.
Indicative of the future, some Pathet Lao politicos, the more moderate members
of the so-called Issara faction of leadership, who had often served as the public
political face for the Pathet Lao in Vientiane, were also removed from their minis-
terial positions in the latter months of 1975, before the formation of the new Lao
PDR government was announced. These purges were indicative of a hard shift to
the left then occurring internally within the leadership of the Pathet Lao itself,

an indication that the "radical faction" of the movement, with its close ties to the Vietnamese, had gained overwhelming control. At its initial National Congress convened in December 1975,

> Suphanouvong was pushed upstairs into the larger ceremonial office of the president of the new republic. Phumi Vongvichit, senior PL representative minister in the coalition government, was demoted from deputy prime minister . . . to second vice-premier and minister for education, sport and religion. . . . Kaison Phomvihan, secretary-general of the LPRP, became prime minister, a concentration of power that made his word virtual law. His principal lieutenant, Nuhak Phumsavan became the first vice-premier and minister of finance. . . . [I]t was clear that any split in the supreme policy-making body guiding the Lao revolution would favor the radicals. (Stuart-Fox 1996: 60–61)

In his speech to the National Congress, Kaysone left no doubt about the future political architecture of Laos. It also reflected an insecurity that characterized his xenophobic and autocratic rule for the next seventeen years. He

> warned that vigilance against the machinations of the enemy had to be constant. The revolution had to "completely liquidate all remaining traces, consequences and power of the neo-colonialist system, [and to] destroy all new manoeuvres and tactics of the imperialist Americans and their lackeys." (Stuart-Fox 1996: 61)

This was not a veiled threat. Kaysone's first year in power proved especially traumatic for many: in addition to the thousands of people incarcerated in primitive conditions in the mountainous extremes of northern Laos, many others, including Buddhist monks sympathetic to the Pathet Lao, were harassed by zealous rank-and-file (often Lao Theung) followers of the communist party.[4] Moreover,

> instead of concentrating on immediate reforms in such fields as health, education and welfare, the LPRP cadres focused their attention on the personal lifestyle of villagers and townsfolk alike. Dress and hair styles, singing and dancing at religious festivals, even the food consumed at private celebrations, all attracted the unwanted censure of so-called "investigation cadres." (Stuart-Fox 1996: 62)

While some later argued that these early excesses, which aroused a negative, but muted, reaction among many Lao Loum, were the work of lower-level cadres and perpetrated without an explicit directive from the LPRP's politburo,[5] other developments revealed the harsh position that had been staked out at the highest levels of the new regime, which were in concert with the kinds of policies put into effect in Vietnam following the communist victory there, although they paled in comparison with the more draconian measures in neighboring Pol Pot's Kampuchea.

After the first several months of Pathet Lao power in 1976, Prince Souphanouvong's public appearances were minimized, but not before he had performed an extremely important legitimating function for Kaysone. Kaysone had warned about the need to destroy all vestiges of the earlier neocolonialist system. So Prince Souphanouvong cooperated in bringing about the abdication of the king and thus the end of the monarchy in Laos. Indeed, Souphanouvong's ceremonial presence in the new Pathet Lao government made the removal of royalty more palatable for the Lao Loum public, despite the fact that

> the abolition of the monarchy constituted the most radical break with former Lao traditional order. . . . As a prince of the royal clan, and a half-brother of the highly respected Souvanna Phouma . . . , Souphanouvong already enjoyed considerable prestige among the lowland Lao. Though not in direct line for the throne, Souphanouvong was credited with previous religious merit which gave him considerable standing within Lao Buddhist society. In addition, he could draw upon his charisma as nominal leader of the Lao revolution, selflessly dedicated to the cause of national independence. To reinforce Souphanouvong's position, former king Savang Vatthana was [initially] appointed supreme counsellor to the president. By abdicating to become chief adviser to the new head of state, the king in effect subordinated his office of kingship to that of the presidency, and transferred something of the remaining magico-religious legitimacy of his person to Souphanouvong, the nominal source of authority in the new regime. (Stuart-Fox 1983: 44)

The symbol of the old nation was now subordinated to the new.

The extent to which Prince Souphanouvong was complicit in what then happened to the king, his queen, and their son, the crown prince, is simply unknown. The Lao PDR never issued an official statement regarding the fate of the royal family.[6] It is likely that Souphanouvong knew, if he was not directly involved, about the decision to send the king and his immediate family to "seminar" in a remote compound near Vieng Xai, and that the Prince had made, himself, a decisive choice between his fidelity to family on the one hand and his fidelity to the party or state on the other. Many others were also asked to make this same type of decision (family vs. state), a decision that, as we shall see, deeply impacted familial land holdings and the concomitant worship of spirits.

Even before the royal family was sent to "seminar" in 1976, the LPRP unveiled a new national symbolic discourse to reflect its break with the past: a new flag (see Plate 4) replaced the old national flag with its three elephants and parasol, a symbolism that referred to the royal origins of the Lan Xang kingdom, and a new national anthem in which references to the Lao race and Buddhism were replaced by references to all ethnic groups. These changes in public symbolism were not cosmetic, but reflected a new ideology of the state that would be asserted doggedly in the years ahead, one that accounted for and affirmed the country's ethnic diversity. Pholsena describes the substance of this new ideology:

> The communists saw their ultimate objective, namely the creation of "socialist man" in a new society, as entailing the conquest of all the difficulties related to the issue of ethnicity that permeated Laos. Their nationalism, by emphasizing the necessity of including all the ethnic groups of Lao society with equal rights and opportunities, may therefore be defined as a polyethnic or supra-ethnic ideology which stresses civil rights rather than shared cultural roots . . . where no ethnic group tries to turn nation-building into an ethnic project on its own behalf. (2006: 4–5)

The old ideology of the state articulated by Lao nationalist intellectuals such as Maha Sila Viravong and Katay, rooted in Lao ethnicity and Buddhism,[7] was now transcended.

Of this new ideology Evans (1990: 7) has written that "the idea of the new socialist man is premised on the sociologically acceptable view that human beings change and adapt to new environments. Change conditions and you change the person." This philosophically instrumentalist approach, as opposed to a "sapiental" posture (in which change, transformation, or adaptation is effected or willed from within the individual),[8] was frequently articulated in the years that followed, especially when it applied to Buddhism. From the Pathet Lao's revisionist historical view, the *sasana* had accommodated itself to previous social, political, and economic conditions, so now it could also conform to the new "scientifically engineered" post-revolutionary socialist society to help achieve the country's new "higher aims."

In Sri Lanka there is a saying that still has currency today. Translated from the Sinhala, it means: "The country exists for the sake of the religion." Maha Sila Viravong's nationalism, which had become textbook reading in the public schools from the mid-1950s through 1975, was substantially no different from this Sinhala Buddhist axiom. This was inverted under the new Pathet Lao regime: the religion would be allowed to exist if it existed for the sake of the state. Pathet Lao propaganda consistently identified the "old society" with self-interest and corruption while championing "the new socialist man [who] replaces these values

with moral rectitude and selfless devotion to others and to socialist edification"
(Evans 1990: 2).

Yet insofar as Buddhist thought has always emphasized selflessness and moral
consciousness as intrinsic to the spiritual quest, these particular values remained
congenial to the new regime and were often cited in its attempts to advance its new
philosophical vision.[9] But the relation between Buddhism and the state, which
I shall address shortly, proved to be far more complex than simply identifying
traditional religious values of useful currency to the political agenda of the new
government.

Yet another, perhaps more accurate, way of indicating how the philosophy of
the new socialist man came to be implemented would be to say, as Evans did some
fifteen years after the revolution, that

> by projecting a sense of national purpose, the government … attempted to sup-
> plant impersonal aims for personal ones. The new system is ultimately policed
> by a political vanguard, the "incorruptible" communist party, in which adher-
> ence to party rules and policy is the key criterion for advancement, not patron-
> age in the traditional sense. (1990: 191)

In this context the Buddhist valorization of "selflessness" was deemed relevant
in explaining the replacement of personal ambition with the impersonal "higher
aims" of the new state power. The higher aims of the state, like Souphanouvong's
decision to forsake family, demanded the preclusion of self-interested or family-
interested priorities. The "incorruptible" communist party came to epitomize the
institutionalization of "moral consciousness." As we have seen, over the decades
of struggle against "the French and American imperialists and their lackeys," the
Pathet Lao had asserted its status of righteousness, its high moral ground in the
conflict with the urban, Westernized elite, by proclaiming its role as the true defenders of traditional cultural virtues. Thus the loyalty demanded from legitimated
authority that was traditionally expressed through the mechanism of tribute was
now transformed into fidelity to the dictates of the morally authorized communist
party, the institution that embodied the ideals of the new socialist man.

The practical aspirations of the new government's ambitions were almost un-
bridled in scope. Gunn summarizes the extraordinary breadth of early LPRP plans
for a new Laos:

> With liberation in 1975, the fundamental problem, aside from defending the
> gains of the revolution, was to usher in the transition to socialism. This was to
> take the form of bypassing capitalism. Following Vietnamese Marxist precepts
> and in line with the prevailing Soviet orthodoxy, the Lao sought to usher in a

triple revolution in the area of productive relations, science and ideology. The time-table for the transition was never made explicit but the pace for the first three or four years of the post-revolutionary period was fast, running into the resistance of those Lao peasants caught up in cooperativization and those minority peasants involved in sedentarization [they were being moved away from slash-and-burn agriculture] exercises. (2003: 271)

Grandiose ambitions led, inevitably, to frustrations and then to adjustments in policy.

During the first ten or twelve years after the revolution the Lao PDR government was assisted by no less than 4,000 advisors from the Soviet Union and other socialist bloc countries (especially Cuba) who worked as economic advisors, mechanics, engineers, teachers, fiscal specialists in centralized planning, medical practitioners, and so forth, in to order to implement various aspects of the grandly formulated plan and, more realistically, to keep a modicum of the country's infrastructure functioning. At the bureaucratic administrative levels Vietnamese filled most slots. The government was forced to import so many foreign specialists because following its political revolution about 12 percent of the population of Laos fled the country. These included not only the educated elite, but also many skilled laborers and technicians.

Due to a series of setbacks, some unpredictable, including adverse climate conditions, and others more predictable, such as resistance to the new agricultural cooperative scheme, economic progress throughout the country was severely slowed down. The retardation of the economy had been abetted, of course, by the absence of Western, especially American, foreign aid that had buttressed the economy for the two previous decades. Thus from 1976 until 1979 the economy of Laos entered a very serious retrenchment, in fact a severe depression. Conditions for everyone, in the city and the countryside, were austere.[10]

While it is clear that Lao Loum supporters of the former Royal Lao Government were the biggest losers in the aftermath of the Pathet Lao revolution, and it is perhaps among this group that resentment against the new government was most intensely harbored, many from the highlands, with the exception of most of the Hmong who had cast their lot with the Royal Lao Government and the CIA,[11] benefited quite positively from the change in regimes. Gunn (2003: 253) wrote that the Lao Theung "are undoubtedly the major beneficiaries of the Pathet Lao victory, especially in terms of military opportunities afforded by participants in the LPFA."[12]

Despite the massive problems that the new regime faced in relocating many of its people and in putting into place the bases for a new political economy, the Pathet Lao seizure of power was truly revolutionary in its immediate social consequences. For example, in 1976 many highland people who had functioned as administrators in the infrastructure of Huaphan Province, where the Pathet Lao operated during the war from its base in Vieng Xai, or had managed factories in the regional towns like Xam Neua, came to Vientiane to work for the new government and to manage its nationalized enterprises, just as many people in Vientiane who had occupied positions of authority were simultaneously sent for "seminar" in the internment camps of Huaphan. After the political events of 1975, a genuine inversion of former social hierarchies occurred as these populations literally crossed each others' paths towards their new destinations. Virtually all scholars who have written in depth about the immediate social consequences of the Pathet Lao revolution agree regarding its outcome. For example, Pholsena (2006: 7) writes: "The French and American-Vietnam Wars abruptly changed their [the ethnic minorities'] historical and social position: from the 'periphery' to the 'center,' from being the 'savage' (or the 'slave') to becoming a 'patriot.'" Stuart-Fox's comment corroborates this view and elaborates upon it by emphasizing how highlanders gained from newly available opportunities for upward social mobility, as they assumed new responsibilities in the fledgling Lao PDR government at many levels:

> The new regime could rightfully claim . . . to have gone further than any previous government in integrating the tribal minorities into the national community. Tribesman had been recruited into both the LPRP and the army in considerable numbers, and filled many positions in the bureaucracy, especially at the local level in tribal areas. Both the party and the army provided avenues of social mobility for the politically ambitious tribesmen such as never existed under the royal Lao government, and a number of minority representatives have risen to positions of authority in the new regime. (1983: 448–449)

Evans, however, depicts an emergent cynicism among the urban middle-class Lao Loum, who reacted to the social inversion that was then occurring in Vientiane:

> The composition of the cities changed as many upland Tai and various minorities came into town with the revolutionaries. In some respects, the countryside reclaimed the cities, and indeed city residents often referred to the PL as *khon pa*, "jungle men," with all the connotations of ignorant country hicks. (2002b: 177)

While the Marxist ideology of the new socialist man and its "polyethnic" ethos were aimed at providing a new supralocal basis for national identity through erasing social and ethnic markers inherited by a "feudal," "colonialist," and "neocolonialist" past, national consciousness was quite slow to emerge in post-revolution

Laos. Ironically, some of the policies and administrative strategies initially put into place by the Lao PDR to facilitate the transformation of the economy and society actually had the reverse affect of stifling the realization of a national identity. Basing his comments on what he observed during the 1980s, Evans says that

> local solidarity tends to prevail over outside allegiances. Despite the state's desire to sink administrative roots in the villages, many of its policies . . . actually militated against supralocal organization. Restrictions on the movement of people and goods forced people back into their local communities. (1990: 188)

Though the new Marxist regime assiduously articulated its new philosophy, and though, as we shall see, it sought to build bridges to a subordinated Buddhist conceptuality among the Lao Loum, by the 1990s Laos remained a Marxist country in rhetoric only. The philosophy of the new socialist man, in turn, especially following the death of Kaysone, was relegated to a historical curiosity.

With this general overview of the 1975 revolution and its immediate social and economic effects in mind, I will now examine the nature and extent of the revolution's impact on Buddhism in particular and on Lao religious culture in general.

State-Making, not Merit-Making

The establishment of the Lao PDR in 1975 marked a watershed for Lao Buddhism. No longer at the center of traditional mandala legitimation scenarios, no longer heralded as a definitive component of modern Lao post-independence nationalism, Buddhists were challenged to find a place for themselves in the post-revolution Lao political context. On its side, the new government of the Lao PDR faced a delicate challenge. While its ideology was avowedly Marxist-inspired, and its practical, material support came from orthodox Marxist Russians and Vietnamese who were anti-religious in disposition, the government remained wary of suppressing Buddhist practice because it might fatally alienate more than 60 percent of its population. Due perhaps to psychological insecurity about its grip on power, or to its realistically founded fears regarding continued armed resistance among the Hmong in the northern highlands, the Pathet Lao did not follow the Vietnamese example of seriously suppressing Buddhism.[13] Nor did it embrace the more radical solution followed by the Khmer Rouge in Cambodia, the total annihilation of religious people. Whatever the precise motivation of its leadership, the new government's approach to Buddhism was somewhat tempered, pragmatic, and bifocal. It could be argued that this approach may have been similar to the general strategy they deployed in relation to the coalition government that they had

toppled in late 1975: to whittle away gradually at the religion and attempt to subvert it from within for their own purposes. It may also have been the case that the
political leadership surrounding Kaysone Phomvihan believed that eventually, if
their policies were successful, Buddhism would eventually simply wither away. But
this is merely speculative.[14] In any case it is clear that the government attempted to
circumscribe Buddhism in the following ways: (1) by limiting or forbidding certain cultic practices that were deemed deleterious to the contemporary economic
interests of the state, (2) by openly criticizing Buddhist ideas that supported these
practices or fostered a nonprogressive economic ethos, (3) by arguing at the same
time that the fundamental goal of Buddhism to assuage the condition of suffering
(*dukkha*) is congruent with the ultimate goals of Marxist socialist ideology, and
(4) by attempting to reform Buddhist thought and practice so that it could more
effectively serve the purpose of realizing the "higher aims" of the state. But this is
not to argue in any way that the communist party sought to forge a kind of "Buddhist socialism" on which to build a new society. The government consistently
legitimated its position by appealing to an orthodox Marxist view of history and
made no attempts to appeal to Buddhist ontology. Rather, what I am suggesting
is that the LPRP attempted to bend Buddhism to the will of the new nation-state.
Rather than eliminate it, the government took the pragmatic position of trying to
use a "reformed Buddhism," now separated from its former task of legitimating
the old social order, for its own socialist higher aims that were embodied in the
vision of its new socialist man.

     In trying to understand Buddhism's place in the new Lao PDR following the
1975 revolution, scholars have not arrived at consensus. This lack of agreement,
I think, reflects the rather inconsistent or bifocal policy that the government put
into play during the early years, a policy that affected different individuals in different ways at different times. In turn, this may account for the quite disparate
statements regarding its status. Thus Pholsena (2006: 63) states that "for more
than fifteen years, the communist regime forbade external expressions of the
former reactionary culture—of which Buddhism and the monarchy were arguably the most potent symbols," and Lafont (1982: 152) reported that "as early
as the beginning of 1976 a number of attacks were mounted against Buddhism.
The teaching of religion and Buddhist morality was forbidden in primary schools.
Teaching in schools for party members emphasized that religion was the opiate of
the people." From these statements it might be imagined that any forms of public
Buddhist expression after 1975 were simply not tolerated in Laos. While it is no
doubt true that many party officials espoused the view that religion, in particular
Buddhism, was an "expression of the former reactionary culture," it is equally clear
that the party actually attempted to reform Buddhism to serve its own interests. So
these statements, at least insofar as they may be construed to imply that Buddhism

was absolutely forbidden a place in the public culture of the early Lao PDR, may be regarded as somewhat misleading.

On the other hand, and in support of Pholsena's statement, though a reformed Buddhism was given a place in the evolving public culture of the Lao PDR, that fact does not obviate the reality of the situation for many individual Buddhists, who felt that they could no longer carry on with their Buddhist-oriented lives under the subversive and sometimes overtly hostile tactics of the new regime. In exactly this vein, Lao refugee monks in Thailand painted a dismal picture of religious life in contemporary Laos. According to one prominent monk who published a booklet in Thailand upon his escape in 1977, "from the moment they attained power, the Lao revolutionaries tried to suppress all spiritual life in the pagodas, obliged monks to share their time between indoctrination and the propagation of communism and attempted to make away with Buddhism altogether" (cited in Lafont 1982: 158). Moreover, there were charges that the state appropriated all monastic assets, thus robbing the *sangha* of its material endowment. The government, in the days of its early xenophobia, had also issued a prohibition against the reading of any religious texts that had been printed in Thailand.[15] Furthermore, as Gunn (1982: 93) writes: "The defection in March 1979 of the former supreme patriarch [*sangharaja*] of the Buddhist clergy in Laos, Phra Dhammayano, would appear to be symptomatic of the enfeeblement of the institution and of dissent within the Buddhist hierarchy." In this connection, and rendering further support for Pholsena's statement, Stuart-Fox has described the Lao Buddhist *sangharaja*'s defection in some detail. It is a sobering portrait.

In March 1979, the Venerable Thammayano, the eighty-seven year old *Sangharaja* of Laos, fled the country by floating across the Mekong on a raft of inflated car tubes. His secretary, who engineered the escape, reported that in Luang Phrabang the *Sangharaja* had been confined to the monastery and had not been permitted to preach. He confirmed that youths were discouraged from joining the Sangha, and that monks taught only what the government [had] prescribed. One important result of the government policy was that, despite official claims to the contrary, there was a serious decrease in the number of monks in the Lao Sangha. The diminished privileges and comforts of the monkhood caused many monks to leave the Sangha; many more fled the country, a number dying in the attempt; others were reported to be in labor camps. . . . In early 1979, according to the secretary of the *Sangharaja*, there were only 1,700 monks in the country, down from 20,000 when the PL took power. Pagodas left with no monks were taken over as schools. Some were even reported to have been used on occasion as barracks and storage barns. Buddha images and other ritual objects from these monasteries were consigned to museums. (1996: 105)

Such portrayals seem to support fully the assertions made by Pholsena and Lafont.

But these portrayals are countered by the assertions of other observers. The Thai followers of the "modernistic" reformer Buddhadasa, for instance, "are of the opinion that since 1975, Lao Buddhism has freed itself of those false beliefs that encumbered the Buddhism of other Indochinese countries. As proof, they point to the prohibition of spirit cult (worship of *phi*). These monks believe that Lao Buddhism is reverting to the Buddha's original teaching" (Lafont 1982: 159).[16] Lafont (158), contradicting what the defecting *sangharaja*'s secretary reported regarding the number of monks in the Lao PDR in 1979, noted instead that in 1982 "the number of monks had remained at pre-1975 levels." He also said:

> It does not seem that the great majority of the *Sangha* believe that Buddhism can be fundamentally opposed to Marxism.
>
> . . . .
>
> Whatever criticism may be leveled against the LPDR, all impartial observers have unanimously reported that pagodas in Laos are used for worship, that they can be visited by the faithful without anxiety, that traditional Buddhist festivals are still celebrated and that anyone can don the yellow robe of a monk without undue difficulty. . . . It could be said that since Buddhism is so popular, it cannot be eliminated. So far, the authorities have preferred to compromise: to treat Buddhism with consideration, rather than to compete with it, especially as the outcome of such a struggle would not be certain. (1982: 155, 158)

On the basis of his visit to the Lao PDR and his interviews conducted with various government representatives, Gunn (1982: 92) agreed with Lafont's assessment: "Clearly the LPRP is attentive to upholding the form of Lao Buddhist ceremonial life: to do otherwise would confirm doubts as to the regime's patriotism and raise serious questions as to its legitimacy in the eyes of the *Sangha*."

So the picture is somewhat clouded, no doubt complicated by the fact that after the revolution some factions of the *sangha* remained committed to supporting the Pathet Lao as "patriotic monks," while others were being victimized by local and national Pathet Lao policies and tactics. It is likely that members of the communist party in Laos were not completely uniform in their disposition towards Buddhism, for the Lao Theung, unlike the Lao Loum, were not Buddhists in the first place. It is also very likely that government policies were not executed in exactly the same manner in every locale. Thus what may have transpired in some localities did not transpire, or were not allowed to transpire, in others. It is now known, for example, that the party leaders in control of the Luang Phrabang provincial government were mostly Lao Theung, and they took an especially harsh approach to Buddhism.

With this mixed picture in mind, I shall reconstruct some key moments and issues regarding Buddhism as they unfolded in the years immediately following the 1975 revolution. I will follow these reconstructions with a discussion about how the new government attempted to reform Buddhist thought and practice.

From the beginning it was clear that if Buddhism was to be allowed a place within the new Lao PDR, it would be at the pleasure of the state's pragmatic policies aimed at creating a new socialist society. That is, its raison d'etre, as far as the government was concerned, would be economic and political, and not religious. Moreover, though the new government would not endorse Buddhist religious practices officially, the *sangha*'s active participation in various government programs could be to the government's advantage, tantamount to the *sangha*'s endorsement of its policies, and such an endorsement could abet the government's aims. Nevertheless the relationship between the *sangha* and the state was hardly reciprocal in nature, unless total subordination can be seen as a fair price to pay for continued existence.

At the first official convening of Lao PDR government in late 1975, members of the *sangha* were conspicuous in their presence, symbolically endorsing the substance of Kaysone's proclamations of the new socialist society.

> Six monks sat in the National Congress of People's Representatives held near Vientiane on 1 and 2 December 1975, which abolished the monarchy and set up the Lao People's Democratic Republic.
>
> At the congress, Kaysone Phomvihane, in presenting his report setting out the tasks of each social group, made the following appeal: "To venerable monks, novices and other clergymen who should, in order to contribute actively to reviving the spirit of patriotic union, encourage the population to increase production and to economize, help in educating people so as to raise their cultural standard, contribute to persuading, educating and correcting those who do not live virtuously or misbehave, so that they become good citizens." (cited in Lafont 1982: 152)

What is interesting in Kaysone's initial statement regarding the role of the *sangha* is that, in addition to a social and economic rationale, he affirmed the moral contribution he expected from the monks. But by framing it so, he suggested that the *sangha* supported the government's moves against anyone who did "not live virtuously or [who] misbehave[d]." This seeming moral alignment between the state and the *sangha* as upholders of the same ethical order had the effect of legitimating actions that the government was then undertaking to ensure its own power. Some would see this as the *sangha*'s co-option in the repression then occurring in Vientiane and Luang Phrabang.

In order to consolidate the relation between the state and the *sangha*, the *sangha* was quickly reorganized administratively. One of the immediate consequences of this move was that some disaffected monks loyal to the identities of their respective sectarian orders decided to leave the *sangha* and return to their villages as laity, or, if they decided to remain monks, they crossed the Mekong into Thailand. In this connection Gunn reported:

> "Patriotic" monks are now grouped into the Lao Union of Buddhists, under the banner of the Lao Front for National Construction. This union hosts annual reunions of monks from all over the country and is said to represent a single and united organization of Buddhists, free from the sectarian divisions of the past. . . . [A]fter the establishment of the new order, many monks belonging to the *Dhammayut* . . . fled to Thailand, although others agreed to cooperate with the mainstream *Mahanikai*. Sectarian differences between the two groups now have been dissolved through their merger into an umbrella group under party direction. (1982: 92)

It was predictable that many of the Thammayut monks would flee to Thailand. Some of the elements constitutive of the "new image" of the Buddhist monk being formulated in post-revolution Laos were quite at odds with the Thammayut's more orthodox understanding of the monastic vocation. In some ways, however, the monastic vocation envisaged by the new Union of Lao Buddhists was actually more consistent with traditional village Lao understandings of the Buddhist monastic vocation, especially in relation to issues involving manual labor and the monk's integral participation in the social and economic life of the village. It was precisely this specific profile of monasticism that the Thammayut Nikay had historically opposed and had sought to reform. Moreover, the royal Thai roots of the Thammayut made its monks obvious objects of suspicion for the new regime; they were easily regarded as vestiges of the old "feudal" order and the "neocolonialist" regime. Under Kaysone's early Vietnamese-dominated administration, Thailand was vilified publicly on an almost weekly basis, and the Thammayut's identification made its monks obvious targets as well.

The new administrative umbrella organization of Lao Buddhists was placed directly under an oversight committee. The committee was comprised of Lao Peoples Revolutionary Party members, and it replaced, in its administrative but hardly spiritual function, the role formerly accorded to the traditional monastic *sangharaja*. The oversight committee reported directly to the Ministry of Education, Sports and Religious Affairs. Thus the Buddhist *sangha* was formally subordinated to the government and the communist party in a manner quite similar to the way religious organizations of any kind were consistently supervised and controlled by various communist governments throughout the socialist world from the 1940s through the 1980s. However, we should recall that the Royal Lao Government had, since 1959, also placed the *sangha* directly and effectively under its own bureaucratic control. In the new Lao PDR, as in the short-lived 1957 neutralist coalition government led by Souvanna Phouma, Phoumi Vongvichit assumed the nominal position of articulating and coordinating the government's plans for the future direction of Buddhism.

A year later, in December 1976, when he addressed the LPRP, Kaysone was even more explicit in terms of what he expected from the *sangha*: monks should actively contribute by transmitting the policies of the party and the state, educating young people, and providing medical care for the population. In this statement even the dimension of the *sangha*'s moral authority in legitimating the government's actions against those who misbehave was eclipsed, and the role of Buddhist monks seems to have been reduced to acting as an appendage of the state carrying out the directives of the party. Now the major function of the *sangha* consisted of being "urged to disseminate socialism among laypeople" (Evans 1998: 59). Indeed, several months earlier in mid-1976, at the very first formal meeting of the Union of Lao Buddhists,

> Phoumi Vongvichit gave the new regime's keynote speech on Buddhism, where he said that in contradistinction to the "old regime which prohibited Buddhist monks from engaging in politics, the new regime encourages it." The Buddha's original path of learning, he claimed, led him to the same conclusion as communists: "the Lord Buddha gave up all his worldly possessions and became an ordinary person with only an alms bowl to beg food from other people. That meant that he tried to abolish the classes in his country and to create only one class—a class of morally conscious people who were respected by other people. It was in this way that the Lord Buddha became involved with politics. . . ." He requested that monks go out and preach in support of the state's developmental programs. (Evans 1998: 59)

It was certainly true that the "old regime" had kept the *sangha* at a distance from the business of politics. But it also seems as if Phoumi Vongvichit and his colleagues in the party leadership had invented a "revolutionary Buddha," an image of their own socialist imaginations to give the *sangha* a clear social role.

Contrary to some reports, Lao PDR government officials today claim that monks were never prohibited from going out to collect alms after the revolution, nor were the laity forbidden to give them alms in support. Whether or not this claim is true, it can safely be said that neither monks nor laity were encouraged to pursue the practice, but instead they were asked to put the wider economic needs of the country before their own immediate concern for spiritual welfare through the making of merit.[17] Expenditures on rituals, village-wide or neighborhood *bouns*, were especially discouraged. Stuart-Fox describes the situation as it unfolded in Vientiane:

> Monks were not directly ordered to work. Though the practice was discouraged, they could go out with a bowl on the morning alms-round—at least in Viang Chan.[18] They received little, however, because the people usually had little left over from their rations and were afraid of being branded religious. Some lay followers still took alms-food to the *wat*, but not enough to feed the monks, who were encouraged to grow their own vegetables. Furthermore, a monk was not eligible for the government rice ration unless he worked, by gardening or engaging in some other productive task—teaching handicrafts, for example, or addressing seminars and meetings on behalf of the government. Another item which monks no longer received from the people was yellow cloth for robes. ... An important overall effect of government measures was to break down the key relationship between monks and the lay community that had sustained the position of Buddhism in traditional lay society ... the traditional Pali formula of homage to the Buddha, *Dharma* and Sangha was all but replaced by repetition of the five ideals of the Lao Peoples Democratic Republic. Since people had little spare time, visits to pagodas, especially in rural areas, were made only on officially sanctioned occasions. (1996: 105–106)

Spending for religious reasons, then, was seen as contrary to the productive relations that the state was trying to foster, especially during the period of severe economic downturn. On the other hand, savings should be reinvested in the means of production. Monks should, if possible, contribute to this means of production themselves. In order to further curb expenditures on religion, especially in an economic climate that in 1976 and 1977 was bordering on desperation,

> the government attempted to extend its influence into [the] ritual domain, and in April 1976 issued detailed regulations on Buddhist festivals. A central feature of the state's political rhetoric at the time related to the importance of thrift for economic development. ... The new regime soon acquired the emotional quality of *boh muan*— "no fun"—the worst possible quality by Lao standards. (Evans 1998: 58)

Evans provides further details of what eventually became a failed policy of trying to curtail, or even to eliminate, important public ritual expressions of Buddhism.

> In Laos in 1977 . . . the communist government banned the traditional *boun bang fay* fertility festival, a syncretic "animist-Buddhist" event held each year just before the monsoon rains. The peasants blamed the following disastrous drought on the banning of the festival, and the reaction was such that the ban was discontinued . . . , but the government continued to promote the work regime that was divorced from the rhythms of the season and religion. (1992: 134)

As might be expected, the lowland Lao Loum did more than simply blame the government for the declining economic conditions of the time. Lao laywomen, in particular, were understandably unhappy about being discouraged from supporting monks through the giving of alms. Many continued the practice despite government admonitions. Giving (*dana*) to the *sangha* while its members are on *pindapata* (alms rounds) is one of the chief means by which the laity gain merit for improving their conditions in this life while positioning themselves for a better rebirth in the next. By far the primary almsgivers to the *sangha* are middle-aged and elderly women. The same principle of who engages in merit-making holds in relation to mothers whose sons join the *sangha*. The merit derived from a son joining the *sangha* is thought to devolve primarily to the mother. Thus from the perspective of many lay Buddhists, the government was not only asking them to sacrifice their economic well-being for the benefit of the state, but it was also asking them to sacrifice the possibility of spiritual well-being by discouraging them from admitting their sons to the *sangha*. Providing food and sons to the *sangha* were the traditional means of realizing the benefit of the *sangha* as the laity's primary field of merit, especially for laywomen. There is no doubt that the government's disposition towards Buddhism was disliked intensely and resisted the most by rural Lao Loum laywoman, for ultimately it was these same laywomen who had the most to lose traditionally with the curtailment of these practices. Indeed, while the government could not foresee this, the failure of their economic plans, which produced a condition of severe want, also short-circuited, from the perspective of pious Buddhist laity, their spiritual hopes as well. As the laity's material means dwindled under the new government, so did their ability to make merit by giving.

In addition to becoming aware of widespread opposition to their policies toward the public ritual practice of Buddhism, there was an additional consideration that tempered the government's treatment of Buddhism and contributed to the politically pragmatic approach that eventually characterized its policy: "In addition to propagating the political line of the LPRP, official Buddhism was of use to the new regime as a further means of maintaining diplomatic contact between states and advancing foreign policy" (Stuart-Fox 1996: 103). Indeed, the diplomatic significance of Buddhism is still made use of today.[19]

In enlisting the *sangha* to its advantage however possible, while limiting Buddhist cultic public expression and material support, the government set about to consciously reform Buddhism, to bend it institutionally and ideologically to its will. The reform of the *sangha* was undertaken in a rather thoroughgoing fashion. Not only was the public ritual expression of Buddhism brought under the state's control, but the *dhamma* of the Buddha was politically reinterpreted as well. Key Buddhist texts for monastic consumption were edited and streamlined in order to conform to socialist emphases. Moreover, the old issue of Buddhism and its relation to the spirit cults was resurrected and a clear course of action determined: Buddhism should be purified of such "accretions." During the early years following the revolution,

> the Pathet Lao drew upon the goodwill many monks had towards the revolutionaries as upholders of traditional Lao cultural values against the materialism and corruption of the West. Monks either volunteered or were prevailed upon to attend political re-education seminars, where they were encouraged to adopt "progressive" attitudes and prove themselves by communicating the policies and decisions of the Pathet Lao leadership to the mass of the people. They were also urged to purge Buddhism of such superstitions as belief in the existence of demons, or of life after death in one of the Buddhist heavens or hells. The accumulation of merit was downplayed; and *karma* was denounced as leading to fatalism and pacifism. The use of monks by the Pathet Lao to spread a political message had a twofold effect: in the short term, the impact of socialist ideology was enhanced by virtue of the traditional respect accorded to monks, especially in rural Laos; but, in the longer term, use of the Sangha led to a decline in social standing. . . . The party argued that Buddhism and socialism had much in common: both taught equality, promoted communal values, and sought to end human suffering. The Buddha was portrayed as a man with a social conscience. But it was also emphasized that, as Buddhism had adapted to a variety of social systems over time, so it had to adapt to socialism—in the way the Party directed. (Stuart-Fox 1996: 78–79)

In retrospect it is quite easy to see the extent to which Buddhist ideas were read through reductionist Marxist lenses. In these rather tortured renderings, a somewhat naive understanding of traditional Buddhist practice and ideas emerges. Buddhism is understood as being almost entirely otherworldly oriented and thus as directing attention away from the immediate needs at hand. It is obvious that these interpretations were proffered by individuals who lacked intimate acquaintance with the manner in which sophisticated Buddhist thought and practice has been understood within the Theravada *sangha* historically or how the practice of Buddhism has been traditionally articulated at the village level. These criticisms came either from urban Lao French-educated elite Marxists or tribal highlanders now in positions of newfound power, which is no doubt why the Lao Marxists understood notions such as *upekkha* as "indifference" rather than as "evenmindedness."[20] Or why it is that they construed *karma* as "fatalism" or "resignation," rather than as "action" that has the potential to change the course of future events. That is also why they singled out as "irrational" traditional cosmological conceptions.[21]

Unfortunately some Western scholars commenting on what happened to Lao Buddhism in the aftermath of the revolution also seem to share a misunderstanding that Theravada's primary religious trajectory has been entirely otherworldly. As a result they have interpreted the *sangha*'s treatment under the Pathet Lao to ensure its this-worldly relevance as a degrading distortion. While the *sangha* may have been subordinated to the Pathet Lao government, and while the teachings of *dhamma* were certainly reinterpreted along intellectually strained socialist lines, I doubt very much that the *sangha*'s degradation in the eyes of lay followers was a consequence of its becoming too this-worldly in orientation. Explanations about how the Pathet Lao completely reoriented the *sangha* from an otherworldly to this-worldly orientation are somewhat innocent, for the traditional Buddhism of the Lao village has always been quite this-worldly in its orientation.

While the soteriology of Theravada may seem otherworldly from a surface reading, especially as presented in many Western textbook accounts, its trajectory, as understood normatively within classic Pali texts such as in Buddhagosa's orthodox commentary, the *Visuddhimagga*, does not lead at all in the direction of an ethereal mysticism. Rather it has always been fundamentally concerned with the cultivation of *sila, panna,* and *samadhi* (morality, wisdom, and concentrated meditation). With regard to *vipassana* meditation, the meditative practice that came to characterize Theravada contemplation, the aim is to become fully aware of the presence of reality-as-it-is, of its transient nature and continuous process of change,[22] and not to seek altered states of consciousness in conditions of deep trance. Even the Lao forest monks of the Theravada tradition, the so-called *vipassanadhura* or *thudong* monks, enjoyed a reputation among Lao laity for being great healers and compassionate actors working for the spiritual edification of the people.

Thus part of the reason that many monks embraced the Pathet Lao perspective was not because they accepted a Marxist ideological critique of Buddhist ideas per se, but because the vocational profile that the Pathet Lao wanted to advocate was actually more in accord with how the monastic vocation had been traditionally understood not only in many canonical and commentarial Pali Buddhist texts but, more importantly, how it had been practically realized in the village context. It is worth remembering again, in this context, that the overwhelming majority of Buddhist monks came from rural villages, not urban settings. Their models for the monastic life had been village monks.

I want to press this specific point further because I think it has been largely lost in the accounts of what happened to the *sangha* after the Lao revolution. The most intimate account of rural Lao monastic life is by Kamala Tiyavanich in her work that focuses on the Lao *thudong* of Isan, the Lao cultural region of northeast Thailand. Her work is based on an extensive reading of traditional hagiographical materials and yields a picture of Buddhist monasticism before and during the process of modernization, including the Thammayut-inspired reforms that were attempted in the first half of the twentieth century. Conditions of that time in Laos itself would have been quite similar to those in Isan, as Hayashi (2003) affirms. So Tiyavanich's portraits of monastic life are especially worth considering. I quote her at length because she makes the case so clearly and directly.

> A common feature of regional [non-Thammayut Bangkok-based] traditions was the assumption that monastics would remain engaged in village life. Regional monks organized festivals, worked on construction projects in the wat, tilled the fields, kept cattle or horses, carved boats, played musical instruments during the Boun Phawet festival, taught martial arts—and were still considered to be respectable *bhikkhus* (monks) all the while. . . . [C]ultural expectations and loyalties of kinship and community made all these activities legitimate ones for monks. . . . Village or town abbots consequently remained very much in the world, devoting their energies to community work that benefited local people. (1997: 23)

To this she adds a description of the specifically religious value accorded to this-worldly work:

> Revered monks of regional Buddhist traditions had always regarded work as a means of practicing the dhamma. They taught by example, by living simply, working hard, and acting ethically. . . . [T]he old as well as the young were engaged in the same kind of work; no distinctions were made. Manual labor such as chopping wood, hauling water, cleaning latrines, sweeping the ground, and thatching roofs was seen as training for mindfulness. (275)

Finally, she says simply that "in the Lao tradition, monks often supervised the villagers' work and worked along them" (221).

Perhaps Pholsena read Tiyavanich's accounts of Lao monasticism, for she writes in essentially the same vein when she depicts the traditional vocation of the Buddhist monk in Laos, though she adds a more expedient motivation and lay perspective in accounting for the manual labor of monks:

> In many regional traditions, laypeople expected a monk to perform hard labor. They expected him to be self-reliant and self-sufficient. When monks were not gifted in oratorical, artistic, or healing skills (which brought in donations), the wat had to survive any way it could. In many local traditions, monks had to work to support the monasteries by growing vegetables, tending orchards, carving boats, or raising horses and cattle. (2006: 24)

Thus when Gunn reports[23] how Khamtan Thepbuali, a spokesman for the Lao PDR, characterizes the Buddhist monastic vocation from a Pathet Lao perspective, there is consistency between what he presents and the pre-revolutionary model of the village monk that I have just drawn from Tiyavanich and Pholsena:

> Khamtan tells of the past labour heritage by monks as carpenters, brickmakers and cultivators, in contrast to what he describes as their general indolence during the "feudal and colonial period." Hence the kind of cultivation work that monks can be seen doing in the early mornings and evenings, he avers, is in accord with the ideology of the people and therefore most suitable. (1982: 93)

Khamtan's Marxist gloss on history reveals his lack of awareness with regard to the nature of the village monkhood during what he has referred to as the "feudal and colonial period." What he describes as the "labour heritage" of monks was practiced in the village right up to the time of the revolution in 1975.

This important commentary aside, what the Marxist ideologues of the new Lao PDR sought was to integrate the work of Buddhist monks into their new economic development schemes. They rationalized this integration by emphasizing that Buddhism and Marxism shared the same basic aims. Whatever criticisms the Pathet Lao launched against Buddhism, these were based on their own Marxist belief that religion, as an instrument of the ruling class, had traditionally contributed to the oppression of the masses. In their view Buddhist monks had traditionally performed the function of legitimizing an oppressive royalty and its attendant feudal structure, so they sought to implement a new program aimed at the rehabilitation of the Buddhist monk. Ironically, though the ideology of the Marxists was quite removed from a normative Buddhist perspective and despite the general philosophical affinities that they emphasized over and over again, the vision of the monk that they sought to inculcate was, in fact, already functionally in place!

Village monks had always been involved intimately in the local political economy of the village. That is, they were traditionally part and parcel of the means of
production.

Lafont's (1982) observations provide a basis for further discussion.

> From the LPF [Lao Patriotic Front] perspective, monks were fully capable as
> citizens of the Lao PDR to be active in politics, education, culture, health and
> the economy, as monks were in former times. . . . If the motivation of detach-
> ment was legitimate at certain times, in the present situation in Laos, it could
> only serve to prolong the existence of the old regime and favour the continued
> oppression of the working classes by those in power.
> . . . .
> The authorities encouraged monks to take part in propaganda on behalf of the
> regime by informing people that there was no incompatibility between Marx-
> ism and Buddhism, and by emphasizing the early revolutionary aspects of Bud-
> dhism mentioned in many texts. (1982: 151, 155)

Again, whether the fault is Lafont's or the position taken by the Pathet Lao, it is
very clear that a precise understanding of "detachment" is lacking in this statement. Detachment has never been regarded in Buddhist texts as connoting an
aloof or unconcerned disposition for the troubles of the world. This is clearly an
orthodox Marxist attribution or a Western misunderstanding. Rather, detachment
has meant detachment from self-interested motives such as passion, hatred, and
delusion (*asavas* or conditioning dispositions that can "ulcerate" the mind) that
create karmic attachments either to the ego or to material possessions. The detachment normatively sought by Buddhist monks is detachment from *ahamkara*
("I-making" or self-perpetuating egotism) and the conditions that create *dukkha*
(suffering) in the world, either for the monk himself or for others. More precisely,
it is detachment from the kinds of actions that generate deleterious (*akusala*) karmic retribution. *It is not detachment from the world or society per se.* From the
earliest pages of the canonical *Vinayapitaka* (Book of Discipline) and its seminal
accounts of the first monastic conversions by the Buddha to the *sangha*, monks
have been enjoined in formulaic fashion to "wander for the welfare of the many."
Thus the ethos of the Buddhist monastic vocation has never been construed as
one of detachment from the suffering (*dukkha*) of the people. On the contrary,
compassion and loving-kindness (*karuna* and *metta*—two of the four primary
brahmavihara "abidings" cultivated in meditation) are meant to constitute the
ethos of the *sangha*'s disposition towards the world. Thus Gunn (1982: 94) is not
at all wrong when he asserts: "There is also much truth in the observation . . . that
what has aided the Pathet Lao in their move to create an egalitarian society is the

Buddhist sanction for the renunciation of worldly goods—at least, it should be added, for the long-suffering peasantry, as opposed to the bourgeoisie, whose life-style implied a fixation on the consumer culture of the metropole."

It is quite clear that the Pathet Lao, despite their misunderstanding of important aspects of Buddhist thought, especially when they emphasized an otherworldly trajectory in Buddhist monasticism, did seek important general affinities that they could profitably exploit. Again Gunn provides us with an especially pertinent example in his report on Khamtan's "official" or representative Pathet Lao view:

> In an official explanation, again as expressed by Khamtan, "the supreme goal of the revolution is to liberate the nation, to liberate the people so that they can escape from *dukkha* [suffering] and to render all men happy." . . . [T]he importance of the monk in new Laos was in "blending Buddhist and revolutionary moralities." (1982: 94–95; brackets Gunn's)

Indeed, the Pathet Lao would consistently portray the Buddha "as a man of social conscience" (Stuart-Fox 1983 445) whose aims, they argued, were fully commensurate with their own. They sought, then, to utilize Buddhist principles to generate a liberating rationale for the state.

Phoumi Vongvichit, in a major policy speech directed to Buddhist monks in October 1976, outlined quite clearly what the new government's intentions were for the *sangha*. This is the most detailed public statement provided by a Lao PDR official in the early years of the regime regarding Buddhism.

> Buddhist monks [should] study politics to consolidate their political background and make it conform to progressive revolutionary politics. This will enable them to more easily integrate themselves into the revolutionary ranks alongside the revolutionary cadres. . . .
>
> Revolutionary politics and the politics practiced by the Lord Buddha have the same goals. They differ only in organization and practice. . . .
>
> In certain countries, Buddhist monks may not become involved in or study politics. I hold such prohibitions to be a deprivation of Buddhist monks. Buddhist monks are regarded as potential cadres of the Lord Buddha who are fighting injustice in the world. . . .
>
> Buddhist monks assigned to teach the people in rural areas must understand the people who attend their sermons. They must select an appropriate sermon to give the people in order to change their line of thinking. If they use only Buddhist politics coupled with examples from ancient times, it may be difficult for the people to understand them, and the people may not be able to relate the example to present day reality. Therefore, they should mix the themes

of current politics and Buddhist politics in giving sermons and use current examples....

The policy of this Party and government is . . . to request Buddhist monks to give sermons to teach the people and encourage them to understand that all policies and lines of the party and government are in line with the teachings of the Lord Buddha so that the people will be willing to follow them. Thus, there will be no lazy people, thieves, or liars in our country. Instead, there will be only diligent people working for the prosperity of the country. If our Buddhist monks can do this, it means that they are contributing to economic construction. (cited in Stuart-Fox 1996: 102–103; brackets Stuart-Fox's)

Commenting on the substance of this speech, Stuart-Fox observes:

Significantly, Phoumi situated himself and his government in the same position as the Theravada kings of old who, in their role as defenders of the faith, occasionally acted as purifiers of the sangha. By retraining monks, the new regime, he said, "will help purify and make Buddhism in this country more scientific than in other countries." (1996: 105)

Here it would seem as if Phoumi Vongvichit had shorn Buddhism of its religious dimension completely, even in its this-worldly apprehension, by subordinating the *sangha* entirely to the political and economic aims of the state. The Buddhist monk's positive potential was understood only in terms of becoming one of the party's cadres. While Stuart-Fox is right in pointing out that the government had situated itself in the role of purifier of the *sangha*, unlike the kings of the past who often tried to preclude the *sangha* from getting too entangled in politics, the government clearly made the case for its intimate involvement. In this the government was not functionally far from the vocational aims of the Sri Lanka Vidyalankara monks of the late 1940s and 1950s in Colombo, who were led by the Venerable Walpola Rahula. They saw politics as an effective and necessary effort incumbent upon the *sangha* in rendering service to the country.[24] Moreover, Phoumi Vongvichit wanted monks to make party policies the actual substance of monastic sermons, mixing moral tales of the *jatakas* with contemporary policies of the government, a wholly utilitarian use of the *sangha*.

While Phoumi Vongvichit's ministry was heavily involved in reforming monastic education, I have not located precise textual examples of these efforts. Lafont, however, makes these general remarks about the new curricular reforms:

In the past, however, monks had studied manuscripts kept in monastic libraries, many of which were apocryphal or tendentious, containing unim-

portant rules incompatible with modern living or encouraging belief in superstition, especially in the cult of spirits known as *phi*. Now monks study
revised texts, rewritten by a committee of monks convened on the initiative
of the LPRP and consisting of representatives from both the former "liberated
zone" and the "Vientiane zone." This committee has been entrusted with the
task of pruning and modernizing both canonical and non-canonical texts, a
project that accords with wishes expressed by reformist monks prior to 1975.
Theoretically, the aim is to purify Lao Buddhism: the result seems to be to
reduce it to three principles—not to sin, to increase one's excellence, and
to purify one's own heart—all of which are compatible with Marxism-
Leninism. (1982: 155)

Lafont seems to be unaware that his final sentence paraphrases of one of the most
famous and often-quoted passages from the *Dhammapada*, verse 183:

> To avoid evil,
> To cultivate good,
> To purify the mind,
> This is the teaching of the Buddha.

If the monastic committee of reform had based their work on these principles
alone, then they would not go far wrong, as far as a Theravada doctrinal perspective is concerned. Yet we get the impression that the Buddhist monks who were
compatible with the Pathet Lao were more concerned with distancing themselves
from traditional Buddhist cosmology, especially from the cult of spirit veneration,
and in aligning themselves with the political hegemony of the government, than
they were with doctrinal purity and precision.

Lafont (1982: 159) has made the following insightful comment: "It is interesting to note that whereas most lay followers have remained faithful to the traditional beliefs of their parents and ancestors, and do not want any change in their
religion, the monks have been more prepared to accept changes imposed by the
new regime in their monastic rules, sacred texts or religious practices." Years later
Evans (1993: 136) would make a similar comment, that "most ethnic Lao party
members remain active Buddhists . . . and this support for Buddhism was not
just political expediency." It would seem, then, that many Lao Loum laity had
a difficult time coming to terms with the new Lao PDR policies regarding religious culture in general, even if they were completely sympathetic in general to the
government.

I shall examine some of the reasons for this, especially in relation to the worship of spirits, but in order to do so more effectively, I shall first address how

efforts to form agricultural cooperatives competed with the cultic and economic significance of the traditional village Buddhist *vat* in the early years following the revolution.

The Agricultural Cooperative and the Buddhist *Vat*

Laos is a profoundly agricultural society, so the collectivization scheme that the socialist government launched, hoping that economies of scale would reverse the current depressed economic conditions, struck at the heart of the old subsistence patterns of rural village life and ultimately engendered serious resistance. In fact within a year of its implementation the government was compelled to reconsider, when it became clear that the transition to collectivization would lead to an even more precipitous drop in crop production, following the very weak levels of production for 1976 and 1977. In the months following the implementation of collectivization in 1978, and for the first time since the revolution, significant numbers of Buddhist Lao Loum farmers attempted to escape the country across the Mekong River into Thailand. The government reacted by suspending the cooperatives, asking farmers to continue their individual cultivation, and shifted its emphasis to establishing trade cooperatives instead, although they simultaneously allowed a small market economy to emerge. Even these adjustments, however, did little to ameliorate the economic decline.

Agricultural collectivization, of course, is a hallmark of socialist-inspired societies. It represents the abolition of private property and the socialization of the means of production. For that reason alone, and in emulation of its socialist models and supporters in Vietnam and the Soviet Union, the Marxist hardliners of the Lao PDR politburo had been enthusiastic proponents of institutionalizing collectivization as quickly as possible. They hoped to bypass capitalism altogether to realize their vision of a truly socialist society. The government was also convinced that collectivization would not only be more efficient in increasing production, but would also increase government revenues as well. Like all Lao governments of the past, the Lao PDR had to cope with a chronic shortage of revenue.[25]

There was another compelling reason for the government to begin implementing agricultural collectivization. "Collectivization . . . was not only seen as a means to achieve economic security but also as an instrument for political consolidation" (Pholsena 2006: 56). Thus in 1978 the government set about, through collectivization, to bring the socialist revolution to the village. In hindsight it is clear that the government did not anticipate how villagers might react to this fundamental reorganization of the local political economy. Nor did they seem fully prepared administratively to implement these changes.

Several serious factors led to resistance among the village Lao Loum. Chief among these was that "the organizational strength of the LPRP was insufficient to reach down into the majority of villages or cooperatives. The leaders of the cooperatives, the managing committees, were drawn from local peasants, who usually owed their allegiance to their fellow farmers and were unused to offering it to some higher organization" (Evans 1990: 151). Such a radical rearrangement of basic economic patterns mounted a serious challenge to fundamental village social patterns. While the Pathet Lao enjoyed much support in the countryside before the revolution, that support was based on its opposition to the government in Vientiane and what Vientiane had symbolized. Support did not necessarily translate into support for a utopian socialist vision, nor was it for the disintegration of the traditional patterns of village life. The problem that the Lao PDR faced in implementing its collectivization scheme was that

> ideas of modern (socialist) cooperation are found on *individuals* participating *equally* and *democratically* in collective activity for mutual benefit. These ideas inevitably cut across traditional concepts of authority and, therefore, promotion of modern cooperatives may lead to the breakdown in traditional solidarity through a challenging of preexisting patterns of authority. In other words, modern cooperatives are likely to destroy the very foundations on which some hope to build (Evans 1990: 203; emphasis Evans's)

As the French introduction of taxes and a cash economy had threatened the traditional economic and moral order in the colonial era, so precisely did the Lao PDR upset the existing moral and economic system with its new collectivization scheme. Not only did a structural dislocation of the family's central position occur, but the cooperative also challenged the *vat* as the new social, economic, and political center of the village.

The *vat*, of course, constituted the central foundation of traditional Lao society in the village. It was the chief institutional venue, which served as the repository of village wealth as well as the chief redistributor of village wealth. In the new economic scheme, the cooperative became the new repository of created wealth and the state its collector, once subsistence had been accounted for. The state became religion's competitor in its quest to gather surpluses beyond subsistence. It was within this grassroots village context of competition that the transformation of Laos into a truly socialist state failed.

Specific social, economic, and *religious* reasons accounted for the failure of agricultural cooperatives.[26] Most broadly, "cooperatives were generally not successful in achieving their aims . . . [because] inside the cooperatives there were continual disputes over the proportions to be retained for collective investment, and payments to members. These disputes strengthened the feeling among

individual peasants that their disposable income, including that available for
ceremonial outlays, had been reduced" (Evans 1993: 134). Related to this, there were
"other problems in the cooperative scheme [that] involved the same pay for un-
even amounts of work within a context where there were no familial affinities"
(Evans 1990: 146). In analyzing the failure of the cooperative schemes, Evans
concludes that the program

> ultimately disintegrated because it tried to rearrange peasant production
> without being able to introduce substantial technological improvements.
> This not only complicated [the] peasants' lives unnecessarily but also led to a
> fall of production, and to the extent that the cooperatives were economically
> unsuccessful there was less income available for merit-making. This added
> significantly to their unpopularity, although it could hardly be construed as
> the fundamental reason for the failure of cooperativization progamme in Laos.
> (Evans 1993: 141)

Evans has argued that the agricultural collectivization scheme failed because it
lacked necessary technology, that it was abandoned because the government realized that it was not economically productive, and that it was unpopular among the
farmers because it inhibited the religious aspirations of individuals and challenged
the basic social foundation of the family. Kaysone himself admitted in an interview
with Evans in 1988 that the basic planning for agriculture in Laos had to begin
with a consideration of the family as its foundation (Evans 2002b: 195).

One other aspect of the problems intrinsic to the government's collectivization
program needs to be noted before I address how it impacted village religious life:
the role of women in Lao society. This aspect of the problem was clearly related to
effects on religious culture as well. In this context Evans has written:

> A clear division exists between the public and private spheres for men and
> women. Men generally speak for the household and are elected or seconded
> to positions of authority within village and political organizations. Women by
> and large are confined to the private, domestic sphere, except for the important
> economic activity of trading. On the basis of these cultural facts, it may seem
> that the cooperatives could hold some advantages for women. But this is not
> so. The formation of cooperatives would entail women handing over control of
> their important social asset, land, to a group that is most likely to be dominated
> by male officeholders. Cooperatives would cause women to surrender some of
> their autonomy. Thus, in Laos, spontaneous peasant resistance to collectiviza-
> tion arising from the heart of the peasant social structure comes from both men
> *and* women because both stand to lose some of their former social prerogatives

by joining a cooperative. The only person structurally situated to potentially gain from such a reorganization is the landless son-in-law who is still under the tutelage of his father-in-law. (1990: 132)

Indeed, traditional Lao Loum land-tenure practices placed inheritance of land into the hands of the youngest female child who, in turn, was expected to care for her aging parents on the family homestead. Older male children married into their wives' families and tilled land under a revenue-sharing arrangement with fathers-in-law. Their hope was to accumulate enough surplus from their labor to purchase their own land eventually. Under the cooperative schemes, women lost control of their lands.[27]

When it became clear that the state had positioned itself to skim off whatever excesses beyond subsistence were produced through cooperative labor, that fewer funds would be available for merit-making (through *dana* provided to the *vat* or for holding festive village-wide *bouns*), Lao women then understood that their spiritual lives were being impoverished. Middle-aged and elderly women are the primary givers to the *sangha* and the ultimate retainers of the family's ability to create wealth. Moreover, women are not just the primary givers of provisions to the *sangha*, they are the ultimate holders of the source of wealth (land) that can be transmuted into merit.[28] Moreover, as the organizers of the domestic households, they are the family members who determine whether or not there are enough funds available within the family budget for the sponsoring of *bouns*. Within the social dynamics of village society, the holding of *bouns* functions as a ritual means not only for articulating prestige, but for the redistribution of wealth throughout the village. Thus Evans writes:

Before 1975 surpluses among Buddhist Lao were often directed into maintaining the vat, and ceremonial expenses and expenditures on festivals are a well-established means of redistributing wealth in Lao villages. By contributing to the vat, the donor acquires religious merit and social prestige. Bouns, which are forms of ceremonial consumption, also earn prestige for the host. (1990: 87)

Evans then proceeds to quote Christian Taillard:

The dynamic of the boun overcomes antagonisms and contributes to the *piep* (good-will) of social life. The individual who accumulates more material goods than others, even at their expense, will then have them redistributed among the community through the vat. This levels the individual wealth and maintains a socio-economic equilibrium between various households. By transposing social competition from a material plane to a spiritual plane, the vat establishes a

new logic of prestige: the more this is striven for, the more wealth is redistributed and the more solidarity is reinforced. (Ibid.)

Then, commenting upon the irony of the government's policy to encourage thrift
while discouraging the considerable expenditure that *bouns* entail,[29] Evans notes:

> After 1975 there was less social pressure on people to compete for prestige by
> throwing bouns, partly as a result of government discouragement and partly
> because people did not want to draw the state's attention to any wealth they
> may have possessed. One could, perhaps, argue that by frowning on the "waste-
> fulness" of religious ceremonies the government inhibited a leveling mecha-
> nism at the village level. (1990: 88)

Thus the government's policy of discouraging *bouns* (in the belief that festivals
siphoned off wealth from the state) actually retarded the kind of solidarity that
socialist ideology tries to engender.

> Buddhist ritual and ceremonies dramatize social and economic reciprocity
> within the village. Thus, merit-making in all its forms plays a basic social role
> in village life, and its disruption threatens to break a vital filament in the social
> fabric of the village. (Evans 1993: 139)

Moreover,

> merit-making is a spur to economic action because wealth facilitates the mak-
> ing of more merit. Hence a significant portion of the peasant's surplus is direct-
> ed towards merit-making primarily because there are no "rational" alternatives.
> In other words, far from being a drag on economic *effort* because of its "other-
> worldly orientation," ... Buddhism acts as a stimulus. (Evans 1993: 133)

From this perspective, what the state failed to do was to provide a more persuasive
rationale for the use of surpluses than merit-making. Much like the rural highlanders during French colonial times, villagers could not understand the tangible
benefits of their conscripted labor. In addition to the fact that cooperatives inhibited the practice of merit-making that had also facilitated village "labor exchanges,"
appeals to the ideology of the new socialist man and state recognition for meeting
production targets were unconvincing substitutes for the spiritual and local social
recognition traditionally gained through ritual performances at the village *vat*.
Simply put, the ideals of the socialist vision did not resonate on the local village
level well enough to compete with the traditional Buddhist worldview articulated

in the religious symbolism and ritual life of the *vat*. This was especially true among women, the principle ritual makers of merit.

Tiyavanich (1997), Hayashi (2003), and Pholsena (2006) describe the *vat* as not only a symbol of the spiritual values of the village, but as an embodiment of its collective wealth and the nexus of its social relations (extrafamilial and to some extent intrafamilial). The government's collectivization schemes threatened the verity of that symbolism and failed to provide a suitable alternative. "Some cooperatives displaced the *vat* temporarily as an important centre for secular village affairs (especially if the cooperative had electricity for meetings at night), but community identity remained fixed on the *vat*, and its status, rather than that of the cooperative, was considered the primary index of a village's standing and accumulated merit" (Evans 1993: 141).

While the *vat* remained a fixture within Lao Loum village life during the early years of the Lao PDR, its position was weakened to some extent through the implementation of various government policies. Indeed, the centrality of the *vat*'s social function had begun to erode even during the waning years of French colonial rule and this decline continued into the period of the Royal Lao governments from the mid-1950s through the mid-1970s, in part because government schools had replaced the *vat* as the usual venue for primary education. By 1975 only 9 percent of primary schools in Laos were still located within *vat*s (Evans 1998: 156). The *vat*'s marginalization was also abetted by the provision of more health centers, which displaced the monk's function as a primary dispenser of traditional medicines.[30]

From 1975 until 1990, *vat* construction or maintenance was minimal. Not only did the government discourage expenditures for merit-making efforts directed toward these purposes, but "most of the wealthy and those with means to undertake projects like this had left in 1975" (Evans 1993: 138).

Against "Superstition"

The contemporary significance of spirit veneration in relation to Buddhist religious village culture is more fully examined in Chapter 5, but in the context of the impact of the Lao PDR government on Lao religious culture following the 1975 revolution, relevant issues arise.

Marxist orthodoxy claims to be rational and scientific. So in Laos a clear line was drawn between Buddhism, seen as a philosophically inclined religion that could be reformed, rehabilitated, and made rational, capable of being readjusted to the new sociopolitical milieu, and the superstitious practice of venerating spirits. Part of the reinterpretation of post-revolution Buddhism involved, therefore, its purification of "cultural accretions" of a superstitious nature. In this the Marxists shared a perspective first articulated by King Phothisarat in the sixteenth century, which reappears among some Thai Thammayut monks of the nineteenth and twentieth centuries, and then again among the "modern" monks of the French-sponsored Institut Bouddhique in the 1930s and 1940s. Buddhadasa's supporters in Thailand also applauded post-revolution efforts in Laos to purge Buddhist practice of spirit veneration.

It is also the case that despite the fact that most ritual specialists of the spirit cults are men (and usually former monks), "the spirit cults are one area in which women have a special preserve" (Evans 1990: 112). If the *sangha* was more willing than the laity to adapt to the new demands of the communist state, it follows that women formed the core of resistance to the state's prohibition against spirit worship. Insofar as the attempt to disassociate the veneration of spirits from Buddhist practice appears to have been *relatively* successful,[31] the effect was to drive "superstitious" behavior out of the temple, at least publicly, and underground into strictly private spaces.

> State hostility to "superstitious" mediums in post-1975 Laos had the effect of weakening or even severing these ties with Buddhism and making mediums the reluctant scribes of the culture's "hidden transcripts." . . . Campaigns against "superstition" in the temples meant that monks were less available to provide fortune telling, interpret dreams, and generally help ordinary people interpret the vicissitudes of their lives. Despite proclamations of a "new dawn" after the revolution, problems of life and death and love did not disappear. Ironically, therefore, with the path to the temples closed off, or at least felt to be closed off, one consequence of the new government's policies was to direct people to the more private, less easily monitored, world of the spirit mediums. Austerity after the revolution also had this effect, as medicines became more scarce and expensive throughout the country. Monks were encouraged to practice traditional forms of medicine, but many people also turned to spirit mediums to help with illness. (Evans 1998: 72–73)

Whether or not the severance of the spirit cults from the Buddhist *vat* per se led ironically to an increase in its vitality or not, the veneration of spirits remains ubiquitous throughout Laos today, but not because it has regained government or monastic acceptance. Rather, my sense is that its "times" and "places" have been more clearly defined as a result of the government's early campaigns to eradicate it. And since the spirit cults seem to have been much less integrated into popular Buddhist religious cult than, for instance, the cults of the *devata*s and *yaksa*s in Sri Lanka, this partitioning was not as difficult to accomplish as we might think. In contemporary Laos it would seem that as long as spirit cults do not intrude too much into the government's public or the *sangha*'s *vat* domains,[32] the authorities seem to ignore them, despite the official ban.

> The LPRP and spokesmen for the sangha maintain their public opposition to "superstitious" beliefs, but today this must be counted as one of the least successful of the regime's campaigns. Immediately after the revolution all forms of astrology and fortune telling by monks were repressed or heavily restricted. With the relaxation of restrictions in the 1980s all of these practices and beliefs have gradually returned. Significantly, in 1993, the long-time supporter of the LPRP and president of the Lao Buddhist Association, Maha Bouakham Voraphet, produced a traditional Lao calendar in which he said: "Lao astrology in the past and now is still a very important tool of the nation and of all Lao people, it is still a useful tool for officials and all Buddhists. (Evans 1998: 68)

Thus

> there remains . . . a certain schizophrenia in state attitudes. While various forms of "superstition" now flourish in civil society, discussion of it is systematically excluded from the state-controlled mass media. This is especially true, for example, of ethnic minority practices of spirit worship. Discussion of similar practices encompassed by Buddhism sometimes sneak through because an ethnocentric Lao cultural state apparatus does not recognize its own practices as "superstitious" [see Photo 3.1]. (Evans 1998: 74–75).

Evans' last comment is especially interesting because it reveals the extent to which Lao Buddhists remain innocent of the manner in which the ontology of the spirit cults has affected their rather unique understanding of Buddhism, especially as it relates to the power of Buddha images, stupas, and the *dhamma*.

In yet another relevant discussion Evans has provided a rather humorous example of how and why the eradication of spirit cults by the state has proved problematic, given the worldviews of many contemporary Lao, including those who were enthusiastic supporters of the revolution.

> The cultural milieu in which the communists were operating, however, could not abide such sharp and uncompromising distinctions between "science" and "superstition." Many cadres, especially at lower levels, had not imbibed the rationalist spirit of Marx and they and their families faced the same vicissitudes of life as most Lao. Thus localized compromises were reached with both mediums and their spirits all over Laos, and some cadres even took the revolution to the world of spirits. During 1977 in Luang Prabang, for example, one such cadre

Photo 3.1 Sculpture and photo of the previous abbot of Vat Xieng Thong, whose spirit is worshiped daily in the *vat sim*, Luang Phrabang

claimed that all spirits attached to temples in the old royal capital were *sakdina* (feudal) and therefore he conducted a ceremony at the shrine of the spirit in his temple to call all of these spirits to court, whereupon he told them that the king had been deposed and sent to seminar and that the spirits too had to change. They could, he said, choose to become monks attached to the temples, they could choose to follow the king to Vieng Xai, or they could choose to leave the country. He then sent the spirits away telling them to think it over and to decide. That night "all the villagers" dreamt that they could hear pandemonium among the spirits. Subsequently, full *boun kong bouat* ceremonies were held to induct some of these spirits into the sangha. A ceremony was also held for sending others to Vieng Xai to be with the king, and "you could hear the sounds of elephants" as they began their journey. No ritual was required for the other spirits who became "refugees" and fled away stealthily. Telling the story in 1996, this former cadre remarked that the fame he acquired from this operation meant that some people still approach him to help conduct purification ceremonies, but he says he is no longer young and bold and no longer has the power to do this. Of course, what he narrated was the story of the revolution transposed onto the plane of ritual, just as his contemporary loss of the power to expel spirits suggests the decline in revolutionary militance and power *vis-à-vis* the realm of the spirits. (1998: 73–74)

While the government campaign obviously proved ineffective in eradicating the spirit cults from Lao religious culture, a campaign that in hindsight was doomed to failure, it is still worth examining the motives for the campaign and its continuing public endorsement by the contemporary Lao PDR. In the first instance, unless the government authorities had decided to ban Buddhism entirely, vestiges of the spirit cult would remain alive in the very practice of Buddhist cultic behavior itself, for the ontology of the indigenous religious substratum continues to inflect the manner in which Buddhism is understood in Laos. The government, however, did not choose to ban Buddhism entirely, but instead tried to reform it to be congruent with socialism. While this congruence could be philosophically forged, it was beyond the government's ability, and the ability of its sympathetic monks, to create new forms of Buddhist ritual expression. Aside from the outright ban on the public veneration of *phi*, cultic life in Laos remained pretty much the same as before the revolution, with the exception that during the early years its frequency abated.

What is more interesting to note, however, is the virulence of the government's attack on the spirit cults. In the words of Mayoury Ngaosrivathana (1995: 154): "After 1975, political campaigns were launched against superstitious beliefs to eradicate such despised 'old-fashioned' and 'pernicious' behaviour." Why did the leaders of Lao Peoples' Revolutionary Party find it necessary to "despise" the spirit cults as "old-fashioned" and "pernicious"? Why such harsh rhetoric against seemingly innocuous ritual practices, especially from a regime facing so many pressing practical difficulties? Why would the prohibition of spirit veneration become such an important matter for the country's new political leadership?

I can begin to address these questions by referring to an article written by Charles Keyes (2002) that reflects on how national memory has been constructed and contested in the Lao cultural regions of northeast Thailand. Keyes describes a public controversy centering upon a young scholar's M.A. thesis written at a Bangkok university. In this thesis there is an analytical account of how a local woman who allegedly resisted Chao Anou's retreating army in the early nineteenth century was later "mythicized" and turned into a city *phi* by the people. Keyes notes how the public reaction was powerfully and politically charged: in public demonstrations the thesis was burned and demands were made that its author be barred from her academic job.

It is the remembering of grandmother Mo as a powerful local spirit rather than national heroine that is far more threatening to the proponents of a Bangkok-centered nationalism than an erudite and meticulously researched scholarly work that few will ever read.

. . . .

That Thao Suranari should be remembered as a powerful local spirit rather than a national heroine is very threatening to those who would have the past recalled only in the service of national unity. (2002: 117, 128)

There are analogous implications that can be drawn from this episode to the immediate post-revolution situation in Laos during the late 1970s when the anti-*phi* campaigns were most virulent. Why might the worship of *phi* be threatening to an emergent sense of national unity? By framing the question in this context, it is possible to see that the motivation for opposing *phi* worship was not simply an expression of Marxist faith, though that element cannot be entirely dismissed because of its relevance to the views of the urban elite leadership. Rather, Pathet Lao revolutionaries, especially Lao Theung, recognized very clearly the deep-seated political implications of the *phi* cults and the need to short-circuit their potential.

Various types of *phi* are essentially "supernaturalized" powers thought to exist in direct relation to corresponding natural and socially domesticated spaces, as well in direct relation to social institutions. Specific *phi* are thought to exercise powerful jurisdiction over forests, rivers, mountains, ponds, rice paddies, and other natural places. More significantly for the discussion at hand, however, other *phi* also are thought to exist as jurisdictional powers for the interests of the family, the village, the district, the *muang*, and for the capital center of the mandala. As I previously pointed out, the indigenous ontology of the spirit cults, a hierarchy of spirits, legitimizes a parallel this-worldly political hierarchy: the *phi ban* empowered the village headman; the *chao muang* was empowered by the *phi muang*; and the king was empowered by the Phra Bang image (what was, in effect, a *phi* mandala or *phi muang Lao*). *Phi* are thus supernatural embodiments of the "powers of place" and the powers of various social constituencies as well. From the perspective of many Pathet Lao revolutionaries, most of whom were drawn from the countryside and quite aware of this traditional mode of religio-political thought, allegiance to and veneration of *phi* could easily be seen as a potential rival threat to the powers of the party.

The Pathet Lao government was extremely xenophobic in its early years. What it was most concerned with publicly was securing legitimate national recognition as the power of the state. It repeatedly denounced all associations with traditional Lao power structures (the monarchy being the most obvious and accessible target) as illegitimate. Buddhism, in turn, was stripped of its previous associations with royal power, subordinated, reformed, "purified," and enlisted to contribute to the state's ideological bidding. What the Lao revolutionary state demanded of its citizens, then, was an unconditioned loyalty. Whoever might be suspected of being less than fully committed was removed from the public scene and asked to attend seminar. Moreover, just as Prince Souphanouvong made an exemplary decision to forsake his family for the apparent benefit of the new nation-state, just as families were initially asked to sacrifice family land for the collectivized agricultural cooperatives, and just as Buddhist monks were asked to transcend their sectarian *sangha* loyalties, so the Pathet Lao demanded an ultimate loyalty to the state. Family, village, *muang*, ethnic and religious identities, all were potentially rival, even dangerous competitors for patriotic loyalty. The new Lao PDR government wanted to eliminate every vestige and symbol of power associated with the former social and political order, particularly any aspects of traditional culture that provided support for that order. The state's hostility to the spirit cults was nothing less than an attack on a traditional ontology of power.

Historiography and the State Cult

By 1979 widespread unhappiness about the government's economic failures, especially but not limited to the 1978 experiment in the collectivization of agriculture and the suppression of popular religious practices, especially the official party line discouraging the holding of *bouns*, did not pass unnoticed by the party's leadership. Instead of a crackdown on dissent, Kaysone responded by proposing the Seventh Resolution of the Supreme People's Assembly of the LPDR, an attempt to foster a renewed sense of acceptance and legitimacy for his Marxist regime. The Seventh Resolution loosened many of the social and cultural restrictions that had been in place since the revolution, including public religious ritual, and seemed to indicate a greater confidence of control over the country's population.[33] It certainly reflected a new strategy: a softening in hostility towards the old order on the one hand, and a bolder, more positive image-building effort for the state on the other.

Concomitant with this more relaxed disposition and confidence, a renewed effort at Marxist historiography began its articulation, one in which ancient indigenous roots from within the modern political boundaries of Laos were emphasized, while an appeal to a broader "Indochinese" revolutionary identity was also mounted. Thus deeper national roots and a wider revolutionary identity were stressed in this emergent historical literature. The new emphases placed greater stress on the importance of Mon-Khmer peoples to the history of the country, perhaps in recognition of the fact that the highland Lao Theung had played such an important role in the revolution and that Laos was now more than simply the homeland of the ethnic Lao.[34]

Goscha (2003) has studied this phase of Marxist historiography in some depth and points out the degree to which it is indebted to Vietnamese inspiration. First he notes how Vietnamese communist historians cited Chao Anou, Ong Keo, and Ong Kommadan as examples of "Indochinese" historical precursors to twentieth-century "anticolonial movements." In these examples it is possible to see how Lao resistance movements were folded into a broader conception of the Indochinese revolutionary struggle. In the same way, the Vietnamese struggle, especially the legacy of Ho Chi Minh, was viewed as part of a wider, broader, or common Southeast Asian revolutionary struggle within which the revolutionaries of Laos had also participated, a specific struggle within a larger whole. "This Indochinese resistance past was linked, in turn, to a wider twentieth century internationalist communist genealogy with the October Revolution of 1917 as the starting point, followed by the formation of the Indochinese Communist Party (ICP) in 1930, the August Revolutions of 1945 and the final revolutionary victories in 1975" (Goscha 2003: 266). Linking Indochina to the wider world revolution was Ho Chi Minh. In turn, linking Laos to the Vietnamese "godfather" was Kaysone Phomvihane.

The political histories formulated by orthodox-minded Marxist historians were framed quite intellectually, more for the consumption of a high-brow leadership level of the party, it would appear, than for the masses. We can imagine the currency of such histories within Parisian parlors.

> Communism, based on the credo of Marxism-Leninism, provided a seemingly coherent explanation for European imperial domination and offered a way out of Darwinian subjugation for the semi- and fully colonized of Asia. More importantly for our purposes, it also offered an internationalist outlook that integrated the Asian anti-colonialist cause into a wider, world revolutionary movement based in Moscow and claiming historical continuity with the French revolution. Lenin's thesis on colonialism helped even more to explain how the expansion of European capitalism had led to their exploitation and the domination of large parts of the world. Marx offered an historical and economic analysis that promised an eventual world revolution based on class struggle and extolled proletarian internationalism as a modern identity beyond national or colonial frontiers. (Goscha 2003: 268)

In terms of what the new Marxist historiography of the 1980s offered the broader public:

> The Pathet Lao account of their "thirty-year struggle" against "French colonialists and American interventionists" was couched in orthodox, Cold War, Marxist terms and told in much greater detail from earlier periods. It was told as a story of heroic struggle against overwhelming odds in the course of which valiant Lao people achieved numerous victories (with the occasional unmen-

tioned help of Vietnamese volunteers) to bring about the first, or national democratic, phase of the Lao revolution. (Stuart-Fox 2003: 87)

In surveying the character and trajectories of modern Lao historiography in
the Lao PDR, Pholsena notes the importance attached to demonstrating the indigenous genius of Lao peoples, the cultivation of a primordial identity, and the
downplaying of migration motifs and links to other countries (other than Vietnam and Cambodia) in Southeast Asia or China. That is, what is stressed is an
autonomous history that leaves out the reality of close linguistic, cultural, and
historical affinities to the Thai and the ancestral homeland in Southwestern China.
The central idea in this historiography is to celebrate the nonforeign (except the
Vietnamese) and to emphasize the transformative historical catalyst provided by
the mission of the communist party. As an example, Pholsena cites the following
paragraph lifted from an essay written by a member of the Lao Front for National
Construction (LFNC) Research Department on Ethnic Groups:

Photo 3.2 Soldiers and peasants, in social-realist-style sculpture, triumph over the American
bombs. Note the "USA" on the bomb that soldier is standing upon, below center. Vieng Xai.

Our party rallied the highland peoples such as those who lived along the Lao-
Vietnamese, Lao-Chinese and Lao-Cambodian borders, and turned them into
a bastion of the revolution. Our Party trained the children and grandchildren
of these ethnic groups, who joined our troops to become political militants on
the ground, guerilla fighters and skirmishers. They then rose to become regular
soldiers equipped with modern weapons of the Revolution. Thanks to the support, the supplies, the care and the collaboration of the ethnic population, the
revolutionary forces took form and spread from the highland and remote areas
to the plains, and surrounded the towns that were the enemy's bases. (cited in
Pholsena 2006: 108)

This approach to history is designed for the consumption of the masses. It was
accompanied, of course, by the populist genre of art known as "socialist realism," wherein male and female peasants, workers, and soldiers, with solemn,
grim, and determined faces look far off into a horizon that holds a hopeful
future. The "people," as revolutionary heroes, are depicted as resolute and valiant
in demeanor, sacrificing their personal lives to overcome steep odds in order
to achieve victory against faceless evil and the greedy imperialistic usurpers of
legitimate power (see Plate 4 and Photo 3.2). This simplistic, cartoonish, patriotic, and naive rendition of political history continues to be articulated in Lao
school textbooks today.[35]

Concerted efforts to integrate cultural history into political history began to
appear about ten years after the revolution.

Around the mid-1980s, we can observe a growing need by the party to anchor
more securely its nationalist credentials by leaning on Buddhism. . . . We therefore begin to see the production of short, somewhat amateurish, histories of
temples or stupas; [for example] histories of the That Luang (Vientiane). . . .
[T]hese conform to an older genre that freely mixes fact with legend. . . . [I]n
the 1990s, as orthodox communist ideology weakened and the state set off in
search of more purely nationalist sources of legitimation, we have begun to see
the writing of booklets which lean on older traditions of historical writing in
Laos, and indeed plagiarize these works. (Evans 2003: 99)[36]

In recognizing the need to integrate cultural history into political history, the
research wing of the Lao Front for National Construction was, therefore, faced
with an interesting problem, somewhat similar to what had faced those who had
been charged with the task of reforming Buddhism. The problem was this: how is
history to be rewritten along Marxist lines when the very substance of that history,
and all of its previous accounts, are not framed in Marxist categories? How, for

instance, is it possible to reclaim the glories of the Lan Xang kingdom as part of the national legacy, a reclamation project that supplies cultural depth and legitimacy to the contemporary nation-making project? Stuart-Fox provides a fascinating account of how the Lao Front for National Construction attempted to grapple with this problem by inventing new guidelines for reading the pre-revolutionary history of Laos constructively.

> In 1996 a new attempt was made to come to grips with the history of Lan Xang. Two conferences of "experts" were organized by the Ministry of Information and Culture, bringing together not only qualified historians and geographers, but also a number of interested ideologues from the Lao Front for National Construction. What was agreed was that history prior to the founding of the Indochina Communist Party in 1930 should as far as possible reflect the state of current knowledge; that is, it need not be written from an explicitly Marxist theoretical perspective. It was also agreed that four kings would be singled out for their contribution to "the two strategic tasks of the country: economic development and national defence. The four chosen were Fa Ngum (for both reasons), Setthatirath (defence against the Burmese), Souligna Vongsa (economic development) and Chao Anou (defence against the Thai).
>
> The decision bore fruit in the erection of a statue of Fa Ngum to mark the 650th anniversary of the founding of the Lan Xang in 1353. The accompanying kilometer-long procession was on a scale seldom seen in Laos. At its head came the sacred Phra Bang Buddha image, former palladium of the kingdom, followed by the "king" on a white elephant and his Cambodian queen, accompanied by hundreds of attendants and warriors in period dress. The symbolism could have hardly been more pointed. History and religion were celebrated in a frank display of Lao nationalism unconceivable in the early years of the regime. The only danger in such a shift, however, was that it might again legitimize a narrow and exclusive ethnic Lao nationalism that leaves little room for minority participation. (2003: 89)

This final comment captures something of the intellectual and political bind facing contemporary Lao political historians. In order to affirm the historical depth of national culture prior to the early or mid-twentieth century, how can an inclusive account be created when virtually all of the literary and material cultural sources, except archeological excavations dating to the first millennium, are either royal Lao or Buddhist in orientation? The attempt to retrieve and reclaim the virtues of specific kings from Lan Xang's history on the basis of their contributions to economic development and national defense is obviously one particular yardstick that has been put into play. But the very recognition of these same kings also inevitably invokes attendant Lao Buddhist cultural values as well. These, of course, are not culturally inclusive in nature.[37]

Evans has pointed out that public national rhetoric in the 1990s reflected a more concerted "rebuddhafication," a term first coined by Grant Evans (1998) to describe the rather dramatic shift in public discourse favorable to Buddhism.[38] Yet one means by which the government has sought to counter the possible divisive effect of rebuddhafication has been to create, simultaneously, a transcendent nation-state cult around the figure of Kaysone, whose death in 1992 marked a major transition in Laos's modern political history.

As I noted earlier, in the waning months of the last coalition government in 1975, and in the earliest phase of the revolution in 1976, Prince Souphanouvong's presence in the Pathet Lao leadership provided symbolic continuity to the nation's royal past. Kaysone's leadership, on the other hand, provided a symbolic link between the Lao and Vietnamese struggles within the Indochinese revolution. Kaysone was educated in Hanoi but was probably first introduced to Marxist ideas through the Viet Kieu community of Savannakhet. Some observers remark that he was bicultural (Lao and Vietnamese). For many of those Lao Loum and Lao Theung party cadres who had been deeply committed to the revolution, Kaysone was a preferred embodiment of the leadership for the Pathet Lao movement, precisely because, unlike Souphanouvong, he was linked neither to the old royal Lao family, nor the nationalist Lao Loum Vientiane elite. Kaysone's ties, instead, were unmistakably to the Vietnamese. His leadership represented a clean break from a feudal and imperialist-related past.

Following the revolution, the degree to which Kaysone had enjoyed the support of the Vietnamese became more apparent than most had previously realized. That the Vietnamese fully endorsed Kaysone as their trusted comrade in the revolution, and fully backed him during the seventeen years of his rule that followed, is materially evident, as Goscha (2003: 291) has noted, in the extent to which the Kaysone Phomvihane National Museum, which opened in 1994 only two years after his death, was made possible by generous grants of Vietnamese government money, labor, and artifacts. Vietnamese support of a state cult centering on Kaysone was unqualified (see Photo 3.3).

At the high water marks of Soviet power, a number of twentieth-century Protestant Christian theologians, including Paul Tillich and Reinhold Niebuhr, commented on how Marxist ideologies and the ritual expressions of socialist political regimes represent a kind of "quasi-religious system," atheistic avowals and pretensions to the scientific quest notwithstanding. Deterministic Marxist readings of history certainly authorize revolutionary movements with a power that transcends time-specific and culturally specific occasions. With its implanted Hegelian dialectical principle, Marxist readings of history explicitly affirm an intrinsic dy-

Photo 3.3 Massive statue of Kaysone Phomvihane in front of Kaysone Phomvihane National Museum, Vientiane

namic trajectory or force that is inherently directive and transcendent. At the same time the cultic celebration of state power is ritually articulated to consummate an ultimate identity, a place in history that is linked to transcendent inevitability. In more concrete terms, this transcendent dimension of the state cult is symbolized to "believers" by means of a state leadership cult. The best example of this kind of state cult continues to be the one related to Ho Chi Minh in Hanoi. Ho's mausoleum is maintained as if it were a sacred place of pilgrimage, where all visitors must conform to an almost pietistic etiquette of reverence. In Ho's contemporary cult it would not be wrong to see elements of ancestor veneration in play, as well as the principles of "place" articulated in Paul Mus's "religion of monsoon Asia." Indeed, Ho represents a national "god of the soil" writ large,[39] insofar as he symbolizes the definitive *events* that have defined the nation's space.

While veneration of Kaysone in Laos is not nearly so obvious or intense as Ho's cultic veneration in Vietnam, it is of the same genre. It demands a kind of faith in the vision of "our leader." It has been promoted through the establishment of a museum,[40] the erection of a plethora of statues throughout the country, the placing of Kaysone's visage on the country's currency, and constant references in official government press releases. On the political symbolism of the Kaysone statues, Evans observes:

> A major activity associated with the cult has been the erection of memorial busts of Kaysone throughout the country. All 150 of these statues were, not surprisingly, produced by North Korea.... [L]arger busts of Kaysone (1.2m) are installed at the provincial level, while the smaller (0.75m) busts are installed at the district level. One can see in this layout shades of the older *muang* structure, with the smaller units being subordinate to and incorporated within larger and more central units, culminating at last in the main statues in Vientiane—in the National Assembly and in the Museum. In August, 1996, three full-size statues made in China were erected: one in Houaphan Province (the old revolutionary base area), one in Savannaket (his birthplace), and one at the Kaysone Museum in Vientiane. The placement of all these statues is an undisguised attempt to symbolize national unity by the new regime. (2002a: 163)

He concludes:

> The Kaysone statues represent the most intensive episode of statue building ever in Lao history. Their proliferation is connected directly to the LPRP's inheritance of a particular type of communist iconography, combined with the need of the party to implant signs of legitimacy and control of Lao territory by using icons of its main political figure. (2002a: 175)

The relative placement of statues throughout the country clearly indicates that the cult of Kaysone has been constructed to invoke the "leader" as a source of iconic authority in the newly imagined national memory. And while the cult may draw on a Vietnamese-cum-Confucian-cum-Soviet inspiration for its articulation, it is also inspired by the legacy of Lao kingship. This is evident, I think, in at least two other ways. First, Kaysone's face is found on all new denominations of Lao PDR money, replacing, of course, the traditional image of the king. Kaysone literally erased and replaced the image of the king in post-revolution Laos as a symbol of authorized national identity. On newer bills Kaysone's face is accompanied by images of important Buddhist *vats*, including Luang Phrabang's historic Vat Xieng Thong on the 20,000 kip note, thus articulating the new move to "rebuddhify" national public symbolism. Second, the public cult of Kaysone, clearly a successor to kingship in its attempt to embody the identity of the nation, is also meant to counter any appeal emanating from the powerful symbolism of Buddhist kingship in Bangkok. For

> the disappearance of the Lao monarch . . . has also led to a blurring of the symbolism of the Thai monarchy in Laos. Hence all over Laos we find images of Thai royalty where once we would have found images of Lao royalty, and it suggests that at least in some respects the Lao have been drawn into the orbit of the Thai realm. (Evans 1998: 179)

To counter the appeal of Thai royalty in the absence of Lao royalty, the Lao PDR has fought a losing battle to restrict the impact of Thai media, a media that is saturated with allusions to Thai royalty.[41] Nonetheless in its efforts to contain the indirect political effects of continuous exposure to Thai culture through television and frequent border-crossings made possible by the construction in 1994 of a new "friendship bridge" between the two countries, the Lao PDR has not completely given up on its efforts to create a perspective in which

> Thailand appears as an anti-model, the core of which is viewed as being contaminated by the ill-effects of capitalism. Laos, by contrast, tries to define itself as a virtuous nation by applying a moral discourse; in other words, by claiming an authenticity lost by Thailand. . . . It is well-known that the influence of the Thai media is a matter of great concern for the Lao authorities . . . some officials have accused the media of playing a significant role in the rise of consumerism, or worse, of crime in Laos. (Pholsena 2006: 52)

Thus the state's promulgation of the Kaysone cult needs to be weighed in this context as: (1) a functional replacement for the national symbolism formerly associated with Lao Buddhist kingship and (2) as an antidote to the possible appeal of Thai Buddhist kingship. The Lao PDR's efforts to promote the cult of Kaysone while at the same time offering a rebuddhafication of national public discourse is a strategy aimed at simultaneously affirming Buddhist symbolism and providing an alternative patriotic symbolism for its non-Buddhist citizens.

Rebuddhafication and Its Ramifications

Rebuddhafication was increasingly deployed by Lao PDR government officials in the 1990s. As early as Kaysone's Seventh Resolution in 1979, a softening in the government's posture towards public expressions of Buddhist ritual was observable.

Stuart-Fox (1996: 84–85) suggests that this softening in relation to Buddhism and other aspects of traditional Lao culture, including dress and language, was due to the fact that the Pathet Lao political leadership was still seeking ways to deepen its legitimacy among the people, particularly in the wake of economic difficulties: "In stressing the need for Laos to build its own particular form of socialism, some Lao were beginning to argue that this had to take into consideration the historical reality of the Lao cultural identity and that it could not be divorced from Theravada Buddhism." Thus an improvement in the economic conditions of the 1980s (due to the implementation of macroeconomic reforms) was accompanied by an easing in the government's attitude towards religion in general.

> By the mid-1980s an efflorescence of Lao Buddhism had begun. Growing prosperity in the towns as a result of economic reforms begun in 1979 and accelerated after 1986, saw money flow towards the *vats* for their repair and for the building of Buddhist monuments, all highly visible forms of merit-making. . . . The revival of Buddhism has been attributed largely to these macro-economic reforms. But I would also like to suggest that an accumulating existential crisis within the Lao leadership contributed to it as well, for as Gellner remarks: "Marxism has nothing to say to personal tragedy and bereavement." (Evans 1998: 63)

Evans, I think, is quite right, especially when the evidence of Kaysone Phomvihane's own death and funeral proceedings in 1992 are considered.

In 1989 the first public statements since the 1975 revolution about the *sangha*, including rules for joining and leaving, were unveiled at an official convention held under the auspices of the United Lao Buddhist Association (ULBA) in Vientiane. At that meeting the ULBA continued to assert its hegemonic role in supervising the *sangha* by vowing to "take the religion forward along the road of socialism under the leadership of the party" (cited in Evans 1998: 65).[42] However, the convention also

> established the right of young men to enter the *vats* so long as they get permission from the local persons concerned; and before leaving the Sangha they must have a good reason and carry it out according to the customs of Buddhism; the Lao United Buddhist Association does not restrict the beliefs of the people . . . but it reserves the right to decide on all problems relating to the work of the Sangha. . . . It reiterated that the organization was opposed to "superstitious" beliefs in spirits and *thevadas* [Pali: *devatas*—deities], and opposed all forms of intoxication and gambling. (Ibid.)

The policies reflect a delicate balance that the party was trying to sustain. While it affirmed that personal religious motivations for joining the *sangha* would be respected, it also declared that "local persons concerned" must also give consent. This ambiguity obviously was designed to empower lower-level party members to determine who might or might not join the *sangha*. The convention's statement also reasserts the party's rights (through its ULBA front) to control the institutionalized *sangha* administratively at every level. That is, the *sangha*'s raison d'etre would remain a matter of how it might serve the higher aims of the socialist state.

While the statement asserts that the ULBA "does not restrict the beliefs of the people," it directly contradicts this assertion by subsequently reiterating its condemnation of "superstitious" beliefs in spirits and deities. This double-speak was predicated on a distinction made between "religion" (Buddhism) on the one hand and "superstition" (spirit cults) on the other.

I have already argued that this distinction between religion and superstition was, in all likelihood, based on political considerations. In returning to the issue briefly once more, I want to highlight the fact that the term "belief" is used consistently in depicting the nature of religion in this most recent Lao context. "Belief," of course, is a thoroughly Western, more specifically Judeo-Christian-Muslim, manner of identifying the essence of religion. All three of these religious traditions are certainly "creedal" in orientation and theological substance. And it is absolutely this very specific sense of being religious, that is, "believing," that Marx and Lenin had in mind when they articulated their critiques regarding the deleterious "otherworldly" effect of religion that prevents the masses from tending to this-worldly problems. In these instances of Western religion, belief very surely connotes faith in a quintessential otherworldly or transcendent power (Christ, Yahweh, or Allah) that enters from the outside into human history. From a Lao Marxist intellectual perspective, understanding religion as a matter of belief provides a convenient way to separate Buddhism from "otherworldly" spirit cults, or "rational religion" from "superstitious *belief*." A rationalized or "scientific" form of "modern Buddhism," the kind that the party sought to foster, does not posit the necessity of a powerful, transcendent, creator type of supernatural being or god. Thus this kind of Buddhism does not direct the people's attention away from this world to another, nor does it compete with the absolute loyalty to the state that the party demands. Instead, Buddhism can be reduced to a complementary practical methodology that shares similar concerns with the state: the eradication of suffering and the promotion of material well-being.

Spirit cults, on the other hand, imply an alternative ontology of power. They command respect and loyalty. In addition to being a product of "unscientific" irrationality, indicative of "backward" cultural dispositions derived from hierarchical feudal society, spirit cults are competitors with the state because of the supernatural power attributed to them, which is "believed in," and furthermore, because they demand a recognition of and a loyalty to other socioeconomic phenomena such as family, village, *muang*, kingdom, and so forth, whose power they symbolize. Today spirit cults remain officially proscribed, but official opposition is more rhetorical than a policy strictly enforced.

With increasing social, economic, and political stability in the late 1980s, not only did Buddhism begin to flourish once again, but the government began to feel confident enough so that it began to release thousands of political prisoners from "seminar," though it was not until Kaysone's death in 1992 that some of those still languishing in prison were finally released. By 1989 the last Vietnamese combat troops were also sent home.[43] In addition, "clearly a more outward-oriented strategy had been in the wind for several years. No doubt with an eye to encouraging international investor confidence in the 'rule of law'" (Evans 2002b: 199).

These events and the new economic "outward-oriented strategy" were well timed, for the events of 1989 that reverberated throughout the "socialist world" demanded a new approach to the country's continuing development. With the fall of the Soviet Union and the transformation of its "eastern block," Laos lost more than 60 percent of its external assistance and a substantial amount of its military aid, though it continues to count on Vietnam for military assistance should the need arise. Like China, North Korea, Vietnam, and Cuba, the socialist regime in Laos did not fall to democratic forces in 1989. But like China and Vietnam, it formulated innovative strategies to transform its economy. By 1991 the government of Laos finally put a formal constitution in place that guaranteed property ownership and regulated international business transactions. This put the Lao PDR in a legal position to attract investments from abroad to infuse the country with much-needed capital. Moreover, Article 9 of the new constitution states:

> The state respects and protects all lawful activities of the Buddhists and of other religious followers, [and] mobilizes and encourages the Buddhist monks and novices as well as the priests of other religions to participate in activities which are beneficial to the country and people. All acts of creating division of religions and classes of people are prohibited.

The careful wording of Article 9, by specifically mentioning Buddhists, recognizes implicitly the special standing of Buddhism in Laos. Yet it also recognizes "other religious followers" as well. But a disposition to bend Buddhism to the will of the state is still implied in restricting religion to "activities which are beneficial to the country." Moreover, it would seem that the statement precluding "division of religions and classes" is a reference to further precluding of the presence of the Thammayut Nikay. Nonetheless, Article 9 legally recognizes institutionalized religion.

In 1992 Laos experienced another watershed event: the death and funeral of Kaysone Phomvihane. Earlier I noted Evans's assessment that one of the weaknesses of Marxism as a practical ideology is that it provides no appeasement for personal existential crises. Kaysone's seventeen years as a political strongman began with a policy of seriously discouraging the practice of Buddhism. Yet remarkably,

> when Kaysone Phomvihane died full Buddhist rites were also accorded to him. Further evidence of this existential crisis among the leadership is revealed by the fact that as Kaysone's health began to fail him he turned increasingly to traditional remedies, which included visiting famous and mystically powerful monks in search of traditional medicines and also religious protection through prayers and amulets. (Evans 1998: 64)

Moreover, Kaysone's funeral was "a significant marker replete with chanting Buddhist monks wherein Nouhak [his longtime associate and successor] even ended the ceremony with 'Comrade, we wish your soul may reach paradise and the state of bliss'" (Evans 2002: 208).

The substance of Nouhak's wish is worth considering closely. First, it contains one of the central contradictions of Lao Buddhism: the belief in a spirit or soul (*khwan*). Philosophically, one of the distinctive markers of Buddhist thought, both in Theravada and Mahayana recensions, is *anatta*, or "without self." *Anatta* is what distinguishes a Buddhist from a Hindu or from practitioners of all other "major" religions. Belief in or attachment to the idea of self or soul is what Buddhists identify as the root cause of suffering (*dukkha*). All beings and all phenomena are regarded as transitory, inherently compounded or conditioned, subject to unceasing uprising and passing away, with no permanent essence transmigrating from moment to moment, or from lifetime to lifetime. That the Lao have continuously held on to the notions of *khwan* and *phi* (soul and spirit), despite more than six centuries of being nominally a Buddhist people, is a remarkable testimony to the persistence of the ontology of the religious substratum, and even more so in this specific instance, given that it relates to the progenitor of official communist party policies that denounced consistently the existence of spirit cults as "backward," "pernicious," and "superstitious." Moreover, Nouhak's reference to an otherworldly "paradise and state of bliss," ostensibly a reference to *nibbana*, betrays, perhaps, the reality of private aspirations of intensely political men, the same men who repeatedly scoffed at these very notions in their public pronouncements. Death often puts life into perspective, even for communist hardliners.

The death and funeral of Kaysone set into motion what Evans has called rebuddhafication of the state's public discourse on national identity. As I have noted, rebuddhafication is not the only public discourse that remains in play, for the party also launched a public cult of Kaysone. It also advertised the nation's ethnic diversity as an exotic feature of attraction when it decided, in the mid-1990s, to enter the international tourism market. But with the rebuddhafication of public discourse, the state began to insert itself literally in the place of the former kings within a number of notable public rites. This will be quite apparent in Chapter 4, when I discuss how the national New Year's rites in Luang Phrabang are currently orchestrated.

The clearest instance of rebuddhafication involves how the That Luang, the grand stupa of Vientiane (see Plate 3), became the new national symbol following the death of Kaysone, replacing the hammer and sickle as the new national insignia. (It is also the signature emblem appearing in the corner of the screen for Lao national television.) A massive annual state-sponsored ritual commemorating the nation is now held each year in November at the That Luang. Insofar as auxiliary rites are held simultaneously at many other stupas throughout the country, it is clear that conceptions of the old centripetal and centrifugal ritual flows of power pulsating throughout a mandala formation have been reasserted once again. Evans refers to the symbolism of the That Luang as "the nation's stillpoint" (1998: 42) in a time of rapid social change and "the central symbol through which the nation remembers itself" (1998: 41). Patrice Ladwig has been even more specific; he refers to the That Luang as "a modern Mount Meru in a modern capital" (2000: 76). Moreover, he says (2000: 82) explicitly that "the cosmic polity associated with the "mandala" or *muang* structure is still very much alive, when we look at the centralized nature of the festival in honor of the *that*: the *Thaat Luang* in Vientiane is the navel in Laos's sacred topography and the smaller stupas in the provinces are linked to the main festival."

While the That Luang has become a new national symbol and the annual national New Year rites in Luang Phrabang are ritual examples of the process that Evans has termed rebuddhafication, the *sangha* is also increasingly identified once again as the embodiment of traditional Lao culture. This reassertion of the *sangha*'s identity is occurring at a time when Laos is opening up to the outside world, and worries have grown again about the continuing influence of modern Thai culture and the transformative cultural influence of the West that is also eroding traditional Lao cultural values. "Thus, at [a] June 1995 conference, Buddhism and the monkhood were being championed as the 'leaders of cultural pride,' and the conference was told that monks are traditionally the keepers of knowledge and culture" (Evans 1998: 67).

Although the government has clearly fostered a process of inserting Buddhism into its national public discourse, the ramifications of this decision are many and significant. In the first instance, two parallel tendencies characterizing contemporary Buddhism in Laos are surfacing that partly contradict each other. One is the officially sanctioned rebuddhafication process that Evans has identified. But the second is a process that reflects a fundamental decrease in knowledge about Buddhism among the population in general and a lessening of ritual involvement as well. In contemporary Luang Phrabang, where I carried out research primarily among Buddhist novices and monks, novices from the countryside arrive in town with a basic knowledge of Buddhism and deepen their understanding while receiving high school educations at the monastic school. But in Luang Phrabang, while they live in a cultural context in which symbols of Buddhism are vigorously promoted by the government and UNESCO, the population of the city itself is becoming increasingly Westernized, due to the intensity with which tourism and the economy related to it are advancing. Indeed, the promotion of Buddhism is very much a part of the Lao PDR tourism strategy.[44] While public national discourse may be marked currently by a rebuddhafication process, it does not follow that urban or globalizing segments of the population are experiencing a renaissance of Buddhist piety.

Another ramification of the increased presence of Buddhism in the state's national public discourse is that it raises questions about the state's intentions for its ethnic minority populations. To what extent does the rebuddhafication process alienate the non-Buddhist ethnic minorities of Laos? Does it signal an implicit plan to emulate what the Thai government has attempted in the twentieth century: to bring the ethnic minorities within the religious and cultural orbit of the nation through conversion to Buddhism? For decades the government of Laos has encouraged many of the ethnic minority people to relocate from their highland villages to the towns of the Mekong River Valley basin into order to better integrate them into the national political economy and to wean them away from slash-and-burn agriculture. The question is whether the rebuddhafication process signals a concomitant attempt to assimilate ethnic minorities into the dominant Lao Loum Buddhist culture. The statistics that I generated in my research (discussed in Chapter 4) indicate that a significant number of Buddhist novices in Luang Phrabang are now of Lao Theung and Lao Sung origins (30 percent combined). Whether there is currently a deliberate effort to buddhacize these populations, it is clear that some assimilation is currently taking place.

Pholsena's book on the contemporary political culture of Laos is an interesting follow-up to Evans's 1998 study. Her central focus is on the manner in which the ethnic minorities are being marginalized in the current political context. This is why Pholsena takes Evans to task in the opening pages of her study.

What constitutes the major theme of his [Evans's] book also constitutes the main weakness of his argument: although he never makes it explicit, his analysis is obviously centered on culture, history and society from the perspective of the ethnic Lao majority. Likewise, the geographic focus of his study is revealing: his case studies are drawn from urban or semi-urban areas; more precisely, from Vientiane and Luang Prabang, both towns with predominantly ethnic Lao populations.... [T]here is no mention of the minorities' feelings regarding the actions of the state or how they make sense of their worlds and interpret the nationalist discourse. (2006: 12)

Regardless of whether her criticism of Evans is altogether fair, Pholsena skillfully manages a thoroughgoing analysis of rebuddhafication. She demonstrates that the state's new understanding of Buddhism is not simply a throwback to the old mandala paradigm, nor is it a recasting of the old 1950s nationalist discourse; nor, finally, is it simply a restatement of the old maxim that Buddhist practice is allowed as long as it serves the interest of the socialist state.

Pholsena begins by noting that

to a certain extent the revival of Buddhism, both at the popular and institutional levels, reflects a remarkable evolution in the government's promotion of national identity in post-socialist Laos. Yet, the phenomenon can be interpreted in several ways: as a step backward in the process of building a modern state or, on the contrary, as the regime's attempt to legitimate its rule, or again as a sign of autonomy from the Western model of nation-state. (2006: 66)

No doubt some ethnic minorities would regard it as a step backwards and some Lao Loum as a necessary legitimation. And there is no doubt, given the landslide of globalization occurring in Vientiane and Luang Phrabang, that some in government see it as a sign of autonomy from Western models.

However the revivified Buddhist presence in public is regarded, it is also clear that in both government and nongovernment circles, the significance of Buddhism within Laotian society is being reconsidered. Pholsena discusses two pertinent examples. In the first instance, she notes how

the Department of Religion of the LFNC [the government's Lao Front for National Construction] published an intriguing article on Buddhism in the *Lao Sang Sat*, the LFNC's official magazine, in 1998. The text differed from official rhetoric as the authors did not try to demonstrate the common ground between the religion and socialist ideals; rather, they stressed the spiritual force of religion in general, and of Buddhism in particular. The article went on to emphasize the role of Buddhism in various areas, such as education and the arts. More surprisingly, it also pointed out the political role of Buddhist monks in the form of kings' advisers, whose kingdoms furthermore were to be ruled by Buddhist principles and commandments. The conclusion is the most innovative as it recognizes that progress in science and technology will never undermine religion. On the contrary, society will always need spiritual support and moral values, no matter how developed it is. (2006: 67)

From this line of thinking it is clear that for some in positions of political authority, religion, Buddhism in particular, is not just accorded a constructive historical role in the nation's past, nor is it seen simply in utilitarian terms as an appendage to the higher aims of the state. It is also no longer regarded as a mode of thought in need of scientific or rationale rehabilitation. Rather, its functions (providing spiritual solace and moral direction) are overtly affirmed, independent of any other pragmatic legitimating political or economic functions. Discernable in this line of thought is a trajectory containing the liberation of religion from its former reductions and subordinations. We can only wonder whether the same line might eventually be extended to practitioners of the spirit cults. This seems doubtful.

Pholsena then presents the substance of a second article, this one published in the French language newspaper *La Renovator* (May 18, 2000), in which the author basically argues for the complementarity of Buddhism and Marxism. I quote from Pholsena's rendering extensively because it recapitulates so many points that I commonly heard in discussion with Buddhist monks and laity in Luang Phrabang. It is a perspective heard from people who simultaneously support the government (and Marxism) and are staunch Buddhists. In this, it is very much a normative and conservative contemporary Lao Loum perspective, one that is concerned not only with communist party excesses of the past, but one also worried about a wholesale plunge into capitalism. It is a quintessential defense of Buddhism within a changing socialist society.

To begin with Khamphao criticizes both the old regime and the Pathet Lao, the former for corrupting Buddhism and latter for misunderstanding it, he then suggests that religion has now been cleansed of its superstitious aspects while the Party has recognized its previous mistakes. Accordingly, in its newly purified form and fully rehabilitated, Buddhism now enjoys an even greater popularity than in the past.

Khamphao then explains that Buddhism, like Marxism, has no ambitions but to change society for the better; neither of them pretends to provide holistic doctrines, which are anyway "useless discourses"; they are not "ideologies"; both simply offer men and women a "recipe" for happiness. The only difference between religion and Marxism, he argues, is merely a question of scale. "Both of them are extremely practical and put practice above everything," Khamphao asserts, no matter what the petty arguments, only the end matters; the Marxists prefer calling this result "happiness" and the Buddhists, "end of suffering." Moreover, Buddhist people, he says, are better able to live in a socialist society because a Buddhist person, some may argue, is not a selfish individual in quest of his/her own salvations, but on the contrary, a person who is more able to feel compassion for others.

The author goes on to argue that Buddhism, like Marxism, promotes socioeconomic development. In doing so, he refutes the commonly held view that the Buddhist concept of renunciation is contradictory to the idea of material well-being. Poverty has been condemned by the Buddha, he writes, as a cause of immorality and crimes. Consequently, to eliminate these negative phenomena, the economic conditions of the population first must be improved. Of course, development must not follow market logic, as that will produce the reverse effect: creating a vicious cycle of needs and desires leading to endless suffering. Accordingly, both Buddhism and Marxism reject the capitalist system that enslaves men and women. Therefore Khamphao happily concludes: ". . . there is nothing surprising in the fact that Buddhism and Marxism get along with each other very well in Laos. It is not so much a political deal as a very natural alliance. Not only do they not oppose each other (for they belong to different parts of human life) but they are complementary, and in some ways they reinforce each other." (Pholsena 2006: 70–72).

The substance of this stance is familiar. Indeed, it is similar to the way senior Buddhist monks at Luang Phrabang's prestigious *vats* continue to articulate the place of Buddhism in contemporary Laos. It represents a skilled practice in acknowledging the legitimacy of Marxist socialism in contemporary Laos while negotiating a presence for Buddhism under the continued hegemonic authority of the state. At the same time it critiques the past distortions of Buddhism by party enthusiasts.

Over and against these two newer views of Buddhism, I take note of yet another, this one reflective of conversations occurring among the senior monks of Luang Phrabang. The view articulated in the *La Revonator* is almost a restatement of the village/scholastic monk side of the old *granthadhura/vipassanadhura* or *gamavasi/ arannavasi* monastic debate that has frequently surfaced throughout Theravada history, a side that is currently advanced by one perspective in the monastic conversation now taking place in Luang Phrabang. This is the socially oriented perspective of the monastic vocation. But another segment of monks take a much more individualistic or personal view of the practice of Buddhism. For them, and they also represent a younger contingent within the *sangha*, meditation is the dimension of Buddhist practice that needs more emphasis in the monastic routine on a daily basis. Social service and the ritual orientation of the monk can even become a distraction from what they regard as the primary aim of Buddhist practice. Monks of this perspective conceive of religion as a dimension of the human experience that is separate from society and culture. In this connection one highly respected and important monk in Luang Phrabang told me: "The most important task confronting the *sangha* today is to disentangle Buddhism from culture." He went on to explain that the government does not have to fear "true Buddhism," because Buddhism is not primarily concerned with society and politics. The practice of Buddhism, he argued, exists in a separate domain of human existence. When I asked him about the moral implications of the Buddha's teachings for society-at-large, he responded by saying: "One doesn't need to be political in order to be moral." At the same time, monks of this persuasion are adamantly against the spirit cults. They see as one of their main tasks an education of Buddhist laity and novices that helps to eliminate these "superstitious" practices that "have invaded the teachings of the Buddha." I would note that comparatively these monks are more highly educated individuals, some having now gained an international exposure. It is clear that they are influenced by other Buddhist monks, from Burma, urban Malaysia, Singapore, and Thailand. They regard themselves as leading a new generation of monks away from the sociopolitical and cultural orientation of Buddhism that has dominated the *sangha* in virtually every epoch of the Lao past.

Ironically, however, the posture of this group of monks is also the by-product of emergent political conditions in Laos. Before the 1990s process of rebuddhafication, party members usually labeled this perspective "parasitic." That is no longer the case. There is now space in Laos for monks to claim an apolitical or politically irrelevant posture by emphasizing an individualistic spiritual quest. I think it is no coincidence that a similar form of Buddhist understanding has also emerged in Burma. In a public context in which Buddhism is accorded great respect, but a public context in which politics is dominated by only one political party, an apolitical and meditation-oriented posture can be tolerated by the state. It is a posture to be respected because it is unabashedly Buddhist, and it is tolerated because it does not represent any political threat to the one-party state. Moreover, inasmuch as it contributes to the image of Buddhism that a tourist-seeking government wants to project, it can even be regarded as an asset. It serves the purpose of "authenticity." It is certainly a profile of Buddhism that many Westerners, with their Western assumptions about religion in place, find congenial.

Conclusion

The ascendant position of Buddhism within the public space of contemporary Laos, however its profile is construed by various Buddhist persuasions, is not entirely an unproblematic phenomenon for the country as a whole. Pholsena notes:

the secular promotion of Buddhism by the government is . . . rooted in a great dilemma: a third of the population is, according to official data, non-Buddhist. . . . [A]lthough Buddhism is no longer the state religion, the party unambiguously commands ethnic groups to abandon their "backward practices," that is, their "animist" rituals which "have bad impacts on solidarity, productivity and life of the diverse ethnic groups as well as the nation" [quote from Lao Peoples Revolutionary Party's Central Committee in 1992]. . . . What we have therefore is the challenge of recognition of minority groups in Laos, on the one hand, and the claim to authenticity in the process of nation-differentiation, on the other. The state has yet to find an answer that would give justice to both demands. (2006: 72)

The legitimate political and economic hopes of the ethnic minorities, despite the fact that much of the Pathet's Lao's revolutionary support historically derived from them, have yet to be addressed effectively. The current bonanza derived from the spectacular growth of tourism has yielded little benefit for them, but instead has been capitalized upon mostly by the Buddhist Lao Loum. Thus, the rebuddhafication of public national discourse cannot sit comfortably with the leaders of the ethnic minorities. Indeed, some informed observers of contemporary Laos assert that

the exclusivity of the party had an effect similar to the exclusivity of ethnic Lao chauvinism, for it effectively denied political participation to a substantial portion of the population. No integration occurred. . . . [B]oth aid and investment in the Lao PDR, as in the Kingdom of Laos, is overwhelmingly concentrated in Lao Loum areas. The minorities have little to show as yet for supporting the revolution. (Stuart-Fox 2002: 20–21)

The Lao PDR, despite the continued allure of the *phu nyai* politics of patronage, recognizes the need to develop the economy by appealing for more international investment and assistance. To that extent it has been somewhat successful by adjusting its national discourse.

As the country progressively opens itself up to the market economy and to regional and international tourism, anti-capitalist and anti-Western imperialist rhetoric is no longer appropriate for galvanizing the population behind the leadership. The discourse of struggle is being displaced by a discourse of lack. The regime now calls for modernity . . . [though] the newly reformulated nationalist discourse is itself unstable and still in the process of development. (Pholsena 2006: 218–219)

Given such "instability" as Laos continues to ponder its national identity, and given how it is imponderable to predict how ethnic minorities will react if more and more gain an education and enter into the mainstream of the nation's political economy (both of which seem to be state priorities), it is difficult to know exactly how Buddhism will figure as a component in future national public discourse. Years ago, before rebuddhafication and the radical restructuring into a relatively open economy, Evans offered the following theoretical principle, one fully congruent with a guiding thesis of this study.

It is clear that major religions can be "manipulated" to promote either capitalist or socialist development. Buddhism in Laos has been interpreted in a way that serves the secular aims of the socialist government, while in Thailand it is used to legitimate a capitalist state. It would be difficult to argue that Buddhism is more predisposed to one form of social organization than another. *In fact, it is most plausible to argue that social, economic and political contexts provide the basic framework in which either reformist or reactionary interpretations of [religion] will be elaborated.* (1990: 207; emphasis mine)

While Pholsena's and Evans's views are helpful in ruminating about the current and future spaces allotted to Buddhism in the Lao PDR, it seems to me that another more basic force is still at work in Laos—the cult of the *phi.* It may be that the persistent forces of the *phi* cult are what actually lie behind the re-emergence of what Evans has called rebuddhafication. What the recent history of religions in Laos seems to suggest is that "politics of the authoritarian kind can coerce religious institutions" (Stuart-Fox, private communication), but in the end, when coercion abates, bedrock principles of religious culture resurface. Stuart-Fox observes (private communication): "Lao in the PDR (and this includes Party members) have never stopped believing [in] the reality of the *phi* world, or the benefits of making merit. It is this persistence that made rebuddhafication possible, and that needs explaining."[45]

What we might also add to Stuart-Fox's perceptive comments is that the cult of Kaysone, the other dimension of publicly orchestrated cultic behavior endorsed by officials of the Lao PDR since the 1990s, can also be understood as a transformation and resurgence of the cult of *phi.* It is the spirit of Kaysone that the state has chosen as its symbol, and the *events* it celebrates are clearly indexed in the Vientiane museum erected in his memory that serves simultaneously as a museum of the revolution and the founding of the state. In some ways we can understand the cult of Kaysone as an attempt to supplant or to supercede the cult of the Buddha as it has been traditionally celebrated in the form of Phra Bang image and its association with Lao kingship. At least, this seems to be the categorical explanation for how the Kaysone cult is read by many in Laos.

CHAPTER 4

Commodities of the Place

Ritual Expressions and the Marketing
of Religious Culture

The spectacular growth of the international tourist industry in contemporary Laos, especially in Luang Phrabang, has been almost as remarkable as the persistence of its spirit cults. If there is any place in Asia that represents the process of globalization, to employ that now over-worn concept, it would be Luang Phrabang. Contemporary Luang Phrabang dramatizes a conflict that many other communities in Asia are experiencing: it has been chosen by the West (in this case UNESCO), in collusion with an impoverished "capital-hungry" government, the Lao PDR, to represent and to market an "authentic Asia." Within one short decade Luang Phrabang has been transformed from a sleepy, small (population about 30,000), neglected backwater town with some recently restored and architecturally unique Buddhist temples, to being one of the hottest attractions on the Asian tourist circuit for Westerners. In 2006 the number of tourists visiting Laos topped one million, about double the number visiting Sri Lanka. In 2007 the number was 1.4 million. Between 300,000 and 400,000 visited Luang Phrabang. Why?

First, because Laos is an exceedingly beautiful country topographically, owing to its mountains, valleys, and rivers, it has been marketed as a destination for "ecotourists." Second, two decades of isolation from the outside world spawns curiosity, and it is common to hear tourists say that they wanted to come to Laos before it changes too much. But I think these two factors may be less important draws than a third. My unsystematic attempt to ascertain the reasons tourists are coming suggests it is a combination of its Buddhist culture and its mixed ethnic population, amidst a relatively "unspoiled" or nonurbanized social context. Finally, Luang Phrabang seems to epitomize the values of "boutique tourism," a search for "a tourism of scale" that promises a cultural experience different from the tourist "mega-sites" in South and Southeast Asia such as Nepal, Bali, Angkor, the beaches and islands of southern Thailand, and so forth. As Trankell (1999: 200) says: "Louang Prabang is promoted on the tourist market as a place of romanticism and royal mystique."

As early as 1979 there was one inchoate plan for marketing Buddhism and Lao culture for international tourist consumption. Almost thirty years ago "Kaysone Phomvihane, Prime Minister and Secretary-General of the LPRP, referred only once to the 'monks of the Buddhist clergy' in his 82 page report on the state of the LPDR from 1975 to 1978, and mentioned the need to 'restore . . . famous pagodas' only with reference to tourism" (Lafont 1982: 159). But the government's conscious attempts to commodify the culture of Laos began in earnest only in the early 1990s.

> The gradual opening up of Laos from the mid-1980s onwards demanded the creation of tourist displays, sites and activities [that] conformed to the expectations of the international tourist industry. This inevitably meant that the Lao had to reach back into the cultural past and revive it, albeit selectively, because so much of that traditional past was permeated by the old regime, the so-called *sakdina* system. Information has had to be produced for tourist consumption and for this, old regime books and pamphlets have been cannibalized, taking care to excise wherever possible references to the monarchy or any positive references to the RLG. (Evans 1998: 130)

Laos has now adopted an aggressive tourism policy that goes beyond simply marketing its ancient ruins. Luang Prabang has, for example, been registered as a UNESCO World Heritage Site.

> Partly influenced by assistance and advice from the Tourism Authority of Thailand, they [the Lao PDR] now also proclaim French-style architecture from colonial times as evidence of the nation's rich culture. They even extol its multi-ethnicity, an issue over which the government has been deliberating for some time, by proclaiming Laos to be "a treasure house of exotic ethnic cultures." (Hayashi 2003: 351)

In this chapter I present my reflections based on seven months of fieldwork in Luang Phrabang between June 2006 and June 2007. My discussion, which focuses on the Buddhist novices of Luang Phrabang and public ritual expressions within the context of two of the most important ceremonial occasions of the calendar year (Boun Phravet and Pi Mai) has been framed by my overarching concern to determine how Lao religious culture is responding to changes in its social and political economy.

Contemporary Luang Prabang

Luang Prabang is auspiciously sited. It is built on a narrow kilometer-long peninsula dominated by a picturesque hill (Phou Si). At the end of the peninsula is the scenic confluence of the rivers Mekong and Khan. Verdant, forest-covered mountains can be seen in every direction (except in the "season of smoke" during March and April when slash-and-burn agriculture commences). Nature has been kind to this place.

During the period of French intervention, nineteenth- and early twentieth-century European and "hybrid European-Laotian architecture [were] introduced to Luang Prabang. However, the original town plan was retained and is still apparent today" (UNESCO 2004: 23). Indeed, Luang Phrabang is regarded as one of the best-preserved cities in Southeast Asia. It is essentially a conglomeration of *ban*, each with its own temple at the core, and many known specifically for the handicrafts that they produced or the vocations that their residents specialized in. Xieng Thong (at the tip of the peninsula), for example, was known for its puppetry, and other *ban* in Luang Phrabang for silversmithing, woodcarving, blacksmithing, papermaking, weaving, and embroidery. (Basketry was an occupation followed by the Lao Theung Khmu who lived in hillside villages surrounding Luang Phrabang proper.) Luang Phrabang articulates an ancient settlement pattern "visible in the archaeological ruins of many important Tai cities such as Sri Satchanalai, Kaphaeng Phet and Chiang Saen" (UNESCO 2004: 17), but it is the only contemporary Southeast Asian city in which this settlement pattern has not been layered over entirely by modernity. "Luang Prabang's Buddhist temples are known throughout Southeast Asia for their distinctive style: tiered roofs and pillared porticos, embellished with ornamentation of the highest quality, including wood carvings, stucco moulding, dry fresco wall painting, lacquer work, and glass mosaic work" [see Plates 5 through 8 for glass mosaics and Photo 4.1 for painted pillars] (UNESCO 2004: 24). Indeed, the aesthetic beauty of its temples remains, in my view, the town's most endearing and enduring attraction.

As the Lao PDR opened itself up to the world beyond its former socialist partners in the early 1990s, its disposition towards Buddhism shifted markedly to a more accommodating and more politically and economically strategic stance. This shift occurred when the government began to ponder issues of "heritage management." In so doing, the government fostered relationships with international institutions and donor countries in an effort to explore the possibility of creating a tourism industry to benefit its stultified economy.

Two years after Prime Minister Phomvihane Kaysone's death and his remarkable funeral in 1992, the Lao PDR Ministry of Information and Culture, with en-

Photo 4.1 Painted pillar on front verandah of Wai Mai, Luang Phrabang

couragement from the French government, hired a French architectural company to assess the quality and scope of the historic buildings in Luang Phrabang. As a consequence the town's thirty-three *vat*s and eleven of its secular buildings were designated as "heritage buildings." The government announced that Luang Phrabang would be regarded henceforth as a "national heritage site." "The building inventory was also used as the basis for determining heritage protection zones and formed part of the supporting documentation to UNESCO for world heritage listing" (2004: 40). In 1995 Luang Phrabang was added to UNESCO's list of World Heritage Sites and officially cited for its "outstanding universal value, representing the harmonious relationship between the built and natural environment, and for the successful fusion of traditional Lao architecture and urban structure with those of the nineteenth and twentieth century French style" (2004: 42).

A year later La Maison du Patrimoine (Heritage House) was set up by the Luang Phrabang Provincial Department of Information with support provided by
the French Ministry of Foreign Affairs, the European Union, and the UNESCO
World Heritage Centre. Under the supervision of La Maison du Patrimoine, "no
monuments may be destroyed and no restorations undertaken that do not conform to original architectural specifications" (2004: 43). In this manner Luang
Phrabang's preservation was initiated with an emphasis on conserving its material
culture.

In addition, a related UNESCO project, called "Cultural Survival in Luang Prabang," was launched to rekindle traditional temple arts and building crafts within
the monastic *sangha*: "Monks, novices and local artisans are participating in this
project which concentrates on skills training in order to ensure the survival and
continued social and economic relevance of the traditional system of fine arts in
Luang Prabang" (2004: 46). Since its inception in 2000 at Vat Xieng Muang Vajiramangalaram (see Photo 4.2), this project, initiated by UNESCO, the Department
of Information and Culture of Luang Phrabang Province, and the Laotian Buddhist Sangha, and funded by the governments of Norway and New Zealand, has
been extremely successful.

It has graduated more than a hundred from its program, many of whom pro-

Photo 4.2 Vat Xieng Muang Vajiramangalaram, Luang Phrabang

ceeded to be part of restoration projects at temples not only in Luang Phrabang, but also at historic temples in outlying provinces as well. Trainees have been taught skills in traditional building techniques, lacquer sculpture, bronze casting, glass mosaic inlay work, mural painting, and woodcarving. The products produced from these newly learned skills have not only been utilized in the refurbishing of temples, but are also for sale to tourists throughout the shops and pavements of Luang Phrabang. The funding for this project ended in mid-2007.

The extensive UNESCO report published in 2004 notes that Luang Phrabang's strategy for its conservation and preservation is based on "the concept of authenticity . . . [that] may be applied to built heritage such as monasteries, palaces, houses, public monuments, and town layout; movable cultural property such as handicrafts; intangible heritage including rituals and traditional performing arts and practices; unique local practices ranging from cooking methods to medical practices to agricultural techniques" (55). It goes on to assert that "authenticity is a particularly complex concept as culture is constantly in flux and draws vitality from the ability to adapt to inevitably changing circumstances. However, while being a difficult concept to describe, cultural authenticity is recognizable and is a key defining feature for World Heritage sites" (53). Although this UNESCO report recognizes that "authenticity" is a "controversial and complex notion," it makes little effort to define authenticity in greater detail or to relate it quite specifically to the culture of Luang Phrabang, other than to cite examples about how the calendrical pattern or dates of certain rituals should not be manipulated for the benefit of the tourist "high season," or that only appropriate materials should be used in restoring old buildings (53). Rather, the report simply makes the case that one knows authenticity when one sees it in specific cases of "built heritage" and "ritual."

One question that arises, therefore, within the context of marketing Luang Phrabang has to do with who will identify this authenticity. And what is clear is that the French have played the leading role for Paris-based UNESCO in determining what is authentic in Luang Phrabang. It is only fair, then, to ask, how authentic is it for the French to be the dominant agency determining what is authentically Lao in Luang Phrabang? Moreover, to what extent would it be correct to say that in some ways, with regard to its conservation and preservation, contemporary Luang Phrabang has re-emerged, at least in terms of its imagined culture, as a new kind of French protectorate? Or to frame the question a bit more emphatically: "Has Luang Phrabang entered a period of 'recolonialization'"?[1] These issues are not unrelated to Buddhism and how it is envisaged within Luang Phrabang. Indeed, some of the harshest critics of Luang Phrabang's *samaneras* (novices) are French expatriates with decidedly Western understandings of what it means to be Buddhist.

To be fair, the 2004 UNESCO report reflects a high degree of awareness regarding the complicated impact of Luang Phrabang's designation as a World Heritage Site. It rightly emphasizes that "Luang Prabang faces the dilemma of ascertaining acceptable levels of change and determining its carrying capacity for absorbing and managing tourism. The challenge is how to avoid compromising the natural, built and cultural heritage of Luang Prabang in pursuit of the benefits of tourism" (2004: 53). Yet this very statement captures the irony of the situation now at hand in Luang Phrabang, a situation quite similar to what has occurred at UNESCO World Heritage Sites in Sri Lanka, such as Anuradhapura and Polonnaruva. Having embarked on an effort ostensibly to conserve and preserve cultural expressions of "universal value," UNESCO, unwittingly or not, has actually functioned as the key catalyst for dramatic cultural and social changes. Recent history records the reality that being deemed a World Heritage Site by UNESCO means immediately becoming a target of development by the international tourist industry. Angkor Wat in neighboring Cambodia may be the best example of this pattern. As the emerging local economy adjoining a World Heritage Site grows (the hotels, guesthouses, restaurants, bars, Internet cafes, massage parlors, travel agencies, souvenir shops, and so forth), the local culture becomes globalized. Or as soon as the World Heritage Site's "universal value" is trumpeted, it is opened up to market forces far beyond local (or UNESCO's) control. Indeed, a social and economic transformation of the given locality is set into motion[2] that has not only serious cultural side effects, but critical environmental consequences as well.[3] The changes occurring in Luang Phrabang over the past ten years due to a rampaging growth of tourism are nothing short of breathtaking in their magnitude.[4] An economic momentum has overcome so much inertia that the government and business interests now have too much at stake to slow the growth. Indeed, given the number of major construction projects currently underway in Luang Phrabang, and given predictions that the number of tourists visiting Luang Phrabang will double in the next four to six years, the pressures now facing the town will only intensify in the future. Officials at UNESCO are aware of the surging tide that they have helped create. After describing some of the social problems that have resulted from the influx of tourism (2004: 59), they state: "The Luang Prabang community must be made aware that if they choose not to follow UNESCO World Heritage guidelines for protecting the essence of the town, one of the consequences may be the delisting of Luang Prabang as a World Heritage site and the loss of Luang Prabang's attractiveness as a global tourism destination." From this ominous warning, it is clear that UNESCO not only intends to protect, but it also has the capacity to punish if it ascertains that local people and their government are unable to cope effectively with the fallout that UNESCO itself has helped to engender.

Though UNESCO is certainly well intentioned, it seems as if it is also unable to cope with the consequences of its actions. Philosophically, its rhetoric not only contains echoes of neocolonialism, but its emphases on "authenticity" and "essence" betray, unfortunately, a naivete about social and cultural historical processes. Both concepts of authenticity and essence are wedded to a primordialist view that assumes that cultures possess intrinsic qualities. If there is a blind spot in UNESCO's approach as it has pertained to Luang Phrabang, it is this: while concentrating its "protectorate" on preserving the "built heritage" and remaining at least conscious of conserving the ritual calendar, UNESCO has not anticipated the transformation of social processes that it has helped engender. Some of its efforts to improve the city physically have been somewhat ill-conceived, given the deleterious impacts these have occasioned on specific social processes.

The *Samaneras* of Luang Phrabang

The vicissitudes of the current monastic scene in Luang Phrabang are better appreciated within the city's new context as a World Heritage Site. The Buddhist monks of Luang Phrabang are primarily *samaneras* (novices), who have taken up robes following their initiation into the *sangha* by means of the *pabbaja* (temporary initiation ceremony).[5] They have vowed to uphold ten precepts: the five cardinal moral principles (*pancasila*)[6] incumbent upon all Buddhists who take refuge in the Buddha, *dhamma*, and *sangha*, and five more minor observations of restraint. While fully fledged *bhikkhus*, those monks of at least twenty years of age who have been ordained by means of the *upasampada* rite,[7] are less conspicuously seen in Luang Phrabang, *samaneras* are ubiquitous.

During the early weeks of my fieldwork in Luang Phrabang, I was uncomfortable with seeing saffron-robed *samaneras* out at Internet cafes late into the night (see Photo 4.3), sometimes handing out their custom-made business cards to bemused tourists, seeing them answering their cell phones, wearing a cigarette behind the ear, chatting with young, scantily attired European, Australian, and North American women, or trolling for tourists' attention outside of their temple compounds in the mid-afternoons after school.

Moreover, I often saw *samaneras* laboring physically in the construction of new buildings within their temple compounds or working in vegetable gardens along the banks of the Nam Khan and Mekong rivers. All of this constituted new modes of monastic behavior for me to comprehend, modes of social behavior that I had not encountered before in Sri Lanka, or anywhere else in Southeast Asia for that matter. In Sri Lanka there are certainly many monks who behave in controversial ways. Some join in public political rallies or demonstrations; some elite monks of major urban temples are driven around in expensive European luxury vehicles, while others have recently made it their business to get themselves

Photo 4.3 *Samaneras* at night in the Internet cafe, Luang Phrabang

elected to the national parliament. One has even hosted a television talk show and written a weekly column for a Sunday newspaper. Moreover, there remains throughout Sri Lanka a persistent buzz (*oppadupa*) about how overtly entrepreneurial some monks have become in promoting the business side of their temples. In other words there is now in Sri Lanka a certain type of "big-time monk" who is out to make his mark on the national political economy. These monks rationalize their involvement in mundane affairs by pointing out that it is "the heritage of a *bhikkhu*" to play a significant role in promoting the well-being of society and advancing the cause of the *sangha*.[8] Sometimes a monk of this sort is referred to sarcastically by concerned laity as "a man in robes" to indicate, sardonically, that donning monastic apparel, or even being ordained as a monk, does not necessarily constitute true monkhood. But these monks are exceptions to the norm. After more than six years of living in Sri Lanka, I cannot remember seeing monks out on the streets at night,[9] soliciting tourists for attention, especially young women, or so publicly engaged in the entanglements or distractions of popular culture.

Plate 1 Phra Bang (image of the Buddha) in New Year ritual context in front courtyard of Vat Mai, Luang Phrabang

Plate 2 That Luang, Vientiane

Plate 3 Sculpture of the revolutionaries in socialist-realist style with Lao PDR flag, in front of Kaysone Phomvihamne National Museum, Vientiane

Plate 4 Glass mosaic of a harvesting scene, exterior wall of Vat Xieng Thong, Luang Phrabang

Plate 5 Glass mosaic of a village and forest scene with animals, exterior walls of the Vat Xieng Thong, Luang Phrabang

Plate 6 Glass mosaic of a gamboling couple, exterior wall of Vat Xieng Thong, Luang Phrabang

Plate 7 Glass mosaic of musicians, exterior wall of Vat Xieng Thong, Luang Phrabang

The public deportment of monks in Sri Lanka remains a serious matter carefully monitored by the laity, and most monks, quite conscious of that fact, generally act accordingly in public.

It is not that the laity and senior clergy of Luang Phrabang are not concerned with *samanera* behavior. Novices reported that they are sometimes berated by local laity for being too boisterous or playful in the streets. Senior monks complain that there are just not enough of them to supervise all of the *samanera*s in their temples. Other senior monks told me that problems in *samanera* behavior were not endemic, but the by-product of disciplinary laxity in a few temples. The concerns expressed to me by senior monks and laity did not surprise me, as the kind of casual *samanera* behavior that I observed was something I suspected was not only new to me, but new to the senior monks and Buddhist laity of Laos as well. To some degree my discomfort was also not simply a matter of juxtaposing the more formal public deportment of monks I have regularly observed in Sri Lanka with the *samanera*s of Luang Phrabang, but it was also a consequence of the fact that thirty years ago I had written a doctoral dissertation on the *Vinayapitaka*, that portion of the Pali Tipitaka concerned with Buddhist monastic law, ethics, and social etiquette. It seemed to me at first that the young novices of Luang Phrabang were completely innocent of this basic charter of conduct for the Buddhist *sangha* that carefully details the social behavior expected of a monk.

But as the weeks and months passed, and I became personally familiar with many novices, recorded some of their life histories, or in some instances visited their villages of origins, I was able to get somewhat more comfortable with what I was observing in town. Or at least I was able to put it into a more charitable context. Moreover, I reminded myself that what I was seeing certainly validated the theoretical maxim that transformations occurring in society at large were sure to be reflected in that society's religious culture. In what follows, it will become clear that as a burgeoning tourist industry is causing major socioeconomic transitions in Luang Phrabang, its Buddhist monastic institutions are being significantly impacted as well. Indeed, they are under considerable pressure.

Yukio Hayashi has written about how the seemingly problematic behavior of young monks is regarded in the Lao villages of northeast Thailand. His comments are an excellent point of departure:

The adult villagers are not unaware of what [homosexuality, eating after noon, touching women during Songkran, etc.] goes on in the temple. Yet they seem to take the practical view that such behavior is normal for young novices. No one spouts dogma on the exemplary behavior expected of a monk. Rather they perceive the monks' role as part of the ritual apparatus for Buddhist rituals, and the novices and young monks enact this role for the villagers. In terms of

outward forms, the purity of the monks in the village must be absolute. The
ethics of the monks' behavior are never questioned as long as they maintain an
attitude of purity on the ritual stage. (Hayashi 2003: 312; brackets Hayashi's)

Tiyavanich makes a complementary observation that indicates why certain types
of "unmonastic" behavior of monks is tolerated by the laity:

> People in villages and towns saw nothing wrong with monks participating in
> boat races, throwing water at women, or playing chess because they knew the
> monks and were in fact often their relatives. Many of the monks were sons
> of villagers who had been ordained temporarily, and their lay providers were
> their parents, aunts and uncles, or acquaintances. But for outsiders—sangha
> inspectors, Christian missionaries, and Western travelers—the regional monks'
> behavior was, to say the least, questionable. (1997: 29)

I find these comments helpful in several ways. In the first place we should not forget that the novices of Luang Phrabang are all between the ages of ten and twenty.
That is, they are first and foremost teenaged Lao boys, most from very rural village
settings, and they are encountering a radically new social world for the first time.
Nothing in their previous experiences can have possibly prepared them for the dimensions of social life that they encounter in Luang Phrabang. One needs venture
only a few kilometers outside of the town of Luang Phrabang to see the stark differences that these young novices must negotiate in making the transition. Unlike
the villages and small towns where most of these *samaneras* come from, Luang
Phrabang is a venue where hundreds of thousands of relatively well-heeled Western tourists now ply its streets. It has become a veritable locus of globalization, for
reasons I have mentioned earlier. Moreover, the people of Luang Phrabang who
live in the vicinity of its thirty-three historic temples are comparatively prosperous by national Lao PDR standards, owing to the stupendous boom in the tourist
trade that they have profited from over the past ten years. For the urban folk of Luang Phrabang, motorcycles, televisions with cable service originating largely from
Thailand (and carrying not only the major Thai TV stations, but CNN, BBC, HBO,
Cinemax, and so forth), Thai popular music, Western clothing fashions, and many
other types of consumer items are now within their reach. Consequently it is not
difficult to imagine that encountering the affluence possessed by Western tourists
and the urban lifestyle of the middle-class Lao of Luang Phrabang must generate a
significant culture shock in the newly arrived teenager from rural-village Laos. *Samanera* behavior not conforming to the ancient Vinaya monastic rules should not,
then, come as a complete surprise. While the novices' behavior is not completely
overlooked, and it is quite easy to initiate some grumbling among the laity, on the

whole they seem to tolerate these young men. Perhaps there is some awareness on the laity's part that the "deviant" behavior they observe in the junior monks is at least partially a by-product of the social environment that they, themselves, have had a significant part in creating and from which they have certainly profited. More than one novice mentioned to me that in Luang Phrabang everyone seemed to be living individually for themselves, unlike the collective ethos of the village. Criticism, though muted, moves in both directions.

More to the point, however, is Hayashi's comment about primacy placed on the ritual role the novices perform. The *samaneras* have become, in addition to Luang Phrabang's aesthetically stunning temples, star tourist attractions due to their daily ritual behavior. Recently some coffee-table books, with very little in the way of insightful explanation, have been published to showcase *samanera* ritual activities in public.[10] During the early-morning *bindabath* (Pali: *pindapata*) alms rounds, it is not unusual, especially during the high season of November through February, for tourists to actually outnumber the laity who line the streets of town to offer sticky rice for the novices' and monks' begging bowls (see Photo 4.4).

Indeed, some of Luang Phrabang enterprising individuals and guesthouses sell packets of sticky rice for tourists to offer to the novices (for about kip 20,000 = $2),[11] along with a briefing on etiquette so that the occasion does not become

Photo 4.4 Enthusiastic tourists photographing *bhikkhus* and *samaneras* on morning alms rounds, Luang Phrabang

too overly wrought with inappropriate tourist behavior. There is also some worry among Luang Phrabang laity that the growing number of tourist guesthouses threatens to displace the laity near major temples so that not enough pious lay Buddhists will be left to support the daily feeding of the novices.[12] Novices report that on some days in the "low season," they are not able to collect enough rice to have a decent morning meal. In any case the *samanera*s, by virtue of *bindabath*, find themselves at the intersection of two economies: the religious economy of merit-making for the Buddhist laity on the one hand and the bourgeoning tourist economy constituted by foreigners on the other. Since they are a "hot commodity" locally, any minor indiscretions occasionally observed can easily be overlooked because of their ritual and economic importance.

But another factor makes the *samanera*s "unmonastic" social behavior difficult to comprehend at first. It has to do with dominant Western or Western-originated perceptions of the Buddhist monastic vocation. In my doctoral work my textual study of Buddhist monastic discipline had led me to a somewhat idealistic thesis, but I still believe it to be embedded in the Vinaya text itself: namely, a monk's outward behavioral social expressions should be regarded as an index of the degree to which the monk has internalized the realized truth of the Buddha's *dhamma*. This is, of course, tantamount to measuring a monk's behavior in relation to an ideal doctrinal or behavioral standard, precisely what Hayashi states is *not* what goes on among the laity in the Lao village contexts he has observed. Unknown to me at the time I was writing my dissertation, my understanding (as well as the Vinaya's idealistic formulation) was quite similar in nature to the dominant Euro–North American image of the Buddhist holy man, a consequence of considering the importance of doctrinal and soteriological formulations in canonical texts almost to the total exclusion of ritual or social orientations. The image of the Buddha that I held at that earlier time was a cross between a Platonic and Confucian gentleman, and I expected the "sons of the Buddha" to be no less. Indeed, the image of the Buddhist monk for most Westerners, one that is usually derived from a study of translated Buddhist texts only or, more likely, one that is imbibed from the plethora of simplistic apologetic writings that flood the spirituality sections of popular bookstores in the shopping malls of Western cities, is linked to the practice of meditation and consequently of serene composure, in the manner of Buddha images preserved in Buddhist art. The contemplative image of a meditative Buddhist monk, of course, stands in stark contrast to the social activities of the young Luang Phrabang *samanera* (see Photo 4.5).[13]

According to monastic officials who oversee the *samanera*s' education in Luang Phrabang, there were 878 novices (in the 2006–2007 high school academic year) in residence at the thirty-three *vat*s of the city, all aged ten to twenty. Between August and December 2006 I arranged interviews with one hundred of them, a sample of

THE FLOATING BUDDHA
ການເຝິກສະມາທິວິປັດສະນາຂອງພຣະສົງຫລວງພະບາງ

Meditation retreats of the Luang Prabang Sangha (2004-2005)
Photographs by Hans Georg Berger
LUANG PRABANG
NATIONAL MUSEUM
OPENING OCTOBER 2006

Photo 4.5 Poster advertising photographic exhibition of meditating *samaneras*, Luang Phrabang National Museum

eleven percent of Luang Phrabang's *samaneras*, or about one in nine. This is what I learned.

At the beginning of my fieldwork I noticed that many *samaneras* were reticent in giving me approval to publish their temple affiliations. I originally construed their reluctance to being so specifically identified as a holdover from earlier days in the Lao PDR when people worried about who might be looking over their shoulder. It is still the case in Luang Phrabang, for instance, that every night guesthouses have to report to the police the names and passport numbers of each guest. While conditions have relaxed in recent years, there is still the sense that "the authorities" are watching and remain firmly in control of this one-party state. But this was not the primary reason for the *samaneras*' reticence. The real reason entailed the fact that the head monks of their *vats* have absolute authority over novices if they want to exercise it, from deciding who will be admitted to deciding who, if necessary, must go. I soon came to see that some novices were concerned that any information I received from them might be used in ways that could affect their relationships to their temple's head monk. So I took no names from the novices, and I promised not to publish specific information regarding the numbers I had managed to interview from each specific *vat*. Suffice it to say that my interviewees came from twenty-two of Luang Phrabang's thirty-three *vats*. Since some were also reluctant to have me publish information about their villages of origin, since that information might also compromise their anonymity, I agreed to publish only the identity of their home provinces. The list appears below, and Map 4.1 provides a visual of this distribution.

Luang Phrabang	56	Huaphan	2
Oudomxay	18	Xiang Khuang	2
Bokeo	5	Luang Namtha	1
Phongsaly	5	Vientiane	1
Champasak	4	Khammuan	1
Xayaboury	4		

Over half of the novices come from Luang Phrabang Province, and a total of eleven out of the country's eighteen provinces are represented in the sample, including all of those provinces contiguous to Luang Phrabang. Given the size of Vientiane's population—it is the capital city and center of the country's commercial activities—I expected more novices from there. But Vientiane has its own well-developed high school for monastic students, one that serves as a fairly effective conduit for its graduates to enter the National University of Laos or one of the smaller new private educational ventures like Vientiane College or Lao American College. Moreover, the people of Vientiane see no advantage in sending their children for education in Luang Phrabang. While the historic temples of Luang Phrabang may be revered, that fact alone is not enough to sway any decision for novices to come to study in Luang Phrabang, which most people in Vientiane still view as somewhat of a backwater and certainly not as a center of education. Rather, what Luang Phrabang represents to its almost exclusively rural novices is a bridge to the wider world represented by Vientiane. In the *samanera* world, the impulse is to head *to* Vientiane and not to come *from* it.

Very few *samaneras*, and virtually none of those interviewed, come from Luang Phrabang town itself. Most are from villages in the outlying regions of the province located on Highway 13, the national trunk road connecting the country from north to south. While Luang Phrabang Province may not look extensive on a national map, it is quite so when one tries to navigate it by any available transportation. For most novices, getting to and from their native village is a major undertaking. In addition to the time required to make the journey, the expense is almost

Map 4.1 Provinces of Laos

prohibitive for most. Consequently, it is not unusual for a novice to go home only once or twice a year, even if his village is only two or three hours away by public transportation from Luang Phrabang. Novices from Bokeo, Phongsaly, Champasak, Huaphan, or Luang Namtha may not go home at all, such is the distance and cost of the journey. In any case Luang Phrabang is clearly an education magnet for those male youth who live in rural northern Laos. Once they arrive, they rarely return home except for a family emergency.

In an attempt to see if there might be any pattern as to whether it would be more likely for eldest or youngest sons to join the *sangha*, I asked each *samanera* to indicate his position within his family in relation to other siblings. I also wanted to know if any of their brothers or their fathers had been *samaneras* or monks. With regard to the oldest/youngest child issue, I could discern no pattern whatsoever: thirty-one indicated that they were the oldest male siblings, thirty-three indicated that they were the youngest, and thirty-four were either in the middle or were the only male sibling in the family. Nine reported that they had brothers who were or had been *samaneras*, and two reported that they had two brothers each of whom had also been *samaneras*. What these figures do reveal is that usually only one son from a family will become a *samanera*. With regard to whether their fathers had either been fully fledged monks or *samaneras*, thirty-three, or one-third of the group indicated that this had been so. Thirty out of the thirty-three, or more than 90 percent of these were Lao Loum, indicating some degree of customary familial *sangha* lineage among that ethnic group. I also learned that the average number of siblings in these families is 3.97, or nearly four per family, further evidence for the continued practice of early marriage among all Laotians and the high percentage rate of population growth that continues to be sustained in rural areas of Laos.

In terms of ethnicity, seventy novices identified themselves as Lao Loum, twenty as Lao Theung, and ten as Lao Sung. I was surprised at this finding. I had expected only an occasional Lao Theung, and certainly had not expected the number to be this high, nor did I have any expectations regarding Lao Sung at all. Lao Theung, and especially Lao Sung, are usually categorized as animists by most scholars or journalists who describe the religious demography of Laos. I also included a question about whether Lao Theung and Lao Sung *should* become Buddhists. This question, of course, was partly based on my earlier assumption that Khmu Lao Theung and Hmong Lao Sung were *not* Buddhists in the first place. In Laos, conversions to Christianity, especially to evangelical Protestant groups, have come largely from the Lao Theung and Lao Sung segments of the population. So the responses as to whether these groups should become Buddhists were very interesting. Fifty-three responded positively to the question, nine negatively, and twenty-seven were ambivalent. All nine who responded negatively and twenty-four of the twenty-seven who were ambivalent were Lao Loum. The rest of the Lao Loum who responded did so positively. The question was aimed at determining the extent to which the ethnically dominant group in the country believes that the minority groups ought to conform or convert, especially because the Lao PDR government has, since the early 1990s, increasingly appealed to Buddhist symbolism and sentiment in its effort to generate national identity. Moreover, there has been a concerted effort by the Lao PDR to encourage Lao Theung and Lao Sung who live in very remote villages to come down from their mountain locales to integrate into the towns where the children can receive a basic education and the adults can engage in occupations other than swidden agriculture. While a significant number of the Lao Loum believe that Lao Theung and Lao Sung minorities should become Buddhists, it is also clear that many, almost half, do not believe that this is an especially good idea. The major reason for the positive response was that becoming Buddhist would be healthy in general for these minorities, since they would be assimilated to the generic national norm. The reasons for the negative or ambivalent responses, however, were not uniform. About half felt that religion is not a matter to force on people and that non-Buddhists can remain non-Buddhists if that is their disposition. But the other half simply thought that Lao Theung or Lao Sung becoming Buddhists was just a bad idea altogether, because the Theravada Buddhist religion belongs to the ethnic Lao Loum historically and because its integrity could suffer if too many Lao Sung and Lao Theung became Buddhist. In responses by three Lao Sung who expressed ambivalence to the question, the rationale for their answers was rooted in the fear that Lao Sung would also lose their own distinctive identity if too many of them became Buddhist.[14] These same respondents also turned out to be novices who had clearly joined the *sangha* for thoroughly expedient reasons.

In each of the interview contexts, every novice was asked to identify the vocation, or the chief occupation, of their families. These broke down as follows:

Farming or related to agriculture	82
Business	9
Government official or employee	6
Driver	2
Undeclared	1

The distribution of these occupations is not much at variance from the 1995 national census figures, which indicate that 85 percent of the population is engaged in agriculture. It also all but guarantees that eighty-two of these novices come from families who are quite unable to contribute much financially, if anything at all, to the maintenance of their sons while they obtain educations at the temples in Luang Phrabang. It also quite clearly signals that these *samaneras* originate from a socioeconomic background not only quite dissimilar from the middle-class urban laity of Luang Phrabang,[15] but light years away from socioeconomies of the tourists they encounter.

Table 4.1 breaks down the occupational backgrounds of the novices further, taking their ethnic backgrounds into account. What the figures in this table show is that there is no appreciable correlation between any specific occupation and general ethnic groupings. In each ethnic group approximately 80 percent of the family households engage in agricultural work.

TABLE 4.1 Occupations of the *samanera* families according to ethnic grouping

	Lao Loum	Lao Theung	Lao Sung
Agriculture	57	17	8
Business	7	1	1
Government officials	4	1	1
Drivers	2		
Undeclared		1	

Each of the *samaneras* was asked their reasons for becoming a novice. They were given multiple options and told that they could choose more than one of the reasons listed or they could provide another. The following reasons were given:

To study and practice Buddhism	95
To earn merit for the family	16
To give economic relief to the family	9
To gain an education	85
To gain merit for oneself	2

It is clear that most novices take the study and practice of Buddhism quite seriously, perhaps much more so than critical expatriates and many Luang Phrabang laity may give them credit for. Only five did not indicate that they had become a novice to study and practice Buddhism. All the same, however, this does not translate into a widely held motivation to undertake the *upasampada* ordination eventually in order to become a fully fledged monk. But what it does mean is that, despite some of the behavior I have described, most novices have great respect for the *dhamma* and believe that spending these years as a novice studying and practicing the religion is time well spent. Not to do so would be to deny the validity of the daily routines of discipline in which they engage. Most arise at 4 a.m. and tend to personal and temple chores before gathering to chant *suttas* at 5:45 a.m. or 6 a.m. in the *vat sim* (image hall). By 6:30 or 6:45, many are out on the streets of Luang Phrabang engaged in *bindabath*. They return to their temples for their early morning meals before departing for school, which begins at 8:00 a.m. Mid- to late afternoons are spent studying. From 3:00 p.m. to around 5:30 p.m., when they assemble again for chanting, the novices have some free time. So the daily regimen involves a good deal of discipline. Their responses to this question signals that they take their own routines of wearing the monastic robe quite seriously.

The second most-cited reason for becoming a novice is obvious: to gain an education. While learning the spiritual teachings and values of the Theravada tradition are no doubt important, the fact is that more than 90 percent will disrobe immediately following their final high school exams. When I asked laity in Luang Phrabang for their reactions to this statistic, they were not surprised, nor were they especially concerned. Some said that it is common for young men to spend time in the *sangha* without the assumption that it represents a life-long commitment. Others were more pointed and said that it is a good thing that so many of Laos's future teachers, businessmen, and professionals will have spent this formative time becoming familiar with the traditions of the Buddhasasana. It will only make them better people and the country a better place. Indeed, spending these years in Luang Phrabang gaining an education is without any doubt the primary mundane reason for becoming a novice. This is unsurprising when the conditions for education in the Lao PDR are considered in general, especially in nonurban areas of the country. As Sisouphanthong and Taillard (2000: 66) report: "38 per cent of the population in country is without primary education. . . . In most of the country more than three-quarters of the population have received only primary education at best. . . . Only in the capital (Vientiane) and Pakse have a significant portion of population received higher education (5% to 16%)." These same authors go on to point out that "the education sector saw a massive increase in the number of pupils and teachers during the 20 years that followed the founding of the Lao PDR [in 1975] . . . [and that] numbers of pupils and teachers more than doubled in primary education" (2000: 134). But the obvious fact remains that a secondary education, with a chance to continue at the tertiary level, is still very unusual in contemporary Laos. Indeed, if the figures in Sisouphanthong and Taillard's *An Atlas of Laos* are accurate, it means that only a quarter of the population graduates from high school in Laos. And only this 25 percent has any realistic hope of transcending the socioeconomic context into which they have been born. In Hayashi's studies of village Lao in northeast Thailand, he reports (2003: 313) that "the villagers cite two motivations that justify ordaining youth. One is filial piety, in which the candidate seeks ordination in response to his mother's 'request' so that his parents can receive merit. The other is the desire to attend curricula of 'adult education' and obtain qualifications equivalent to those acquired at secular schools."[16]

While Hayashi's second reason (education) is certainly validated by my findings, at first it seems surprising that only sixteen out of my hundred interviewees cited merit for the family as a reason for becoming a novice. Perhaps this can be explained by the fact that the question was put to the novices themselves, and not to their parents. Ngaosrivathana[17] and Hayashi have both stressed the importance of this motive. It may well be that if this question were put to the novices' parents, the positive responses would have been much higher. The same would hold true for the other motivation cited for joining the *sangha*: economic relief for the family. The perspectives of parents are no doubt quite different from the perspectives of novices. Moreover, this question might be read not only with regard to the short-term matter of economic relief, but also in relation to the long term, given the propensity of Laotians to expend great care on aging parents. This concern is specifically linked to the beneficial expectations that accompany acquiring a secondary education.

I asked the novices about their vocational aspirations once they finish with their monastic education, and they responded as shown in Table 4.2. It is very instructive to compare the occupations of the novices' families with their vocational aspirations. Not a single one of the eighty-two who come from farming or agricultural families aspires to that livelihood, findings that also imply most of them have little motivation for returning to any village setting, including their own. Joining the *sangha* is clearly understood not so much as it is portrayed in the Pali *suttas* and Vinaya, as the proverbial "journey into homelessness," but as a move into life in the city.[18]

Another notable finding is that the number of *samanera*s aiming for business careers is twice as high as the number of *samanera* families with business occupations. That only five indicated that they wish to work in the tourism industry is also quite significant, I think. Given Luang Phrabang's saturation with tourists and tourist-related businesses, that option would obviously occur to any of them.

TABLE 4.2 Vocational aspirations of Luang Phrabang *samaneras*

Business	21[a]
Teacher	12[b]
Monk	8[c]
Government official *(panak ngan)*	8[d]
Doctor	5
Policeman	4
Artist/crafts/designer	3
Retail employee *(kountammadar)*	3
Lawyer	2
Musician	1
Interpreter	1
Undecided	32

[a] 5 specified "tourism"
[b] 3 specified university professor
[c] 2 specified *dhamma* teacher
[d] 1 specified Communist Party member; 1 a "politician"

Therefore the allure of the tourism industry may not be quite as compelling for *samaneras* as some have thought. Yet in reality many of them will eventually work in tourist-related jobs.[19]

Of the one hundred novices surveyed, only eight expressed a desire to remain as a monk and to seek the *upasampada* higher ordination when they reach the age of twenty. This figure would probably surprise most tourists and Westerners in general, given their idealistic images of Buddhist monks. The fact is that when many young Lao become novices, they have no intention of remaining a monk for life. While it is not quite the case, as it is among the Thai and Burmese, that most young males are expected to spend at least some of their youth as novices—this is almost a rite of passage—it is a frequent occurrence in Lao society as well. And unlike in the Sri Lankan context, there is little stigma attached to disrobing. Indeed, a novice can expect his village to add *thith* to his name, an honorific denoting his time spent in the *sangha*. There is prestige in having served in the *sangha* for any length of time, and little dishonor, if any, in disrobing.[20]

When the vocational aspirations of the *samaneras* are broken down into ethnic groupings, the most notable finding is the level of high aspiration among the Lao Sung novices. While two were undecided, two said they wanted to be doctors, three said they wanted to be teachers (one a university professor), one said he wanted to be a Buddhist monk, and the one who wanted to go into business indicated that he wanted to be a manager. What we can infer from this is that many Lao Sung youth who become novices understand that they can or should significantly parlay the education they are currently receiving. Or perhaps it may be that in becoming *samaneras*, already an unusual move for them, they are more imaginative in pondering their future.

Each novice was also asked if he regularly talked with tourists in Luang Phrabang, as well as why he did so. Of the hundred, sixty-eight regularly engaged in talking with tourists, and thirty-two did not. Multiple options were provided for the reasons of those who did, and their responses break down as follows:

To practice English	71
To learn about others' cultures	39
To receive money	35
To learn other languages	3

If these findings are representative, more than two-thirds of Luang Phrabang's *samaneras* regularly converse with tourists. This may not seem like a remarkable statement, but prior to coming to Luang Phrabang most of the novices had rarely seen a person of Euro-American origins before, and had more rarely still engaged in conversation with them. But now interacting with tourists has become a normal pattern in their daily lives, and many are not at all shy in striking up conversations. The substance of these conservations, however, are usually utterly mundane; they almost always begin with the *samanera*s asking about the tourists' countries of origin, how long the tourists plan to stay in Luang Phrabang, what other countries they are visiting, whether they have any brothers or sisters or if they are married, how old they are, and so forth. Tourists almost always ask the novices why they became Buddhist monks. I suspect the fact that 95 percent of the novices answered my question about why they became a *samanera* with the answer "to study and practice Buddhism" is partially a by-product, or almost a reflexive response, given the frequency with which tourists ask this question. Insofar as their answer is fielded positively by tourists, it has been, in turn, reinforced in the minds of the *samanera*s. The *samanera*s, after all, want to project a good image while engaging the tourists. Often they will ask if the tourists want to see the interior of the *sim*s of their temples, and sometimes they invite the tourists to come back to the temple late in the afternoon to hear a round of chanting. Indeed, this routine has become part and parcel of the tourist experience in Luang Phrabang. I observed it time and again, day after day.

Curiously, according to the data I tabulated, more novices (seventy-one) said that they talk to tourists because it represents a possibility for them to practice their English than the number of novices who actually said that they talk to tourists regularly! I can only surmise that what this means is that some of the novices construed the question to mean: "*If* I talked to tourists, I would do so in order to practice English." *Samanera*s understand well that English is the lingua franca of the modern world. One went so far as to tell me that his English teacher at the monastic high school had recently said: "If you want to learn French, then you will be able to speak to the French. But if you learn English, you will be able to speak to anyone." Before the 1970s there was no question that French was the second language for Lao to acquire if they had such a rare opportunity or luxury.[21]

A little more than one-third of the *samanera*s in total, or more than one-half of those who indicated that they talk to tourists, say that they do so in order to get money. I myself was sometimes badgered about money, even quite insistently, in my interactions with some novices, to the point where I sometimes felt like I was being regarded as a cash cow. I heard numerous long stories of woe from some of them, stories that had obviously been told before or thoroughly rehearsed to create the desired affect of sympathy. These stories, or accounts, were normally elicited by the question about future vocation. The novices would preface their responses by "if I had money, I could continue studying." Offering to show tourists the interior of their temples or inviting them to hear their chanting is often motivated, I think, by the hope that, in return, the tourist will express thanks and sympathy through a monetary gratuity. The gratuity is, more often than not, solicited.

There is no doubt that a few of the novices are really quite skilled in extracting money, sometimes relatively large sums, from tourists. Some can be wily in their use of pressure tactics or guilt. Many use e-mail to maintain contact with tourists and to continue their solicitations for money. Yet most are genuinely poor, especially if they are among the eighty percent from the agricultural sector, and they have little hope of much, if any, support from home. Indeed, some of their families expect them to send money back to the village if they are successful in getting their hands on it in Luang Phrabang. Other than tourists, the *samaneras'* primary source of funds comes from accompanying ordained monks on ritual occasions to chant at the houses of affluent or middle-class laity in the Luang Phrabang vicinity. All *samaneras* share in the donations made by the laity to the group. For most novices, however, this is not enough money to pay their examination fees, buy sandals for walking to and from school, pay for transportation for the occasional visit to their families, buy school supplies, or supplement their diet of sticky rice with fruits or vegetables. Moreover, their solicitation for funds for further education is also necessary for many of them. The current tuition for most students attending the National University of Laos in Vientiane is about $600 a year. The private colleges charge around the same. This amount is far beyond the reach of most Laotians, whose annual per capita income amounts to far less.

When I asked *samaneras* why they thought that tourists should give them any money at all, many asserted that it was a form of *bindabath* or making alms rounds. Some of them hold the view that tourists have vast sums of money, which in comparison to their own financial situations, of course they do indeed. It seems unfair, some of them say, that such people should have so much money and that they themselves should have access to so little. And, of course, this is also quite true.

I asked the *samaneras* if they thought that the presence of tourists was good for Buddhism in Laos. Fifty-eight said yes, eleven said no, and seventeen expressed ambivalence. I then followed up immediately by asking the novices if they felt that tourists were good for Luang Phrabang. Seventy-nine answered yes, four said no, and thirteen were ambivalent. But some of the *samaneras* were confused in ascertaining the intent of the first question. I had asked it because some senior Buddhist clergy have expressed apprehension about what may become of the religion as the country rushes headlong into development. Tourism, of course, is one of major routes to development chosen by the Lao PDR, so I wanted to know if the novices felt that the presence of so many tourists might have a deleterious effect on the health of the religion. Some novices were clear in stating that the tourists were a distraction, and some, in their ambivalence, said that there were some tourists who were very kind and good, while others were impolite, indifferent, or arrogant (*khiimo*). The novices tended to personalize the question, quite understandably, based upon their own experiences of interacting with tourists. But some thought that the exposure to Buddhism might have a positive effect on these foreign tourists. They understood the question to mean: "Is the presence of Buddhism good for tourists?" What can be gleaned from comparing responses to each of these questions is that whereas most novices think that tourists are good for Buddhism and Luang Phrabang, they are more hesitant about tourists being good for Buddhism.

Considering all of this, I believe we can expect nothing but intensified change within the *sangha* in the future in Luang Phrabang. Many of the temples and their novices are under enormous pressure from the globalization process occurring all around them. As more Western tourists crowd the town, Western conceptions of Buddhism will continue to exert a further effect on the monks and novices in terms of how they respond to Western expectations of what a monk should be. Perhaps the phenomenon of the "virtual Buddhist monk" is not far off. At the same time monastic interactions using the information technology available at the many Internet cafes in town will also continue to create its effects. When I asked one of the leading abbots a question about the greatest problems facing the *samanera*s in Luang Phrabang, he misunderstood my question and thought I had asked him about his greatest problem in dealing with the *samanera*s. Though I had really wanted to ask that question directly of him too, I had been reticent to do so because of its very sensitive nature these days in Luang Phrabang. But with this bit of inadvertent luck, I got his answer, which I found very pertinent and pointed: "what they see on the websites of the Internet."

Boun Phravet: Ritual Expression in Contemporary Luang Phrabang

While *samanera*s and exquisite temples are the most conspicuous expressions of present and past Buddhist religious life in Luang Phrabang, formal rites for the purpose of making merit remain the most important aspects of religious culture for the Buddhist laity. The ritual descriptions by Tambiah (1970) and Hayashi (2003), who focused their ethnographic analyses on the ritual dimensions of Lao religious culture in village Isan or northeast Thailand,[22] though removed in time and space from present-day Laos, were invaluable to me in ferreting out the significance of a myriad details in the ritual life among the Lao Buddhists of Luang Phrabang and in gaining a more analytical understanding in regard to the principal Buddhist rites of merit-making that dot the annual religious calendar, an annual religious calendar observed on both sides of the Mekong consisting of twelve festivals (*hit sipsong*) held on the full moon days of each month.[23]

Tambiah was not exaggerating when, in his opening remarks about Boun Phravet, he wrote that "*Bun Phraawes* is the grandest merit-making ceremony in the village" (1970: 160). Planning for weeks, more likely months, made possible the orchestration of what, in early February of 2007, amounted to a three-day-long merit-making festival at Luang Phrabang's historic Vat Xieng Thong. Before the festival even began, an impressive and beautifully arranged array of gifts to the *sangha*, consisting of slippers, woven baskets, plastic buckets, thermoses, umbrellas, silver begging bowls, pillows, blankets, cushions, candles, incense, and other paraphernalia of use in monastic life, were displayed on several canopied low wooden tables in front of the monks' living quarters in the *vat*'s courtyard. Signs attached to the canopied tables of gifts indicated that some of these elaborate and expensive donations were being given in absentia by Lao laity now living as far away as North America or Australia, in addition to pious laity from Luang Phrabang, Vientiane, and Bangkok. Hayashi's study (2003: 121) also indicated that villagers regarded Boun Phravet as the most important merit-making festival of the year. Only Kathin, the October/November full-moon observance marking the end of *vassa*, the rain retreat season, when new robes are given to monks, comes close to rivaling it. The situation is no different in Luang Phrabang. Boun Phravet is the premier rite of the year for making merit, whether the laity who are giving reside locally or abroad.

In my description of the festival, I shall compare what I observed at Vat Xieng Thong's Boun Phravet with Tambiah's observations of nearly forty years ago, even though Tambiah's study was conducted in a relatively remote Lao village (Ban Phra Nan) in northeast Thailand downriver from Vientiane, a decidedly rustic venue. In contrast, Luang Phrabang's Vat Xieng Thong is arguably one of the most important temples in the entire Lao culture area[24] and is situated in a progressive urban setting. It is also situated within the Lao PDR, where the *sangha* is formally under the auspices of the government's Department of Religious Affairs.

The name of this festival derives from *boun* or *bun* (the Lao term derived from the Pali *punya*, meaning "merit"), *phra* meaning "buddha" or "bodhisattva," and *vet*, a shortened Lao form for Vetsandon or Pali Vessantara. So the festival signifies the ritual merit-making occasion (*boun*) that consists of a reading of the *Vessantara Jataka*. The *Vessantara Jataka* is the longest, most detailed of the 550 ever-popular "birth stories" among the Lao[25] that illustrate the bodhisattva's perfection of virtues in his previous lives on his long path to becoming the Buddha of our era. Listening to it is not only regarded as a supreme merit-making endeavor, but also serves as an inspiration for the perfection of giving as well. As Prince Vessantara in his penultimate rebirth, the bodhisattva is a royal prince who perfects the virtue of selfless giving (*dana*).

While almost epic in detail and drama, the story can be encapsulated, though surely short-shrifted, as follows. Because a neighboring country is suffering from severe draught, *Vessantara* gives away to that country's solicitous brahmin priests his prize white elephant, who possesses supernatural powers to make rain. Vessantara's countrymen are so aghast at this magnanimous act of charity (that will come at their eventual expense) that Vessantara's father, the king, has no choice but to banish him from the kingdom. Before leaving, Vessantara also makes "the gift of seven hundreds" (seven hundred slaves, elephants, horses, buffaloes, chariots, and so forth), and then, as he leaves the kingdom accompanied by his devoted wife and loving children, he also gives away his own horse and chariot to another set of suppliant brahmins. After a long journey on foot through neighboring kingdoms, he comes into the forest where he chooses to live a life of asceticism. In his wife's absence and surmounting great reluctance and pain, Vessantara gives away his children to a conniving old brahmin who has been cajoled into securing them by a greedy, young wife. Finally Vessantara even agrees to give away his faithful wife to yet another brahmin, who is really Indra (king of the gods) in disguise. At this moment Indra reveals himself, announces that all the deities are in awe of Vessantara's single-minded pursuit of perfecting his acts of generosity, declares that Vessantara will surely become a Buddha in his next rebirth, and tells him that he will receive back his wife, children, and kingdom in seven days' time.[26]

Historically this *jataka* has been a favorite not only for the laity, because it extols the power of merit made through the virtue of giving (the nature of their very own primary religious ritual and ethical acts), but of royalty throughout the history of the Theravada world as well. In another book I have discussed in some depth how the *Vessantara Jataka* forms the centerpiece of visual liturgies painted on the interior walls of eighteenth-century Kandyan Buddhist *viharas* in upcountry Sri Lanka. These temples, known as *rajamahaviharas*, were royally supported and maintained by pious Sinhala as well as Tamil Buddhist princes and kings,[27] in the same manner that Vat Xieng Thong has been supported by Lao royalty over most of the past four centuries. Indeed, many scenes of the *jataka* are also painted on the interior walls of the royally constructed *sim* at Vat Xieng Thong as well (see Photo 1.2). The *Vessantara Jataka* obviously appealed to many Theravada kings in other countries of South and Southeast Asia, but the Lao and Khmer[28] are unique in ritually reciting the *jataka* in this particular manner. I know of no similar practice historically among the Sinhalas in Sri Lanka or among the Burmese or central Thai. Though the origin of this ritual recitation is now lost to history, it must have been initiated at the behest of a Theravada-inspired king. Sixteen framed paintings depicting various scenes from the *jataka* remain within the Luang Phrabang National Museum, the former royal palace of the Lao kings. Thus it is clear that this *jataka*, along with *Phra Lak Phra Lam* (the Lao *Ramayana*), enjoyed a legacy of royal attention from Luang Phrabang's lineage of kingship to the time of Lao kingship's disestablishment.

The conclusion of Tambiah's analysis of Boun Phravet provides a convenient point of departure for my observations about ritual:

> To recapitulate some of the main conclusions reached in respect of the *Bun Phraawes* festival: it is the major festival of the village performed after harvest time at a time of plenty. It is a grand merit-making ceremony in which the villagers make liberal gifts to the monks and the *wat*, listen to the most celebrated story of the Buddha as *Phraawes* [Vessantara] engaging in acts of selfless giving which represent the ultimate in self-sacrifice, and, by analogy and transfer, they acquire merit. Structurally the Bun Phraawes festival divides into three sequences. First comes the invitation to Phraa Uppakrut, the swamp monk, to attend the festival; he is associated with protecting the village and ensuring rains. I interpret this as man's communion with and the taming of natural forces. The second phase is the invitation and propitiation of the ... *thewada* [deities; Pali *devata*], who are regarded as benevolent agents of Buddhism. This phase represents man's reunion with the upper benevolent spirit world. Uppakrut mediates with nature, the *thewada* with the divine. The ideologically central part, enacted in the third phase, is merit-making and recitation of and listening to the great story (*Lam Phraawes*). This sequence recalls and enacts Buddha's life in this world: it recalls a heroic past and allows present-day humble humanity to participate vicariously in that past. The three structured sequences represent a hierarchy of values in which the lower world of nature and the upper world of divine angels [sic] take their place in service of Buddhism. (1970: 302)

Later in his study Tambiah juxtaposes Boun Phravet with Boun Banfai (the rocket festival), the latter another full-moon rite directed toward the propitiation of the town's or village's guardian *phi* to ensure fertility during the coming agricultural season.

> The comparison between *Bun Phraawes* and *Bunbanfai* reveals that the two ritual complexes stand in opposition and complementarity, and state a dialectical relationship between two quite different positions taken by villagers in regard to man's relationship with nature and the divine. The first as a Buddhist ceremony and the second as a *phi* cult bring out the following contrasts. *Bun Phraawes* is staged in terms of the pious Buddhist ideology of merit-making; in this festival the two main categories of actors are monks and lay elders, who occupy the most important statuses in the village. Merit-making is accompanied by a grand fair, thus combining the moral pursuits of monks and elders with the pleasure derived by youth.... *Bunbanfai* is staged in terms of the ideology of the guardian spirit cult, in which favours are sought in exchange for offerings.

> The ritual officiants—*tiam* and *cham*—practise ecstatic techniques. Possession
> represents the descent and entry into men of powerful supernatural agents in
> order to aid them. The ceremony concludes with ritual licence in which village
> statuses and the respective hierarchies are dissolved temporarily before the next
> agricultural cycle starts. (1970: 303–304)

Having read Tambiah's accounts before observing Boun Phravet at Vat Xieng
Thong, I was immediately made aware not only of many significant differences,
but of the great consistencies that exist between them as well.

The most important difference is that the ritual celebration at Vat Xieng
Thong was not accompanied by a village fair. Tambiah had made much of the significance of the fair in Ban Phra Muan, noting not only how various participants
alternated their presence between *vat* and fair, but also how because monks came
from many other *vat*s and laity came from villages far away, Tambiah's Boun
Phravet "establishes the nature of festive Buddhism as a supra-local religion"
(1970: 168). Though the Boun Phravet that I observed was not accompanied by
a fair that would attract laypeople from afar, especially the young, many monks
from other temples in Luang Phrabang did attend and played important roles
in the central recitation rite itself. In addition, some of the elaborate donations
for the monks came from laity abroad, and a significant amount of money was
donated to the temple by laity in Bangkok, signaling the continuing attraction
of Vat Xieng Thong as a genuine merit-making venue and further illustrating
Tambiah's comment that Boun Phravet helps articulate and sustain Buddhism's
supralocality.

The three sequences of Boun Phravet to which Tambiah and Zago (1972: 290–
297) refer were certainly present and formed the basic structure of the three days
of festivities I observed in 2007, although not in the same order that Tambiah
describes. In Tambiah's village, the second sequence, the offering of one thousand
balls of rice to the *thewada* deities, one for each verse of the *Vessantara Jataka*, occurs at 2:30 in the morning before the *jataka* is recited. Ostensibly this is to invite
the *thewada* to be present so that they, in turn "would make the villagers 'live well
and in health' (*ju dee mee haeng*), that rain would fall as usual and much rainfall
might be expected (*fon fah cha dee*)." Tambiah notes that there is no other ritual
occasion in which the *thewada* are directly propitiated as "the sole recipients of offerings" (1970: 164–165). At the Vat Xieng Thong Boun Phravet, the recitation of
the *Vessantara* was held over a period of two days, and the *thewada* were venerated
at 2:30 in the early morning of the *second* day with the candlelight processions of
the thousand balls of rice. While in other Lao ritual contexts, there are traditions
about the need for only one monk to recite the entire *jataka* within one day's
time, at Vat Xieng Thong the ten hours of recitation occurred over a two-day pe-

riod rather than one, and no less than ten monks, including the chief monk, who commenced the recitation with his uniquely sonorous style, shared the honor of the task for an hour at a time. Moreover, the chief monk, novices, and laity I interviewed about the significance of the thousand balls of rice also gave an alternative explanation. The giving of the rice to *Vessantara* and the *thewada* was said to generate merit that could either be enjoyed for oneself, or it could be transferred to deceased relations, especially to one's parents. Hence at this Boun Phravet, merit is made not only for oneself, but it is shared with those no longer able to make it for themselves. The food itself was later distributed to anyone who was hungry, and after that to animals, especially the ubiquitous roosters and hens of Luang Phrabang, in the belief that that this might increase their fertility as well. If this last understanding is correct, this dimension of the rite, which has to do with fertility in Tambiah's account, has been preserved in this particular way in a contemporary urban context.

Tambiah comments on one more relevant detail. He mentions that the rice balls given to the *thewada* were ritually deposited into wicker baskets symbolizing *kalpa vrksas*, the heavenly wishing "trees that gratify the desires of men" (1970: 165) often alluded to in apocryphal texts such as the Pali *Anagatavamsa Desana* or the *Metteyasutta*.[29] They are often symbolically referenced in Laos and constitute an especially conspicuous presence within Burmese temple contexts as well. Tambiah describes their importance in this way:

> In popular Buddhism, they are said to represent the four trees that will blossom at the four corners of the city [Ketumati] in which the next Buddha, Maitreya, will be born. They will produce all kinds of delicious fruits in fabulous quantities. . . . The money trees that appear in merit-making rites may also be seen as associated with this symbolism. (Ibid.)

Money trees are often seen in Lao religious rites in Luang Phrabang, including during propitiation rites for various *phi* and commemorative rites for deceased family members. Money decorated the elaborate canopy in Vat Xieng Thong's *sim,* where the monks were seated during their recitations of the *Vessantara Jataka.* But no other money trees per se were to be found in the precincts of Vat Xieng Thong during this Boun Phravet. Instead, many of the rice balls of the early morning rite, which were later distributed to the chickens of the town, were placed in the small decorative sculpted trees that surround the *sim,* in this way sustaining the symbolism brought to our attention by Tambiah.

With the exception of some other minor variations, the structural outline and ethos of the village Boun Phravet that Tambiah described some forty years ago is thoroughly recognizable in its contemporary Luang Phrabang rendition, testimony to the persistence of ritual forms. But there were two other events held in conjunction with the Vat Xieng Thong version that are quite noteworthy and revealing.

The first is the fact that a new *sala*, the construction of which had begun the previous summer, was consecrated on the first morning of the rite, after Phra Uppakrut's invitation had been accomplished the previous evening. In the company of about fifty elderly laity, about ten of whom were *upasaka*s (laymen) seated in front and about forty of whom were *upasika*s (laywomen) seated behind them, twenty *bhikkhu*s led by the chief monk, while holding a white cord of rope, chanted *sutta*s and administered the taking of the eight precepts of restraint by two white-clad *mae khao* (ascetic women devotees). In effect, this morning ceremony initiated the series of rites that constituted the days of merit-making that were to follow. According to the head monk, both the impetus and the money for the new building were generated by pious Buddhist laity from Bangkok. At the very end of the festivities, during the third evening, the names of these Bangkok laity and the amounts of money that they had contributed were read out by the head monk over the temple's amplified sound system. This beautifully appointed new building consisted of an open meditation and sermon hall on its elevated top floor and six living quarters, two of which were immediately occupied, by the precept-taking *mae khao*. These quarters are to be used by laity taking precepts in the future whenever Vat Xieng Thong hosts multiple-day festivals like Boun Phravet. Because the construction of the new *sala* was regarded as a grand merit-making process, it was only appropriate that its consecration occur during the most meritoriously auspicious ritual event of the year.

The second episode that signals an important difference from what Tambiah described was the performance of *upasampada* (higher ordination) for two monks, an elaborate rite held in the afternoon of the first day at the *sim*. I had not expected this, for Tambiah had reported that ordination rites for monks in his Lao village occurred during the Boun Banfai festival, and in Zago's account (1972: 57–64) *upasampada* occurs during a different month of the calendar. In fact Tambiah commented extensively on the rich symbolism and rationale for holding this important monastic rite at the beginning of Boun Banfai, going so far as to identify *upasampada* as the first sequence of ritual performance that commences the entire Boun Banfai festival.

> The first sequence . . . [is] the ordination of novices and monks. A major reason why ordination takes place at this time is that part of the merit acquired is transferred to the swamp and village guardians. This expresses not so much the conversion of the spirits into Buddhist agents (as *Bun Phraawes* does with

Uppakrut) but that the human actors as Buddhists transfer some of their moral worth to the spirit guardians as offering in order to solicit favours. (1970: 291)

Since the elements of the village guardian *phi* cult are not included within the context of the *upasampada* rites celebrated during Boun Phravet at Vat Xieng Thong, a rationale other than the reciprocating exchange between guardian *phi* and laity must be sought. Tambiah actually provides part of the rationale himself in a later commentary:

> The ceremony for the elevation and honoring of monks occasionally performed together with ordination embodies rich meaning: the monk is purified by water which flows through the *Naga's* [serpent's] throat. Here the *Naga* is directly perceived as a Buddhist agent, and the analogy is that just as the *Naga* in this ritual purifies a monk, so may the swamp and village guardians fertilize the fields. . . . It is evident that in this ceremony [pouring water into a wooden receptacle in the shape of a *naga* that is then poured onto the monk's body] that the *Naga* is seen as a friend and guardian of Buddhism; at the same time, since he is associated with rain and fertility, the ceremony connotes the sacred *Naga* enhancing and cleansing the monk who is being honoured. Since the drama is staged at a rain-invoking festival we are justified in asserting the equation: just as the *Naga* pours water on the monk to increase his sacredness, so may the rain fall on the fields and increase their agricultural fertility. But note the paradox: in the case of the monk it is his non-sexual sacredness that is increased; in the case of the layman their material prosperity and fertility. . . . The monk is a mediator and vehicle, and it is precisely his access to sacred life-renouncing power that is transformed into life-giving powers for the layman. (1970: 290–291)

The reason for this dual function is that *nagas* have always been symbols for both purity *and* fertility in Hindu and Buddhist religious cultures: thus the *naga* symbolizes purity (and its protection) in relation to monks and temples on the one hand and fertility in relation to the laity's fields and their agricultural pursuits on the other.[30] Moreover, *nagas* are often associated with temporal beginnings or spatial transitions in Indian myth and architectural symbolism. In one of the most well-known Hindu creation myths, which has been adapted throughout the religious cultures of Southeast Asia, Visnu churns the Ocean of Milk with the primordial *naga* on which he has been recumbent between world intervals in order to initiate the re-creation of the physical or phenomenal world. Thus the *naga* is seen as the divine instrument that Visnu utilizes in creation. In terms of the *naga's* significance in spatial symbolism, the *naga's* elongated body is most often found constituting the railings for entrances to temple compounds, usually on

Photo 4.6 Naga balustrade, Wat Nong, Luang Phrabang

each side of central staircases, with its many heads (sometimes five and sometimes seven; see Photo 4.6) fiercely facing the mundane world.

In this spatial context the *naga* is protecting the purity or sanctity of the temple and marks the boundary between the mundane space outside of the temple and the sacred space within. From this the symbolism of pouring water through the body of the *naga* onto the monk's body just before the start of the ceremony marking his rebirth in identity as a monk is fairly apparent. Zago remarks (1972: 59) that the novice is actually referred to as a *naga* or "Nak" as this stage. This is the moment marking transition from *samanera* to *bhikkhu*, from novice to fully fledged monk. The monk is symbolically purified by the waters of regeneration that pass through the *naga*'s body just as he is about to make his transitional "rebirth." The same ritual symbolism can be seen during the New Year rites in Luang Phrabang when the Phra Bang image, as well as other important Buddha images, is bathed in exactly the same manner, by water poured through a *naga*'s body: the image of the Buddha is purified during the transition from the end of one year to the beginning of the next.[31] This preliminary aspect of the *upasampada* rite occurs outside and in front of the *sim* just before the monk is questioned about his eligibility to formally enter the *sangha*. His ritual bath of "*naga* water" occurs within a square space enclosed by saffron cloth, so he remains hidden from the laity and other monks during the liminal purification process. When he emerges from this enclosed or hidden space, he has donned a new robe, symbolic of his new status in the monastic fraternity. On the particular occasion I saw, when the candidate for admission to the *sangha* returned to the *sim* on an especially provided red carpet, he was pelted with rice and candy by lay well-wishers.[32]

Auxiliary ceremonies notwithstanding, the central event of the Boun Phravet festival remains the recitation of the *Vessantara Jataka*. During the ten hours of its recitation over the following two days, many laity listened attentively, some for the entire period, others coming and going after sections were concluded and different monks took up their part of the task. Most of the audience (approximately three-fourths) were very elderly women, the remainder being elderly men and a few middle-aged women. While Tambiah mentioned that the style of listening he observed was "casual," I observed most of the laity listening patiently and intently, with their hands folded together in pious attention. After the consecration of the new *sala* on the first day, young women who had been preparing a sumptuous feast all morning had brought trays of food to serve first the monks and then the laity following the ceremony. On the second day of the *Vessantara* recitation, the same kind of elaborate food presentation was brought into the *sim* proper, but with no break in the recitation of the *jataka*. The preparation and serving of food was also a merit-making event. Following the conclusion of the recitation around 3:00 p.m. on the third day, more gifts, mostly robes, were given to the monks in attendance, and Boun Phravet was finally brought to its conclusion.

One of the most salient differences I observed from Tambiah's account has to do with the demography of people who attended Boun Phravet in Luang Phrabang. Perhaps the village fair that Tambiah reports being held simultaneously guaranteed a much broader cross-section of population in Ban Phra Muan forty years ago. Certainly, the celebration of Boun Phravet in that context would have also signaled the more thorough integration of Buddhist rites and "secular" life in the village social experience. Tambiah stressed how the villagers, young and old, alternated between the religious ritual and the village fair. At Vat Xieng Thong there was no reason to be present *except* to listen to the *jataka* and to reap the merit thereof. There were no other competing interests in play. Indeed, the chief monk later told me that one of his own personal concerns had to do with "keeping the Buddhasasana separate from cultural traditions" because they have become so entwined. I would hesitate to say, however, that the more exclusive religious nature of the ritual proceedings at Vat Xieng Thong signals the walling off of religion into a sacred sphere opposed to a profane one, in the manner frequently attributed to the pattern of religion within the context of "Western modernity." For Luang Phrabang in spatial and temporal terms and on a daily basis, is suffused with the presence of monks and novices chanting, going on *bindabath*, frequenting the Internet cafes, and so forth, as well as going about their other normal types of business. The temples dominate the settlement pattern of the population, the sounds of their ritual activities are as diffused into the town as those of the airplanes overhead ferrying the tourists in and out. The boundaries between the sacred and the profane are very porous. Tourists are as often seen entering the temples as novices are seen entering the Internet cafes. Despite the pious abbot's desire to keep religion separate from culture, the weight of the contemporary social process prevents that from occurring. Perhaps this is why some Westerners have a more difficult time, as I first did as well, comprehending contemporary monastic behavior. It seems out of place, given their compartmentalized view of religion. But the chief monk's attempt to refine Boun Phravet religiously in this historic temple setting did, I suspect, make the occasion a far more sober, "mature" event than the celebratory ethos that Tambiah described.

Some of the *upasaka*s and *upasika*s present during the Boun Phravet recitations at Vat Xieng Thong were locally prominent laity and longtime supporters from Xieng Thong village itself. But others were simply elderly laity from other *ban* in Luang Phrabang. But why was there such a preponderance of elderly people, a phenomenon also seen in Sri Lanka on monthly *poya* (full-moon days) when laity don white clothes and observe five or eight precepts within the temple compound: abstaining from food after noon, listening to sermons, chanting melodic refrains, and engaging in meditation? Is it simply because the elderly have more time, having retired from their jobs and raised their children? Is it that their generation predates the establishment of the Lao PDR, after which participation in merit-making rites was initially discouraged and then looked upon largely with indifference by the government authorities? Or could these elderly laity simply be Buddhist analogues to the ancient Indian paradigm of *vanaprastha,* the third stage in life, when one devotes more time to religious devotion in anticipation of one's next rebirth? It may be a combination of all these considerations, but I think the last is probably the one most consciously affirmed by the elderly merit-making participants of Boun Phravet. Making merit is a form of preparation for the next rebirth where further progress on the path prescribed by the teachings of the Buddhasasana can take place.

Pi Mai: The Lao New Year

In contemporary Luang Phrabang it is almost impossible for anyone, Lao or foreign tourist, to escape some form of participation in the New Year (Pi Mai) festivities, the collective ritual articulations of which affirm the substance and parameters of the entire social and cosmic order as traditionally conceived.

Hayashi (2003), Tambiah (1970), and Zago (1972) all have said that neither laity nor monks regard the New Year's rites as significant for merit-making. Indeed, Pi Mai is not about merit-making at all, but focuses on the renewal of order, both social and (at least traditionally) cosmic (Zago 1972: 297–306). As in New Year's ceremonies the world over, Luang Prabang's New Year's ethos is now decidedly and almost wholly secular in orientation, with only degrees of the sacred still in play. But it is precisely these vestiges that, as a historian of religions, I am primarily interested in considering.

The annual Pi Mai celebrations in Luang Phrabang are observed in mid-April and have been written about in great length by many capable scholars, so I have chosen not to recapitulate in any great detail what is already so well analyzed and easily accessed. I shall present only certain salient observations to indicate how changes in the political economy and society of Laos are clearly reflected in contemporary religious culture. Readers interested in greater depth, nuance, and detail should consult Trankell's (1999) and Zago's (1972) account.

The creation mythology introduced in Chapter 1 still serves as the traditional narrative backdrop for the New Year's rites celebrated in Luang Phrabang. The central events of the New Year's festivities in 2007 consisted of the Miss Lao New Year Beauty Pageant, which concluded on the first day of the festival, the market held on the morning of the second day on the main road in front of the provincial government buildings, the main ritual procession the afternoon of the second day from the beauty pageant grounds (the old football stadium) to Vat Xieng Thong, the construction of sand stupas on the far bank of the Mekong opposite Luang Phrabang and the return ritual procession from Vat Xieng Thong on the third day, and finally the ritual lustration of the Phra Bang image on the morning of the fourth and final day of festivities.

In writing about the significance of the Miss Lao New Year Beauty Pageant, Trankell notes how the event first came about not only as a result of influence from Thailand, where beauty pageants have become a veritable cultural craze, but as a strategically calculated substitution for the performance of the *Ramayana*, since in post-revolutionary times, the *Ramayana* contains too many associations in Luang Phrabang with its now deposed kingship. She notes that

> the winner of the contest (*nang sangkhan*, Miss Lao New Year) represents the tutelary spirit of the New Year and is seen as the incarnation of the *sanghkan* (the horastic animal sign of the year). In the New Year procession, she performs in the main parades mounted on the animal of the year, surrounded by her fellow contestants. (1999: 204–205)

Trankell goes on to note that the beauty contest was first introduced in 1973 by the mayor of Luang Phrabang, who had read a story about how a former king had been ceremoniously venerated by his seven daughters. The mayor had found the substance of this story, therefore, quite fitting for celebrating the beginning of the Lao New Year and thought that the holding of a beauty pageant could convey the spirit of the story's motifs. Be that as it may, the most significant dimension of Miss Lao's ritual duties, at least as I see it, is that she now performs some of the ritual duties formerly undertaken by the king, including the most auspicious and symbolically powerful of all, the lustration of the Phra Bang image. In addition, by virtue of the symbolism that she has been accorded, she embodies the "welfare of the community" for the following year, just as former kings were emblems of the welfare of their kingdoms. I will simply note that the other festivities, including the morning market, the two parades that attempt to symbolize collectively the hierarchical presence of all Luang Phrabang people according to ethnicity (with the tourists bringing up the rear!), and the building of the sand stupas on the banks of the Mekong (amidst blasts of rock music and a jungle of temporarily constructed beer and food stalls, copious amounts of both items being heavily consumed), are heavily patronized. But what I want to focus on, given this discussion, is the symbolism of the Phra Bang within the totality of these proceedings. The statue remains the most symbolically potent vestige of traditional Lao religious culture that is invoked during the New Year's rites. I have already written extensively about what the Phra Bang had come to symbolize in the old Lan Xang kingdom.[33]

On the morning of the fourth and final day of the New Year festivities, the Phra Bang is brought in procession from the old palace (now Luang Phrabang National Museum) to the front courtyard of adjacent Vat Mai. The costumed Luang Phrabang ancestral *phi*, together with their tamed stepchild lion (see Chapter 1 for their roles in Luang Phrabang's foundation myth), first worship the image, thereby indicating their recognition of the ultimate power of the Buddha and their enlistment to his cause (see Photo 4.7).

After monks chant Pali *suttas* from inside the *sim* of Vat Mai, the ancestors are the first to pour water into the *naga* from which it cascades over the Phra Bang, the lustration symbolically purifying and renewing the power of the Buddha. The ancestral *phi* are then followed by the four most senior abbots of the Buddhist *vats* in Luang Phrabang, representing the *sangha*'s legitimation of the proceedings. They are followed by a series of government officials: those representing the national government of the Lao PDR, the Luang Phrabang provincial government, the local mayor, and finally the *ban* chief. These government officials, together with Miss Lao and her attendants, are the first laity given the opportunity to worship the image and to offer their lustrations.[34] What is most significant in the contemporary context is the insertion of Lao PDR government officials and Miss Lao into the aspersion proceedings. This insertion not only indicates their official endorsement of Buddhism, since their patronage represents the consent of the state, but

Photo 4.7 Luang Phrabang ancestral *phi* (guardian spirits and tamed lion) bow before the Phra Bang image during rites celebrating Pi Mai (New Year), Luang Phrabang

it also represents their role as replacements for Laos's disestablished royalty. The hierarchy of the symbolism in this annual rite of purification and renewal is still quite apparent, despite the absence of royalty since 1975. As the king protected and purified the power of the Buddha, and in turn was protected and purified *by* the Buddha, so the same relations are symbolically expressed between the government officials and Miss Lao on the one hand and the Buddha on the other. Order and prosperity are sustained symbolically by virtue of this rite of reciprocation.

Frank Reynolds has interpreted the general symbolism of the New Year's rites as they were conducted before the 1975 revolution in the following way:

> The rites themselves, which almost certainly go back to the fourteenth century, center around the lustration of the image, an act which seeks to assure the coming of the rains, the renewal of the magical power of the image, and its continued beneficence toward the community. For our purposes it is crucial that these lustrations are performed both by the masked dancers representing the primal ancestors (the *devata luang*) and by the king. Since, in addition to its other functions, the lustration is an act of veneration and commitment, the participation by the ancestors signals the acceptance by the whole community of Laotians, past, present, and future, of the supremacy and authority of the image (and hence of the Buddha whom the image represents). In the same vein the lustration by the king confirms his own acceptance of the Buddha's authority and prepares the way for the ceremony which immediately follows, the oath of loyalty to him (the king) taken by the nobles. (1969: 86)

From this Reynolds proceeds to unpack the symbolism of the Phra Bang's lustration in relation to other calendrical rites celebrated annually in Luang Phrabang and then ferrets out the specifics of the sociocosmic hierarchy that all of rituals these affirm in toto.

> When one telescopes these various ceremonial episodes which we have discussed—and in fact they are telescoped in a variety of different ways in the ritual context itself—the lineaments of a strongly hierarchical religio-social ideal can be discerned. The three jewels of Buddhism, the Buddha, Dhamma, and Samgha, appear at the peak of the hierarchy, providing the ultimate norms which regulate the structure and circumscribing the cosmos in which it operates. Below the three jewels and within the world which they define stand the *devata luang*, the ancient divinized kings, and the living monarch who is himself at least potentially divine. Under them are ranged, on one side, the lesser spirits and demons which they have "tamed" and drawn into the service of Buddhism and, on the other, the hierarchy of court nobles committed to the ruling king

and responsible for the implementation of his rule of Dhamma. Next in the order come the commoners who are organized in socio-territorial units established by the ancestors and given particular segments of the Dhamma which it is their special responsibility to maintain. Finally, at the bottom of this ideal order, but through their original association with the territory still necessary participants in it, are the aborigines of the area, the Kha. (1969: 87–88)

Reynolds's account seems to include his reflections upon the two processions that form an important dimension of New Year's rites. Even today, within these processions are found representatives of the various "commoners" and "*kha*" who collectively make up the totality of the Luang Phrabang community.

The royal aspects of the New Year's proceedings have obviously vanished since the 1975 revolution, along with the banishment of the royal family in 1976, but Trankell has examined the royal protocols at the Luang Phrabang National Museum, formerly the royal palace (see Photo 4.8), and has reconstructed the sojourn of the king's annual "cosmological journey" that followed the Phra Bang's lustration. In this journey, which marks the first movements of the New Year on behalf of

Photo 4.8 Luang Phrabang National Museum, formerly the palace of Luang Phrabang royalty

the community, Luang Phrabang's ancestors are also venerated and the Buddha's central authoritative presence repeatedly commemorated throughout the kingdom (at least symbolically). These are the first acts undertaken in the New Year, thereby reconfirming the fundamental order of the kingdom within the cosmos as a whole. According to Trankell,

> the king started his cosmological journey, on the day after the reception of the New Year, at the religious center, the Vat Xieng Thong. There he was offered the purifying bath before entering the temple for worship, which included bathing the Buddha image [Phra Man]. During the course of the following days, he first traveled south to the village of Sangalok. Located at the mouth of the Nam Dong River, where, according to legend, the "grandparents" (ancestors) died after killing a dragon monster that had threatened the kingdom [see Chapter 1]. Sangalok is also said to be the first stop of the Prabang upon arrival in the kingdom, as well as being, in more recent times, a Khmer village which supplied the royal guards and policeman. The following day the journey goes north, where the king should make a stop on Don Khun island outside the tributary of Nam Xeuan in order to receive the aspersion, and to enjoy a short rest, as an act of commemoration of the event when the Lord Buddha arrived at this place. The same day the journey continued north, up the river to the sacred caves of Vat Tham Thing just opposite the Pak Ou where the bathing ritual was repeated before the king returned to the city.
>
> The important ritual elements in the king's cosmic journey include traveling along the south/north axis and the offering of water of successively higher social and cosmological levels. The journey constitutes the symbolic recreation of the kingdom in connection with the Lao New Year. (1999: 194–195)

From the interpretive accounts of Reynolds and Trankell, it is impossible to miss the fact that the traditional New Year's rites were fundamentally about regenerating cosmic power and hierarchical social order through rites of purification.

In light of this interpretation, what can be said about how the New Year's rites have changed since the disestablishment of Lao royalty and the political ascendancy of the Lao PDR? Answering this takes us some distance in generally assessing the condition of religious culture in northern Laos today.

Evans's observations in *The Politics of Ritual Memory* provide an excellent starting point.

> Reconstructing all the historical transformations that have occurred in the New Year rituals fall outside of my aim here, although it is clear that they were in a slow process of amalgamation and change. What we are mainly interested

in is the direction of the change. Purification rites of the city previously conducted by parades of the king's elephants have disappeared, as have rites connected with minorities. . . . But nothing has taken their place. Thus the direction or change is towards simplification and secularization of the ritual process through the highlighting of the beauty pageant element. The suppression of the role of the king in the ritual was the cause of a rapid and dramatic simplification and secularization of the ritual process. (1998: 137).

Evans extends these observations to say:

As we have seen, after 1975 in Luang Prabang the very elaborate traditional New Year rituals contracted drastically. Significantly, this occurred during the term of a Hmong governor who retired in the 1980s, who now tends to be blamed for the excessive rigidity of communist policy in Luang Prabang. The deposed king could play no role in the rituals, and as far as I can ascertain from informants, the *kha* [Khamu] lost their role. Only after 1989 when the government began to open its doors widely to foreign capital and tourism was there an attempt to revive some of the pomp of the traditional New Year rituals. (1998: 147)

And finally:

The now defunct rituals which gave prominence to the *kha* and which suggested a profound kinship relationship between them and the Lao have not been replaced by any rituals of equivalent depth. Minorities today in Laos, while legally equal, find themselves in a position similar to minorities in many other Asian countries—they simply provide ethnic flavor for the tourist industry. Furthermore, this works for only some "colorful" minorities like the Hmong. The Khamu, however, who played such a crucial role in the rituals of Luang Prabang do not have this color and therefore they are likely to drop completely out of sight. (1998: 151)

Evans's observations supplement my own from 2007 in moving forward to answer the fundamental question that has been posed. In reading the accounts by Reynolds and Trankell, one might get the impression that Pi Mai is celebrated in Luang Phrabang with great solemnity and sacredness because of the grand social and cosmic issues that seem to be at stake. Indeed, it is likely that in the decades and centuries past, the processions and lustrations were conducted with high sacrality and sobriety. But Evans is right to emphasize that since 1975 there has been a definite movement towards secularization and simplicity. I would add that I think the direction includes elements of profanity, ribaldry, or bacchanalia as well. Only the formal lustration of the Phra Bang image on the fourth day at Vat Mai is conducted with any degree of solemnity. And yet it is conducted amidst such a welter of photo-flashing tourists that its sacrality has also been sacrificed, to some extent, at the altar of tourism. The previous three days of Pi Mai in 2007 were nothing short of a continuous war of water: squads of young Lao fanned out patrolling the streets in pick-up trucks thoroughly dousing any and every person in proximity, with no exceptions provided. In addition, virtually every intersection in the town was manned by young men and women armed with buckets of water and bags of powder, grinning menacingly as they attacked whomever attempted to pass by. The amount of water tossed during these three days was rivaled only by the amount of Beer Lao consumed. The only other ritual occasion I have seen in the past that comes close to the licensed mayhem I witnessed during these days in Luang Phrabang is the celebration of Holi in India. In this Lao instance, however, I could not ascertain any elements of ritual reversal, except for the general fact that the normally exceedingly polite and even-minded people of Laos had become temporarily unhinged.

The ritual processions through the streets of Luang Phrabang were conducted within the context of this war of water. All of the participants in the processions, including members of the *sangha*, Miss Lao New Year and her entourage, the costumed ancestral *phi* or *devata luang*, representatives from each of Luang Phrabang's *ban*, Khmu and Hmong people, and even the quite loud, sodden, and boisterous tourists, were thoroughly inundated with water and doused with powder as they made their way through the streets of the city. By the end of the procession, all participants were soaked to the skin, and many were colored over completely from the bursts of powder that had peppered their journey. This was no solemn affair reestablishing order and hierarchy, but a carnival atmosphere of lighthearted licensed anarchy. Of course, many New Year's celebrations the world over are similar in nature. In the West, one only needs to recall social behavior on New Year's Eve to find an analogy. The chaos of the end of the year finally gives way to the reestablishment of some semblance of order at the beginning of the new. But in Luang Phrabang, it is not an exaggeration to say that, at least in public, the accent is now on the chaos rather than on purification and order.

But the public processions in Luang Phrabang deserve further comment, for in 2007 they were remarkably inclusive. The processions were headed—and I have no idea whether this was countenanced by officials or not—by five effeminate men who were dressed as women and who sauntered and stumbled in semi-dance steps in front of the costumed ancestral *phi* and their accompanied costumed stepchild lion. These young men, of course, bravely received the first blasts of liquids and powder to be hurled at the procession. Following the costumed ancestral *phi* were Lao Loum residents of Luang Phrabang, followed by a large contingent of the *sangha*. None of these were spared a healthy drenching/powdering either. Miss Lao, on an elevated float, came next with her attendants, who in turn were followed by representatives from outlying villages. These villagers carried with them silver, stick-character effigies of *phi*, the only anthropomorphic (or semi-anthropomorphic) representations of *phi* that I observed during my months of living in northern Laos. Finally, contingents of Khmu, Hmong, and tourists brought up the rear of the procession. In each section, with the exception of the *sangha* and Miss Lao's contingent, a significant percentage of those in the procession had entered into advanced states of inebriation. But what struck me most about the procession in general, apart from its casual and irreverent ethos, was its remarkable inclusiveness. While, as Evans has noted, the formal rituals that symbolically emphasized the place of the "Kha" may have been discarded, there was still a place for everyone, including the tourists, in the reconstituted New Year processions in Luang Phrabang.

I also think that any sense of a holistic or synchronized ritual process governing the entirety of the proceedings has been largely lost, if it was ever present even in the more traditional past. Few people seem to attend all of the festivities. The only participants consistently present at all the ritual venues, with the exception of the sand-stupa-making, were the ancestral *phi*, members of the *sangha*, and Miss Lao and her contingent. And even so, the members of the *sangha* who participated in the processions were not the same as those who participated in the Phra Bang's lustrations. But it is still worth pondering the contemporary significance of these three elements.

While I agree with Trankell that Miss Lao and her contingent are structural and symbolic replacements of the king and royalty in these proceedings, I also think that Evans's observations about secularization, and my own sense of the ethos of contemporary Pi Mai need to be factored in as well. That is, while scholars may suggest a deeply rooted symbolism indicative of a transformation of royal associations, Miss Lao is, obviously, a beauty queen first and foremost in the eyes of the contemporary public. She has been chosen not just because she represents the community in the manner in which kings may have done formerly (which I doubt is a thought consciously entertained by many in Luang Phrabang today), but because she is judged to be a talented and beautiful young woman, or the epitome of Lao femininity, as it is adjudged in contemporary Laos.[35] As much as beauty contests are increasingly viewed with skepticism and criticism in the West, where some think they contribute to the exploitation of women purely as sex objects, in South and Southeast Asia they continue to gain popularity. What I want to point out within the context of the New Year's rites in Luang Phrabang, however, is that after the beauty pageant has ended, Miss Lao's presence at every occasion that follows is complemented by the attendance of the *sangha* and the ancestral *phi*.

They are the three elements consistently present at all formally organized occasions constituting the remainder of the festivities. Members of the *sangha*, of course, may be said to represent the epitome of ideals constitutive of Lao masculinity, despite their formal detachment from sex (which no doubt constitutes a paradox). The ancestral *phi*, one feminine and one masculine, represent the primordial sexuality of the community. I suggest, therefore, that the presence of these ritual actors, even within the context of secularization, continue to symbolize the continuing *vitality* or viability of the Lao community in the past and present, all nominally continuing to be subject to and beneficiaries of the power of the Buddha as symbolized by the Phra Bang. Collectively, all four elements (Miss Lao, the *sangha*, the ancestral *phi*, and the Buddha) symbolize the vital powers of the changing place, degrees of secularization notwithstanding.

There is no doubt that the Lao New Year celebrations in Luang Phrabang have become increasingly commodified for domestic and tourist consumption. Anyone trying to book a room at a guesthouse in Luang Phrabang during the four days of festivities may as well be in Bethlehem on Christmas Eve. The increasingly raucous ethos of the occasion reflects a party spirit writ large, consistent with the increasingly relaxation of various social prohibitions in contemporary Laos. The current regime, though still nominally Marxist, can longer be accused of being "the party of no fun." At the same time, and even though they are perhaps sustained by the government for expedient economic purpose, the traditional symbols of ancestry and the Buddha, the nominal ontological powers of the place, continue to be affirmed in the presence of socially constructed masculine and feminine ideals. This is not to argue that the ideals themselves are not changing substantively. But it remains an open question in this evolving context as to what the community of Luang Phrabang is about to become, what the Buddha will mean to it, and what ideals the masculine *sangha* and feminine Miss Lao will truly embody in the future.

Conclusion

After several months of living in Luang Phrabang, I left in a wistful state. In the two and half years since my wife and I had first visited, the changes occurring in this lovely little city had been spectacular in nature. Transformations in Luang Phrabang's pace, ethos, and raison d'etre were easily seen, especially on the historic peninsula separating the Nam Khan and Mekong rivers. The social and cultural impacts brought about by the new economic opportunities afforded by international tourism were not only palpable, but I thought profound. Certainly the major temples of Luang Phrabang are now fundamentally changed insofar as their monks and especially their *samaneras* now interact intimately on a daily basis with foreigners from other parts of the world. While Vientiane is more likely to experience changes due to its proximity to Thailand, Luang Phrabang is experiencing a different sort of change. It is being even more directly impacted by its encounter with things Western. I have tried to demonstrate how UNESCO, tourism, and the world of NGOs have helped to foment change, wittingly and unwittingly. With regard to both the routines of *samaneras* and the celebrations of Pi Mai, the influence of tourists is significant.

I am not sure, however, that Boun Phravet has been impacted in the same way. As the primary occasion for the making of merit during the ritual calendar year, it seems to maintain its primary rationale without being redirected by the demands of tourists. While some *samaneras* have turned themselves into a commodity of sorts, and while the provincial and central governments of Laos have promoted Pi Mai for ostensible tourist (read economic) reasons, Boun Phravet retains its fundamental religious ethos. It remains an occasion when economics is subordinated to religion in that gifts are made to the *sangha* to sustain its spiritual well-being, not for material gain. The ritual exists for the sake of the religion, whereas Pi Mai and the behavior of some of Luang Phrabang's monks and novices seem to be motivated almost exclusively by monetary concerns.

CHAPTER 5

The Spirit(s) of the Place

Buddhists and Contemporary Lao Religion Reconsidered

> In traditional Lao society . . . , the search for meaning was aimed
> not at the satisfaction of intellectual curiosity concerning the
> intentions of an unknown author of a uncertain past, but rather
> the fulfillment of practical needs in their performance and
> consumption in the present.
> —Peter Koret, "*Luep Phasun*"

> The Muang [people] themselves are not of a particularly
> reflective or philosophical temperament. Although they are
> Buddhists, they are not given to pondering the ultimate
> nature of things.
> —Richard B. Davis, *Muang Metaphysics*

Throughout this study I have consistently referred to the persistent worship of *phi* as a cultic propitiation that is ubiquitous within Lao religious culture. I outlined the ontology and political significance of *phi* for the social organization of the *muang* in the first chapter, and in the following chapters I have indicated how spirit cults came under pressure by normative-minded and politically driven Buddhists during the time of the Lan Xang kingdom, during the late French colonial period, and by orthodox Marxists following the revolution of 1975. Yet several pertinent issues remain. In this concluding chapter, my approach shifts from the diachronic trajectory followed thus far to discuss more fully, in synchronic fashion, the current relationships that obtain between Buddhism and the spirit cults. I want to look more closely at the reasons why the veneration of *phi* continues with such vigor in the Lao PDR.

I will also discuss, by way of comparison, the process that Hayashi (2003) has labeled Buddhacization; that is, how the spirit cults have been transformed within an increasingly predominant, emphatically Buddhist-dominated religious culture in the Lao regions of Isan (northeast Thailand). I want to contrast this Buddhacization process in Isan with the manner in which important aspects of Buddhism continue to be construed through the prism of the spirit cults within the contemporary Lao PDR. In contrast to what seems to be happening in northeast Thailand, the process in the Lao PDR appears to be what I will call the "inspiriting" of Buddhism. What I am suggesting here is that though Buddhism and the spirit cults are expressions of two separate ontologies, a mutually or potentially transformative dialectic obtains between the two. Zago (1972: 378–383), like Tambiah (1970), sketched out the nature of this dynamic almost forty years ago in his structural analysis by noting how the relationship between Buddhism and the spirits could be understood as "*une symbiose harmonieuse*" (Zago 1972: 383). While that may be true to some extent, what will also become quite clear is that, unlike in Sri Lanka, the indigenous cult of supernatural *phi* in the Lao PDR has not been thoroughly rationalized according to the Buddhist theory of karma, though this kind of Buddhacization process is definitely occurring in the Lao region of northeast Thailand. Rather, what persists in the Lao PDR is a more pragmatic or instrumental understanding of power and of how the power of *phi* can be manipulated positively or defended against.

I began this study by stating that the persistence of the spirit cults in Laos, despite the presence of Buddhism for more than six centuries and despite the contemporary pressures of political transformations and socioeconomic modernization, has been remarkable. In this vein and in terms of just how deeply rooted the spirit cults remain within Lao religious culture, Gunn has gone so far to argue that

> it can be said that in Laos, obeisance to the spirit world, to a degree [is] unsurpassed in other Southeast Asian Theravada Buddhist societies. . . . [T]he real continuity in tradition (and this must be borne in mind when considering post-revolutionary Laos) is manifest in the attention given to the *ban* . . . and *muong* . . . deities. . . . At this level of analysis, it is the Theravada tradition that represents the major discontinuity in Indianized Southeast Asia; in Laos above all, it is the heritage of the guardian *phi* and hence the continuity of the T'ai tradition that represents the underlying common denominator. (1982: 81)[1]

How clearly Gunn's assertion about Buddhism's challenge to the spirit cults is readily seen in Hayashi's (2003) study of religion in contemporary villages of the Lao culture areas of northeast Thailand. There he observes a process whereby Buddhist practices are essentially replacing spirit cults, albeit they are transforming Buddhist practices in the process. But this same kind of process does not seem to be occurring in Laos.

If the spirit cults have been more persistent or more deeply rooted in Lao religious culture than in any other Southeast Asian cultural context, I would argue that this is because Buddhist explanations of power, protection, or suffering have not become as diffused, rooted, or functional as they have in most parts of Burma, central Thailand, and Cambodia. This is because the institutionalization of Buddhism has been identified with royal support, and royal power per se has been weaker in Laos historically than in these other Southeast Asian political contexts, due in part to a more decentralized indigenous polity rooted in *muang* social structures. The political history of the Lao, with the exception of the sixteenth and seventeenth centuries, supports this line of thought. Buddhism simply was not as thoroughly diffused throughout the regions that became contemporary Laos.

As to why most observers have not recognized the deeply rooted historical, political, and social significance of the persistent spirit cults in Laos, Condominas (1973: 272–273) has argued simply they have not actually looked hard enough for it, "being themselves members of the world religions, including Buddhists. Also, because it is not as conspicuous as the vat centered religion of Buddhism, but rather centered only on a hut hidden in the forest." While that may be the case, I shall attempt to ascertain in some greater detail perhaps another cause for the pervasive, continuing significance of the spirit cults of the Lao, a cause that also goes beyond the relative historical weakness of the Lao royalty in thoroughly promulgating Buddhism to the exclusion of the spirit cults.

I begin in the context of recent Lao PDR political history by reasserting an important point that was suggested in the abstract by Ernest Gellner and then spotlighted by Evans with reference to the sudden public appropriation of Buddhist thought, ritual, and symbolism by leading Marxist officials in Vientiane at the time leading up to and including the funeral of communist strongman Kaysone Phomvihane in 1992. Evans stressed the relevance of Gellner's point that Marxist ideology provides little, if any, solace in moments of personal existential crisis. As a worldview it is almost totally irrelevant in addressing matters of personal, psychological concern, owing to its almost exclusive and mechanical focus upon class analysis, deterministic economics, and overriding emphasis on the subject of the state. Marxism is concerned with power of a kind different from those associated with either karma or the spirit cults. Perhaps that is the reason why Kaysone's death and funeral occasioned the beginning of a public reaffirmation of Buddhism in Laos, for Marxism lacked the capacity to articulate what his death actually meant to the Lao nation, a nation dominantly constituted by Buddhists and so-called animists. In searching for a wider and deeper meaning, even the Marxist hardliner Lao had to return to Buddhism and the spirit cults for a suitable ritual vocabulary, for socialism is simply not religious in character. It does not answer some of the deeper questions in life for people who remain religious in outlook.

In asserting this, I think it is possible to begin to understand why the cults of the *khwan* and *phi* have also remained functionally so indispensable from a traditional Lao point of view, especially since 1975. The fact of the matter is that most people in Laos, apart from a very small number of communist party ideologues, whether they were Lao or highlander, continued to interact with spirits throughout the post-1975 period, even though the state officially regarded such interactions as crimes.

Not only is Marxism ill-equipped to handle personal and existential crises and social transitions, but Marxist thought itself had actually been quite poorly transmitted throughout Laos. Even if Marxism became a comprehensive guiding ideology for a few, most people, especially at the village level, never gained a clear understanding of its basic tenets. In contrast, almost every liminal moment of life's transitions in Lao culture continues to be marked by the performance of a *basi* ceremony, which ensures that *khwan*, or the vital essence of the individual, overcomes alienation or vulnerability and, once reintegrated, results in a social and psychological equilibrium for the individual (see Appendix 2). In addition, the powers of various *phi* are called upon daily for protection to navigate through difficult moments of transition or stress. Recentering the *khwan* and placating the *phi* remained the basic ritual technologies in place for virtually all Lao, in spite of vigorous efforts to discourage such practices after the 1975 revolution. Marxism simply never penetrated village culture to the extent that it could displace the ontology and function of the spirit cults. Important Marxist texts were never even translated into Lao. Its instrumental efficacy was never established.

In the post-Kaysone era of greater public relaxation and ritual expression, both *khwan* and *phi* spirit-cult orientations, in addition to Buddhist practices, are again ubiquitous. The spirit cults are even sometimes trumpeted in current government tourist literature as symbolizing what is quintessentially Lao. Thus for now the future of the spirit cults is assured as a cultural expression in which Lao may once again, like their posture towards Buddhism, take public pride.

Phi and Place

One question I was frequently asked in casual conversations with middle-class Lao Buddhists during my months in Luang Phrabang was whether I believed in *phi*. Given the direction in which these conversations inevitably turned, it finally occurred to me that those asking me were usually people who were convinced of the powerful presence of *phi*. Moreover, these types of conversations were far more likely to occur with women than with men. If I answered the question negatively, which I tended to do at first, the topic of conversation seemed to change quickly to an unrelated issue. But if I professed an agnosticism about the existence of *phi*, which I tended to do after having lived in Laos for some time, then story after story about encounters with the various powers of *phi* would ensue, especially if the conversation took place in a group setting. Everyone had testimony to contribute. One pattern that emerged was how almost all troubling experiences arising from encounters with *phi* were usually reported as *events* that had occurred outside of the home or the immediate family context, that is, in another less familiar *place*.[2] Forests, hotels, or guest houses were the most frequently mentioned venues.[3] Almost without exception, troubling experiences caused by *phi* had engendered sobering fears and, as a result, the need to seek some form of counteractive protection.

While my casual conversation partners were relatively urbanized, middle-class people, their stories about *phi* and the genuine fears they experienced were not at all at odds with how Tambiah characterized the views of Lao villagers in Isan forty years ago or with Zago's general descriptions from the Lao PDR in the 1970s. Tambiah wrote that villagers "view malevolent agents more as disorderly forces emanating from the unpredictable external nonhuman world or the world of the dead than as originating amongst the living contemporary fellow villagers and kin" (1970: 332). I found this to be a very important observation that eventually helped me to understand why Buddhism and the spirit cults remain two separate forces in play. *Phi* represent powers from an extrahuman supernatural plane of existence, and because their powers were not regarded as of human origin, their forces require the expertise of a specialized ritual practitioner. Because the actions of *phi* are unpredictable, they fall outside the Buddhist regime of karma, the inexorable principle of cause and effect. It follows from this that *phi* are not necessarily influenced or placated by the ethical behavior of human beings. This does not mean that *phi* are not of human origin. In fact, many of them are. But what it does mean is that their power cannot necessarily be controlled through the power of karma. So while *phi* may have become *phi* as a result of karmic retributions originally stemming from their human actions, their actions <u>as</u> *phi* that cause either misfortune or fortune for the living are *not* necessarily karmicly based or induced, but may be more a matter of caprice. Thus the protective power of *phi* is more likely to be elicited through bargaining and bribes than by undertaking ethical action to please them. Or they may be cajoled by the superior magical power that is often associated with Buddhist Pali mantras, Pali-inscribed amulets, and so forth. The possibility that *phi* will use their power to punish is also just as likely to be elicited by neglect or failure to show proper respect as it is by unethical behavior in relation to other human beings.

It took a while for me to realize how this Lao understanding is at deep odds with the manner in which misfortune and fortune are explained in the Sinhala Buddhist religious culture of Sri Lanka or in the Pali *sutta*s where all types of explanations for suffering (including the dynamics of astrology and sorcery) are ultimately attributed to the process of karmic conditioning (Holt 2004: 175–180).

In addition, the understanding that the Lao *thewada* deities reside permanently in their own special heaven, from which they undertake benevolent actions, is also an understanding that persists quite independently of the dynamics of *samsara* as normatively envisaged in Buddhist tradition. In the Pali literary and Sinhala cultural contexts, all *devata*, like all other sojourners in *samsara*, are impermanent, playing out karmic acts, and they are all subject to rebirth. Even their powers to react benevolently in response to human entreaties are understood to be a consequence of their own karma accumulated as human beings. Thus the Lao understanding of *thewada*, like that of *khwan* and *phi*, also appears to be unique.[4]

It is precisely for these reasons that I have argued that a Buddhist karmic rationalization has not thoroughly penetrated, rationalized, or domesticated the spirit cults of Laos. While some *phi*, such as the tutelary matrilineal or territorial spirits, appear to be responsive to ethical human actions, most other types of *phi* seem to remain free agents, as it were, beyond the control of ethically conscious or karmicly driven Buddhists. Perhaps this is why some Buddhists deny the existence of *phi*, for the powers of *phi* cannot be rationalized by appeals to a bedrock Buddhist karmic explanation.

Phi remain outside the dynamics of Buddhist cosmology because the ontological basis of *phi* power has a quite separate origin. In his study of Muang people in Nan, close Tai kindred to the Lao, Davis (1984: 76) affirms this same finding: "The archaic Tai category of 'spirits' (*phi*) . . . is not fully integrated into the Buddhist cosmology. Folk cosmology does not locate spirits in any particular level of the . . . World, nor does it make any attempt to reconcile . . . [them with] Buddhist principle."

Yet the ontology of the *phi* spirit cults continues to dominate the religious episteme of the Lao, despite the avowals of most Lao that Buddhism is given pride of place (Zago 1972: 381). During the final month of my stay in Luang Phrabang, I had a long conversation with a middle-aged Lao woman who had recently converted from Buddhism to an evangelical form of Protestant Christianity. During the past year she had taken employment with an NGO that, while ostensibly focused on poverty alleviation, was ultimately concerned with converting village Lao and highland minorities. When I asked this woman why she had converted, she told me that as a Christian she is now well protected from *phi* by "the biggest spirit of all" and so has come to live with a measure of peace in her life. When I asked her if by "the biggest spirit of all" she had meant the "Holy Spirit," she answered emphatically, "Yes!" In thinking over the significance of this conversation, I came to the following considerations. The first was that Christian missionaries have been quite adept in terms of the manner in which they have presented the "power" of the Holy Spirit. Rather than arguing against Buddhism, they have correctly read the religious terrain that they hope to transform as one dominated by the spirit cults. Moreover, those evangelical and pentacostal forms of Protestant Christianity that emphasize the power of the Holy Spirit can probably be expected to prosper in Asian religious cultures that, like Laos, are characterized by persistent spirit cults.[5] It seems that my conversation partner actually exemplifies a primary thesis of this book: she interpreted the cardinal principles of religion, in this case Christianity rather than Buddhism, through the prism of a spirit-cult ontology. It then made sense to me that, if the Phra Bang image could have been functionally or analogously understood as a kind of powerful *phi* mandala or *phi muang*, then the Holy Spirit could also be rendered as a type of powerful, transcendent *phi*. The spiritual power claimed by Christians in the form of the Holy Spirit was being construed as a form of effective protection in the same manner in which aspects of Lao Buddhism have been rendered. Just as most Lao see no conflict between being Buddhist and venerating *phi*, so my friend saw no conflict in continuing to believe in *phi* and becoming a Christian. Indeed, her rationale for becoming a Christian was determined precisely because she believed that the Holy Spirit provided the most effective way of gaining protection from malevolent *phi*. From these types of conversations I came to see more clearly how and why the dominant function of popular religious culture in contemporary Laos remains, even in a Christian context, a matter of enlisting benevolent powers for the purpose of seeking protection against unpredictable forces that emanate from unfamiliar *places* and their associated malevolent *phi*. I also began to see how the cult of *phi* functions as an instrumental efficacy. And this, in turn, lays bare the principles of spirit-cult ontology.

In Hayashi's studies of village Lao, he identified a plethora of *phi* who are clearly associated with various forms of territoriality. There are, first of all,

> the *phi sia* (lit. "spirits of genealogy"), spirits of a deceased mother and father, which protected each household's living space. These resided in one of the pillars of the house and watched over household members. People thus had guardian spirits in all "spaces" related to their daily lives—the fields, the house, the kin group, and the village compound—to guard them from malevolent spirits' unpredictable mischief and from misfortune. (2003: 113)

Perusing through his extensive glossary, we find the following types of *phi* and their definitions:

Phi ba: mad spirits
Phi ban: village spirits

Phi borisat: evil spirits of unknown genealogy
Phi fa: celestial spirits [*thewada*]
Phi hai: spirits of the field
Phi na: guardian spirits of the paddy field
Phi pa: spirits of the forest; untamed spirits
Phi puta: village guardian spirits worshipped for generations
Phi sia: spirits of deceased father and mother
Phi taihong: dangerous spirits of those dead due to violent death or suicide
Phi thaen: sky spirits
Phi thammasat: spirits of the natural environment
Phi thiaowada: guardian spirits who protect family members
Phi tonmai: spirits of the trees

In addition Davis (1984; passim) not only discusses most of these specific *phi,* but also refers to others including *phi ka* (who possess women), *phi dam* (who are ancestral *phi*), *phi am* (who cause nightmares), and *phi pay* (spirits of deceased women who died in childbirth). For protection against these types of *phi,* it is necessary to appeal to the spirits of the place that one inhabits.

Here is Tambiah's description of how the protective power of *phi* are expressly related to the familiar terrain of the household or the field and to other types of territoriality in general:

There is also the large category of highly miscellaneous spirits which reside in mountains or rivers, or are allotted to particular locations, that is, they are nature spirits.... Within the sphere of intra-village activities, *phi rai phi naa* (spirits of the rice field) are said to attack villagers. The belief is that each field has a resident spirit, and it is not unusual for farmers to set up shrines for them in their respective fields.... Field spirits are essentially the guardians of the fields, and farmers dutifully make offerings at their field shrines before ploughing and after harvest. Field spirits are in this respect secondary and individualized counterparts of the guardian spirits of the village, who protect the collective agricultural interests of the entire village and are propitiated before ploughing and after harvesting. The offerings to the field spirits by individual farmers are made immediately after the collective offerings to the village guardians. Thus in a sense the *phi naa,* as spirit owners of the fields, are *guardians of household property rights, who are promised and given their fees for their protective function. But clearly they are not moral agents when they cause individual afflictions, for they are seen as acting capriciously when they cause harm.* (1970: 316–317; emphasis mine)

Finally, there are other important types of *phi* that also need to be mentioned here in relation to their relevance to territorial power. One of the most important, of course, is the *phi muang*, the spirit associated with regionally affiliated villages (see Chapter 1). Condominas says that

> the term *phimeuang* refers to a spirit who resides in the capital of a principal-ity (*mueang*) and whose jurisdiction is its entire territory. The *phimueang* was initially brought into being by the construction of a *lakmueung* ("pillar of the principality") which involved the voluntary self-sacrifice of a pregnant woman who was then transformed into the guardian spirit of the principality.... [I]t is this spirit who received the subsequent annual sacrifices ... [which] involved no human sacrifices; rather, the cult called for the annual sacrifice of a water buffalo. (1973: 255)[6]

It is quite obvious from Tambiah and Condominas that the cults of the *phi na, phi puta, phi muang,* and *phi ban* are intricately connected to fertility and thus to the continuous general well-being of the region and village community. I want to focus in particular on the cults of *phi* of this kind, those who are regarded as the protectors or guardians of villages or regions, for these cults of guardian deities constitute the clearest instances of what Mus was referring to in his discussion of cadastral deities in the "religion of monsoon Asia."[7] Their cults also form the venues within which the process of Buddhacization has so clearly occurred, the process that Hayashi has been so concerned about within the Lao village culture of Isan, and the process I want to contrast with "inspiriting" in the Lao PDR.

Hayashi, Tambiah, Zago, and Condominas have each written extensively on the cult of the village guardian deity, the deity of territoriality par excellence. What each of these scholars has emphasized is how the village guardian deity is so closely bound up with the original and enduring identity of the village per se.[8] Having established the village, the guardian spirit is now seen as a fundamental power interested in sustaining it.

Condominas compares the fertility function of the Lao village deity with the earth goddess Nang Thoranee (see Photo 5.1).[9] He emphasizes (like Hayashi) how the village guardian deity is usually presented as an ancestral couple who first set-tled the village long ago, a theme seen so clearly in the New Year myths and rites I have described in Luang Phrabang:

> The functions of the *phiban* overlap somewhat with those of Nang Thorani, a goddess of the soil, whose concern is the agricultural fertility on which harvests depend. However, whereas Nang Thorani is generic and functionally specific, the *phiban* is a *genius loci*, the god of a specifically defined area, the protector

of the fields, the forest, and the ponds which make up that area, and also the people who live off it. While the *phiban* can be a single individual, it is more often a married couple, whence the double hut. In most cases, the guardian spirit appears to derive from the first settler in the area or the founder of the village, together with his wife. (1973: 258)

Tambiah provides a yet more elaborated perspective that emphasizes how the guardian spirits have been kept quite separate from Buddhist ritual cult. His ob-

Photo 5.1 Recently dedicated sculpture of Nang Thoranee opposite the Luang Phrabang Provincial Offices

servations support my assertion that the spirit cults have not been penetrated or
rationalized thoroughly by Buddhist thought and practice.

> In Ban Phraa Muan there are two supernatural agents who, though they fall
> into the category of *phi*, have an elevated status. They are called *Tapubaan*
> ("grandparent" or ancestor of the village) and *Chau Phau Phraa Khao*. Both
> may be referred to as *chao phau*, and in village conception and attitudes they
> are as much a respected deity as *phi*. They are different from a number of ma-
> levolent and capriciously acting *phi*, from whom they are distinguished. On
> the other hand, certain category distinctions separate all *phi* from *thewada* . . .
> thus it may be said that *thewada* are opposed to *phi*, who in turn are differenti-
> ated into elevated guardians (*chau phau*) and malevolent spirits (*phi*). . . . [I]
> n relation to Buddhism, the villagers view *Tapubaan* and *Chau Phau* cults as
> belonging in a separate and even opposed domain of action (just as, at another
> level, the *thewada* are opposed to the *phi*). Thus it is clearly recognized that
> Buddhist monks do not take part in the *phi* cult, for they "belong to a separate
> party." . . . As one informant put it, "Monks are human beings, *chau phau* are
> *phi*. Monks never chant for *chau phau*; they are called upon to chant when hu-
> man beings die" (i.e., to conduct mortuary rites, a major ritual function of the
> monks). Buddhist religious action is phrased in terms of the ideology of merit;
> but when one propitiates *Chau Phau* or *Tapubaan*, villagers explicitly consider
> the transaction as a *bargain*, an offering made to gain a particular favour, gener-
> ally to remove an affliction caused by the *phi*. (1970: 286–287)

While Buddhist monks may keep their distance from the ritual transactions involving *phi*, a disposition that I ascertained was observed (at least publicly) in the
temples of Luang Phrabang as well, villagers understand space or territoriality in
such a manner that even the Buddhist *vat*, the venue of the Buddha, *dhamma*, and
sangha, is understood as a space that needs to be afforded protection by a relevant
phi.

> *Tapubaan* is the "owner" of the village (*baan*); villagers sometimes elucidate
> this ownership literally in the sense that he was the original owner of the land.
> *Chau Phau Phraa Khao* is, on the other hand, the guardian of the *wat*. Thus
> their domains of authority, *baan* (settlement) and *wat* (temple), are important
> village ecological and socio-religious distinctions. (Tambiah 1970: 264)

While respective "domains of authority" may indicate important socioreligious
distinctions, what is of greater interest here is the fact that a guardian spirit of
the *vat* has been generated as a necessity by the villagers, thus indicating again

the manner in which the nature of "Buddhist space" has been construed through categories of spirit cult ideology in Laos. I shall explore further this type of phenomenon later on in this discussion, but for now I simply want to underscore how the archaic ontology that Mus highlighted continues to operate "even within the most learned religions" of this contemporary time.

Yet before pursuing that theme, I want to discuss how Buddhist practice in Isan is displacing some aspects of the spirit cults, but being transformed in the process itself. I will speculate further as to why this process is occurring in Lao cultural areas in northeast Thailand but not in the Lao PDR.

Buddhacization in Isan

In the 1820s and 1830s the Bangkok Chakri mandala had exerted its power over the Lao people of the Vientiane and Plain of Jars regions by forcibly removing about 80 percent of them to the Khorat plateau, the region that eventually became Isan, following the gunboat diplomacy of the French in 1893. In that new geopolitical world of boundaried nation-states, Bangkok immediately adopted policies related to standardizing the Thai language and reforming the Buddhist religion, policies designed to further integrate these transplanted Lao into the central-Thai-based national cultural ethos. Then after 1975 about 350,000 Lao fled Laos, half of whom eventually settled in Isan. Due to the centrality of Buddhism to the religious culture of the ethnic Lao, half of all the Buddhist *vats* in Thailand today are now located in Isan, along with one-third of the nation's population. These demographic facts—that about one-third of the population in Thailand is "Thai-Lao" and that one-half of the nation's Buddhist *vats* are Lao—led Hayashi (2003: 5) to call Isan "the most robust Buddhist region of the country." Yet Lao religious culture, as we have seen, cannot be simply equated with Theravada Buddhism. The spirit cults intrinsic to Lao religious culture also accompanied the Lao population to Thailand.

In order to abet the process of enfolding the Lao into central Thai linguistic and religious norms in the interest of creating national solidarity, and confident of "the superior potency of Buddhism over animistic threats," a premise that "is taken as axiomatic in Thai Buddhism" (Kirsch 1977: 259), "the Thai government [in 1929] issued a proclamation prohibiting spirit worship and urging people to take refuge in the Triple Gem" (Tiyavanich 1997: 178). While taking refuge in the Triple Gem was certainly not novel for the Lao of Isan, the Thai expectation that Lao would immediately jettison their worldview anchored in the epistemology of the spirit cults was simply overly idealistic, if not naive. Rather than simply declaring spirit veneration illegal or criminal, a different tact had to be devised by the Thai authorities to achieve their aims. Their approach was this: Lao Buddhists had to be convinced that Buddhist practices by themselves contained such powerful methodologies that they rendered the function of the spirit cults obsolete. In addition to this strategy, the Bangkok-based Buddhist establishment set in motion a complementary campaign aimed at reforming the rustic Lao village monks of the Mahanikay order to conform more completely to the Vinaya monastic rules. These efforts continued throughout the twentieth and even into the twentieth-first century.

Since the early 1980s the Japanese anthropologist Yukio Hayashi has been studying the consequences of Thai efforts to enculturate the Lao of Isan. He has acknowledged and built upon earlier anthropological insights contributed by Tambiah, but he has also tried to make use of a different type of analysis, one that more fully recognizes how historical changes affect social process (2003: 20). While applauding Tambiah's contributions and noting that his three major ethnographic studies have served as a salient point of departure for a generation of scholars focusing on Thai Buddhism, Hayashi argues that Tambiah's treatment suffers from an overemphasis on systematic synchronization. By that he means that Tambiah was overly enthusiastic in drawing parallels and correspondences between various rites to the extent that his "use of structuralist standards to identify systematic categories abstracts the social process within which the bearer of religious knowledge and those concepts [are articulated], [and thereby] exclude[s] the practical subject that creates meaning" (2003: 21). That is, Hayashi argues that Tambiah failed to account for how religious knowledge was actually processed by certain types of villagers within ritual settings.

Hayashi argues further that the work of many scholars of Theravada Buddhism has suffered from a methodology that assumes that the literary canon is a basis or essence of the religious tradition and then proceeds to find correspondences of the literary world in the cultic expressions of village life.[10] While Hayashi admits that there is, of course, a place for the literary and doctrinal in village life, he argues that such an approach is unnecessarily narrow in attempting to understand the broader significance of religion.

I agree with Hayashi's criticism in this specific regard. Reified texts and finely articulated doctrines are highly evolved forms of religious expression that are more reflective of a formal interpretation of religious culture than the generators of religious culture per se. That is, text and doctrine are highly derivative religious expressions, not usually progenitors. Approaches overly dependent upon sacred texts and doctrine also tend to be static, insofar that they usually assume a fixed understanding of religious tradition, while tradition, a phenomenon of time itself, is always dynamic in nature, evolving in a constant process of change and adaptation.

Hayashi argues further that in addition to considering the teachings of venerable texts, it is just as important, if not more so, to "look at the history of people's daily life" from an interdisciplinary perspective transcending the confines of a single academic discipline (2003: 22). Finally, rather than pursuing macroanalyses abstracted from single village studies, seeking to identify a dialectical relationship between "great" and "little" traditions, and so on, Hayashi advocates the study of several particular village sites within their *regional* social, political, and historical milieus. His study of the village Lao religious culture in Isan constitutes an examination of one such regional milieu.

The crux of Hayashi's extended study of several Lao villages over a twenty-five-year period is the process he identifies as Buddhacization, a process that he sees unfolding especially in relation to the spirit cults. In fact Hayashi observes a competitive conflict of sorts breaking out in Isan villages between the cults of the guardian spirit of the village on the one hand and the guardian spirit of the *vat* on the other. I could not locate such a conflict occurring in Lao Loum village contexts within the Lao PDR. For purposes of comparison in relation to Lao villages in what is now the Lao PDR, I cite Condominas, who, although he wrote before 1975 (1973), accurately reflects what I believe still remains the case today.

> [In] terms of its unifying function the *ho phiban* [the shrine to the village guardian deity] might be viewed as something of an animist equivalent of the vat. . . . The vat represents the Buddhist principles which govern men directly, whereby the *ho phiban* represents the land on which the village is established and from which the villagers obtain their food and principal resources. (1973: 257–258)

Then in reference to the ritual specialist who presides over the village's veneration of its guardian spirit, Condominas adds: "The *chao cham* comes to pray to the spirit for the prosperity of the village on every fifteenth day of the waxing and waning moons, a schedule that coincides with the Buddhist holy days" (261). Earlier Condominas says:

> One may think that, because of his responsibilities to the village guardian spirit, the *chao cham* might set himself up as a rival to the head of the village pagoda. This does not occur, however, for actually the *chao cham* is usually a good Buddhist who would never believe that the rites he performs in honor of the village spirits run counter to his worship of the Buddha. In fact, before the *chao cham* goes to the *ho phiban* to honor the spirit, he goes first to give alms to the monks. (258)

While Condominas's description of the relation between Buddhism and the spirit cults accurately reflects the continuing situation now in play in the Lao

Loum villages that are still part of the Lao PDR, the situation in contemporary
Isan is now quite different. Indeed, Hayashi understands, especially in light of
the concerted Thai national effort to discourage the worship of *phi*, that the *ho
phiban* and the *vat* have become increasingly involved in a relationship of conflict. While the *ho phiban* may continue to have salience for the most local of
multiple identities realized by villagers, the Buddhist *vat* is clearly the institution
that connects the villagers to the rest of the country and to the outside world.
In Tambiah's terms, the *vat* enjoys the merit of "supralocality." Hayashi heartily
concurs:

> The shrine to village guardian deity built in the forest, which locates the village
> boundary, is a constant symbol reminding the villagers that they are members
> of a particular settlement. The village temple is the polar opposite. Although
> situated within the village, it transcends it by such characteristics as its open-
> ness to strangers. The history of migration within this region shows that Bud-
> dhist temples in the Thai-Lao villages of northeast Thailand operated as a social
> apparatus joining the village to the external world. . . . The temple is perceived
> as an arena for creating a network of relations, the most suitable place for out-
> siders to visit when entering the village. In contrast, the forest temple [of the vil-
> lage guardian spirit] is not offered as a venue for this type of practice; its nature
> is as a place for pure individual practice and its purpose is in direct contrast to
> the collective nature of the village temple. (2003: 357)

It is very interesting how Hayashi asserts that it is through the village temple that
the greatest forces of change are being introduced into most villages. Not only is
the *vat* the conduit through which elements of the outside world are introduced
into the village at an increasingly intense pace, but it is also the possible channel
for young men, especially as monks or *samaneras*, to gain an exit from the village.
This is true in the Lao villages of Lao PDR as well.

> Buddhism is becoming increasingly prominent in all aspects of village religion
> . . . [in a] process by which the world religion of Buddhism is indigenized within
> village society and the parallel process by which indigenous beliefs are incor-
> porated within village society and Buddhism. . . . [Within this context], the *mo
> tham* [a specific type of ritual specialist] emerged through a conflict between
> Buddhism and indigenous beliefs that occurred at the regional level. (Hayashi
> 2003: 201)

The emergence of the *mo tham*, a new type of ritual specialist or holy man,
is a very interesting phenomenon to consider, for he seems to embody the very

process of Buddhacization that Hayashi has spotlighted. The *mo tham* does not venerate spirits, nor does he try to mobilize or channel their power. Rather he exorcizes, heals, and affords protection from spirits through specifically Buddhist means. In other words he performs functions formerly the province of *phi* ritual specialists by appealing to the power of *thamma* [Sanskrit *dharma*; Pali *dhamma*] instead. That is, he is bridging the ontologies of Buddhism and the spirit cults. In most cases the *mo tham* appears to have formerly been a Buddhist monk or at least a *samanera* for an extended period during his youth. He is usually now middle-aged, if not elderly. His having spent a number of years in the *sangha* accounts, in part, for his knowledge of *thamma* and effective use of mantras.[11]

Typically, Hayashi says, when villagers are asked about the meaning of *thamma*, they are usually quite vague. Yet they are quite aware that the *mo tham*'s power to command and control the power of *phi* by means of the *thamma* depends upon his having in his previous life as a monk adhered strictly to the Vinaya rules or to his continuing observance of the *pancasila* (the basic five-fold morality concerning abstinence from killing or harming, adhering to the truth, not appropriating what is not given, observing sexual continence or propriety, and abstaining from intoxicants) (2003: 238). What becomes quite clear from this, then, is that power is understood, or Buddhacization is based upon, an ethicization that empowers the practice of magic. Or to put the matter more clearly, *magical power is derived from ethical practice.* Moreover, Hayashi reports that *mo tham* are intent upon actually converting *phi* to the Buddhist ethical regime while at the same time they are impressing upon their clients the need for them to be instilled with the power of *thamma* themselves through the observance of the ethical *pancasila* precepts.

> *Thamma* used by the *mo tham* is a force wielded to withstand the evil spirits that are the power of the world beyond. It is recognized as a physical force capable of subjugating the opposing forces of the world beyond. If however, the *mo tham* expels an evil spirit from a client's body using *thamma*, he does not kill it. In contrast to evil spirits, it is clear that *thamma* is not a destructive power that erases existence. . . . The mechanism for driving out evil spirits, however, is to convert them to Buddhism, to bring them into the Buddhist world and thereby render the power of the world beyond impotent. . . . [T]he subject possessed by an evil spirit must be a Buddhist for the exorcism to succeed. . . . [T]he precepts are first administered to the client and then to the spirit, after which it is expelled. (2003: 243)[12]

But this is only a small part of the story that is unfolding. In one village Hayashi studied, the *mo tham* has abolished all rites concerning guardian spirits, expelling them from the village and constructing a village pillar in the center. There are many names for this village pillar but all of them are commonly understood to mean the "center of the village" or the "pillar dedicated to *thamma*," literally "Buddhist dharma." (2003: 95)

Later in his discussion Hayashi analyzes more closely the significance of this transformation:

While the *mo tham* . . . who destroyed the shrine to the guardian spirit have some relation to the system of knowledge concerning evil spirits, they are enacting a historically new religious role in the region because they had little exposure to the indigenous spirit cults that came before. This clearly demonstrates a transition in the religious world of the Thai-Lao village. (2003: 98).

Indeed!

Hayashi also reports that in one village the cult of the guardian spirits was not only abolished, but that the very location of the former guardian spirit shrine was selected as a site for a second "forest temple." He notes that changes in mortuary rites occurred at the same time, from cremation to burial (at the forest site).[13]

Hayashi (2003: 297) says that the forerunners of the contemporary *mo tham* phenomena were wandering ascetic (*thudong*) monks who in the earlier decades of the twentieth century visited these Lao villages frequently and were usually accorded the highest respect.

Kamala Tiyavanich (1997) has studied the traditional biographies (or hagiographies) of these *thudong* monks and has reconstructed their posture in relation to the issue of the spirit cults. The Bangkok-based Thammayut order had attempted to recruit many of these wandering Lao monks in support of their programs of reform aimed at the Lao Buddhists of Isan. From what Tiyavanich reports, it is clear that the process of Buddhacization began far earlier than the contemporary period that Hayashi has analyzed.

One issue that Tiyavanich makes clear is that although the wandering *thudong* monks were enlisted to do the bidding of reform by the Bangkok Buddhist establishment, and especially to wean the laity away from venerating spirits, the *thudong* themselves never relinquished their own beliefs in the existence of *phi*.

When *thudong* monks preached against ghosts or spirits [at the behest of the Thai Thammayut order], it was not because they doubted their existence; rather they opposed the practice of bribing the spirits with sacrificial offerings. Indeed, the idea that different kinds of spirits abided everywhere (in forests, trees, rivers, mountains, caves, earth, sky and animals) was convincing to wandering monks, who had experienced meetings with some of these spirits in their visions. (1997: 209)

Thus the *thudong* saw as their mission not the eradication of belief in *phi*; rather, what becomes apparent is that they agreed to their mission because they believed that Buddhism provided a more effective means for protection against the power of *phi*. The *thudong* firmly believed that the power of *phi* needed to be confronted and overcome personally. It constituted an important dimension of their religious quest. *Phi* were regarded as a given fact in the forest, the milieu within which these transient and homeless monks had chosen to practice their discipline. Tiyavanich asks:

What gave thudong monks confidence when wandering alone through dense forests or high mountains? In addition to strong mindfulness, four convictions were instrumental in protecting them.

First, they believed in the merit of the *thudong* practice: if they strictly adhered to *sila* [morality] and its precepts, the *dhamma* would protect them....

Second, the thudong monks had trust in their *ajan* [mentor]....

Third, the monks had faith in the law of *kamma* and the good they had done by not harming any creatures ..., [a] belief in the power of *metta* [loving-kindness].[14]

A fourth source of the thudong monks' confidence was their belief that tigers, wild elephants, and snakes were *devatas* or guardian spirits that had disguised themselves as animals and had come to test the depth of a monk's understanding, and faith. (1997: 92–93)

Tiyavanich (1997: 80–81) also describes how *thudong* monks advocated the mantra "Buddho" in order to overcome fear in the forest and how, in turn, these monks taught the mantra to lay villagers as a form of protective power. She also reports (163) this about the leading *ajan* (mentor) of the monks whose biographies she studied: "Man [his name] told them [villagers] that if they recited 'buddho, dhamma, sangho' mentally, no ghosts would be able to withstand the power of these words."[15] Moreover,

to convert people from spirit worship [at the behest of the Thammayut] the wandering monks attempted to replace the custom of making sacrificial offerings with the custom of taking refuge in the Triple Gem.... This indispensable ritual [combined with meditation on "buddho" and taking the five precepts] provided the villagers with a means of protection against punishing spirits. (1997: 201)

In describing how villagers regarded one particular *thudong* monk after he had taken up as his abode and place for meditation in the very hut formerly used for venerating the village *phi*, Tiyavanich says that eventually "it was almost as if the villagers were treating him [the *thudong* monk] like a substitute spirit" (213).

Tiyavanich's observations capture, almost in microcosmic fashion, the process of Buddhacization that Hayashi has identified. It is not so much that the Isan Lao have stopped believing in the power of *phi*. Rather, the power of *phi* has been contained within Buddhist practice. This Buddhist power, embodied by the *mo tham*, and by Buddhist monks and laity alike who observe their practice ethically, has been increasingly understood as an efficacious means of warding off the dangers emanating from the spirit world. Rather than fighting malevolent spirits with the power of benevolent spirits, Buddhacization means fighting spirits with Buddhist practice, especially through the invocation of powerful mantras and by means of the observance of a karmicly fortuitous ethical regime.

Inspiriting Buddhism

While the *dhamma* deployed by *mo tham* ritual specialists in Isan is clearly understood as a kind of ethicized protective and healing power, it is also true that among the Lao in the Lao PDR, the Buddha and the *sangha* have been "inspirited." The three aspects of the *triratna*, or "Triple Gem," form, of course, an interrelated whole: the Buddha's *dhamma* is embodied and transmitted by the *sangha*.[16] While the didactic content of the *dhamma* is concerned with cultivating virtues to arrest the process of karmic conditioning in *samsara*, the power of the *dhamma* has not been intellectualized among the Lao laity, nor has it been understood primarily within the context of the normative Buddhist soteriological quest. Rather, among the Lao, it is deployed either for protection from *phi*, or more generally to help ameliorate experiences of suffering in the world, arguably the whole point of Buddhism in the first place.

I have emphasized how the *dhamma* has been put to use as a protective and healing force by Lao Buddhists in Isan, but now I want to contrast this understanding by illustrating the process of "inspiriting." I will do this by discussing how the other two aspects of the *triratna*, the Buddha and the *sangha*, have been understood in the Lao PDR. But first I shall take a very brief look at how the *vat*, the venue of the *sangha*, has also become an inspirited space for Lao laity. I have already commented extensively on the significance of the Buddha as a *phi* mandala or *phi Lao muang* embodied in the Phra Bang image of Luang Phrabang, so after discussing the *vat*, I will then discuss another primary symbol of the Buddha's presence, the stupa or *that*. What these discussions will show is that, within the Lao PDR context, the spirits of the place continue to inflect understandings of

Buddhist principles. While the spirit cults may be in the process of becoming bud-dhacized in Isan, Buddhism continues to be understood primarily through the lenses of the spirit cults in Laos.

Condominas has captured succinctly the continuing social and social psycho-logical significance of the *vat* for the village:

> The village monastery has multiple functions serving not only as a religious structure, but also as a warehouse for the village, its forum and community center, a shelter for travelers, and so on. But above all, the monastery is an ex-pression and symbol of the village unit, for in most cases the village has either conferred its name on the monastery or taken its name from it. (1973: 254)

Though Condominas was writing in 1973, I find his observations remain quite accurate for rural Laos even today, more than thirty years after the revolution. The *vat* and the *ho phiban* (the "shrine" of the village guardian spirit) share a similar function in relation to the village insofar as both are nominal symbols of the vil-lage's identity. Within the indigenous logic of territoriality, therefore, it should not be surprising that the *vat* is also presided over and protected by a *phi vat*, in the same way that the *ho phiban* is a shrine regarded as a venue of power that protects the village. And just as Hayashi and Condominas have noted that the identity of the village guardian *phi* is usually traced to the original ancestral settlers of the village, so, as Condominas (1973: 259) points out, "the *phikunvat* is none other than the spirit of the original abbot of the monastery. This example indicates how two notions we consider distinct—'ancestors' and 'guardian spirits'—may in fact be only one."

During my months of living in Luang Phrabang and in my many visits to its myriad *vats* (and to several *vats* in Vientiane as well), every *sim* I visited contained a bronze or plaster image dedicated to the original abbot of the *vat*, in addition to an image, or often a photo, of its most recently deceased abbot (see Photo 3.1). These images are objects of daily veneration. It is clear that the conceptuality of presiding territorial *phi* and ancestor veneration, two principle elements of the in-digenous religious substratum, have been deployed to constitute how the sanctity of *sangha*'s venue is preserved.

But there are other ways in which the vitality and sanctity of the *vat* are articu-lated and nourished. At Vat Xieng Thong in Luang Phrabang I was also told by one of the longtime resident senior monks that the temple's participation in the an-nual August boat races between various *vats* on the Mekong and Nam Khan rivers is a symbol of the vitality of the *phi vat*.[17]

While every *vat* is presided over by its venerated guardian *phi*, it is also the case that every *vat* contains a stupa symbolizing the presence of the Buddha and smaller votive stupas containing the cremated ashes of various pious laity as well. The stupa for the Buddha is always located in a position of central prominence, while the votive stupas of the deceased laity are invariably located alongside of one of the compound walls marking the *sima* or boundary of the *vat* (see Photo 5.2).

Ladwig (2000 and 2002) has written two insightful essays that contain cogent observations on the confluence of *phi* and stupa veneration. I shall cite the major

Photo 5.2 Votive stupa at Vat Phra Keo, Vientiane

issues that he has raised, for they confirm the thesis I am trying to illustrate in general: that among the Lao of the Lao PDR, central aspects of Buddhist thought and practice continue to be understood through a prism of principles intrinsic to the ontology of the indigenous substratum of Lao religious culture.

I have already noted how important images of the Buddha, especially the Phra Bang, are understood to contain a spiritual power that, when protected and purified, serves as a source of vitality for the mandala, *muang*, or *ban*. In the *vat*s of Luang Phrabang, virtually every temple has in its possession a Buddha image to which great power is attributed.[18] While the cults of Buddha images have been central to lay Buddhism and political legitimations since perhaps as early as the fourteenth century among the Lao and Thai, the stupa or *that* has also been an enduring symbol of the Buddha's presence. The cults of images and stupas have their roots in ancient India. What I am interested in ascertaining here is the unique understanding of the power of stupas among the contemporary Lao of the Lao PDR.[19]

Ladwig (2002: 121) has referred to "the *thaat* (stupa) as a funeral monument [that is] also a mediating nature between classical Theravada Buddhist conceptions of death and those related to a pre-Buddhist ancestor cult of the Tai." Rather than "mediating nature," I would prefer "confluence" in this context, for two separate traditions regarding the dead are meeting in how the Lao ritually venerate their stupas. In what would at first appear to be an instance of Buddhacization, Ladwig notes that

> significantly, the edifices with the Buddha's relics were usually erected in or near places which were formerly occupied by different gods and spirits like *phi* ("spirits," "ancestor") or *naak* (nagas = "mythical serpents"). Sometimes, these supernatural beings were expelled, as the spirit living on the ground where the *Thaat Luang* of Luang Prabang stands today, but usually they were transformed into the guardians of the *that*. . . . [W]e can assume that this was a common strategy for the erection of stupas in the whole of Laos. (2000: 73)

What this process has actually resulted in is not Buddhacization, but rather what I would call the inspiriting of the stupa. In India and Sri Lanka the function of the stupa is normatively commemorative in nature. It symbolizes a passive sacred presence of the Buddha that can become an object of meditation, or an object of veneration, the act of which can generate merit. In the lay Lao context, however, the spirit of the stupa is an active force that not only protects the stupa itself, but can also be tapped for protection by those who venerate it. As Ladwig has indicated, sometimes the *phi* formerly associated with the spaces that stupas have come to occupy are enlisted as protective forces for the stupas themselves.

While *phi* can be associated with stupas representing the Buddha's presence, votive stupas erected for pious lay deceased are also associated with *khwan*. As Ladwig observes (2002: 122): "There are intriguing parallels to be found in the Laos' indigenous ontology, because some *thaat* are believed to have 'life essence' (*khwan*), a quality they share with humans, houses, buffaloes and so on. . . . Furthermore . . . , they seem connected to a specific spirit (*phii*)." The "specific *phi*" connected to the votive stupa found within Buddhist *vats* is always an ancestor of the deceased. The stupa is, in a sense, much like a family plot in a Western cemetery in that it may contain the remains of more than one family member. For the living, the stupa represents a link to the dead. Again, Ladwig observes:

> The ancestral *phii* of the deceased inhabit the *thaat* and are, in an active sense, present there. They prolong the deceased's life here on earth. The *stupa* forms a body for them that is constructed in accordance with the Buddhist cosmology. The relics contained in the *stupa* not only possess the "essence" of the dead, but through their new body connect the world of the living and the dead. Buddhism and the cult of ancestors are inseparably merged here in the form of the *stupa* as in so many other areas of the Lao worldview. (2002: 127)[20]

What this means collectively, then, is that the *vat* has become a venue for the practices of venerating *phi* and ancestors. In this case *phi* and ancestor are one in the same. Ladwig has put the matter this way: "When we recall that the *thaat* is equally a representation of the dead as an ancestor, then the *wat* has to be viewed as a type of ancestral tomb that unites all the deceased of a village at the center of the social space" (131). The *vat*, therefore, is the venue for the village that not only unites the powers of the Buddha, *dhamma*, and *sangha* as active presences, but these same active presences are understood and apprehended through the agencies of various *phi*. Thus when pious Buddhist laity come to the *vat* to engage in the cultic veneration of votive stupas, the *khwan* and *phi* of the family are joined not only in relation to generations of family members, but also in relation to the *triratna*. Family spirits and the spirits associated with the Buddha, *dhamma*, and *sangha* inhabit the same sacred or spiritual space.

Ladwig has also observed (2000: 74) that the central stupa signifying the Buddha in the *vat* "can sometimes equally be regarded as the center of a *baan* (village) or *muang*," equivalent to the *lak* or post in the center of the village that usually signifies the home of the *phi ban*. He asserts: "Seeing the stupa from that perspective, we are directly reminded of the idea formulated by Paul Mus (1975), who proposes that in the context of the 'Indianization' of southeast Asian religions the different ('animistic') deities of the soil were gradually integrated into the cult of the stupa and other forms of images which were originally reserved for depicting Buddhist and Hinduist [sic] deities" (Ladwig 2000: 74).

But rather than understanding this phenomenon as a kind of syncretism, which Ladwig tends to do, I agree with Tambiah that the ontologies of Buddhism and the spirit cults are separate but complementary, and with Hayashi that what has occurred is a matter of mutual transformation rather than an integration or synthesis. While Hayashi has documented a process whereby Buddhism is transforming the spirit cults within the context of the village Lao in Isan, in Luang Phrabang, and in other Lao cultural regions of the Lao PDR, what continues to occur is instead an inspiriting of Buddhism in which central aspects of the *sasana* (here the Buddha represented by images and stupas, *dhamma* represented by texts and incantations, and the *sangha* represented by the *vat*) continue to be interpreted through the lenses of the indigenous spirit cults related to both *khwan* and *phi*.

Conclusion

What implications do these two processes (Buddhacization and inspiriting) have for understanding the various contemporary players in Lao Buddhist religious culture? Buddhacization in this context refers primarily to how the indigenous religious culture has been interpreted and transformed by Buddhists. Inspiriting refers to the manner in which aspects of Buddhist practice have been interpreted and practiced by people whose epistemology is dominated by the ontology of the spirit cults.

Towards the end of *Buddhism and the Spirit Cults of North-East Thailand*, Tambiah offers a remarkably clear and insightful statement about the relation between the monk and layman. The heart of it is contained in this lengthy but adroit observation that helps us further to understand the processes of Buddhacization and inspiriting:

> Monk and laymen stand in a particular relation. The monk, by virtue of his asceticism and way of life, is practically aggregated to the world of death and final release. The layman is not, and is emphatically in this world. Through proper ritual procedures the monk as mediator and specialist can transfer Buddha's conquest of dangers inherent in human existence, transmuting it into prosperity and mental states free of pain and charged with merit. But at the same time, ethical effort and right intention are required from the layman; the most conspicuous manifestation of this is making merit by materially supporting the monks and temples.
>
> All this brings out a duality in Buddhist ritual and religious action that I have tried to cope with. Let me state three dualities or paradoxes which derive

from the trinity—Buddha, *Dhamma, Sangha*—itself. The Buddha has achieved *nirvana* and does not live; the Buddha or, better still, a material representation of him—his image or relics—has spiritual potency. The *Dhamma*, as sacred texts, relate primarily to the conquest of life, desire, and the seeking of release and salvation by attaining *nirvana*; the sacred texts have the power to confer blessings of a good life on ordinary mortals. The *Sangha* and its monks represent human beings who have renounced life and are seeking salvation through the practice of austere religious technology; the monks are as well human mediators who have access to mystical powers, deriving their sources which represent negation of life, but which are pre-eminently of a life-intensifying character when transferred to the laity. Supernatural power of a certain sort is located in the other world of the dead, and it can be reached only through the practice of asceticism and through asexual mediators. (1970: 211)

Tambiah's analysis is worth commenting upon at some length, but I will limit my remarks to two observations.

The first is that Tambiah has idealized the profile of the Lao monk by relying too heavily upon a model of Buddhist monasticism that, while certainly embedded within the Pali corpus, does not correspond to the profile embodied by most *bhikkhus*, at least in most village settings within Lao cultural areas, especially in the Lao PDR. Most Buddhist monks in the village context are far less preoccupied with practices of asceticism and more thoroughly engaged with the worldly dimensions of socioeconomic and political life than Tambiah's rendering suggests.

Second, and more important for the discussion at hand, I suggest that in elucidating the three fundamental paradoxes related to the Buddha, *dhamma*, and *sangha*, Tambiah has also identified and then underscored the potential for the respective processes of Buddhacization on the one hand and inspiriting on the other. Buddhacization is clearly in play when those normative aspects constitutive of, or related to, the soteriological quest (the first side of each paradox Tambiah has identified) are used to interpret the significance of the this-worldly living of lay religious life (the second side of each paradox). A particularly good example of Buddhacization in this sense is provided in one of Tiyavanich's lucid observations about Lao monks:

> *Revered monks of regional Buddhist traditions had always regarded work as a means of practicing the dhamma. They taught by example, by living simply, working hard, and acting ethically. . . . [T]he old as well as the young were engaged in the same kind of work; no distinctions were made. Manual labor such as chopping wood, hauling water, cleaning latrines, sweeping the ground,*

and thatching roofs was seen as training for mindfulness. (1997: 275; emphases mine).[21]

Thus manual labor is valorized as part and parcel of the soteriological quest leading to *nibbana*.

An excellent and closely related example of the converse process at work, that is, of how the monk's activity or labor is rationalized from a predominantly lay perspective inflected by the ontology of the spirit cults, is also provided by Tiyavanich in the following passage:

> The hard labor in which monks as well as villagers participated was usually done during the slack period or the beginning of the agricultural cycle. Village monks and abbots either helped villagers cut down trees and work the land or did this all themselves. *Since villagers were often afraid of being punished by spirits who guarded the forest, having monks work along side gave them a sense of security. In the Lao tradition, it was the monks and novices who repaired and did the clean-up work at sacred stupas. . . . Local people refused; they believed that anyone who touched, scrubbed, or climbed the stupa would sicken.* (1997: 26; my emphasis).

Thus the same physical labor of the monks is from one perspective a matter of practicing *dhamma*, but from another perspective it is what a monk needs to do so that the laity will not incur the malevolence of *phi*. Two separate religious understandings interpret the same monastic action. At the present time it appears that the former interpretation predominates in northeast Thailand, while the latter does in the Lao PDR. It may be a grand overgeneralization, but it seems as though in the tug of war between Buddhism and the spirit cults, Buddhism has seized the upper hand in Thailand, while the spirits remain ultimately vested in Laos.

The Lao Loum communities in the Lao PDR have not been subjected to the same kind of ideological pressures from their central government during the past thirty years that the Lao in the Isan region have been by theirs. Not only have they not been pressured to become authentically "Thai," they have been subjected consistently to anti-Thai propaganda and the ideological vicissitudes of Marxism ("the new socialist man") as well. Still, neither of these efforts (the anti-Thai or the Marxist) have significantly altered the religious dispositions in most Lao Loum villages. Rather, it should be quite obvious to any careful observer that the cults of *phi* and *khwan* remain quite firmly entrenched. While Buddhism is increasingly affirmed in the public life of Laos, the spirit cults are also recognized by many as a characteristic that distinctively delineates the Lao. Moreover, while the process of modernization (or globalization or Westernization) is quite evident among many of the newly emerging middle class in Vientiane and Luang Phrabang, the inspiriting of Buddhism continues apace and relatively unabated in the village. If anything, it could be argued that the soteriological dimension of Buddhism, with its emphasis on meditation and merit-making, is giving ground to a more instrumental view grounded in observance of the spirit cults. Clearly the Pathet Lao and the communist party have always espoused an instrumentalist view of Buddhism. Certainly the new generation of capitalists seeking to market Buddhism as one of the great tourist attractions for Luang Phrabang and Laos also take an instrumentalist view. It is not so surprising to conclude, then, that the traditional village instrumental view of the inspiriting of Buddhism will continue vigorously into the foreseeable future. Indeed, it would seem that this predominantly instrumentalist view of pragmatic power among the Lao is the deep-seated cause for the persistence of the spirit cults and that in Laos it will be extremely difficult to exorcize the spirits of the place.

APPENDIX I

Transformations of the *Ramayana*

The *Ramayana* is arguably the best-known epic throughout South and Southeast Asia.[1] It has been adapted in Hindu and Buddhist cultures from northwestern India to Indonesia. It would be difficult, if not impossible, to locate royal courts in any part of the world influenced by Indic culture that did not embrace and then produce a localized version of the *Ramayana*.[2] The epic has become, in a sense, every South and Southeast Asian king's royal story.

The most famous version today remains Valmiki's Sanskrit *Ramayana*,[3] a north Indian version from the Ganges River valley dating roughly to the second century BCE, but probably a text based on many antecedents already in play at that time. It is important to note that Valmiki's version—certainly the most internationally renowned because of its translation into Western languages—cannot be regarded as a root text from which all other versions have developed. The history of the epic's various versions in disparate regions of India and elsewhere is far too complex and obscure to allow for this. No doubt several different versions were exported to Southeast Asian cultures at various times throughout history. Nonetheless, a comparison between the Lao version and Valmiki's proves generally instructive, as respective emphases in each can tell us what may be unique about Lao royal culture. The story's specifically Buddhist reading within the Lao Theravada context also contributes to its uniqueness. I first provide a short summary of the Valmiki version in order to set up a brief discussion of the Lao version.

Valmiki's story is about a *dharma*-minded prince who falls victim to his father's promise to a secondary wife that her son, rather than Rama, should assume the throne of Ayodhya, though it is Rama who is the rightful heir. As part of his father's promise, Rama observes fourteen years of asceticism while in exile in forest hinterlands. To uphold his regretful father's honor, Rama dutifully obeys and departs for the forest accompanied by his loyal younger brother Lakshmana, and the ever-dedicated Sita, the princess whose hand Rama has won in a martial competition by performing astounding feats of strength with his trademark bow. Rama's younger half-brother (not Lakshmana), despite the clever wiles of his mother, refuses to assume the Ayodhya throne out of his love and respect for Rama. Meanwhile, as Rama, Lakshmana, and Sita wander in the forest, various episodes unfold including, most importantly, Rama's encounter with Surpanakha, a demonic *raksasi* in disguise, who attempts to seduce him. In reaction, Surpanakha's nose is sliced by Lakshmana. When her true identity is revealed, she flees back to her home on the island of Lanka, where she reports the encounter, including a vivid depiction of the beautiful Sita, to her older brother Ravana, the ten-headed mighty king of the *raksasas*, who has gained his great power through the practice of ascetic devotion to Siva. On hearing Surpanakha's description of Sita, Ravana is deeply aroused. His imagination of Sita's beauty becomes obsessive, and so he contrives a plan to gain her as his queen. He magically conjures a golden stag that briefly appears before Sita, who in turn is immediately enamored and wants to possess it as her companion. To please Sita, Rama searches in vain for the stag deep into the forest for a long period of time, leaving Lakshmana behind to protect Sita. When Rama does not return, Lakshmana draws a protective circle around Sita, recites a holy prayer, and sets off in search of Rama. Ravana then appears and abducts the frightened and resistant Sita. As he carries her away through the skies back to his capital in Lanka, Jetayu, king of the eagles, encounters the two and vainly tries to free Sita. He is defeated and fatally wounded. Rama and Lakshmana soon return and learn of Sita's fate from the dying Jetayu. The two set off for Lanka determined to win back Sita. On their way many episodes occur, but the most important is the recruitment of Hanuman, the courageous monkey-king, who invests Rama with his loyalty and his army for the inevitable battle with Ravana. On a reconnaissance mission to Lanka, Hanuman finds Sita, who all the while has foiled Ravana's amorous advances. Hanuman tells her of Rama's plan for her rescue. When his presence is discovered, a fight ensues in which Hanuman's tail is set on fire. As Hanuman jumps from house to house in Ravana's capital city, all of the houses are set on fire, and the city is completely burned up. Ravana is enraged. Hanuman reports all to Rama and Lakshmana, who then lay out their plans for their invasion. When they are prepared for the final assault, they are aided by Vibhisana, a dharma-minded younger brother of Ravana, who has seen the virtue of Rama's cause. The two armies clash, a terrible war is fought, culminating in an epic battle between Rama and Ravana. Ravana is finally defeated and in his dying words acknowledges the righteousness of Rama. He is given a solemn "state funeral," and Rama appoints Vibhisana as king of Lanka. Rama and Sita are temporarily united, but the question of Sita's purity in Rama's absence remains. She willingly agrees to enter a sacrificial fire to prove her virtuous purity and devotion, after which Rama, Sita, and Lakshmana return triumphantly to Ayodhya.

I shall first discuss the manner in which the main characters of the text are portrayed in the Lao version, a method that provides some insight into the specifically royal Lao ideals articulated in the *Phra Lak Phra Lam*. I will then comment on the specifically Theravada Buddhist character reflected in the Lao redaction.

Like Valmiki's Sanskrit *Ramayana*, the *Phra Lak Phra Lam* is also focused on familial relations, only much more intensively and intimately. Sahai argues that an elder/younger brother rivalry between various family members pervades the entire text (1996, 1: 35) and roots the presence of this continuing tension throughout the story partly in the mythic and historical political past of Lao kingdoms. He first recalls the myth of King Borom from the *Luang Phrabang Chronicle* in which this divine primordial king divided up the world among his seven sons, with the eldest receiving Xieng Dong Xieng Thong (Luang Prabhang): "The principalities were ranked elder or younger according to the seniority of its ruler. . . . Luang Prabang was the elder *muang*, Champasak was the younger *muang*, because its prince was the younger brother of the king of Vientiane" (33). In the same vein, Sahai goes on to note that Thailand commonly assumes an elder-brother stance vis-à-vis Laos (34), but that the *Phra Lak Phra Lam* positions Laos as the older brother to Cambodia. If tensions between mandalas are in play in the text, they are not Thai-Lao, but Lao-Khmer. The *Phra Lak Phra Lam* has the king of Indraprasthanagara ("the city and abode Indra" [king of the gods] but also referring to the this-worldly cities of either Angkor or Phnom Penh), Tapa Paramesvara ("the supreme lord of yogic asceticism," or Siva) giving his kingdom to his younger son, rather than his older son. (The parallels with Valmiki's text are obvious.) Annoyed, Siva's older son departs for the north and sets up his own throne in Vientiane. Obviously, the inference of this episode is that proper lineage of divine kingship, based on principles of seniority, now runs through Vientiane rather than through Angkor (or Phnom Penh) or, rather, through the Lao rather than the Khmer.[4] There is, then, at least in part, a political inspiration for the manner in which the text was framed locally.

In terms of structure and content, however, the greatest difference between Valmiki's *Ramayana* and the *Phra Lak Phra Lam*, lies in the fact that the Lao story contains a long first part that is absent in Valmiki's version. This is the story of Ravana's abduction of Canda, the daughter of the king of Vientiane, who turns out to be Ravana's older cousin, since Ravana is the son of Siva's younger son who was given the kingship of Indraprasthanagara (Cambodia). Canda also turns out to be Rama and Lakshmana's older sister, since the two brothers are born to the king of Vientiane as the result of a request made to Indra that his daughter's abduction be righted through divine intervention. Indra is only too happy to comply with this request, since previously Ravana had magically impersonated Indra and had seduced his wife, Indrani. Sahai notes that the legend of Rama's elder sister is found in versions of the *Ramayana* less well known than Valmiki's from eastern and northwestern India and that one of these versions may have served as the basis for the entire first part of the Lao text. In the concluding comments of his introduction to the *Phra Lak Phra Lam,* Sahai argues that

> this Valmikian legend [from either eastern or northwestern India] has been used in the Laotian story to depict the Mekong Valley, to ventilate the ethnic tension between the Lao and the Khmer and to introduce the concept of sibling rivalry. . . . Structurally the text is based on a double theme of abduction, those of Santa [Canda] and Sita by Ravana. The narrative describes the Laotian perception of Mekong and Indochina through the first abduction. Through the second, the text outlines the cultural linkages between Laos, Cambodia and Sri Lanka. (1996, 2: 51)

By these comments we are introduced not only to what Sahai perceives to be the central focus of the Lao text (sibling rivalry), but also the possible geopolitical perceptions that informed the text within the context of its contemporary localization.

Thus in the Lao version we are presented with not one, but two abductions by Ravana. Moreover, we witness two instances of rectification by Rama in response. In the first abduction, the scene has been set when Ravana usurps the rule of his grandfather (Siva)[5] and father in Indraprasthanagara and proceeds to abduct his elder uncle's daughter, Nan Canda, for marriage, without any ritual formalities, an especially problematic turn of events since she is also elder to him. This, then, further sets the stage for the king of Vientiane's appeal to Indra for help by having two divine beings born as his sons to avenge Ravana's crime. What follows, of course, is the appearance of Rama and Lakshmana and the eventual defeat of Ravana in battle. Rama recaptures Canda, so that Ravana is forced to fulfill all of the required pre-marriage rites, including paying a proper bride price, in order to right the wrongs he has committed. In fact, in the process he officially becomes Rama's older brother-in-law in addition to the fact that the two are first cousins.

In contrast to Ravana, during the course of his expedition to Indraprasthanagara to recover Canda, Rama sets the example of contracting good and proper marriage alliances of his own with a number of families of princes and chieftains. He reestablishes the Lao social balance by arresting the reversals perpetrated by Ravana on the elder-younger sibling relationship. Sahai also notes that when Rama takes several wives of his own, it is only after he has properly asked for the hand of each woman in question and paid the proper bride price.[6] Rama contracts marriages with no less than twelve wives, while his brother Lakshmana contracts seven. Of Rama's wives, one is a niece of his brother Lakshmana and another the daughter of the headman of a Kha tribe. Rama also marries the women of those he defeats in battle. "Some of Rama's sons [eventually] marry Lakshmana's daughters, though it is clear that sibling marriage is preferred to cross-cousin marriage" (Sahai 1996, 2: 54).

Every one of these events is quite foreign to Valmiki's *Ramayana* and reflects what is unique to the Lao rendition. While Sanskrit culture, and many castes in India, traditionally approved of cross-cousin marriages, sibling marriage was regarded as incest, as it was for Lao commoners. In India, while the *Ramayana* was understood as a text of fundamentally royal significance, it has wide appeal historically beyond elite court cultures. Moreover, the ethos of Valmiki's *Ramayana* is nowhere so overtly political in tone or focus as the *Phra Lak Phra Lam*. Personal loyalty, a kind of pre-*bhakti* devotion to divinely inspired realizations of a more cosmic *dharma*, transcends such this-worldly concern for the diplomacy of politically correct or strategic marriage alliances. Personal fidelity or devotional piety is more the order of Valmiki's text, a theme that would seem to preclude the many marriages by Rama and Lakshmana as well. Clearly, Lao royalty placed a much greater premium on intrafamilial marriage where possible, but also on diplomatically conducted strategic marriage alliances.

In the second part of the *Phra Lak Phra Lam*, which focuses on the abduction of Sita, we learn that she is also closely related to Rama, being Rama's niece both patrilineally and matrilineally (Sahai 1996, 2: 54). Sahai adds that "the Laotian version follows a non-Valmikian tradition contained in the Jain works, the *Vasudevi Hindi* and the *Uttarapurana* in which Sita was born of Mandodari, the wife of Ravana" (19). Readers familiar with Valmiki's *Ramayana* will be surprised to learn that in the Lao rendition, Sita is, therefore, a daughter of Ravana! This means that in the Lao version Canda (Rama's elder sister) is Ravana's wife, who has given birth to Sita. The Lao redaction, therefore, seems to be much more intended for a limited royal or court audience. Its protagonists cannot easily be abstracted and generalized to assist in didactic lessons of general social and cultural order. The text seems as much aimed at the behavior of political elites as it is at promulgating the Buddhist virtues that also informed ideals of Lao royalty of the time. Before dealing with the substance of the Buddhist ideals implanted in the text, we should note a series of further comparisons.

Comparing the profiles of Ravana in Valmiki's *Ramayana* and the Lao text, Sahai says this specifically:

The *Valmiki Ramayana* and the *Mahabharata* do not contain any reference to the former life of Ravana . . .[but t]he Laotian genealogy of Ravana tracing his origin from the *brahma*-couple contains an illusion to his link with Brahma of the Hindu pantheon. His association with Siva is also evoked by introducing Paramesvara/Isvara as his grandfather. . . . In the *Rama Jataka* [*Phra Lak Phra Lam*], Ravana is not a ten-headed demon of the Indian epic. He is the prince and heir of the royal dynasty . . . handsome, powerful and audacious. He is the *enfant terrible* of the royal family. . . . He abducted his cousin, the elder sister of Rama from Vientiane. His mother advised him to return the girl who he had brought without formally begging for her hand and paying the bride-price for her. But he did not listen to her words, overpowered by passion and obstinacy, though as a *maha brahma,* he had accumulated spiritual merits, wisdom and knowledge of Buddhist doctrine. In this respect, the Laotian portrayal reminds us of Valmiki who focuses on the prideful in Ravana's character. (1996, 1: 14)

It is true that the Lao continued to emphasize the theme of Ravana's pride, but they also further humanized Ravana. While of divine origin, as claimed by all Lao royalty, Ravana is also the royal spoiled brat, who, in addition to transgressing social custom, defies his mother's counsel and ignores the very virtues of knowledge he has obtained in gaining his position of power. Because he is self-centered, he is also the perfect antithesis of Buddhist values. In the end, after his second and final defeat by Rama, he gets what he karmicly deserves:

In the Valmikian narration, Ravana's funeral rites are performed. But in the Laotian text in which the Buddhist concept of sin [better: karma] predominates, Ravana, after his fall in the battlefield is immediately caught by the four guardian angels [sic] of hell and instantly thrown into the pot of hell. In the Laotian narrative, there is no scope and time for Ravana's funeral. (Sahai 1996, 2: 44)

This stands in sharp contrast to Valmiki's end of Ravana, in which Ravana comes to realize the *dharmic* truth that Rama embodies, an event that seems to prefigure his possible ultimate redemption.

Sahai also supplies us with a litany of comparisons focused on Sita:

The Valmikian narrative of the abduction of Sita has been considerably modified by the Laotian text. The Valmiki *Ramayana* mentions Surpanakha as the instigator [as a result of being rejected and humiliated by Rama and Lakshmana]. She incites Ravana to abduct Sita after Lakshmana mutilates her nose and ears. According to *Phra Lak Phra Lam,* Ravana plans the abduction of his own initiative after perceiving with his divine eyes Rama's success in winning the hand of Sita. He sets [forth] from Lanka to abduct her. The abduction does not take place in the forest in the course of the exile of Rama (an episode omitted in the Laotian text), but on the island of the foster-father of Sita from where Rama was taking his bride to the city of Vientiane. (1996, 2: 24)

Ravana's abduction of Sita not only redounds more seriously and directly on Ravana, and therefore makes the weight of his karmic actions that much heavier to bear, but the fact that Sita is abducted from her foster-father's island while Rama is actually conducting her to Vientiane for their marriage, heightens the sense of Ravana's crime: family space (the foster-father's island) is truly disrespected, and the family sense of time (the impending marriage rites) is insulted as well.

Sahai cites further variations between the Valmiki version and the Lao: the motif of Sita's body heating up as a protection against Ravana's amorous advances; Sita accusing Lakshmana of not helping Rama enough, such that she implies that Lakshmana might have designs on her himself; and the earth goddess (Nang Thoranee) protecting Sita in the same way that Lakshmana does in the Valmiki version by drawing a protective circle around her (1996, 2: 25). Sahai notes further that in the Valmiki narration:

> After Vibhisana is installed as King of Lanka, he goes to Sita and conveys Rama's desire to escort her well-dressed and decorated. . . . But in the Lao narration, Sita decorates herself well and then departs for the camp of Rama escorted by Ravana's widow (Rama's elder sister Canda) and the people of Lanka. It is Canda, widow of Ravana, who offers Sita to Rama for marriage in accordance with Lao tradition. (43)

Canda, in turn, again in Lao fashion, is remarried to Vibhisana (44), the brother of the deceased. The *Phra Lak Phra Lam* also includes a scene of Sita adoringly drawing Ravana's portrait, which, while not included in Valmiki, is also found in Gujarati, Bengali, Kashmiri, and Sinhala recensions. All of these texts, including the Lao, then, infer some culpability on Sita's part. Yet the Lao text discards the Valmiki version of Sita being held susceptible to criticism because of the time she spent in exile in Ravana's company, and Rama's subsequent demand that she prove her purity by undergoing *sati*.

But perhaps the greatest difference between Valmiki's version and the Lao lies in the Lao text's suffusion with Buddhist ideals. Rama is, after all, styled the bodhisattva in a previous rebirth. Indeed, the *Phra Lak Phra Lam* is also known as the "Rama Jataka."[7] While Sahai stresses how intrafamily issues predominate in accordance with Lao royal family customs, the text is also meant to be a didactic device in the *dhammic* inculcation of karmic retribution. Ravana's demise and its aftermath illustrate the central teaching of karma, but throughout there are many other instances that illustrate the pervasive presence of this central teaching. Three examples of the seemingly countless instances of karma at work in the Lao version include: (1) Hanuman's representation as a son of Rama, the result of Rama's taking on the form of a monkey for three years in order to burn up the karma of past deeds (Sahai [1996, 2: 27] says that this theme possibly could be traced back to versions of *Mahabharata* in which Siva and Parvati take on the form of monkeys and give birth to Hanuman); (2) Rama is injured because one of Ravana's arrows pierces his heel, a vulnerability coming to fruition because of past karmic actions; and (3) Sita is said to have been overpowered in her mind due to karma when she pursues the golden stag conjured by Ravana.

Rama's actions are also seen in Buddhist fashion in many other ways. One is the manner in which he manifests his compassion for those he has defeated in battle. The bodhisattva faces the challenge of a red-crested *naga*-king and, after defeating him, grants him pardons through his great compassion. He also repeatedly makes known the *pancasila*, or the five-fold basic morality associated with the *cakkavattin* ideal and the cardinal ethical principles at the heart of the monastic Vinaya. Upon passing the River Hin Boun, the bodhisattva pardons an elephant-king and teaches his entourage the five moralities. Similarly the bodhisattva pardons the white-bull king and proceeds to teach him the *pancasila* as well. On the bank of the Lohini River, when his horse kills a forest-spirit couple, the bodhisattva proceeds to teach the horse about the importance of *ahimsa*, noninjury to all forms of life. Rama thus embodies *sila*, or the principle of ethical consciousness, much more emphatically than Valmiki shows him upholding *dharma* as sociocosmic order.

Rama is not only a champion of moral virtue and a master over the natural world, but he also refuses to take the wife of a water *phi* he has just vanquished. Whether or not this reflects the legacy of Phothisarat's attempt to eliminate the *phi* cults, especially among the royalty, it is a curious addition to the Lao text, one reflecting a proclivity to keep the cults of spirits separate from royal Buddhist culture.

Sahai underlines the presence of Theravada doctrine with regard to the centrality placed on the efficacy of human life, that is, how the text is comparatively so anthropocentric in nature.

> The major characters, Ravana, Rama, Lakshmana, Sita are divine beings from the different stages of heaven reborn in the world of mortals . . . but they are [now] normal human beings in the Mekong valley, since according to the Theravada belief prevalent in the valley, in tune with one's stock of merit, a person attains the highest stage of heaven and then descends to be reborn in the world of mortals after that accumulated store is diminished. (1996, 2: 52)

While that may be the case, it is also axiomatic in Theravada that the human realm is the only realm in which karma can be generated, where actions really count in terms of cosmic and soteriological significance. Thus for the bodhisattva's rebirth to result in progress on the path toward his final rebirth, when he realizes perfect enlightenment, the events of the story must take place in the human realm of *samsara*. Perhaps this is the most significant of the Buddhist transformations, insofar as the rebirth of Rama itself has been subordinated as a previous life of the Buddha, one less advanced than Vessantara, and of course, antecedent to the final life of Gotama the Buddha. In Hindu tradition the Buddha was frequently depicted as an avatar of Visnu, but in Theravada Laos, as in Sri Lanka, the heroic Rama is but an episode in the long career of rebirths of the bodhisattva in which he is seen as perfecting his virtues in anticipation of buddhahood. In this manner, the specifically Lao understanding of relations between royal siblings, marriage alliances, and the special place in Buddhist tradition afforded to Vientiane, are all legitimized within the ultimate Buddhist imprimatur.

As with all other *jataka*s, the story is told by the Buddha himself and the characters correspond to those central characters associated with his final rebirth as Gotama. Obviously Rama is the Buddha, and Ravana is his archenemy, Devadatta. Other correspondences are serially identified (see Sahai 1996, 1: 10–11).

At the very end of the *jataka,* the magical power of the text is extolled in a fashion often found in other Buddhist textual traditions (Theravada and Mahayana alike): by hearing the text, the listener will eventually enjoy becoming a *cakkavattin,* or become Indra, and ultimately experience *nibbana*; or by copying the text, the copier will become an object of veneration in his own right. The text should be narrated, as well, especially to children and grandchildren. "Thus the *Rama Jataka* was raised to the status of a sacred text ... [and] ranks next to the Vessantara Jataka whose reading has taken the form of a religious festival in which merit is earned from listening" (Sahai 1996, 1: 11).

Sahai notes that the *Phra Lak Phra Lam* continued to be copied in palm-leaf manuscripts well into the first half of the twentieth century and was traditionally recited as a *jataka* by monks during the rain retreat season (*vassa*) "at different monasteries along the Mekong Valley" (1996, 1: 1–2). The manuscript that Sahai appears to have been working from is one that is preserved in the National Library in Bangkok. The *Phra Lak Phra Lam* is not found in the traditional collection of 550 Pali *jataka*s and seems to have been missed entirely by Louis Finot in his survey of Lao monastic texts in 1917.

The *Phra Lak Phra Lam* continues its association with Lao royalty in contemporary Luang Phrabang, despite the fact that the last king disappeared from the city in 1975. Gilded wall sculptures depicting scenes from the story can be found adorning the *sim* of Vat Mai, which was rebuilt in the early twentieth century and is now the venue for the annual Pi Mai (New Year) lustration rites of the Phra Bang image. A *Ramayana* mural was also painted on one side of the interior walls of the diminutive *sim* at Vat Long Khun, a *vat* located across the Mekong River from the royal palace where kings to be would spend several days in private meditation

Photo A.1 Mural painting of *Ramayana* episodes on the interior wall of the *sim* at Vat Long Khun, Luang Phrabang

Photo A.2 Decorative depiction of Rama and Sita on door of royal funeral carriage house at Vat Xieng Thong, Luang Phrabang

before their formal ritual inaugurations (see Photo A.1). The exterior sides of the royal "funeral house," located within Vat Xieng Thong, are decorated on all sides with gold-gilded scenes from the *Ramayana* (see Photo A.2).

Traditionally, episodes of the *Ramayana* were performed as part of the New Year's celebrations in Luang Phrabang. Before the 1975 revolution,

> the most important parts of the repertoire of the court ballet were episodes from the Lao version of the Ramayana. . . . With the victory of the revolution in 1975, the Pra Lak Pra Lam was no longer felt suitable to figure in the state rituals of the New Year. This does not imply, however, that the Pra Lak Pra Lam has lost any of its local realism and political implications. As late as 1979, the Culture Ministry of Laos presented the Ramayana ballet before foreign and Indian visitors, saying "we still draw inspiration from this epic. Ramayana is the symbol of the proletariat while Ravana speaks for the capitalist-colonialist powers. Rama and Hanuman are creators of the guerilla warfare." (Trankell 1999: 202, 204)

Trankell goes on to note how a beauty contest is now substituted for the performance of the *Ramayana* at the Luang Phrabang national New Year's festivities. "It was apparently felt that the nomination of Miss Lao New Year better fitted the growing emphasis on a common national identity in Laos than did episodes from the classical Ramayana" (204).

In the early 2000s scenes from the *Phra Lak Phra Lam* have been commercially produced in dance performances held three or four nights a week by high school students for tourists in an audience hall on the grounds of the Luang Phrabang National Museum, the last king's residence which he "gifted" to the people in the last months before he disappeared. Some efforts are also under way to recreate the puppets and puppetry that once were a part of the royally sponsored Ramayana ensemble.

APPENDIX 2

The Cult of *Khwan*

If there is a ritual that is ubiquitous and quintessentially Lao, it is the *sukhwan basi* (pronounced "bah-see") ceremony. It is performed for virtually all important occasions marking an individual's life passages: pregnancy, marriage, childbirth (shortly thereafter), an impending ordination into the *sangha*, the assumption of any important social or public position, significant homecomings (welcoming) and departures (bon voyage), the beginning of an institution, or any time that marks a definitive transition from one phase of life to another. The basic function of the ritual is to restore the *khwan* (vital essence) by recalling it to its home in order to achieve once more an invigorated balance, a purity or comportment necessary to negotiate an impending transition, transformation, or undertaking. It is a ritual of integration and reintegration at junctures of liminality. The hope expressed within the rite is that it will induce health, productivity, general well-being, and long life.[1]

The term "*khwan*" itself is nearly impossible to translate. It has been rendered as "life-soul," "vital essence," "inner spirit," "life-force," "psychic energy," and so on. While *phi* are external forces that animate the natural and projected supernatural world, the *khwan* is internal to each individual person, attached to a specific human body, and yet it can leave the body or become alienated from it. It leaves the body when it is frightened, sick, or in trouble, or when the mind is in an unsettled or disturbed state. It may also wander if distracted, in effect becoming "lost." If it wanders into hostile or unwholesome locations, it may be harmed. When it leaves the individual, especially for prolonged periods, the consequence may be suffering, disease, and misfortune. Its departure cannot be observed, but is known only through the effects of its absence. The *khwan* itself is actually believed to be constituted by thirty-two different *khwan* that are identified with various organs or parts of the body, but it is usually treated as just one.[2] No one I encountered in my conversations about the *khwan*—and I attended many *basi*—could enumerate more than a handful of the thirty-two parts. In any case, as Tambiah notes below, though it is related, the *khwan* should not be confused with "consciousness" (*vinjan*) per se.

The *khwan* must be understood in relation to *winjan* [consciousness]. The *winjan*, also a spiritual essence, resides in the body. But it is different from *khwan*. The *khwan* can leave the body temporarily, thereby causing illness, but it can be recalled and mental and physical health thereby restored. At death the *khwan* leaves the body for good, followed by the *winjan*. The *winjan* leaves the body only at death. In fact, death is described as the escape of *winjan* from the body. After death, people are not concerned with the *khwan*, only with the fate of the *winjan* and its subsequent transformations. . . . *Khwan* is associated with life and the vicissitudes of life; *winjan* is associated with death and the vicissitudes after death. Both are spiritual essences that animate life; the *khwan* actively and the *winjan* passively, or the former as a variable substance, the latter as permanent. Their poles are reversed at death. The *khwan* dies for good (or becomes passive), but the *winjan* disengages itself from its mortal coil and leads a separate existence. (1970: 58–59)

This formulation, at least as Tambiah has articulated it, may represent a partial concession to Theravada thought. The *vinjan* is identified as conditioned ephemeral consciousness that transmigrates in the journey of *samsaric* reincarnation, while the essentially substantial *khwan* does not. On the other hand, the *basi* ceremony "does not involve the kind of ethical action on the part of the recipient required in the case of merit acquisition, but is accomplished by virtue of the elders' ritual action and transfer of mystical power vested in them" (Tambiah 1970: 224). Thus the *basi* ceremony is not a Buddhist merit-making rite in any sense. Instead, it invokes a complementary ontology of power rooted in Lao indigenous religious culture. Though the transfer of mystical power from the chanting of Pali words and mantras may have their source in a Lao understanding of the power of the Buddha's *dhamma*, the metaphysical basis of the *khwan* is clearly not Buddhist in substance and orientation.

The liturgy of the *basi* is highly variable, but it typically begins with a veneration of the *thewada* and *phi*. The *phi* identified are usually the local natural powers, but sometimes may also include the *phi* of deceased family members or ancestors. The purpose of the veneration is not so much to summon their powers to assist in the recalling of the *khwan*, but to acknowledge their cooperative presence as part of the extended spirit world so that they will not interfere deleteriously in the process that is about to unfold. If anything, the ritual is about extracting the *khwan* from its possible contamination from contact with *phi*. Abhay provides a typical version of a *basi* liturgy:[3]

This is a very propitious day, a very appropriate one, the day when the victorious King re-enters his Palace.

This is the day we have chosen to put on this tray hard boiled eggs, potatoes, tubers, coconuts, chicken legs. All these choice morsels together with some good bottles of alcohol, apart from other delicious dishes.

The time is propitious and we have invited the great scholar to sit before this tray and to call the soul.

Come back, oh soul, come along the path which has been cleansed and is now open to you;

Come home;

Wade through the river if it only comes up to your chest;

Swim if the river is deep;

When you arrive at the ray, don't hide in the huts;

When you come up to the tree stump, do not rest your head on it.

Do not fear when you come near;

Have no fear of ghosts or *Phi*.

Come, oh soul, if you have eaten with the *Phi*s, vomit it,

If you have been chewing with the *Phi*s, spit it out;

You must come back on an empty stomach, and eat rice with your uncle, and eat fish with your ancestors!

[Abhay: According to tradition, each of the thirty-two parts of our body has a soul. The celebrant does not forget this. He then calls the soul belonging to the head to return from the Akalita heavens . . . (soul of the legs, etc.)]

Come back this day, oh soul who has gone to a new birth in the uninhabited village where live the twin-tail snakes, and where reign the goddesses with two knots of hair.

Do not linger on the way, neither with the *phi*s or in the mountains;

Come home, to your home made of smooth planks, covered with thick hay and of which the foundation piles and the timber of its framework has been pulled by the mighty elephants;

Come back to this stately abode where you shall not be short of anything, where you shall not be ill-treated either by your uncles or parents, where all will love you as gold and cherish you as a precious stone;

[Abhay: then follows the blessing]

Be as strong as the antlers of a stag, as the jaws of the wild bear or husks of an elephant!

May your life last a thousand years, may your riches be abundant in every kind, elephants, horses, victuals and wealth!

Should you suffer with fever, may it disappear!

If you are a servant, may you be free . . .

May you be all powerful the world over!

May everything yield before you and may you be free from want!

May you have long life, health, happiness and strength! (1959: 130–131)

Abhay notes that the *sukhwan* always then extends into a *ngan* or "a night of celebration and love." The *basi* I attended were usually the formal ritual component of larger familial celebrations (marriage, homecoming, new job, and so forth) that did indeed include a big, long party that lasted several hours during which copious amounts of alcohol were consumed and a great deal of singing and dancing were enjoyed. But the formal *basi* ritual itself lasts for only about a half an hour. It always includes the infusion of power into a white cord or string by means of an elder chanting his sacred words, usually in Pali. In turn, each participant ties a cutting from the cord onto the wrists of the person or people who are being feted. In effect, this constitutes a kind of individual and collective blessing by the community that has gathered. While the liturgy chanted effects the integration of the *khwan* with the individual, the tying of strings represents the integration of the *khwan* with the community.

Tambiah has written extensively about the meaning of *sukhwan basi*:

> The *sukhwan* . . . is a prophylactic *cum* therapeutic ritual. The *khwan* . . . leaves the body in certain situations; its flight from a person connotes a particular mental state, an agitation of the mind. The *khwan* must be recalled and aggregated to the body in order to make the person whole. We can translate this as follows. A part of me, my spirit essence, becomes alienated from me and disperses into the outside world; it is as if my mind is elsewhere. It is significant that, in the texts cited, the spirit essence is thought of having gone to that part of the external world which is the very opposite of society and human habitation (village—the forest, cave, mountain, river—lured there by the animals of the forest). How insistently the ritual calls the *khwan* from these places! In other words, the escape of the spirit essence from an individual is suggestive of the escape of a person from his village and community members into the forest and its non-human inhabitants. Typically, we note that the *sukhwan* is an imperative at certain rites of passage (ordination and marriage), at situations of reintegration into the village or social group, or at moments of actual or potential departure from them. These are contexts wherein the interest of the village, or elders, or family require the individual to bring attention to bear on the situation at hand and to conform to norms, assume a new status, or return to a previous status. From society's point of view in these situations there is the danger that the individual may actually withdraw from its requirements or be unhappy about, or unequal to, fulfilling them. When the elders call the *khwan* and restore it to the body, it is they who are charging the celebrant with the vital social force of morale, and they thus enable the celebrant to accept and bind himself to what is expected of him. (1970: 243)[4]

Notes

Preface

1. Thanks to the bibliography on Laos compiled by the famous anthropologist, Charles Keyes, at http://www.lib.washington.edu/Southeastasian/blaos.html, the many historical writings of Martin Stuart-Fox, and the anthropological and historical studies by Grant Evans (see bibliography).

2. Especially the premier study of Lao religious culture, Marcel Zago's *Rites et ceremonies en milieu Bouddhiste Lao* (1972).

Introduction

1. Ian Harris (2005: 188), in reference to understanding Buddhism within the context of neighboring Cambodia, writes: "There has been a reluctance, particularly among Western scholars, to accept Buddhism as a localizable 'total fact.' What I mean by this is that when we look at Buddhism, we are apt to see only its philosophical and scholastic superstructure. Now, in its Asian heartlands, intellectual endeavor has always tended to be part of a specialized and restricted domain, but Buddhism has also operated on a far wider level to sustain and inform the cultures with which it forms a whole. . . . Buddhists are not, and have never been, people outside history." In related fashion Catherine Bell (1992: 186) argues that the study of sophisticated belief tenets is often simply a study of expressions that can be attributed only to an elite class of religious adherents, chiefly because "coherent and shared systems of belief will occur among a relatively small class who specialize in them and will not readily drift down to be shared by society as a whole." As pages of this study unfold, it will be seen how I agree with the perspectives of Bell and Harris on these issues.

2. See especially Malandra (1993); and, in general, McArthur (2002).

3. Mandala polity is a well-worn and debated territory for scholars of Southeast Asia. From what I have written, it should be clear that I have followed Tambiah (1976), Geertz (1981), and Wolters (1982 and 1999) in my general rendering. See McDaniel (2002b: 166–172) for a resume of mandalic "galactic polity" germane to northern Thailand. Stuart-Fox (1996, 1997, and 1998) uses the term to describe royal Lao hegemonies, but does not explain its Indic background and dynamics. Hence my brief resume has been included in this introduction.

4. Martin Stuart-Fox points out that one "point about French colonial policy is that it effectively preserved tribal cultures from continuing Lao Buddhist influence. Divide and rule stopped Buddhacization of minorities" (private communication).

5. For aerial maps of the scope and intensity of the American bombing missions, made possible by the release of classified documents by President Bill Clinton during his fall, 2000 visit to Vietnam, see Taylor Owen and Ben Kiernan, "Bombs over Cambodia: New Light on US Air War," http://japanfocus.org/products/details/2420

6. See also the population figures of ethnolinguistic groups in the Lao PDR provided by Hayashi (2003: 34).

7. In addition to this statistic, see the most recent economic figures for 2006 compiled by the Asian Development Bank at www.adb.org/documents/ado/2007Lao.pdf.

8. Evans (1998: 162) cites a mid-1990s issue of *The New Education* that "reports that 38 percent of primary teachers have had no training, while retention rates at the primary level are also low: 'on average throughout the country, of the students who enter the first grade only 27% reach the fifth grade, in places which are richer such as in the Vientiane municipality, students who entered first grade in 1987–88 numbered 23,664 of whom only 11,223 reached fifth grade in 1991–92, that is 47%.'" It goes on: "the number of people who cannot read nor write has grown, and according to surveys around 40% of people between 15 and 40 years are illiterate."

9. The slash-and-burn season commences in March and runs about five or six weeks into April before the celebration of Pi Mai (the Lao New Year). The Lao PDR government Ministry of Agriculture and Forestry reports that the amount of acreage given over to swidden practice has been reduced by about 20 percent from 2001 through 2006 and that the ministry has plans to eliminate the practice entirely by 2010 (*Vientiane Times*, March 6, 2007, p. 2.) Given the dependence of the Lao Theung and Lao Sung on this traditional form of agriculture in the mountain highlands, this seems an optimistic goal.

10. Surely this 1995 figure for Vietnam as an indicator for its present economic development in comparison with Laos cannot hold, given the rocket-like development that has occurred in Vietnam during the past ten years. Moreover, the Lao PDR reported in January 2008 that per capita income for 2007 was $678, up from just $443 in 2006 (http://www.voanews.com/lao/2008-01-04-voa3.cfm?rss=topstories)

11. Cited in the *Vientiane Times*, January 18, 2007, p. 3.

12. Unfortunately, the *Vientiane Times* does not tell us whether this number includes novices. I suspect it does not, given the ratio of monks to temples (4.5:1) indicated by these figures.

13. Morev (2002: 399) supplies a different set of figures provided by the government's Lao Front for National Construction in 2002 in which 150,000 Christians are estimated and a "few thousand" adherents of Islam (400). Morev also notes the reported existence of some 250 "nongovernmental organizations with religious affiliations"; he writes that "most of these groups have used 'humanitarian aid' as a pretext to get into Laos" where "they work primarily in the regions inhabited by the non-Lao

national minorities such as the Khmu and Hmong" (400–401) to spread evangelical forms of Christianity.

14. See Morev (2002) for an overview of religion in contemporary Laos as of 2002.

15. While this is the conventional view of Theravada history as derived from *vamsa* or chronicle literature, it is more than likely that the Theravada was initially introduced to the Lao through the earlier Mon Buddhist community.

Chapter 1: Powers of the Place

Epigraph: (1975: 7).

1. It is also not uncommon to hear the very same refrain about Buddhism and identity from Burmese, Thai, Khmer, and Sinhalese.

2. The principle exception to this are the "grandmother" and "grandfather" guardian *phi* of Luang Phrabang, whose cartoonish figures form an important presence in the annual New Year (Pi Mai) rites during the month of April. Yet they too are not fashioned anthropomorphically at their central shrine within Vat Aham in Luang Phrabang. Nang Thoranee, the earth goddess (and therefore not quite a *phi*) is another exception.

3. Swearer and Premchit (1995) and Keyes (2002) have provided fascinating studies in the Thai context in which local female deities with some historical bases have been transformed into heroic Buddhist guardian deities of larger urban areas or cities. In these contexts, images have been crafted for their public representation. Moreover, we can also find in both Thai and Lao contexts public images of the earth goddess Nang Thoranee (in Sri Lanka, Bhu Devi). While the inspiration of the former originally may have been motivated by beliefs in the *phi* cult, the latter is a Thai-Lao adaptation of an ancient Indian Buddhist cult. For an excellent comprehensive study of Nang Thoranee, see Elizabeth Guthrie (2004). In any case, none of these goddesses would now be popularly regarded primarily as *phi*. That is probably why they are anthropomorphically represented.

4. *Devalaya*s or deity shrines in Sri Lanka are usually open to the public at least twice a week on Wednesday and Saturday mornings, although the larger and most famous shrines that cater to a national clientele, such as Kataragama or Alutnuvara, may be open every day of the week.

5. Condominas (1973: 254) agrees: "In general the phi do not require any substantial public ritual structures comparable to the Buddhist monastery."

6. In some ways the cult of Nang Thoranee, though she is not a *phi* per se, functions as a protective cult for the Buddhasasana, see Elizabeth Guthrie (2004).

7. Harris agrees: "The *phiban* [village deities of Laos] are geographically more specific and functionally less well-defined" (2005: 257). Indeed, the fact that they are "geographically more specific" is a key insight in recognizing their archaic yet continuing function for Lao religious culture, as we shall see.

8. This observation would seem to argue against, or perhaps constitute an exception to, Stewart Guthrie's argument about anthropomorphism in his *Faces in the Clouds* (1993).

9. The French scholar Condominas (1973: 272) also sees the relationship in this very same way: "This common religious core [of the spirit cults] has been penetrated only superficially by exogenous world religions, and has been less than profoundly affected by other cultural elements taken over seemingly *in toto* by the peoples of Southeast Asia."

10. The art historian Robert DeCaroli (2004) has also argued cogently that the rise of Buddhism, at least insofar as it can be understood through a study of sculpture and popular literature (especially the *jatakas*), needs to be understood within the context of a religious culture dominated by spirit cults.

11. Originally published as "Cultes Indiens et Indigenes au Champa," *Bulletin de l'Ecole Francaise d'Extreme Orient* 33 (1933): 367–410.

12. Another effective summary of the contribution Mus made is provided Davis (1984: 273): "In a distinguished essay, Paul Mus has traced the outlines of a prehistoric religious system which at one time flourished throughout the whole of Monsoon Asia, including southern China, Southeast Asia, and India. This religion consisted of ritual interaction between a localized group of people and an impersonal, intangible earth deity or spirit of the soil. The spirit embodied the fertility of the earth within the territory inhabited and cultivated by the group. In time, says Mus, the local deity came to be identified with some natural object, such as a tree or stone. Later still, the cult of the territorial spirit assimilated the ancestral cult of the local chief. At this point, dynastic and territorial concerns became fused, and statehood was made possible."

13. In commenting on Mus's argument some forty years later, Condominas (1973: 255) relates it more specifically to the Chinese context: "The cult of territorial spirits is common to the T'ai peoples of Southeast Asia, whether Buddhist or not, and bears some resemblance to the Chinese veneration of the earth god." I think that Mus's argument has to be kept separate from the theory of "soul stuff" and "men of prowess" that Wolters (1982 and 1999) has attributed to "pre-Indianized" Southeast cultures. Wolters's theory misses the correspondences of power between the supernatural and the human and then makes some questionable links to Hindu conceptuality by identifying *sakti* with this "soul stuff." More likely, it is linked to the kind of "rule by ritual" described by Lucien Pye (1985: 39–46) and the "bureaucratic cosmology" described by Bell (1992: 128–129) and McMullen (1987: 181–236) that is clearly evident in Chinese culture.

14. See Bechert (1966–1973); Southwold (1983); and Gombrich and Obeyesekere (1988) for a thoroughgoing discussion of these respective terms that refer to a reform-minded and rationally composed understanding of Buddhism. See also Holt (1991b) for a critique of this nomenclature.

15. Tambiah (1970); Hayashi (2003); Terwiel (1978a, 1978b); Condominas (1968, 1973); Tiyavanich (1997); Davis (1984); and Zago (1972 and 1976).

16. Harris (2005); Edwards (2007); Marston and Guthrie (2004) for the Khmer; and Spiro (1967) for the Burmese.

17. For a more elaborate summary of these points, plus the manner in which Mus understood them as relevant to the Vietnamese struggle against the French, see Bayly (2000).

18. See Eliade (1996).

19. This principle can also be observed in relation to how the lineages of clans were later understood as protected by *phi ka* or *phi dam*, the "clan spirit." See the extensive discussion in Davis (1984: 54–65).

20. As Mus asserts:

> The correspondence between the two wings of monsoon Asia extends to practices of remarkable complexity. You are aware that in China, with the strengthening and expansion of the social order, the ancient cults of the soil finally produced a magic duplication of the map of the country. To each one of its rural or urban centres there came to be attached peculiar genies among whom was instituted a hierarchy that reproduced on the supernatural plane the administrative divisions of the country. The genie of the district centre would give orders to those of the townships and take them from the genie of the capital. The emperor and his dynastic earth-god stood at the head of this "government of the beyond", divided among ministers. The emperor even appointed and dismissed local genies.
>
> Indology, preoccupied with its classical reminiscences and its Indo-European interests, has, as far as I know, almost completely neglected to use the scattered but ancient and specific documents which would attest, on the Indian side, [to] very similar beliefs. In the *Jataka*, the *Sutta* and the *Atthakatha* of the Pali tradition may be found all the elements of the government of the beyond: the family genie is responsible to the genie of the town, and he in turn to the gods presiding over the four quarters: these, finally, obey Indra whose divine city is represented on earth by the capital of the kingdom, in a sense its material "double." (1975: 19)

21. Davis (1984: 54) points out that the "transmission of property through women is closely connected to the cult of domestic spirits," a fact that explains why the cult of the household *phi* is focused on preserving the purity of women's sexual behavior.

22. Davis (1984: 54) notes that "uninhabited territory is not conceived as being part of any particular *muang*, and the mountain wilderness which is the border between two *muang* is like an empty space. Conceptually, a forest is the opposite of a *muang* in that it is uninhabited." Justin McDaniel notes that it is from the forest that many holy men and sorcerers emerge, precisely because their powers have not been domesticated (private communication).

23. I use the term "ritualization" in Bell's (1992: 74) sense of referring "to the way certain social actions strategically distinguish themselves in relation to other actions . . . , for creating and privileging a qualitative distinction between the 'sacred' and the 'profane,' and for ascribing such distinctions to realities thought to transcend the powers of human actors."

24. Wolters (1982 and 1999) prefers to refer to individuals like the *chao muang* as

"men of prowess." This manner of characterization is helpful as it is understood that the "prowess" in question is a consequence of what Mus means by "doubling."

25. But Michel Lorrillard, the current leading historian of ancient and medieval Lao material culture, remains skeptical on this point (private communication, June, 2007). Moreover, Davis (1984: 29–30) asserts that the style of kingship in Angkor was much more autocratic and hierarchical in nature than the conceptions of chiefdom found among the Muang of northern Thailand and possibly the Lao.

26. Later known as Xieng Thong Xieng Dong, and after that as Luang Phrabang.

27. Michael Vickery, in closely analyzing two nineteenth-century Lao texts—one with relevance to a *muang* in Isan (northeast Thailand) and another to Xam Neua during the early nineteenth-century rule of Vientiane's Anou—has tried to mitigate what he calls the "mantrification" of mandala discourse in Lao historical inquiry. He seeks to address anew the primary issue of "whether the political economy of early Southeast Asia resulted in rulers being more concerned with control of land or control of people" (2003: 3). In this wide-ranging and carefully argued article, he makes a strong case that economic circumstances sometimes made various kingdoms "land hungry" or that founding myths, such as the foundation myth for Ayutthaya, imply a search for land and not just for people (5). Vickery's argument can stand as a corrective to those studies that simply reduce all dynamics between center and periphery as a matter of mandala ideology, when, in fact, the specifics of a given context of political economy were usually far more complex.

28. Lorrillard has written extensively on this problem. He regards the Fa Ngum saga in the *Nithan Khun Borom* as a narration of a "completely artificial nature" (2006: 140) and notes that "the first factual data in the chronicles that can be proven historically is the promulgation by King Phothisarāt of an edict against spirit worship in 1527" (141). As to how or why the Lao invented the Fa Ngum saga to proclaim their connection to Khmer Angkor, he writes:

> The role of the Khmer and Mon cultures in the development of the Thai civilizations of Sukhothai, Ayuthya and Lān Nā is historically recognised, because it can be established that direct contact existed between these different cultures. The Lao were also aware that the Buddhism they were practising was connected to an ancient form of the religion, which was foreign to them, though the link was only perceptible through material and artistic culture. We can be sure that the first Lao populations to arrive in the middle valley of the Mekong settled on the sites which many centuries previously had been occupied by the Mon. This is especially so in the case of Vientiane and the region of Vieng Kham. . . . We are equally sure that these Lao discovered Mon Buddhist remains, because they reused them. For instance, large steles dating from the second half of the first millennium and bearing the stylised image of a *stūpa* were reemployed from the beginning of the sixteenth century, for the engraving of Lao inscriptions. As the memory of this distant past had vanished, tradition replaced it with a myth that preserved the idea of the presence of a foreign element. This became known as *khom*, a vague term covering all the Mon-Khmer.

The Lao tradition of the introduction of Buddhism from a southern source could thus, in a certain manner, maintain the memory of another historical truth, one that is more distant and so less tangible. (147)

29. See also Tambiah (1970: 29), who says: "No doubt the birth of the first Laotian state was facilitated by the fall of Sukhothai"; and Stuart-Fox, who provides more detail:

> At its furthest extent, Lān Nā under Mangrāy included much of northwestern Laos, the valley of the Nam Ou and parts of Xainyaburī province. It was a powerful Theravāda Buddhist *mandala* incorporating tributary Shan *meuang* to the west, Leu *meuang* to the north, and Lao *meuang* to the east, with the core of the kingdom comprising the valleys of Chiang Mai and Lamphun. The disintegration of the Sukhothai *mandala* and the temporary weakness of Lan Na, coinciding as it did with the continued decline of Angkor, provided opportunities for new centers of power to become established around the middle of the fourteenth century. This long struggle between the two Siamese *mandalas* permitted both Lan Na and Lan Xang by the end of the fourteenth century to establish themselves as powerful competing *mandalas* able to place limits on any further Ayutthayan imperial ambitions: Lan Na by absorbing the semi-independent *meuang* of Phayao and Nan; Lan Xang by drawing together the scattered Lao *meuang* of the Mekong basin. The Khmer kingdom was struggling to hold its own against the growing power of Ayutthaya, and was instrumental in encouraging formation of a competing Lao *mandala*. (1998: 35–36)

30. For an excellent analytical discussion of the *then* or *thaen* as "supreme deities," see Zago (1972: 173–182).

31. Zago (1972: 180) says that the supreme *then* is often identified as Indra. The reorganization of the world described in the following paragraph is accomplished under the aegis of Indra's son, Khun Bulom, who becomes the progenitor of Lan Xang kingship.

32. This last section of Aijmer's summary seems as if it has been adapted from Archaimbault (1959: 386–393).

33. In his comments on the descent and genealogy of the divine, royal lineage of the Luang Phrabang kings, Stuart-Fox (1998: 36–37) adds this in relation to the titles they bore: "According to the genealogies recorded in the Lao chronicles, a line of fifteen princes bearing the title *Khun* (probably of Chinese derivation meaning "Lord") ruled in Meuang Sua. These were followed by six rulers with the title *Thao* (a Tai word indicating a member of the nobility). Loss of the probably more prestigious title *Khun* may suggest that Meuang Sua had fallen under the control of some powerful *mandala*: possibly the Angkorian empire. A second change of title through the addition of *Phraya*, literally 'he who upholds', a term derived from Pali, probably indicates not a change of dynasty, for the former title was retained, but a change of hegemonic overlord, and suggests that the rulers may have been Buddhist."

34. Davis (1984: 34) notes a similar motif in relation to the aboriginal Mon-Khmer among the Muang of Nan and notes that as in Luang Phrabang, "it was common in Tai principalities for a detachment of aboriginals to participate in the installation rites of a prince, in order to affirm both the legality of the installation and the authenticity of the aboriginals' first claim to the territory."

35. Indeed, a glass mosaic mural depicting the arrival of Fa Ngum together with the Phra Bang image dominates the central hall of the king's former palace in Luang Phrabang.

36. Harris points out that Lan Xang was not alone in stylizing itself after Khmer Angkor: "Evidence that the Thai came to regard Cambodia as a repository of important cultural and religious knowledge is plentiful. . . . The Thai . . . quickly came to embrace the Angkorian principles of statecraft, Khmer was adopted as the language of the aristocracy, and the court operated with a terminology derived from both Khmer and Sanskrit. . . . The legacy is also revealed in the importation of the *Ramayana* into royal circles and in the fact that, until well into the nineteenth century, most Pali texts that were used in the Theravada monasteries of central Thailand were written in Khmer script" (2005: 32–33). Unfortunately, Harris is mistaken in this last assertion, as most Pali texts were written in the *khom* script (Justin McDaniel, private communication). Nonetheless, practically the same general description of Khmer influence on central Thailand can apply to Lan Xang as well.

37. Stuart-Fox cautions against reading the text too literally for the following reason: "According to the Lao chronicles, the first Lao imperial *mandala* was founded by Fa Ngum in 1353 with its capital at Xiang Dong Xiang Thong (later to be named Luang Phrabang). The chronicles tell how the conquests of Fa Ngum effectively incorporated a number of previously independent *meuang* situated on the middle Mekong and from the Nam U to the rapids of Khon into a powerful, centralized kingdom. It is necessary, however, to treat this account with some caution, for given the reach of neighbouring powers (Champasak and the Mun River basins were still predominantly Khmer) and difficulties of communication, the kingdom must at first have been both less extended and more loosely constructed than appears from sources dating from two centuries later" (1998: 36).

38. Stuart-Fox (1998: 37–44) has assembled a fairly complete outline summary of Fa Ngum's saga, cribbed from various versions including the *Luang Phrabang Chronicle*, for his book, *The Lao Kingdom of Lan Xang*. In the following pages, I shall basically rely upon his outline, noting his considered analytical commentary on its political ramifications as well, before proceeding to a discussion about its religio-historical significance.

39. The title "Phraya" that his grandfather held indicates that by the early fourteenth century the titular head of Muang Sva was regarded as more than simply a powerful *chao muang*, for the honorific "Phraya" indicates a more exalted status.

40. This symbolism of thirty-three seems to indicate divine associations. In Vedic lore, Indra, king of the gods, is accompanied by thirty-three deities in heaven. So a speculative implication here may be that an allusion is being drawn between Fa Ngum and Indra.

41. Stuart-Fox elaborates:

Losing no time, Fa Ngum turned his attention to the east where his armies seized three small *meuang* owing allegiance to the Emperor of Dai Viet. The Vietnamese, concerned over the threat of a Cham attack, responded by dispatching a diplomatic mission bearing rich tribute to negotiate on the frontier. According to Lao sources, two potentially conflicting criteria, clearly reflecting different notions of sovereignty, were used to demarcate Lao and Vietnamese spheres of control. One embodies the Lao priority of jurisdiction over people: all *meuang* inhabited by people living in houses with verandahs built on piles would be recognized as owing allegiance to the Lao king; those living in houses built on the ground owed allegiance to the emperor of Vietnam. The other reflected concern to define territory: the "flow of rainwater," west or east of the Say Phu Luang cordillera would decide which land would be Lao or Vietnamese. (1998: 39–40)

42. "These forms of legitimation rested on an animist worldview that owed nothing to Buddhism, a worldview similar in many respects to that still held by the tribal upland Tai of northeastern Laos" (Stuart-Fox 1998: 51).

43. In a clarification of his position, Martin Stuart-Fox (private communication) writes: "For the peasantry . . . , Buddhism was appealing not for the path it outlined for escape from *samsara*, but for its superior power over *phi*. So Buddhism was interpreted through the prism of the *phi*, in magical, not doctrinal terms."

44. I would not have been so surprised had I remembered the prominence of Buddha images in the *Jinakalamalipakaranam*.

45. See Godakumbura (1970) for a description of the *perahara*.

46. See Holt (1991a: 176–201); and Duncan (1990).

47. See Strong (2004) for the best assessment to date regarding the power inherent in Buddhist relics.

48. By contrast, compare Donald Swearer's detailed description of the consecration of Buddha images in northern Thailand in his *Becoming the Buddha* (2004), consecrations that render the Buddha image powerful indeed.

49. This is a very unfortunate choice of phrase, as it relegates the understanding of *dukkha* (unsatisfactoriness), the problematic nature of *samsara*, and the Buddhist quest to overcome it by means of the Noble Eightfold Path, to a thoroughgoing Christian idiom. "Sin" is not a good translation for *dukkha* and "saved" connotes a means of "grace" acquired from a divine power without.

50. Again, "redemption" is not quite the right word here for the path leading to *nibbana*, since for most Buddhists progress on the path is a matter of karma or merit derived from self-effort. Moreover, I think what Stuart-Fox actually has in mind here would be better expressed in the phrase: "universal history of the Buddhasasana."

51. See footnote 50.

52. Jayavarman VII styled himself as a *bodhisattva* reflection of Avalokitesvara.

53. Evans (2002b: 7) writes incisively on this point: "Sacred centers, and not sacred

territories and boundaries, were the preoccupation of these polities, which were made up of personal networks focused on the king rather than territorial units. The king's innate spiritual power attracted followers, and had to be shown to attract even greater numbers of followers, as expansion in the known world demonstrated prowess and spiritual potency. This spiritual prowess was not automatically transmitted to sons, however, thus the death of a king threatened to unravel the structure of personal loyalties making up any particular mandala."

54. The *Mahavamsa* (18–19; pp. 122–135) contains an account of how a cutting from the original *bodhi* tree from what is now Buddha Gaya in Bihar was brought to Anuradhapura by Sanghamitta, the daughter of Emperor Asoka, who establishes the *bhikkhunni sangha* on the island. A later Pali text, the *Mahabodhivamsa* is an account of how saplings from the tree have been distributed to sacred places throughout Sri Lanka. The practice of planting saplings taken from the original tree is thus an ancient practice, symbolizing the spread of the Buddha's *dhamma*.

55. In his extensive study of textual transmission in La Na, Veidlinger (2007) frequently refers to the progenitors of the Lan Na *sangha* traditions as being Sri Lankan Sinhala *vipassanadhura* forest monks.

56. As Stuart-Fox writes in characterizing the historical interlude between Fa Ngum and Xainya Chakkaphat Phaen Phaeo in the late fifteenth century:

> From Sam Saen Tai [Fa Ngum's eldest son who succeeded him] on, little more than ages and titles, names of queens and numbers of children, and such significant events as wars and the construction of temples are included. We know next to nothing about the characters of kings, let alone other powerful officials. No independent memoires or histories have come down to us, if any were ever written. There are no personal papers or pamphlets which might provide the historian with insights into the social and cultural life of the court, let alone the popular culture of markets and villages. No records remain of court finances or trade flows. (1998: 58)

57. Evans (2002b: 14) points out: "As far as we know, there was no established order for a son's succession and therefore if a faction in favour of one particular son was not clearly dominant upon the death of the king, murderous disputes could break out among the rival claimants to the throne." Moreover, Stuart-Fox (1998: 63) has characterized the years that were to follow in this way: "We can best understand the events of these years by seeing them as the reflection of a desperate power struggle between opposing factions at court, each endeavouring to manipulate the succession in their favour."

58. "The battle to protect Xiang Dong Xiang Thong is the only section of the later chronicles related with the same kind of detail we find in accounts of the campaigns of Fa Ngum. But these are events which happened a bare twenty-five years before the earliest (1503) version of the *Nithan Khun Borom* and there must have been many still alive who remembered them vividly. . . . The pillage, rape and destruction wrought by the invading army can only be imagined, as hard-won food supplies were seized, houses burned, and whole village populations fled into the jungle. As Lao defences

collapsed, the elderly King Xainya Chakkaphat fled south to Xiang Khan where he abdicated in shame, leaving his second son, Prince Thaen Kham, to rally the shattered Lao forces. . . . According to the Lao chronicles, all credit for the eventual heroic defeat of the Vietnamese was due to the young prince" (Stuart-Fox 1998: 66).

59. See Holt (1991a: 99–116); and Holt (2004: 45–61).

60. Referring to the precolonial context in general, Pholsena (2006: 21) says: "Contacts between the ethnic Lao and these upland populations were primarily economic, and studies have demonstrated that there has always been a tradition of interdependence between the various ethnics groups, mostly through exchange."

61. For a resume of these *jatakas*, see Saddhatissa (1979).

62. It is also from this time that the earliest dated inscription in Lao (rather than Pali) was composed, written upon the base of a Buddha image in *tham* (from *dhamma*) script. This script, Shan in nature and influenced by the Mon, was utilized particularly for writing out Buddhist texts (Tambiah 1970: 30).

63. *The Chronicle of Luang Prabhang* also refers to Angkor as Indraprastha (Sahai 1996, 1: 20); Justin McDaniel writes that Chiang Mai is understood as Indraprasthanagara in northern Thai literature (private communication).

64. The *Rama Jataka* clearly expresses a preference for sibling marriage over cross-cousin marriage.

65. For a detailed study of Lan Na's Pali literary culture during the time of its own fifteenth- and sixteenth-century "golden age," see Veidlinger's *Spreading the Dhamma* (2007). We can assume that Veidlinger's observations on writing, orality, and textual transmission in contemporary Lan Na are, in general, an accurate reflection of similar dynamics in sixteenth-century Lan Xang.

66. Lorrillard (2003: 190), in commenting on this stele, says that Lan Xang epigraphy seems to be directly related to La Na epigraphy and to the *tham* alphabet used for the writing of Pali as well.

67. Stuart-Fox comments:

> The immediate reason for this was probably strategic, to distance his capital from the new rising power of Burma and to be in a better position to counter Ayutthayan threats against Lan Na, but the shift would anyway have been necessary sooner or later for it reflected the changing demographic, economic and strategic balance in mainland Southeast Asia in general, and in the *mandala* of Lan Xang in particular. Over the previous two centuries, Lao settlers had continued to migrate south and west, down the valley of the Mekong and onto the Khorat plateau, through establishment of satellite villages of outlying *meuang*. Even though settlement remained sparse, the Viang Chan plain, the middle Mekong and the Khorat plateau as far south as the Xi River basin together supported a far greater population than the narrow valleys of northern Laos. Population growth went hand-in-hand with improved farming techniques and increased internal exchange, not least between upland minorities and lowland Lao. As the balance of population shifted south, so too did the center of gravity of Lao economic and political power. (1998: 76)

68. Here I am intentionally invoking Buddhist-mindedness to associate Phothisarath's dispositions with what Clifford Geertz (1971: 60–62, 102–107, 114–117) has termed "religious-mindedness." By religious mindedness, Geertz meant to draw the distinction between individuals who "hold truths" rather than experience "being held" by them. "Religious-mindedness" celebrates belief itself rather than what belief asserts. That is, the difference between religious-mindedness and "being religious" is that religious-mindedness is an intolerant scripted orthodoxy that imposes a divinely attributed design on to reality, while religiousness, on the contrary, encounters the reality or quality of the sacred that is present within experience itself.

69. For a more detailed account of the issues and context in fifteenth-century Sri Lanka, see Holt (1991a: 109–117).

70. Parakramabahu VI's reign from 1412 through 1467 represents the last time that the island was united under one political rule from the time of his reign until the disestablishment of Kandyan kingship by the British in 1815.

71. Stuart-Fox notes that the "best example [of this] is Vat Si Meung in Vientiane, where the *lak meuang* is in the centre of the temple" (private communication).

72. The Vinaya is that portion of the Tipitaka that contains the formulations that constitute the rules of monastic discipline ritually recited and celebrated every two weeks on the new and full moon by all monks who have undertaken the *upasampada* ordination rite and who reside within a consecrated *vat*. Collectively as Buddhist juris-prudence, the rules of discipline are an ideal expression of *dhamma* in relation to the social behavior of monks. See Holt (1981).

73. This intensification is evident quite clearly when important trajectories of le-gitimation related to Lan Na's royalty and the *sangha*, especially as these are evinced in the *Jinakalamalipakaranam*, are compared to the legitimation scenarios operating in Lan Xang: the importation of a lineage of forest-dwelling Sinhala monks derived from the Mahavihara tradition in Sri Lanka, the emphasis placed on planting *bodhi* trees, and especially the emphases on accounts of Buddha images, some purported to be of Sri Lankan origins. These are precisely the trajectories emphasized in the legitimation scenarios of Lan Xang.

74. Because the Siamese believed that it was bad luck to have both the Phra Bang and Phra Keo in the same city (Stuart-Fox, private communication).

75. Even before "revolutionary history" was written, we can observe the impor-tance of Anou to the memory of the Lao in the grand glass murals on the parlor walls of the Luang Phrabang palace, where Anou's revolt is depicted in a splendid display dating to the early twentieth century.

76. For exceptionally perceptive analyses of contemporary Thai and Lao readings of the Anouvong rebellion, see Keyes (2002) and Grabowsky (1997).

77. "Men of prowess" is a phrase first coined by Wolters (1982 and 1999) to further characterize his "big man" political theory, in which "soul stuff" accounts for power. I much prefer Mus' explanation, for reasons made clear earlier.

78. Grabowsky (1997: 148) points out that That Prince Damrong Rachanuphap, an inveterate Thai nationalist scholar of the early twentieth century, has argued that the

Thai had completely trusted Anou before he launched his military move. This interpretation, no doubt, assists the interpretation that Anou's "rebellion" was traitorous.

79. Grabowsky (1997: 148–150) reviews the various motives attributed to Anou's decision to invade the Khorat plateau: to restore the *status quo ante* before 1778 or even 1709; "to liberate the numerous Lao war captives whom the later Rama I had deported from Vientiane in 1778 and resettled in Saraburi, Suphanburi and other provinces"; or "a preventive war against a lingering Thai aggression"; and so forth.

80. "By conservative estimates, in the first three decades following the conquest of Vientiane, at least 100,000 Lao were forced to leave the eastern bank of the Mekong and resettle in territories on the western bank of the river or in the interior of the Khorat Plateau" (Grabowsky 1997: 150).

81. Grabowsky (1997: 151) suggests that the depopulating of the Lao from the upper Mekong may be one of the reasons why Ho invaders of the late nineteenth century were "able to shake the Lao states like Luang Phrabang and Siang Khwang so effectively.... In this light, the continuous immigration of the 'Lao Sung' [almost entirely Hmong from southern China] can be interpreted as an indirect result of the forced resettlements of Lao populations into Isan and Central Thailand."

Chapter 2: Interventions from Afar

1. While technically incorrect, it is possible, however, in contemporary Laos to hear the Phuan referred to as "Phuan Lao." Linguistically, the Phuan also belong to the Tai-Kadai family of languages. They have been Buddhist at least since the time of the Lan Xang mandala, so their linguistic and cultural affinities to the Lao Loum are similar to the Lue: they speak a closely related dialect of Tai and are nominally Theravada Buddhists.

2. Ivarsson (2003: 241) notes: "These [Siamese] endeavors cannot be associated with policies aimed at establishing a geographically bounded state with fixed borders and undivided sovereignties. Rather, within the framework of interstate relations of the premodern period, they represented an attempt to maintain territories east of the Mekong as a 'buffer zone'—or as an 'overlapping margin.'" The descendants of many of these people, studied by Hayashi (2003) and Tambiah (1970), have retained many aspects of Lao religious culture.

3. Stuart-Fox (1998: 140) elaborates: "In the first half of 1885, joint Siamese-Lao armies converged on the Huaphan region and the Plain of Jars, only to retreat in the face of modest if stubborn Ho resistance. Annoyed by this failure, King Chulalongkorn determined to annex all regions formerly tributary to Luang Phrabang, together with as much of the Sipsong Chu Tai [Huaphan] as possible, and to incorporate them within the Siamese state." Chulalongkorn's strategy backfired, however, when his forces kidnapped a close relation of a Haw strongman, whose revenge led to the destruction of Luang Phrabang.

4. All of the historic temples in Luang Phrabang, with the exception of Vat Xieng Thong, were destroyed.

5. In this regard Evans (2002b: 37) notes: "All across the Tai world in the early nineteenth century . . . a broader sense of change was reflected in a sudden spurt of 'library-building' inside temples and the compilation of histories. A stronger sense of a Tai world versus a Vietnamese or Burmese world was reflected in these chronicles. . . . The modernization projects launched in Bangkok by King Mongkut, and in particular by King Chulalongkorn, accelerated the centre's consciousness of differences with the periphery, which it saw as increasingly *ban nok* or 'country bumpkin,' uncivilized and steeped in superstitions unfitting to a modern age. This came to apply especially to the northeast and its poor peasantry, the 'Lao', and by extension to the rest of Laos. Thus it was modernization that produced a more widespread consciousness of being Lao or Siamese."

6. During the nineteenth century, though Bangkok claimed suzerainty over Luang Phrabang and Champasak as vassals, "the Lao Sangha was independent of the Siamese hierarchy" (Stuart-Fox 1998: 137). Stuart-Fox notes that links between Luang Phrabang and Bangkok appeared to early European observers to have been quite tenuous.

7. McCoy (1970: 68–70) elaborates: "It was not their interest in Vietnam, Laos, or Cambodia which involved the French, but rather their interest in China—in particular, the vast potential of Chinese markets. The French had watched with envy while Britain had secured enormous profits through domination of the China trade. . . . Saigon was not only a suitable port, but it had the advantage of being close to the mouths of the Mekong, which the French believed would give them their backdoor to southwest China."

8. Further, Larcher-Goscha (2003: 225) writes: "Pavie's research into the royal chronicles [more accurately, royal archives] of Luang Phrabang had been primarily designed to find a way to legitimize French colonial rights in the region, where strictly 'Laotian' borders had never existed. Pavie would later provide his government with arguments for its territorial claims by establishing the ancient tributary relations of Lao principalities to Annam. Having established a protectorate over the former Vietnamese Monarchy and Annam, no one could be upset when the French affirmed that they would maintain the exercise of these traditional Vietnamese rights as a way of justifying her expansion into Laos."

9. Stuart-Fox (1996: 17) writes extensively about how this impacted Lao self-understanding: "French interest in Laos was always from the perspective of Vietnam. Authorities in both Paris and Hanoi saw Laos not as a political or geographical entity in its own right, with its unique history and culture, but rather as a component of Indochina in which Vietnam held pride of place." In terms of how this was articulated within French colonial historiography, he writes: "The necessity of French protection that colonial historiography instilled into two generations of Lao thus stands in stark contrast to the reality of French intentions for Laos. On the one hand, Laos remained administratively distinct from Vietnam; on the other, in French eyes, its destiny was to be ever more linked to Vietnam—to the point of eventual inclusion as a mere hinterland for Vietnamese settlement. French colonial historiography was designed to demonstrate the role of France in 'saving' the Lao (or some of them at least) from Siamese

domination, not to reveal French intentions to reduce them to a more complete sub-servience to (French) Vietnam. French colonial history, by stressing the protective role of France in preserving a separate Lao identity, both justified and reinforced colonial domination. The Lao were taught that they needed France: any challenge to French authority would threaten the very existence of Laos and the Lao people" (Stuart-Fox 2003: 81).

10. Pavie became commissioner general of Laos in 1893.

11. Charles Keyes (2002: 132, n. 13) notes: "The understanding of Siam/Thailand as a 'nation' populated by 'thai' began only in the late nineteenth century as a con-sequence of the influence of Western 'racial' thought and the imposition of colonial power, especially the French."

12. Because of his demonstrated diplomatic dexterity, August Pavie achieved near sainthood in French historiography and public culture. "The biographers of Pavie re-minded all that Laos had become French without violence or the spilling of blood. . . . As such, the conquest was excused and excusable, since it had the consent of the very parties concerned. Pavie embodied the model of an ideal and seductive colonialism, contractual from the start and having no other goal but to fulfill 'a civilizing mis-sion'. . . . This was a nation that had been colonized justly, since her protection had been solicited from below, demanded and accepted by the local populations (Larcher-Goscha: 2003: 227). Moreover, "Auguste Pavie becomes the historic symbol of Franco-Lao 'friendship' (*amities/mittaphap*): the peaceful conqueror of Lao 'hearts' and the saviour of this *peuple doux* threatened by expansionist Siamese 'designs'" (Goscha 2003: 266). Later, non-French historians did not view Pavie in such favorable light. McCoy (1970: 68), for instance, wrote: "Pavie believed himself the father of all Lao and called them 'my dear children' in his letters. He and his successors treated the Lao as charming but incompetent children, denied them all effective political authority, and kept them in a state of prolonged national adolescence." He adds: "Although Laos' first governor, August Pavie, had promised the King of Luang Prabang his autonomy, the French governor assumed absolute authority, and the artificial distinction the French made between indirect administration in the Kingdom of Luang Prabang and direct administration in the rest of Laos was little more than a legal fiction" (78).

13. In Burma and Sri Lanka, the disestablishment of kingship threw the monastic *sangha* into a crisis mode. In 1815, when the British disenfranchised the last Kandyan king, the Sinhalese also entered into a treaty with the king of England, who promised to "protect the religion of Boodoo." But as the king of England was simultaneously the formal head of the Church of England, within a few decades the British parliament, under pressure from its Christian constituency, rescinded the commitment. As a con-spicuous sign of their bad faith following the signing of the Kandyan Treaty, the British built St. Paul's Church within the parameters of Kandy's "temple square," less than a hundred meters from the Dalada Maligava (Temple of the Tooth-relic) and abutting the presence of the Visnu, Natha, and Pattini *devalayas*. Without its primary royal pa-tron, the *sangha* fell on hard times for at least fifty years as it scrambled to redefine itself along new lines. For an excellent resume of the Buddhist *sangha*'s fortunes during the

nineteenth century in Sri Lanka, see Kitsiri Malalgoda (1976). For the aftermath of the Burmese royal disestablishment, see E. Sarkisyanz (1965) and Mendelson (1975).

14. See McDaniel (2008: passim).

15. Hansen (2007: 83) reports similarly in Cambodia that "a prevailing view of texts was of physically potent objects that affected the spiritual well-being of the individuals who handled them; their exact contents were of lesser importance. Texts were understood to be sacred much in the same way as relics, which embodied physical elements of the Buddha." Moreover, as Zago (1976: 126) has noted in commenting upon an attempt after 1956 to have the entire Tipitaka published in Laos in Pali, an effort that resulted in only three of a projected eighty-eight volumes: "It would have been in any case of very limited use, being published only in Pali. The literary sources of Buddhism, therefore, remain inaccessible not only to the lay population but also to the better part of the clergy." This situation stands in contrast somewhat to Cambodia insofar as the entire Tipitaka was eventually translated into the vernacular Khmer due to the tireless efforts of Suzanne Karpeles from 1925–1941 (Edwards 2007: 203 passim). Karpeles was later "retired" from her position by the fascist Vichy government owing to her Jewish lineage.

16. Similarly in Cambodia, these related elements of Buddhist political culture were known as *sdic* (king), *sangha,* and *srok* (district—or in the Lao vernacular, *muang*); see Edwards (2007: 167–169).

17. So Evans (2002b: 71) notes: "When the French took over Laos there was no sense of a Lao nation among the population that fell within the boundaries that they mapped. Even for the French, Laos was, at that time, more a cartographic reality than a social or historical one. But it was the French who brought the idea of a modern nation to Laos, and this idea would slowly grow among the population over the following 50 years."

18. Regarding the French disposition towards "native traditions" in Laos, McCoy (1970: 73–74) adds: "In reality, the French borders meant absolutely nothing to the people of Laos. What the French thought of as a clearly defined political unit was one of the most racially politically complex areas of Southeast Asia. . . . Indeed, in their insistence in defining Laos in terms of the Mekong basis the French *completely ignored existing political structures* and carved a colony out of segments of existing states and federations" (emphasis mine).

19. Consequently Sri Lanka now has one of the most educated populations, one of the highest (if not the highest) literacy rates in all of South and Southeast Asia, and an established class of professionals in the fields of education, law, medicine, and so forth.

20. Evans comments on the contemporary condition of education in the Lao People's Democratic Republic:

> All commentators on Lao education remark on the rapid quantitative growth in pupils and schools after 1975 . . . , but they all also comment on the dramatic fall in the quality of education. The government was determined to place a primary school

in every village, and a rapid expansion in the number of secondary schools occurred as well. This, of course, meant the establishment of many "skeleton schools" (much as there would later be "skeleton cooperatives") in order to fulfill the commands which came from above. Many of these schools were flimsy bamboo structures with a (usually young girl) "teacher" who had had a few years of primary education. Facilities, not surprisingly, were worst in the countryside and in mountain areas among the minorities. This expansion of education was not only limited by the lack of money for capital equipment, such as buildings and books, it was also severely hampered by the lack of qualified teachers. Indeed, one consequence of the revolution was that Laos lost up to 90 per cent of its already miniscule education population as refugees. (1998: 157–158)

21. McCoy provides his perspectives on how it was difficult to recruit French administrators for service in Laos:

Throughout more than a half-century of colonial rule, the kingdom of Laos remained a quaint neglected backwater of France's Indochina empire. While 40,000 Frenchmen crowded into Saigon and the Mekong Delta to compete for jobs ranging from governor to traffic cop, the French colonial administration often found it difficult to get enough men to fill the meager 100 positions that were allotted to Laos on the general Indochina budget. Those Frenchman who did agree to go to Laos went for a short term, having been promised that they would be remembered on the promotion lists in later years for having endured this hardship. This attitude was reflected in their work, for French colonial officials in Laos generally spent most of their time chasing the local women, seeking or avoiding addiction to alcohol or opium, and dreaming of their return to Saigon or Hanoi. (1970: 67)

22. How the French financed their Lao administrative operations, for example, supported the lifestyles of their civil servants, remains a controversial topic today. "French colonialism established opium monopolies in Indochina as a way of financing its administration, and in 1918 opium accounted for 15 per cent of colonial tax revenues" (Evans 1990: 33). "Through its 5,000 opium dens and shops the opium monopoly generated between 20 and 50 per cent of all of Indochina's revenues from 1898 to 1925 and was largely responsible for the economic development of the economy" (McCoy 1970: 86). In this way, the French may have anticipated the American CIA, which, in the 1960s, was accused of abetting the trafficking of heroin in Southeast Asia to finance its "secret war" in Laos. Kremmer (2003: 170) writes: "In the 1960s, the planes of the CIA Airline, Air America, were used to transport opium to Saigon for processing into heroin and subsequent sale to U.S. troops. The CIA claims it had no idea that the contraband was there." For discussion of the massive and still controversial investigation, see McCoy (1991). Others, such as Warner (1996), point out that the CIA had all the funding it wanted from Washington in order to carry out its mission, and so profits from heroin trading would be superfluous. But profits

would not have been superfluous to various others seeking to take advantage from this racketeering.

23. Evans (1998: 143) notes that slavery was formally abolished under the French, yet it also should be noted that corvee labor among the hill tribes functioned as a type of involuntary temporary slavery. In essentially the same vein as Stuart-Fox above, Mc-Coy (1970: 80) adds: "The French used traditional racial hierarchies where they were strong, reinforced them where they were weak, and created them where they did not exist. . . . In addition to being portrayed as "primitive," the "Kha" were also represented as rebels (*peuple insoumis*) in contrast to the ethnic Lao who complied more readily with the French administration's wishes (partly because they were better treated, in relative terms)."

24. "The French view of the Lao as charming but insouciant and lazy was a significant factor underlying French readiness to use Vietnamese in the administration of Laos" (Stuart-Fox 1996: 30).

25. A look at the census figures that Evans (2002b: 71) provides indicates that in six of Laos's urban areas in 1943 (including Vientiane, Luang Phrabang, Savannakhet, and Pakse), the Vietnamese counted for a full 60 percent of the urban population in the country, while the Lao were only 30 percent.

26. With reference to the long-term ramifications of the expatriate Viet Kieu, Lockart (2003: 147) further observes: "Western scholars are unanimous that no real Lao revolutionaries emerged before ["The Red Prince"] Souphanouvong in 1945. Future LPRP [Lao Patriotic Revolutionary Party] leaders like Kaysone [who emerged as the party and government strongman following the 1975 Pathet Lao takeover], Singkap and Nouhak at this point in time were at most climbing on board the party train through contacts either in Vietnam or among the Viet Kieu communities in Laos, and even after Souphanouvong seems to have owed his position (and probably much of his success) to his Vietnamese connections."

27. It is clear that the idea of a "greater Indochina," superceding the identities of Vietnam, Laos, and Cambodia, an idea that owes its origins to French colonial administrative structure, was exploited by the Vietnamese leadership in the struggle for the establishment of the Southeast Asian socialist states. Moreover, even after the 1975 takeover by the Pathet Lao, "much of both the framework and the discourse of Lao historiography is of Vietnamese inspiration" (Lockart 2003: 152). The French, of course, had no clear awareness about this impending legacy of their colonial policies.

28. In a detailed study of the Lao colonial highlands, Gunn (2003: 6) describes the matter generally: "Even in the most remote village of a colonial backwater, peasant behavior was influenced from the outset of the imperialist encounter, as much as by the laws of capitalism (unequal exchange and surplus accumulation) as by the transformations engendered by the imposition of the colonial bureaucratic state. Stated another way, the decisions taken by the boards of directors of metropolitan enterprises, the *Societies* in the French context—had as much if not more impact on colonial subjects at the periphery as the agents of colonial state power, the governor Generals, *Residents*, and their local collaborating agents."

29. *Digha Nikaya* (*Dialogues of the Buddha*) 3: 80–94.

30. "The Lao elite, from the royal family of Luang Phrabang down to the minor chao mueang, collaborated with the French—at first in opposition to Siam, but subsequently in what they conceived to be their own interests in maintaining a continuing French presence. Opposition to the French administration came not from the ethnic Lao, obedient to their own leaders, but from ethnic minorities, the Lao Theung and the Lao Sung, objecting to the imposition of taxes and corvee labor. Suppression of these uprisings, which to the French were madness, was in the interest of both the French authorities and the Lao elite" (Stuart-Fox 2003: 82).

31. In a similar vein, Gunn (2003: 258) argues that "minority peasant movements in Laos were, if anything, more anti-colonial, anti-capitalist than anti-feudal." Moreover, the basic problem engendered by French policies was "the fundamental wrenching of peasant producers from an essentially tributary formation to capitalist-engendered networks of surplus accumulation" (259).

32. At almost the same time that this particular resistance in Laos was transforming into a millenarian movement, a similar millennial movement, known as the Saya San rebellion, broke out in Burma, a violent rebellion that took the British about two years to control; see Sarkisyanz (1965: 160–165). For a relevant collection of essays focused on many aspects of the cult of Maitreya, especially in East Asia, see Hardarce and Sponberg (1988). For a review of millenarian movements in Cambodia in the late nineteenth and early twentieth centuries, see Hansen (2007: 55–64).

33. Pholsena (2006: 130) cites rhetoric like this from the *Vientiane Times* in 1999. I can attest that it remains essentially unchanged in the many references I noted while reading the same newspaper during 2006–2007.

34. Gunn (2003: 143) adds more specificity noting which particular revolts against the French have been singled as part of the historical lineage inherited by the Pathet Lao. "Pathet Lao historiography dates the nationalist movement in Laos from a popular armed insurrection led by the Lao 'patriot,' Phao Ka Douat in 1901, eight years after the French conquest. Other ethnic rebels deemed sufficiently important and 'patriotic' to rate mention are Ong Keo and Ong Kommadan, the leaders of armed insurrection on the Bolovens plateau which lasted from 1901 to 1936, the armed resistance of the Lu minority under the leadership of Chao Fa of Muong Sing (1914–1918); the resistance of the Tai in Sam Neua (1916), and the Hmong rebellion of 1918–1922 led by Tia Fa Patchay."

35. Commenting on precisely this issue in the Cambodian context, Hansen (2007: 111) says: "From an administrative standpoint, highly educated, respected monks and scholars who advocated a demythologized Buddhism and were trained in modern scientific worldview and pedagogical methods were more reliable religious leaders."

36. Gunn's (2003: 2) thesis supports this conclusion. He argues that "the overall dissolution effect engendered by the colonial tax, corvee, and *prestation* (labor due) system was much more dislocative of traditional and social relations in this backwater than has hitherto been appreciated. The otherwise unexplained phenomena of the majority participation of these hill people in a modern movement for social and especially

national liberation under the banner of the Pathet Lao movement . . . is brought into perspective." McCoy's (1970: 92) conclusion is also congruent: "All of these revolts ultimately failed because they were scattered, isolated events which usually involved only one segment of one region of the mountain populations. . . . These revolts would remain localized outbursts of countless racial and regional splinters until a somewhat larger movement could unify their dissidence and harness it to a higher cause. Unwittingly it was the French who supplied this cause."

37. Vat Sisaket, however, in being spared destruction, had been the Thai administrative headquarters in Vientiane after the city had been destroyed in the Chao Anou debacle. Thus there was in fact a very distinct historical political legacy regarding this space.

38. As we noted earlier, the French established only one public secondary educational institution during their entire tenure in Laos.

39. One interesting finding is that Finot could not find a complete edition of the Tipitaka intact not only in any one location, but collectively throughout the entire country.

40. Hansen (2007) has studied in depth the movement that led to an emphasis on the Vinaya code of conduct in a reforming *sangha* context occurring at this same time in Cambodia. She argues that this effort, led by Finot, Coedes, Karpeles, but especially their two Khmer protégés, Chuon Nath and Huot That, constituted a "religious modernism [that] emphasized rationalism, authenticity and purification. They advocated new methods for Buddhist education and for the translation, production and dissemination of new versions of Buddhist texts which they 'purified' from the grammatical and interpretive corruptions and accretions that had occurred over time" (2007: 3). She goes on to say: "The Khmer Buddhist modernism that emerged in Phnom Penh in the first few decades of the twentieth century, I argue, is best understood in ethical terms as a rationalist shift in Buddhist intellectual sensibilities about temporality and purification, a shift that gave a heightened significance to everyday actions and relationships of ordinary individuals in the here and now of modern life" (ibid.).

41. French nomenclature, quite unfortunate in this instance, is especially apparent in the name provided for this institute. Theravadins never refer to themselves as followers of the "Little Vehicle" or Hinayana tradition. Instead, they use Theravada. The term Hinayana was consistently invoked in Mahayana-inspired texts, most notably the *Saddhamapundarika* ("Lotus") *Sutra*, to distinguish the "Great Vehicle" (indicating a more broadly conceived understanding of the various paths that can lead to the enlightenment of all sentient beings) from the "Little Vehicle" (indicating a more narrow-minded, self-oriented path). "*Petit vehicule*" is a French translation of what Theravadins regard as a Mahayana propagandistic term.

42. Durkheim (1995: 28–31).

43. Hansen (2007: 125) points that T. W. Rhys Davids regarded even the morally based *jataka*s as reflecting the social life and popular beliefs of the Aryan tribes, who "were passing through the first stages of civilization" and as "a priceless record of the childhood of our race."

44. Indeed, the French imposed travel restrictions on all monks to prevent them from traveling to Thailand; see Edwards (2007: 113); and Hansen (2007: 116).

45. French authorities were arguing that "if the protectorate government does not succeed in creating an autonomous Laotian individuality—at least among those who have received education—then they will feel themselves increasingly attracted towards the neighboring country [Thailand] and this situation will create new difficulties" (Evans 2002b: 78).

46. Evans (2002b: 82) notes that this renewed French support of Luang Phrabang royalty drew critical reactions from an emergent, secularized faction of the Lao elite.

47. Stuart-Fox provides an effective overview of the leadership of the emergent Pathet Lao:

> Like many of the Lao Issara leaders, this [urban] group [those including Souphanouvong] formed part of the social elite of Laos, having connections with the royal house of Luang Phrabang and a number of prominent families of central and southern Laos. Their education had been in French colonial schools, and by virtue of their birth and training all could have looked forward to participation in government or administration. The second group of revolutionaries came of very different origins. None was socially well connected. Most, with the exception of Kaysone Phomvihan, had relatively little education; all had been involved in some way with the rash of small anti-French guerilla bands that sprang up, particularly in southern and central Laos, towards the end of 1945 [or earlier]. Leaders of these groups were brought together in August 1946 under the auspices of the Viet Minh to form a "Committee of Lao Resistance in the East." Some members of this Resistance committee were montagnards (ethnic minorities). (1996: 55)

Stuart-Fox goes on to note that although Souphanouvong and Phoumi Vongvichit were eventually given the positions of prime minister and deputy prime minister of the later Lao Patriotic Front, real power was vested in Kaysone and Nouhak, both of whom were long-serving members of the Indochina Communist Party (ICP). When the ICP broke into three parties in 1951, representing the revolutionary struggles in Vietnam, Laos, and Cambodia, Kaysone became the general secretary and Nouhak second in the Lao Politburo hierarchy. Because of their history of working with the Vietnamese, they enjoyed total support from that quarter. Moreover, the Viet Minh sometimes cast a more suspicious look at the "royal" communists (Souphanouvong and others who had been a part of the Lao Issara).

48. This posture of American foreign policy was firmly in place during the presidency of Franklin Roosevelt but was mitigated under Harry Truman following Roosevelt's death in April 1945. It is quite ironic, given the spectacular turn of events that ensued, that "in September 1945, during a brief period when Americans were supporting anticolonialist Asians, a U.S. general flew [Prince] Souphanouvong up to Hanoi to introduce him to another promising Asian nationalist, Ho Chi Minh. The two men quickly formed their own alliance behind the Americans' backs. Ho sent Soupha-

nouvong off to Laos on foot with an escort of armed Viet Minh soldiers to organize a resistance against the French" (Warner 1996: 70).

49. "After the re-establishment of French political control in 1946 forced the Lao Issara government into exile in Thailand, it was left to the monks who remained in Laos to fan nationalist sentiment and to organize Buddhist festivals in support of the independence movement" (Stuart-Fox 1996: 88).

50. At the First International Conference of Lao Studies, held at Northern Illinois University in May 2005, the opening ceremony began with a solemn salute to Maha Sila Viravong's legacy of scholarship for the field of Lao Studies.

51. He was so "Thai" in his perspective that when he wrote about the Chao Anou chapter of Lao history, he actually framed it as a rebellion, rather than as a liberation struggle, an aspect of his historical work that never settled well with his Lao nationalists.

52. Justin McDaniel (private communication) writes that "his grammar actually worked to remove many of the unique elements of Lao morphology and syntax, because he grew up speaking an Isan-Lao-Thai dialect."

53. Indeed, Lao *phongsawadan* = Pali *phongsa* + *vamsa*.

54. Chalong Soontravanich (2003: 111) adds: "*Phongsawadan Lao (A Lao Chronicle . . .)* is perhaps the best known history of Laos written by a Lao historian, inside and outside Laos. Completed in 1953 and published as a textbook by the Lao Ministry of Education in 1957, *Phongsawadan Lao* became a standard textbook for Lao history for most Lao students to at least 1975."

55. See Rene de Berval (1956).

56. On this issue in general, Stuart-Fox (1998: 187–188) has commented: "It was only the coming of the modern state and nationalism (via French colonialism) that saw the creation of a different sense of time among the elite, and the emergence of a concept of linear history of the nation, which after independence was increasingly communicated to the masses through education, propaganda and ritual. But the weakness of the Lao state both under the RLG [Royal Lao Government] and the LPDR [Lao People's Democratic Republic] has meant that this new consciousness has remained relatively weak and slippage between legend and the modern idea of history is pervasive."

57. "For Katay . . . , it was the persistent reality of Mueang Lao as it existed in the hearts of all Lao that formed the basis for reconstitution of a unified Lao state. It was not French power that had unified 'this polycephalous nation, this latent Confederacy of States'. In fact just the opposite. France had failed to create a unified Lao state because she had failed to unite the protectorate of Luang Phrabang with the rest of French-administered Laos. It was left to the Lao Issara immediately after World War II to restore Mueang Lao as a modern nation-state" (Stuart-Fox 2003: 84).

58. See Holt (2004); Holt (1996); and Tambiah (1992), in which it is argued that the exclusive political posture of defining the state that was adopted by modern Sinhala Buddhist nationalists is basically a post-independence nationalist phenomenon and that the vast majority of Buddhist kingships in the past were far more inclusive in orientation.

59. That the encompassing, or the assimilation and integration, of the upland

people remains a priority of the contemporary Lao PDR government is clearly seen in its continuing efforts to attract both Lao Theung and Lao Sung upland peoples to the country's river basin towns that are traditionally the domain of the Lao Loum, where educational, health, and other government services are more readily available and where these highland peoples can be more readily pulled away from their subsistence slash-and-burn agriculture and integrated into the emerging political economy. This is one very interesting instance in which contemporary concerns for national integration and the health of the environment have coalesced.

60. Zago (1976: 123) observed among Vientiane's urban elite Lao in the 1960s that "the concept of a sacred society is giving way. The myths of the past are losing their symbolic power and are no longer as effective as they once were. In summary, a process of desanctification is under way; for some it is a conscious process; for others, just a fact of life."

61. Zago (1976: 122), writing about the condition of Buddhism in Laos in the 1960s and early 1970s, seems to confirm this: "Political parties and individual politicians will often seek to present themselves as devoted Buddhists in order to enlist the sympathy and support of monks, but the government and the majority of officials attempt to limit or channel the political influence of the latter."

62. Evans (2002b: 98) has described the undeveloped nature of Laos's infrastructure at the time of political independence: "In the mid-1950s Laos had around 5600 kilometers of roads, of which [only] 800 were surfaced and therefore [about 85 percent of the roads were] unusable in the rainy season. In 1945 there were only nineteen registered vehicles in the country, a figure that had risen to around 100 by the early 1950s. The Mekong River and its tributaries constituted the main travel arteries, but only in some instances were boats driven by motor power. Air transport was minimal, and telecommunications [were] confined to the main centres. Telephone calls to provincial centres would not be possible until 1967."

63. See Castle (1993) for the most reliable military history of the region from the 1950s until 1975.

64. Here is how Dommen describes just one of many conflicts that Souvanna Phouma faced as a result of an American diplomacy that was ideologically driven by the fear of communism:

> In late 1956, after Souvanna Phouma had worked to arrive at a coalition government with the Pathet Lao, he was told by the U.S. Ambassador that the "U.S. was unable to respond favorably to the Prime Minister's appeal for support since it considered the entrance of Communists into the Lao Cabinet would threaten Lao independence. . . . Souvanna Phouma's position was based on the premise that national unity was the priority objective. . . . The RLG was convinced that not all the PL leaders were communists, but included many who, for various reasons, had joined the organization encadred by communists. The best, and indeed the only, means of making it possible for them to escape the communists was to include them as a minority in the government." (1964: 252–253)

65. Many Vietnamese had left Laos in 1946 following the declaration of independence by the Lao Issara government led by Prince Phetsarath. This had forced the French to bring in many of their own bureaucrats to administer the colony.

66. On this specific point regarding military salaries, Evans (2002b: 112) adds: "By 1958 army salaries, which were paid for by US aid, had become the main source of liquid cash in the Lao economy and were driving commercial development. Despite this, the Lao army remained a young, poorly trained force."

67. Twelve years earlier, in another book, Evans wrote the following assessment of the American aid program:

> In the first four years of independence the Lao government received $166 million of aid from the United States, and a further $125 million was programmed to establish Lao armed forces.... The traditional aristocracy and their relatives were well placed to reap the benefits of this U.S. aid bonanza, and some of them grew very rich by channeling aid to suit their own purposes. Some diversified into businesses such as banks, airlines, movie theaters, hotels, construction and transport items. Yet little of the influx of U.S. dollars cornered by them was invested in productive activities, and much was dissipated in luxury spending.... American aid did not create a viable indigenous capitalist class, but it was wonderful new source of "tribute" for the traditional elite. (1990: 34–35)

Evans final comment here is quite insightful insofar as it reflects the manner in which indigenous conceptual categories fielded new social, cultural, and in this case, economic imports. On a theoretical level, this is the same dynamic I have tried to illustrate in terms of how the Lao fielded their understanding of Buddhism through indigenous conceptual categories that were already in place.

68. Evans (2002b: 144) points out that proportionately fewer Lao Loum joined the Pathet Lao than did Lao Theung.

69. Dommen (1964: 266) observes: "It is difficult to avoid the impression that officials in Washington, having failed in their attempt to prevent a coalition, set about to sabotage the coalition and to ensure the downfall of Souvanna Phouma even when the latter adopted a staunchly anti-communist stance."

70. The Pathet Lao was cleverly deceptive in disguising the extent of its communist leanings during these early years. Stuart-Fox explains:

> The formation of each of the three coalition governments had the effect of maintaining a differentiation between the two groups within the Pathet Lao. Negotiations and participation in all three coalitions were left almost exclusively to the Issara group, [those] who were able to converse in the same educated language and negotiate on an equal footing with their royalist neutralist or rightist counterparts. This had the effect of dividing the Pathet Lao leadership into those known personally to members of the Royal Lao government and those virtually unknown. Conclusions reached about the Pathet Lao attitudes and thinking hardly took the

latter into account, despite positions of authority and influence held by such little understood figures as Kaison [Kaysone] and Nuhak. The traditional political influence wielded by the upper classes was taken for granted in Viang Chan and thus there was always a tendency to discount the role played by Resistance Committee members [such as Kaysone and Nouhak, who later emerged as the real powerbrokers behind the scenes]. The political organization adopted by the PL in 1956 encouraged this by exploiting the prestige and popularity of Suphanuvong. ... [F]requency of contact allied to family ties and similarity of background and education, plus the generally moderate position taken by the PL in fulfilling their role in various coalitions, led to a widespread belief, especially in neutralist circles influenced by Suvanna, that the PL were nationalists first and communists second. (1996: 55)

71. Souphanouvong's appointment to his ministry (Plan, Reconstruction and Urbanism) followed the same logic in that it gave the rural-based Pathet Lao control and access to important government plans precisely in an area that the Pathet Lao had previously had no exposure.

72. In relation to lay Buddhism under the Pathet Lao, Zago (1976: 126) offers this interesting comment: "One may find more of a critical spirit, however among adult Buddhist groups, whose members will more readily refuse to accept a given interpretation, and will express the desire for more far-reaching reforms, and a more radical implementation of the original Buddhist ideal. This tendency for lay associations to assert themselves in a meaningful way on both local and the international level is evidently even stronger in the liberated zones of the Pathet Lao."

73. In the meantime the United States had withdrawn its aid to Laos in 1958 in a move that contributed to the downfall of Souvanna Phouma's National Union coalition with the Pathet Lao.

74. Stuart-Fox (1996: 89) believes that this government strategy of importing Thammayut monks from Thailand backfired because "this had the effect of further dividing the sangha" along the lines of either Thammayut or monastic identities.

75. Martin Stuart-Fox (private communication) notes that the "increase in the number of monks was in part to escape being drafted into the army."

76. "The rapid social and cultural changes [from the late 1950s through the early 1970s] in the cities, especially Vientiane, were a cause for anxiety to those who saw them eroding traditional norms, and Buddhist monks in particular began to produce texts preaching the need to protect Lao culture" (Evans 2002b: 153).

77. Tiyavanich (1997: 274) makes it clear that attempts by the Royal Lao Government to recruit monks for rural development were similar to the policy developed in Thailand in the 1960s and 1970s: "The [Thai] military government in the mid-1960s and the sangha authorities decided that monks should take part in rural development to help combat the threat of communism. In an effort to win over villagers, the Thai government attempted to make the monks' roles more relevant to the daily lives and problems of the rural people by allowing monks to perform tasks that would contrib-

ute to the community development. Ironically, modern state Buddhism had previously condemned monks who were involved in these matters."

78. Evans (2002b: 122). Evans provides a detailed summary of the complex and often convoluted Lao political developments from 1958 through 1963 (105–128).

79. On this issue Warner (1996: 380) quotes G. McMurtrie Godley, the U.S. ambassador to Laos during the peak years of fighting, who offered this epitaph. "We used the Meo [Hmong]. The rationale then, which I believed in, was that they tied down three first-rate North Vietnamese divisions that otherwise would have been used against our men in South Vietnam." Warner adds: "Though Operation Momentum began with a different motive, to help defend Laos, America ended up sacrificing the tribals and the lowland Laotians for U.S. goals in Vietnam. These allies, or proxies, were abandoned once the war was over, and the results were a permanent stain on America's reputation" (ibid.).

80. There is some question about the ethnic constituency of the CIA's secret army, which is usually identified as being overwhelmingly Hmong in composition. "Vang Pao provided a breakdown of the ethnic composition of the nine Special Forces battalions under his command in the late 1960s: 48% Hmong, 27% Lao, 22% Khamu and 3% Yao, far from being a 'Hmong Secret Army'" (Evans 2002b: 142). Yet these figures must also be read with skepticism, given Vang Pao's record of dishonesty and corruption compiled not only during the war years in Laos, but after 1975, when the CIA provided him a safe haven in the United States. Vang Pao was repeatedly arrested in the United States, first on corruption and racketeering charges in Los Angeles during the 1980s, and then in June 2007 he was arrested again, along with nine accomplices, for plotting to acquire sophisticated weaponry for an attack on the Lao PDR government. Ironically, Vang Pao's 2007 arrest was orchestrated by the CIA. On a different note, Gunn (2003: 240) points out a rather bizarre fact that "the U.S. ability to re-channel the traditional revolt of the Hmong was inordinately enhanced by the role of a certain U.S. Agency for International Development personality, Edgar "Pop" Buell. His ability to call on airborne supplies in the highlands created a veritable cargo cult. By the 1960s a full-blown millenarian movement developed among Hmong refugees. Evans (2002b: 150) observes: "Estimates are difficult, but between 1960 and 1970 perhaps 20 per cent of the Hmong population had died as a result of the war in the region. The CIA turned increasingly to Thai mercenaries to augment Van Pao's battlefield strength and by 1973 there were approximately 18,000 of them in Laos."

81. Evans described the crucial events in 1968 and 1969 that led to the massive bombing of the Plain of Jars in Xieng Khuang Province:

> In the north, up until 1968 the war seesawed seasonally. Vang Pao's forces had the tactical advantage of air support that during the wet season allowed them to strike at will stranded communist forces whose ground communications and supplies from North Vietnam were hindered. During the dry season, the communist forces counterattacked. . . . Then came the Tet Offensive and Vang Pao was forced to give up his positions in Houaphan Province and lost about 10,000 trying to retake them.

... The battering suffered by Vang Pao's forces led to an expansion of the use of air power in the northern region. This was facilitated by the October 1968 temporary bombing halt of North Vietnam called for by President Nixon [this is not quite correct because Nixon was not elected until November 1968 and not inaugurated until late January 1969]. Consequently in the first half of 1969, in addition to the hundreds of daily bombing runs over southern Laos, the rate of air strikes in the north escalated from 20 flown previously by the Royal Lao Airforce T-28s, to between 200 and 300 per day, flown mostly by US aircraft based in Thailand. ... Nonetheless, the PL moved to take the Plain of Jars holding it temporarily in the summer of 1969 before Vang Pao could regain it in September. The number of refugees grew to about 150,000. But knowing they couldn't retain the area during the dry season, a mass evacuation began and an unprecedented carpet bombing of the Plain of Jars ensued, as well as in Houaphan. (2002b: 147–148)

82. *Vientiane Times*, March 30, 2007, p. 1.

83. Hayashi (2003: 44) has collected personal histories from Laos describing "lives lived as fugitives from destructive violence. The Lao and other ethnic groups made decoy villages to draw American fire, tilled their fields at night, and held weddings and other celebrations in the forest. The external threat forced those living in the country, both Lao and non-Lao alike, to work together for survival. This experience, rather than socialist dogma, resulted in a multiethnic, egalitarian, and fraternal style socialism held together by the common thread of mutual assistance."

84. The legacy of the American bombing continues today because 30 percent of the bombs dropped were unexploded. In 2006, 25 exploded, killing 16 and injuring 33, and in the first two months alone of 2007, 14 exploded, killing 15 and injuring 23. According to Lao officials, an average of about 150 people have been killed every year from unexploded ordnance since the bombing stopped in 1973; see the *Vientiane Times*, March 30, 2007, pp. 1–2. It is difficult not to agree with Gunn (2003: 246) when he says: "In fact, given the cruel and barbaric record of the U.S. during the Second Indochina War in literally bombing Laos back into the stone age, the shoe is on the other foot. Today, it behooves [sic] the U.S. and the Western community to cooperate unconditionally with the Lao PDR in compensating for the war-damaged economy and appalling human and ecological losses suffered as a direct consequence of the bombing."

85. "Politically, all the governments involved—the Americans, the Thais, and the royalist Lao on one side, the Pathet Lao, the North Vietnamese, and their backers, the Chinese and Soviets, on the other—reached the same conclusion about the Geneva accords. As much as they would have liked to publicize their enemies' violations of the accords, they had more to gain by keeping their own roles quiet. So, by tacit agreement, they all outwardly pretended to abide by the accords—cynically guaranteeing the peace and neutrality of a weak country while keeping it polarized and at war" (Warner 1996: 135). See also Stuart-Fox (1996: 47); and Evans (2002b: 146).

86. Phoumi Vongvichit described the Thammayut Nikay in the following way: "A Thai reformed sect of Buddhism, introduced in Laos about 1941–1942 and used by

the American imperialists and Thai reactionaries for their aggressive activities . . . [a sect] which has succeeded in implanting its ideas only in a few pagodas in the suburbs of Vientiane, and in Southern Laos . . . [a sect] within which an important number of monks and faithful patriots have disclosed the schemes of the enemy" (cited in Lafont 1982: 149; brackets Lafont's).

Chapter 3: Question of Place

1. The American embassy in Vientiane continued to function uninterrupted, not only during the volatile months of the 1975 revolution, but throughout Vientiane's diplomatic isolation from 1975 until the late 1980s. It never closed.

2. For published accounts of extended incarcerations and forced labor within Pathet Lao prison camps established in Huaphan Province in the vicinity of Vieng Xai, see Kremmer (2003) and Bouphanouvang (2003).

3. During its first year in power the Pathet Lao government discovered an acute need for various forms of technical and educational expertise. It therefore released many "low-security-threat" individuals, who provided urgently needed services.

4. Regarding the hostilities in the early months of the new regime, Evans (1990: 186) has commented: "Attributed by many observers to the atheism of communist doctrine, the hostility appears to have had complicated ethnic roots as well. Several informants have claimed that the most aggressive anti-Buddhists were soldiers and militants from ethnic minorities who were not Buddhists and who in fact identified the religion with the former, 'oppressive' regime." In addition to ethnicity, class was also a factor.

5. See Lafont (1982: 152).

6. But Kremmer's investigative journalism (2003) reconstructs a story divulged by a political prisoner who survived seventeen years of detention in a Vieng Xai camp. He claims to have witnessed the royal family's incarceration in an adjacent compound and was aware of their eventual deaths occurring before 1980, deaths which were due, he avers, to the extreme conditions of their confinements.

7. Evans (1990: 186) writes in a similar vein: "A nationalism in Laos that was dependent upon Buddhism consequently risked being seen by other ethnic groups as a form threatening cultural domination rather than a vehicle of national integration. . . . By contrast, the major achievement of the Pathet Lao was its ability to project itself as a nationalist force. Its long period in the mountains meant that it not only recruited among the ethnic minorities, but also had to elaborate a nationalist ideology that clearly recognized them as part of the Lao nation." In another context Evans (1998: 57) adds: "Buddhism lost its status as a state religion, and the government announced that 'every Lao citizen is allowed to practice any religion he wishes.' . . . Inevitably this also meant a reorientation of state ritual away from religion towards purely state-based secular rituals."

8. See Southwold's (1983: 181–201) discussion, which contrasts "instrumental" and "sapiental."

9. On this point Evans (1993: 136) has written: "The concept of the ascetic, selfless person working for a higher existence is the folk model of a good person in rural Laos, and this model influenced the new regime's concept of the 'new socialist man.'"

10. The serious downturn in economic conditions was compounded by other factors. Sisouphanthong and Taillard (2000: 13) write: "The difficult process of nation-building left Lao PDR with two legacies. First, the country had to repair the damage done by the war, which had displaced a quarter of the 1973 population (730,000 people) within national borders and caused 12% of the 1986 population (414,000) to leave the country. Between 1975 and 1979, the return of 550,000 people to their provinces of origin was organized, despite transport difficulties." Thus the postwar loss of 12 percent of the population and the resettlement of no less than 15 to 20 percent of its people presented the government with a gargantuan logistical task, given the context of its efforts to reform the national economy at the same time. Stuart-Fox and Bucknell (1982: 453) add that the government's new policy of forcing the "resettlement of tribal people at lower altitudes in order to protect virgin forests" alienated many of the Lao Theung and Lao Sung, precisely those people who had supported the Pathet Lao during the years of struggle. Moreover, "overly close political ties with Vietnam, the presence of thousands of Vietnamese troops in Laos, and the personal contacts leading Lao communists have with Vietnam (by descent, marriage or education) . . . had the effect of compromising Pathet Lao nationalist credentials, and . . . caused widespread popular suspicion and resentment."

11. The Hmong lost about half of their 40,000-man-strong army during the war. "Another 125,000—or about half the total Hmong population of Laos—resettled after the war in the United States" (Kremmer 2003: 31). Some Hmong stayed behind and mounted a resistance that sporadically caused problems for the LPDR into 1978 (Evans 2002b: 177), and small, lightly armed remnants occasionally mounted limited skirmishes even into early 2000. The severity of the Pathet Lao's counterattacks on the Hmong still reverberates today. In June 2006 an American journalist convinced a group of 140 Hmong still holding out in the remote mountains of the north that political conditions in the contemporary Lao PDR had changed sufficiently that they could lay down their arms and begin living a normal life. When the group came out of the mountains, the journalist was immediately expelled from the country for "interfering in internal affairs," and the Hmong were placed in a detention center. I have been unable to ascertain what happened after this event.

12. Because "the brunt of the bombing . . . fell on the Lao Theung, or the people of the mountainsides, . . . [and] American bombardment resulted in the deaths of more than 8,000 people and razed more than 350 villages in Xieng Khouang province alone" (Kremmer 2003: 31), the Lao Theung were among the most enthusiastic and loyal supporters of the new regime and its programs.

13. The Vietnamese did not need to be as concerned about institutional Mahayana or Theravada Buddhism, since its presence in Vietnam was not nearly as ubiquitous as in Laos.

14. In Vientiane's Kaysone Phomvihane National Museum, there are photographs

from the late 1940s though the 1960s of Kaysone posing in the company of Buddhist monks.

15. Justin McDaniel (private communication) points out that "there are thousands of Thai Buddhist publications available in Lao monasteries, and many of them were printed before 1975. They were not banned or burnt en masse."

16. For an overview and critical assessment of Buddhadasa and his significance as a modern Thai reformer of Buddhism, see Jackson (2003).

17. "People were discouraged from alms giving and organizing festivals in monasteries because these were considered wasteful" (Evans 1998: 59).

18. Lifelong residents of Luang Phrabang told me personally that monks were never prevented from going on alms throughout the town and that the laity continued to support them every morning by giving them shares of rice, even during the leanest of economic times during the mid-1970s.

19. For instance, during 2006 the Lao PDR hosted official government visits by Sri Lanka's speaker of Parliament, a visit that paved the way in 2007 for the prime minister of Sri Lanka. During both visits official press releases from the Lao PDR government emphasized how Laos and Sri Lanka share a common set of religious and cultural values embodied in the practices of Theravada Buddhism.

20. "[According to Khamtan], national reconstruction under the new order demands that every monk, 'must not rest with arms crossed, pretending to live in *upekkha* (. . . equanimity), as this attitude is tantamount to perpetuation of the old regime by favouring the oppression of classes under the dominant class.' Rather, he continues, the monk must share in the tasks of the nation and of the people, as one who has the rights and duties like any other citizen" (Gunn 1982: 93).

21. Justin McDaniel (private communication) notes that pamphlets articulating this kind of criticism of Buddhism between 1975 and 1984 were not produced within the *sangha* itself.

22. Still the best study on the subject remains King (1992).

23. From Gunn's (1982) article it is impossible for me to ascertain whether Gunn interviewed Khamtan directly or whether he is reporting from Savang Pinith's summary of Khamtam Thepbuali's "The Lao Sangha and the Revolution" published in *Bulletin d'Ecole Francaise d'Extreme-Orient* 64 (1977): 317–323.

24. See Senevitatne (1999: 130–188) for an extended discussion of this movement. The key difference, however, is that Rahula was arguing for a Buddhist socialism and not for the utilitarian subordination of Buddhism to a one-party socialist state.

25. In fact this is still the case today. According to U.S. embassy officials, the Lao PDR government in 2006 claims to have collected only about $100 million in tax revenues to fund its various operations, a paltry sum in relation to what is needed.

26. The consummate study of the failure of the cooperatives is Evans (1990).

27. Tambiah (1970: 12–13) notes regarding this pattern in Isan: "Ordinarily a newly married couple lives uxorilocally for a few years in the house of the wife's parents as members of the family household. A change takes place when the next sister gets married; the older sister and her family may build a house for themselves in the parents'

compound, or move out altogether and live neolocally. This change is usually synchronized with other changes: no more are the couple part of the parental household, economically dependent upon them and also contributing their labour to the parental farming enterprise. The wife's parents informally transfer some land to the couple so they can farm independently, and to establish themselves as a separate household. . . . The youngest sister lives with the parents as the stem family and inherits and succeeds them in occupying the parental house and farm."

28. Evans writes:

> In Laos the situation of women differs in a number of crucial respects from that of women in the Vietnamese and Chinese family structure. The female-centered nature of the Lao domestic group is structurally quite different from the male dominated ones in the countryside of its northern and eastern neighbors, and this gives Lao women comparatively some power and influence in the family. In Laos, women have some power by virtue of their possession of land and the general practice of matrilocal residence. Their ability to dispossess their husbands through divorce tempers male tyrannical tendencies, and the fact that the husband often moves into a situation where he is surrounded by a network of his wife's relatives and friends attenuates his social and political command over her. Lao women also have a much greater say in their choice of spouse than do either Chinese or Vietnamese women. Arranged marriages among the Lao peasants are rare, although, of course, the parents wield considerable informal influence over the choice of a partner. (1990: 131).

29. Evans (1993: 140) cites an example of a *boun* that cost some five years' worth of income and notes that thirty of these were held in a district near Vientiane in 1982 despite government calls for thrift.

30. One of the paradoxes in the immediate aftermath of the 1975 revolution was that for a few years, because so many teachers had fled the country or had been sent to "seminar" for "re-education," the new regime had to rely more upon Buddhist monks to jumpstart its decimated educational system. For the first two years or so after the revolution, more education was conducted at the *vat*.

31. Indeed, most of the senior monks with whom I spoke in Luang Phrabang were very clear in this regard and were quick to criticize those very few other monks who continued to traffic in spirits. At least this is how the matter was presented to me. Justin McDaniel (private communication), however, writes that "this is the public face the Sangha puts on for foreigners. Even the most modern monks I know think long and hard about spirits."

32. A very notable exception to this would be the national public New Year's ceremonies held in April at Luang Phrabang. Not only do costumed ancestral *phi* of the city play a conspicuous role in venerating and lustrating the Phra Bang, but "stick-figure" *phi* symbols are worn by villagers marching in the main parade that processes on the town's main street on the day preceding the Phra Bang's ritual lustration. Evidently local government authorities have chosen to include these elements of the *phi* cult in

the overriding interest of tourism. Moreover, I often observed the inconspicuous presence of spirit veneration in a number of *vat* courtyards in Luang Phrabang. Beyond this, the worship of *vat phi*, the spirit of either the founding abbot or the most recent abbot remains an important dimension of cultic life at most temples (see Photo 3.1).

33. By this time Hmong resistance in the northern highlands had lost its former vigor.

34. Commenting specifically on this aspect of the early Lao Marxist historiography, Stuart-Fox (2003: 85–86) writes: "The revolutionary movement was portrayed as having deep historical roots in popular resistance to foreign domination. Dissent replaced descent as the principle of continuity and legitimation. . . . Lao Theung and Lao Sung opposition to the imposition of French colonial rule was glorified as standing firmly in the tradition of radical rejection of all forms of elite domination. Pathet Lao historiography thus provided ethnic minorities with a role in the construction of revolutionary Lao nationalism that was far more central than their marginal place in the neo-traditionalist historiography of the royal Lao regime."

35. Evans (2003) is especially critical of the lack of analytical and historical discourse in post-revolutionary Laos. Here are four comments from a recent article he has written concerning the intellectual poverty of Marxist Lao historiography: "Marxism did not lead to the opening up of new questions about Lao history, but rather the closing down of genuine intellectual inquiry" (97); "Serious intellectual life inside Laos stopped, and those who wished to continue serious research had to do so privately or surreptitiously, at least until the beginning of the 1990s" (100); "Laos witnessed a double regression, an intellectual one and a social one. Only in the 1990s did we begin to see some recuperation both intellectually and socially. But the stark fact remains that Lao historiography in the 1990s is even further behind the intellectual progress of the Thai intelligentsia than it was in the early 1970s. . . . The new regime has produced very little of value for historians of Lao society" (98); and finally, "Lao historiography remains constrained by the political straightjacket imposed by the LPRP. The discarding of communist ideology in favour of nationalism has not seen any diminution of dogmatic analysis. . . . [H]istory writing in Laos is paralyzed by politics" (104–105).

36. Noting how Marxist historiography now sought to link itself to the Lao cultural past, Stuart-Fox (2003: 88) notes: "The Lao PDR saw itself, as had the Royal Lao regime, as heir to the legacy of Lan Xang, with all that implied about deep historical roots and national identity."

37. Indeed, the problem has registered deeply with some minorities, especially in these contemporary days after the relative opening up of the economy. For an example of this sentiment, an informant told Pholsena: "Let me tell you, my niece, those who've got the power don't care about the ethnic peoples! It's all for the Lao Loum, and only for the Lao Loum. But we are honest people, we don't benefit from favouritism. It's not the Party-State's fault, but the fault of those who apply the doctrine!" (Pholsena 2006: 208). Pholsena (215) goes on to say that during the revolutionary period, cultural diversity, equality of opportunity, and unity against a common enemy were all stressed. But this initial attempt at transcending ethnicity to create a national identity has been

continuously undermined by the current regime so that being an "ethnic person" is turning into a stigma (ibid.). She argues that the earlier values have been sacrificed in the era of the "the new economic mechanisms."

38. See Evans (1998) for a fuller explanation of the significance of this term.

39. Evans (1998: 27) also seems to think that ancestor veneration enforced by the influence of latent Confucian sensibilities are, in part, responsible for the emergence of the cults of Ho and Kaysone.

40. "The Kaysone Memorial Museum was opened on 13 December 1994, Kaysone's seventy-fourth birthday anniversary, its purpose being, as one party magazine stated, to 'train members of the younger generation to succeed in and perpetuate the cause of the party. It will honor the nation to which Kaysone Phomvihane devoted his entire life for the sake of building the beloved fatherland and to make it a wealthy and strong nation serving the well-being of the Lao people of all ethnic groups (*Laos* 1/1995)" (quoted in Evans 1998: 32).

41. "Thai media is ubiquitous and accessed by every level of [Lao] society, including the country's leadership.... There is no competition between [Thai and Lao television] media: 70 to 75 per cent of the population in Laos watch Thai television programmes, compared to 20 to 25 per cent who watch Lao broadcasting" (Pholsena 2006: 52–53).

42. Evans notes that the constant references to "socialism," which thereafter were replaced by the "development system" (*labop ganpattana*) indicate that the timing of the meeting antedates the collapse of the Soviet Union and the subsequent political transformations that occurred throughout the socialist world.

43. This was the same time that the Vietnamese withdrew from neighboring Cambodia.

44. Regarding the current Lao effort to rebuddhacize, Pholsena, quoting Trankell (1999), writes (2006: 49): "This display of cultural productions for the local population and for the tourists [is a matter of the] 'marketing of culture that consists of simultaneously preserving the cultural heritage, negotiating the Lao national identity, and putting it on stage for commercial purposes.'"

45. Stuart-Fox (private communication) notes how Kaysone "in the last year of his life, when he knew he was dying, . . . regularly met with a famous former monk for meditation; [moreover,] before the Kaysone Museum was built, his house in the km 6 compound was kept as a memorial to him. When I visited the house, I saw burned-down incense sticks before some small Buddha images and asked my guide if the Secretary-General had burned incense. 'Oh no,' came the reply, 'someone else did it for him.'"

Chapter 4: Commodities of the Place

1. Lior Bear, a contemporary anthropologist of tourism, in a private communication, January 28, 2007.

2. "The World Travel and Tourism Council (WTTC) estimated that in 2003 the employment generated by the travel and tourism industry nationally in the Lao PDR

was 145,000 jobs or 6 per cent of total employment. By 2013, it is estimated that tourism will create 269,000 jobs or 9 per cent of total employment. . . . While official figures record the number of persons with salaried jobs in tourism agencies and related services, they do not, for example, take into account persons earning a living from handicraft production and restaurants or from construction jobs created by new tourist hotels or the expansion of airport or other forms of transportation. Staff employed in new business ventures, such as internet cafes and souvenir shops that have opened recently in response to increased numbers of visitors, are also missing from the figures" (UNESCO 2004: 61).

3. "While tourism is not the only causal factor, tourism and associated development have definitely intensified environmental problems. [Specifically], landowners have filled in ponds to extend or construct new buildings thereby jeopardizing fragile ecosystems . . . wetlands and waterways are also being seriously damaged due to the dumping of raw sewage and other waste products, which in part can be traced to tourism. Guesthouses, restaurants and laundries generate substantial amounts of wastewater, which is not currently being adequately managed . . . there is no doubt that without adequate and enforceable regulations dealing with waste, the transportation system and wetland and waterway issues, the environmental conditions in Luang Prabang will be seriously threatened in the future. . . . Many residents of Luang Prabang link the increase in crime and drug abuse to the rise of tourism in the town and perceive that these will increase as tourism numbers grow" (UNESCO 2004: 66–70).

4. The number of tourists visiting Laos has risen in staggering fashion: from only 600 arrivals in 1988 to 636,361 in 2003 (UNESCO 2004: 59). The number of tourist arrivals in Laos climbed over 1 million in 2006 and was expected to exceed 1.2 million in 2007 and 2 million by 2010 (*Vientiane Times*, January 22, 2007, p. 3); tourism actually soared to 1.4 million in 2007 (http://www.voanews.com/lao/2008-01-04-voa3.cfm?rss=topstories).

5. See Holt (1981: 115–116) for a reprise of this initiation rite according to its classical articulation in Pali sources.

6. Including the practice of *ahimsa* (not to injure or kill living beings), *sacca* (to seek the truth and to eschew falsehood), to take only what is given to them, to be sexual ascetics, and to abstain from intoxicants.

7. For a description based on the Pali Vinaya source, see Holt (1981: 106–124). As for the number of fully ordained *bhikkhus*, the leading monk of the *sangha* in Luang Phrabang estimates their number at around 500, though my sense is that it is actually fewer than this.

8. H. L. Seneviratne (1999) has explored this issue at great length historically and analytically, including Bhikkhu Walpola Rahula's manifesto published *The Heritage of a Bhikkhu* (1974).

9. I may not be altogether fair in comparing the "night life" of the *samaneras* in Luang Phrabang to the behavior of Sri Lanka's monks, for the same observation can be made in relation to women's behavior as well. That is, in Sri Lanka, unaccompanied women are rarely seen at night, except in the capital city of Colombo, and even there it

is not common. In contrast, Lao women do not face this same behavioral restraint and freely move about during the evening. Yet more than one layman in Luang Phrabang mentioned that *samaneras* should not be outside of the temple after 5:00 p.m., and if they have evening classes, these should be held in the temple and not in locations that require them to be out on the streets.

10. See, for instance, Hans George Berger, *Laos* (2000) and his *The Floating Buddha* (2007).

11. One visitor from Holland in town to celebrate her son's wedding to a local Lao woman told me of an experience that captures the "hustle" of *bindabath*. After paying 20,000 kip and placing the rice into the monks' bowls, further unsolicited dollops of rice were placed on her banana leaf with loud demands for another 20,000 kip by an agitated hawker.

12. Around 300 *samaneras* participate in *bindabath* each morning. Per agreement, certain streets beyond a temple's *ban* are allocated for the novices of specific temples, a division of labor as it were.

13. My comment is no way intended to demean the importance of meditation. It is only meant to note that meditation has been greatly overemphasized by many who have sought to characterize the profile of Buddhist monasticism. A strain in Buddhist monasticism has always emphasized the importance of *samadhi*, or the subordination of ethics (*sila*) and wisdom (*panna*), rather than seeing these elements of the path as truly interdependent. But for many Westerners, Buddhism equals meditation. One well-intentioned, French-influenced Western NGO that recently set up shop in Luang Phrabang has provided funding for what it hopes will be an annual two-week "*vipassana* forest meditation retreat" for Luang Phrabang's *samaneras*. It has also funded the creation of a kind of Buddhist catechism booklet for *samaneras* to read in English, as well as a simple Pali-English dictionary and an illustrated primer on how to practice *vipassana*. One of its other projects has been to work with European expatriate and local professional photographers to mount an exhibition, entitled "Floating Buddhas" (!), at the Luang Phrabang National Museum, an exhibition that consists of photos of young novices in moments of deep meditation. This NGO has also provided the means for local schoolchildren to visit the exhibition so that they, in addition to the tourists, can see how Buddhism can be "authentically" practiced. Finally, it has provided the money to build a "meditation boat" so that monks will be able to practice meditation during a river cruise, away from the distractions of Luang Phrabang. This naïve but well-intentioned intervention dovetails nicely with the creation of a marketable image for Luang Phrabang that at the same time reasserts a normative image of what constitutes "real Buddhism," as opposed to "Lao folk tradition." Indeed, there is a continuing conversation among the senior monks of Luang Phrabang regarding the degree to which meditation should be emphasized. For the moment those who espouse the traditional *granthadhura* (learning and social service orientation) seem to hold the upper hand over the *vipassanadhura*, though the latter are certainly benefiting directly from this latest Western intervention.

14. In this regard Zago (1976: 125) was correct when he wrote that among those

from "minority groups [who] become Buddhists, one additionally notes a loss of ethnic identity and a tendency for the people to regard themselves as Lao."

15. Thirty years ago Zago (1976: 122), writing from his base in Vientiane reported:
"Recruits to the religious life are almost exclusively products of the countryside lacking public education facilities. Rarely does one come across a young monk whose father is a government official or ranking military officer." That pattern is certainly still
verified by my Luang Phrabang sample taken in 2006.

16. Elsewhere Hayashi (2003: 106) notes four types of ordained novices: those ordained (1) temporarily, as is custom, (2) as an offering to make merit for deceased
parents, (3) as a "return gift" for recovery from illness, and (4) to gain an education.

17. Ngaosrivathana (1995: 148–149): "Many parents are convinced that the ordination of a son will guarantee them a better place in their next lives; parents are said
to be 'lifted into heaven on the yellow robe of their son. . . .' The mother, in particular,
can gain enough merit through her son to achieve *nirvana*." Ngaosrivathana then cites
Zago (1972: 34): "If a son becomes as monk after marriage, parents believe that their
daughters-in-law will take away part of the merit they deserve for caring for their son
all those years. Hence, women of different generations, with often conflicting social
roles, as wife and mother must further compete out of necessity . . . to obtain the maxi-
mum merit from their sons and husbands. . . . A woman must get a monk to turn the
wheel for her. Only thus can she manipulate the system to her advantage."

18. Hayashi makes a similar finding among novices in the Lao villages of northeastern Thailand. "Although young monks learn the existence of the Buddhist afterlife
from adult worshippers who focus upon it as they prostrate themselves before the
monks on the ritual stage, unlike the adults, they do not see it as a reality. When they
are not performing rituals in which they confront the laity, their aspirations for the
future are oriented straight towards the temporal world" (2003: 314).

19. A very high number of waiters and busboys in Luang Phrabang's restaurants are former novices, as are a number of tourist guides working for local travel
agencies.

20. In early April, just before and during their final examinations, I spoke to a few
samaneras within days of disrobing. I wanted to know if they had any apprehension
about informing their abbots of their decisions. None expressed any whatsoever.

21. As noted in Chapter 2, the introduction of the French language and sociocultural values also introduced a new worldview to the Lao elite of Vientiane, but also to
the small elite, especially associated to Lao royalty, in Luang Phrabang. It is still not
unusual today to find middle-aged or older middle-class Lao in Luang Phrabang who
are fluent in French but not in English. The phalanx of returning French people connected to UNESCO and some Lao elite expatriates who have returned from abroad
has resulted in a minor renaissance of French in Luang Phrabang, but on the whole the
French language is simply being overwhelmed by English. However, English is not spoken very well by many, even by the novices who have spent four years trying to study it
in high school while sharpening their skills in encounters with tourists. My own conversations with Lao English-language teachers in charge of teaching the novices were

always quite stilted, often only half-understood, and usually very less than satisfying. What this indicates is that even if *samaneras* "speak to tourists in order to learn about other cultures," the quality and level of information that they receive, given the tourists as sources and the novices' language comprehension, is quite limited indeed.

22. There are three other accounts of Boun Phravet that need to be mentioned here: Marie-Daniel Faure, "The 'Bun' Pha-Vet (4th Month Festival), in Berval (1959: 294–297), Condominas (1968: 119–125), and Zago (1972: 290–297). However, the first is largely apologetic; the second, while detailed and erudite, is mostly expository; and the third, perhaps the most detailed and analytically keen, is generic and not related to any specific locale. So I have relied especially on Tambiah's account for comparative purposes, despite the fact that his study was located in a Lao Isan village.

23. Tiyavanich (1997: 26) points out the Lao in northeast Thailand continue to practice the same cycle of twelve annual festivals (*hit sipsong*) observed in Laos and goes on to say that "religious ritual was similar to those in the upland Lao kingdoms of Luang Prabang and Vientiane. Each Lao polity (*meuang*) had its own rituals, but . . . all Lao rituals were motivated by a search for fertility: the source of protection, renewal and rain." In this context, merit can be understood as yet another form of fertility, albeit spiritual in kind.

24. Its continued status in contemporary Laos is symbolized by its appearance on the 20,000 kip note.

25. In addition to the canonical 550 Pali *jataka*s, Saddhatissa (1979: 329) mentions the *Pannasajataka*, "a collection of fifty apocryphal *jataka*s" known to have been in wide circulation in Cambodia, Thailand, and Laos during the first half of the twentieth century. He provides summaries of seventeen of the most popular in this collection. The existence of this "auxiliary collection" further indicates the popularity of the *jataka* form among the Khmer, Thai, and Lao. Tiyavanich also discusses the primacy of the *jataka*s in the lives of the Lao in Isan or northeast Thailand: "Prior to the imposition of modern state Buddhism [in northeast Thailand], monks of the regional traditions used *jataka*s ('birth' stories) along with myths, legends and folk tales to convey dhamma. . . . The sangha inspectors' [of the royally sponsored Thammayut sect] reports provide evidence of the widespread popularity of jatakas in all regions. . . . The report is typical: 'Most monks preach about alms giving, generosity, precepts, and moral conduct. Basically, the monks' sermons consist of *jataka*s, especially the Great Birth Story' [*Vessantara Jataka*]. . . . In the northeastern region, where the Lao Buddhist tradition prevails, 'Lay people . . . prefer to listen to folk tales and *jataka*s, not dhamma sermons that expound doctrine. It is the villagers who choose the sermon they want to hear. They invariably choose folk stories such as Sang Sinchai, Phra Rot Meri, Phra Jao Liaplok, as well as the Wetsandon Chadok' [*Vessantara Jataka*]" (1997: 30–31).

26. This is a very skeletal summary. The most readable English translation of the text, accompanied by an excellent analytical introduction, is found in Gombrich and Cone (1977). A much more detailed summary of the *jataka*, with painted illustrations from eighteenth-century Kandy, can be found in Holt (1996: 81–89).

27. See Holt (1996: 81–89).

28. Edwards (2007: 100) notes that the recitation of the *Vessantara* was held at the end of the *vassa* rain retreat season in Cambodia and notes an eighteenth-century Khmer inscription that refers to the popularity of its recitation among the laity at Angkor.

29. See Holt and Meddegama (1993) for a translation of this text; and Saddhatissa (1979: 328) for a summary of the *Metteyasutta*.

30. In Tambiah's analysis he provides an outline summary of Heinrich Zimmer's well-known psycho-metaphysical explanation of the symbolism of immanence associated with the *naga* on the one hand and the symbolism of transcendence associated with the aviary *garuda* (Visnu's *vahana* or "vehicle") on the other. See Zimmer (1946: 74–76).

31. See the description by Nginn (1959: 266–271).

32. When I later asked the chief monk about the details of the *upasampada* rite, I was told that *upasamapda* could be held at any time of the year, though Boun Phravet and the two months leading up to Pi Mai, the Lao New Year, were usually regarded as the most auspicious time. He also mentioned that what I had observed (the "*naga* water" purification episode) at Boun Phravet was unusual and performed only on very special occasions. More frequently, a *naga basi* ceremony is performed instead to prepare the novice for *upasampada* proper. In the *naga basi* ceremony, while the *samanera* is still dressed in the white clothes of a laymen, the power of the *naga* is summoned in a *sukhwan* rite to assist in returning the candidate's *khwan* (spiritual essence or soul) completely to the body so that he is in perfect spirit and body balance at the time of *upasampada*.

33. On the authenticity of the Phra Bang image now in Luang Phrabang, Evans writes:

> Around this time of year in Luang Prabang a story has circulated every year since the disappearance of King Sisavang Vatthana, and one can hear it further afield. The story speculates about whether the Prabang today is real or just a copy. Rumor has it that the communist government removed the real one and placed it in a vault somewhere. I have heard this story many times, and this time in Luang Prabang one person assured me she had heard it from an official in the Ministry of Information and Culture in Luang Prabang, and therefore it had to be correct. Perhaps even more astonishingly, during an interview with me in May 1996, the vice president of the Lao sangha said, yes the Prabang in Luang Prabang is a fake. He claimed that in 1976 Sali Vongkhamsao, then attached to Prime Minister Kaysone's office, went to Luang Prabang with an entourage and brought the Prabang back to Vientiane, the seat of government. This story was obviously formed around the assumptions of traditional cosmology which assumed that now that the communists had taken over they were the heirs of its powers. Of course, I have no way of confirming the rumors one way or another. But what is important about this story from an anthropological point of view is that it suggests that people somehow feel that the ritual since 1975 has become debased and is even "fake," too. The fact that the person telling you the

story of the Prabang being a fake will go and pay homage to the Prabang during the New Year ritual confirms this interpretation, showing that the rumor reflects on the ritual as a whole rather than the object itself. It is also a comment on the collapse of the monarchy, on the pressure that Buddhism came under in the early years of revolution, and perhaps even a comment on the illegitimacy of the Lao government. For possession of the Prabang historically has been an objectification of the legitimacy of the Lao monarchy. The idea of it being a fake therefore withdraws this legitimacy from the communist regime. (1998: 139–140)

34. Evans provides a detailed account of the Phra Bang's lustration from his observations in the mid-to-late 1990s:

The parade of the Prabang from the old palace to Vat May remains one of the central religious activities of the New Year in Luang Prabang. This holy relic, the palladium of the former kingdom, after appropriate rituals by leading members of the sangha, is carried down the steps by museum attendants . . . , and placed in its palanquin, at which point scores of tourists with their cameras converge on the statue to photograph it, while older Luang Prabangese in traditional dress watch the spectacle nonplussed. Just before the descent of the Prabang, the foreign minister, Lengsavad and the *chao khouang* of Luang Prabang line up on the steps of the palace, also dressed in traditional *sampots*. Previously it would have been the king who followed the Prabang to Vat May, and begun its purification. Now a high official in the LPDR fills his shoes. . . . Over the next few days almost every family in Luang Prabang has at least one person go to pour water over the Prabang, despite the fact that the official New Year celebrations are over, and on the final night there is a veritably orgy of merit-making. But at the side of the temple as traditional orchestra strains to be heard over taped music, and attempts at traditional singing founder, to the disappointment of one older Luang Prabang man who lamented that older styles of singing rounds between men and women were being lost. The Prabang is then returned to the old palace on 18 April. Just inside the grounds, a new resting place for the Prabang, begun under the old regime, is being built with its main sponsor being the Lao government and business. (1998: 138–139)

35. The valorization of women in Southeast Asian Theravada Buddhism has received some recent attention in the works of Leedom Lefferts (1999) and others. In the conclusion to his "Women's Power and Theravada Buddhism," Lefferts writes: "Women also (re)produce the means by which all Lao and Thai Buddhist laypeople—men as well as women—obtain salvation." In other words, the very commonly held view in the West that women play only a highly subordinated role and are largely excluded in the religious cultures of Southeast Asia is now being contested. As I have observed throughout my fieldwork, the entire ritual system obtaining between the laity and the monks is completely dependent upon women.

Chapter 5: The Spirit(s) of the Place

Koret (2003: 200); Davis (1984: 300)

1. In a quite similar vein, Harris notes that in Khmer cultural contexts, "insofar as the land belonged to anyone, it belonged to the spirits of ancestors (*neak ta*). This meant that kings and other important personages did not claim ownership of the territory of Cambodia. Instead, they consumed it" (2005: 49); see also Zago (1972: 185–188).

2. Davis (1984: 43–52) writes extensively about household *phi*, spirits who oversee sexual propriety within the *heuan* (household) and are known to punish any transgressions that occur within the matrilineally defined sleeping space of the home. But, of course, these kinds of sexual transgressions would never have been brought up by women in the group conversations I have mentioned, especially not in conversations with a *falang* (foreigner) like me present. See also Zago's (1972: 189–190) brief discussion of *phi huan*.

3. Indeed, as Davis (1984: 81) has noted that among the Muang of Nan, "the word 'forest' has negative and often pejorative overtones. Contraband articles such as bootleg whiskey and unregistered firearms are called 'things of the forest wilderness' (*khaung paa khaung theuan*). Undisciplined and immoral people are designated in the same fashion. To 'go to the forest' (*pai paa*) means, in addition to its literal sense, to defecate or to enter a cemetery. The forest is the domain of aboriginals, wild animals and malevolent spirits." The same principle of undomesticated and potentially dangerous space may be applied to modern guesthouses as well, in the sense that these are usually inhabited by foreigners, who are basically unknown or unfamiliar social entities. A number of middle-class Lao in Luang Phrabang told me stories about malevolent *phi* in which the locations were either hotels or guesthouses. That is why, they say, the *phi huan* of the guesthouses need to be propitiated each day by their owners.

4. In an ordinary village formulation the *thewada* constitute a relatively undifferentiated category of divine benevolent agents. Tambiah noted (1970: 59) that this is quite unlike the Pali (and I add Sinhala) contexts, where a pronounced hierarchy exists and gods are known quite individually. Moreover, for the Lao, the origin of benevolent *thewada* deities is nonhuman. They are never reborn and are thus beyond the conditioning process of karmic retribution. That they can be enlisted to help diagnose problems caused by *phi* is also unique to Lao religious culture, insofar as all karmic actions in *samsara* are normatively understood within the Pali corpus of texts as being generated from the human sphere of *samsara*.

5. Previously I had concluded that the recent rise of spirit cults in Sri Lanka had been accompanied by a concomitant increase in conversions to evangelical and pentacostal strains of Christianity that stress the power of the Holy Spirit.

6. Condominas goes on to note that the practice of sacrificing a buffalo continued until 1975 at Vat Phu in Champasak and as recently as the 1940s in Vientiane. He also notes that it was once regularly performed in Chiang Mai as well. Davis (1984: 166–167) describes the "buffalo sukhwan" (sacrifice) among the Muang of Nan.

7. Tambiah (1970: 335) clearly distinguishes between those *phi* who have a distinguishing territorial aspect or identity, and malevolent *phi* who are seen as acting capriciously against individuals. "The major contrast is that the guardian spirits have a collective village significance as controllers of agricultural fertility and rain, and in this respect the cults addressed to them have a territorial and communal aspect. The malevolent spirits only act capriciously against individuals, and the rites addressed to remove their influence primarily concern the victim and his household, not necessarily the wider kingship group or the territorial community."

8. Hayashi writes:

In every village, a religious structure was built on the outskirts of the forest and another within the village: a shrine to house the village guardian spirit and a Buddhist temple, respectively. . . . In contrast to the practices centered on the Buddhist temple, which are most common throughout the country, the definition of "village guardian spirit" differs from village to village. Literally translated, the word *phi puta* means "spirit of both paternal and maternal grandfather," and accordingly tends to be interpreted as "ancestral spirits," but this is not always the case. Some people claim that it is the spirit of a specific person—one of the first settlers who opened the village, although the name has been forgotten—and others believe it is a spirit who lived in the forest before it was cleared and was changed into a benevolent guardian spirit by the first settlers. (2003: 93)

9. Tambiah (1970: 52) cites Alabaster's translation from Thai sources of the story of Nang Thoranee, who mounted a defense of the Buddha against the attacks of Mara's horde on the night of his enlightenment. When the Buddha calls forth the earth goddess as a witness to his attainment of enlightenment, she "sprang up from the earth in the shape of a lovely woman with long flowing hair, and standing before him answered: 'O beings more excellent than angels or men! It is true that when you performed your great works you ever poured water on my hair.' And with these words she wrung her hair, and a stream, a flood of waters gushed forth from it. Onwards against the host of Mara the mighty torrent rushed . . . and his whole army fled in utter confusion, amid the roarings of a terrible earthquake, and peals of thunder crashing through the skies." In Sri Lanka the defense of the Buddha against Mara's army is a famous episode associated intimately with the cult of Visnu. According to various mythic traditions, Visnu, Upulvan, or Dadimunda are credited with a martial defense of the Buddha against Mara and his army (Holt 2004: 102, 115–116, 126–127, 266–268). Elizabeth Guthrie (2004) has completed a masterful and comprehensive Ph.D. dissertation on the cult of Nang Thoranee in Southeast Asia.

10. Richard Gombrich's *Precept and Practice* (1971) comes immediately to mind as the primary example of this type of approach deployed in the Sinhala Sri Lankan context.

11. Hayashi (2003: 131; parentheses Hayashi's) reports that "every *mo tham* keeps *hun phatham* (*khun* being derived from the Malay *guna* meaning incantation) or

thamma (dharma; literally the teachings of the Buddha but here meaning "buddha-cized" protective power) in their main sleeping room on a *han phatham* (an altar or worship shelf enshrining the buddhacized protective power) similar to the one in the village pillar. . . . Protective powers, which are considered to be derived from Buddhist teachings, have replaced village guardian spirits as the medium of ensuring peace and security in the life world."

12. This is, of course, quite different from the manner in which Tambiah (1970: 330) had explained how the power of Buddhist *paahm*s (ritual specialists) was con-strued during his earlier time. In Tambiah's time and context, the power of the Bud-dhist exorcist was understood as completely magical and not ethically based at all: "The power of the exorcist's incantation is rooted in the belief that, although he does not know their meaning, they are taken from Buddhist texts (*paritta mantra, gatha*) and therefore regarded as powerful, subjugating the powers of malevolence."

13. However, Hayashi (2003: 97) reports that the transformations occurring in Lao villages of Isan are not entirely due to the singular efforts of this new type of religious practitioner, the *mo tham*. They are also the consequence of demographics, including the migration of outsiders into the Lao village milieu.

> Judging from the situation in each village since its founding, however, those villages that have retained a shrine to the guardian spirit have a greater number of clansmen who are related to the original founders. In villages where the shrine has been de-stroyed, the number of subsequent migrants exceeds the number of original settlers so that the people who built the shrine and their kin are a minority, or the *cham* who performed the rites and his relatives have left the village. . . . [Moreover,] later migrants [to the village] claim that they are protected not by a spirit, but by *dharma* (*thamma*). Thus the local guardian spirit, a part of village history from the time it was founded, was replaced by a Buddhist protective power that has no relation to the paddies and homes that originated in the forest. In this "religious reform," most of the Thai *tai* relate that no conflict occurred between the original settlers and themselves. . . . In the religious life of the village, local differences in belief and practice have been extinguished within the framework of the state religion of Bud-dhism. (2003: 86–87)

14. Later in her discussion Tiyanvanich (1997: 125) says that "adhering to the dis-ciplinary rules was an essential element in the teaching of *thudong* monks who drew confidence from the belief that purity and asceticism acted as protective shields." From the monks' perspective, discipline was a natural outgrowth of deep meditation practice and an advanced stage in self-purification (271).

15. In her study of the Shan, Nicola Tannenbaum (1987: 694) notes a similar phenomenon of Buddhacization occurring: "Buddhism converts the morally neutral power of tattoos, precept keeping, and meditation into an ethical power that people have because of their virtue."

16. Tambiah has nicely captured the relationality of the *triratna* in what follows

and then underscores how the actual powerful effect of hearing the *dhamma* counts for more than its actual discursive content among the laity.

> What the three "refuges" or "gems" of Buddhism state is that the Buddha, the all-enlightened one, was the source of the sacred words; the *Dhamma*, the doctrines preached by the Buddha and inscribed in the texts, are themselves holy objects in their own right, which when recited or indeed even when simply used as ritual objects can transmit virtue and dispel evil; and the *Sangha*, the monastic order whose ordained members practice good conduct, is the appropriate agent for the recital of the sacred words and performance of the accompanying ritual acts of transfer. ... One fascinating problem in the technology of the ritual is the paradox that the actual words recited deal with the great acts of renunciation of the world by the Buddha, but the grace transferred by virtue of their recitation is an affirmation of this world. (1970: 198)

17. This belief is not limited to the Lao. Harris (2005: 65) notes that in the Khmer context boat racing is not only for the prestige that it brings to monasteries if victorious, but the racing boats are said to represent the nourished spirit of the monastery. Tiyavanich (1997: 27) has a related view of the significance of boat racing: "Boat racing contests with monks in one boat and women in the other symbolized the same ritual male-female opposition and expression of fertility. Boat racing was specifically linked to the growth of rice. Good harvests depended on the rain and having the right amount of water in the fields. If the paddies were in danger of flooding, it was commonly believed that boat racing and singing would drive the water down."

18. Harris (2005: 680) notes that in Cambodia many Buddha images are thought to be the venue for spirits, especially female protective ones.

19. For a general yet cogent interpretive analysis of the symbolism of the stupa in Laos, see Zago (1972: 349–353); and especially Gabaude (1979).

20. Moreover, "through a mimetic ritual strategy, the deceased receives a new body after his death in [the] form [of] a *that kaduuk* reliquary. The funeral monument has to be conceptualized as a living representation of the deceased, housing its spirit and [is] therefore some kind of ancestral shrine" (Ladwig 2002: 130).

21. I underscore once again that Lao village monks hardly fit the template of a renouncing ascetic living a hermit-like life exclusively devoted to contemplative meditation. Village monks were and are always thoroughly integrated into the socioeconomic life of their villages, especially in Laos and especially after the 1975 revolution. Perhaps one could buddhacize their involvement by attributing the contributions of their hard labor to the practice of *karuna* or compassion for the laity. But more likely, their work is a matter of simply contributing directly to the back-breaking work that needs to be done in an agricultural subsistence economy in a village where most of the inhabitants are related. While a number of scholars have noted the nature of village monkhood, none have provided descriptions as graphic as Tiyanvanich:

A common feature of regional traditions was the assumption that monastics would remain engaged in village life. Regional monks organized festivals, worked on construction projects in the wat, tilled the fields, kept cattle or horses, carved boats, played musical instruments during the Bun Phawet festival, taught martial arts—and were still considered to be respectable *bhikkhu* (monks) all the while; cultural expectations and loyalties of kinship and community made all these activities legitimate ones for monks. . . . The wat was in fact the center of lay Buddhism. In regional traditions, the monastery served many functions necessary to community life. It was the town hall for meetings, a school, a hospital (monks provided herbal medicine and took care of the sick), a social and recreational center, a playground for children, an inn for visitors and travelers, a warehouse for keeping boats and other communal objects. And a wildlife refuge (if the wat was near a forest). Village or town abbots consequently remained very much in the world, devoting their energies to community work that benefited local people. (1997: 23)

Appendix 1

1. The discussion that follows is derived chiefly from the analytical reflections offered by Sachchidanand Sahai in his two-volume study, *The Rama Jataka in Laos* (1996).

2. For an excellent resume and discussion of representative versions of the *Ramayana* in South and Southeast Asia, see Richman (1991).

3. For translations from the Sanskrit of Valmiki, see Valmiki (1984–1991), translated by Goldman, and (1957–1962) translated by Shastri.

4. That Vientiane, rather than Xieng Dong Xieng Thong or Luang Phrabang, is named as the location of the Lao kingdom, gives us a general clue regarding the dating of this text. It could not precede the reign of Photihisarat (r. 1520–1547), the first king who resides in Vientiane, nor does it seem likely that it would date to his reign, insofar as it was only during the reign of his son Xetthathirat (1548–1571) that the center of the Lan Xang mandala was officially shifted to Vientiane from Luang Phrabang. Nor is it likely to be later than Surinyavongsa's long seventeenth-century rule (1638–1695). Both of the latter two reigns witnessed the fruition of the literary arts in Vientiane, so it is possible that this version dates from the mid-sixteenth century to late seventeenth century.

5. This is a very familiar motif in Sanskrit *purana* literature: a wrongly motivated devotee of Siva, intent on gaining power over the world, practices *tapas* (asceticism) to a degree that his power outstrips even that of Siva. Siva is forced to appeal to the other gods, usually Visnu, to assist him in bringing the usurper under control. This is the general pattern we witness in the first section of the *Phra Lak Phra Lam*, in which the Vientiane king appeals to Indra for divine assistance to correct the breach in *dharma* that Ravana has committed by abducting his daughter Canda.

6. Sahai (1996, I: 37) provides another note of interest here—marriages be-

tween siblings were authorized only in the Lao royal court and were forbidden for commoners.

7. There is another Pali *jataka* that recasts the first part of the *Ramayana*: the "Dasaratha Jataka," one of the 550 stories included in the canonical Pali *jataka* collection. For a discussion of its comparative significance, see Frank Reynolds (1994).

Appendix 2

1. Thorough descriptions of the ritual cult of *khwan* are found in French in Zago (1972: 149–170). My account is primarily indebted to Tambiah (1970: 223–251).

2. Ladwig (2002: 122, n. 5) suggests, given the number 32, that this theory is "probably modeled on Hindu and Buddhist conceptions of the body." While one can see some parallels with the *laksana*s and *atman*, the dimension of "essence" makes the parallel with Buddhist conceptions somewhat problematic. Though there is, of course, a long tradition of Brahmanism first emanating from the royal courts, I would suggest looking more in the direction of Chinese cultural contexts as well when looking for the religious origins of *khwan*. On this, see especially Granet (1977: 80–90, 149–151).

3. For three *sukhwan* liturgical texts used in *basi* celebrated before *samanera*s undertake the *upasampada* ordination, for weddings, and for pregnant women, see Tambiah (1970: 244–251).

4. "The exorcism ritual represents a different therapeutic situation, in which the exact reverse of the elements of the *sukhwan* ritual is represented. Here a person is mentally and physically ill because an alien external agent has entered him, which produces in the patient an alienation from society. The ritual technique here consists of persuading the patient to define his illness by naming the attacking agent, thereby enabling the patient to re-establish contact with society. The remarkable aspects of this theory of mental illness and therapy is that its cause is externalized and objectified in an outside force or agency. The patient thus is not held responsible for his illness; nor is it seen as being caused by events or processes generated inside the human organism. He does not carry the burden of guilt or personal responsibility" (Tambiah 1970: 336). Here it is clear that the notion of karma has not been universally applied, unlike in Sinhala Sri Lanka, where even a possession may be seen as at least partially caused by karma.

Bibliography

Abhay, Thao Nhouy. 1959. "The Baci." In *Kingdom of Laos: The Land of the Million Elephants and of the White Parasol*, ed. Rene de Berval, 128–131. Saigon: *France-Asie*.

Aijmer, Goran. 1979. "Reconciling Power with Authority: An Aspect of Statecraft in Traditional Laos." *Man* (new series) 14: 734–749.

Archaimbault, Charles. 1959. "La naissance du monde selon les traditions Lao: Le mythe de Khun Belom." In *La naissance du monde*. Sources orient. I. Paris: Editions du Seuil.

———. 1964. "Religious Structures of Laos." *Journal of the Siam Society* 52:57–74.

Asian Development Bank. 2007. www.adb.org/documents/ado/2007Lao.pdf

Bayly, Susan. 2000. "French Anthropology and the Durkheimians in Colonial Indochina." *Modern Asian Studies* 34:581–622.

Bechert, Heinz. 1966–1973. *Buddhismus, Staat und Gesellschaft*. 3 vols. Frankfurt: Institut fuer Asienkunde in Hamburg.

Bell, Catherine. 1992. *Ritual Theory, Ritual Practice*. New York: Oxford University Press.

Berger, Hans George. 2000. *Laos: Sacred Rituals of Luang Phrabang*. London: Westzone Press.

———. 2007. *The Floating Buddha*. Luang Phrabang: Printed privately.

Berval, Rene de. 1956. *Presence du Royaume Lao*. Special Issue of *France-Asie*. 12, nos. 118–120 (March–May 1956). Translated into English and published in 1959 as *Kingdom of Laos: The Land of the Million Elephants and of the White Parasol*. Saigon: *France-Asie*.

Bizot, François. 2001. "La place des communautés du Nord-Laos dans l'histoire du bouddhisme d'Asie du Sud-Est." *BEFEO* 87, 2:511–528.

Bouphanouvang, Nakhonkham. 2003. *Sixteen Years in the Land of Death: Revolution and Reeducation in Laos*. Bangkok: White Lotus Co. Ltd.

Boutsavath, Vongsavath, and Georges Chapelier. 1973. "Lao Popular Buddhism and Community Development." *Journal of the Siam Society* 61:1–38.

Castle, Timothy. 1993. *At War in the Shadow of Vietnam: U.S. Military Aid to the Royal Lao Government 1955–1975*. New York: Columbia University Press.

Coedes, Georges. 1925. "Documents sur l'histoire politique et religieuse du Laos occidental." *Bulletin de l'Ecole Francaise d'Extreme Orient* 25:1–201.

Condominas, Georges. 1968. "Notes sur le bouddhisme populaire en milieu rural Lao." *Archives de sociologie des religions* 25–26:81–150.

———. 1973. "Phiban Cults in Rural Laos." In *Change and Persistence in Thai Society*, ed. William Skinner and A. Thomas Kirsh, 252–273. Ithaca, NY: Cornell University Press.

Cousins, Judith, and Alfred McCoy. 1970. "Living It Up in Laos: Congressional Testimony on United States Aid to Laos in the 1950s." In *Laos: War and Revolution,* ed. Nina S. Adams and Alfred W. McCoy, 340–372. New York: Harper and Row.

Davis, Richard. 1984. *Muang Metaphysics: A Study in Northern Thai Myth and Ritual.* Bangkok: Pandora.

DeCaroli, Robert. 2004. *Haunting the Buddha: Indian Popular Religions and the Formation of Buddhism.* New York: Oxford University Press.

Dhammapada. 1987. John Carter and Mahinda Palihawadana, trans. New York: Oxford University Press.

Digha Nikaya. See Rhys Davids.

Dommen, Arthur. 1964. *Conflict in Laos.* New York: Praeger.

———. 1991. "Lao Nationalism and American Foreign Policy, 1954–9." In *Laos: Beyond the Revolution,* ed. Joseph J. Zasloff and Leonard Unger, 243–274. New York: St. Martin's Press.

Duncan, James. 1990. *The City as Text: The Politics of Landscape Interpretation in the Kandyan Kingdom.* Cambridge: Cambridge University Press.

Durkheim, Emile. 1995. *The Elementary Forms of Religious Life.* Trans. by Karen Fields. New York: The Free Press. Originally published 1912.

Edwards, Penny. 2007. *Cambodge: The Cultivation of a Nation, 1860–1945.* Honolulu: University of Hawai'i Press.

Eliade, Mircea. 1996. *Patterns in Comparative Religion.* Introduction by John Clifford Holt. Lincoln: University of the Nebraska Press. Originally published in 1958.

Evans, Grant. 1990. *Lao Peasants under Socialism.* New Haven: Yale University Press.

———. 1993. "Buddhism and Economic Action in Laos." In *Socialism: Ideals, Ideologies and Local Practices,* ed. C. M. Hann, 132–147. New York: Routledge.

———. 1998. *The Politics of Ritual Memory: Laos since 1975.* Honolulu: University of Hawai'i Press.

———. 2002a. "Immobile Memories: Statues in Thailand and Laos." In *Cultural Crisis and Social Memory: Modernity and Identity in Thailand and Laos,* ed. Shigeharu Tanabe and Charles F. Keyes, 154–182. Honolulu: University of Hawai'i Press.

———. 2002b. *A Short History of Laos.* Chiang Mai: Silkworm Books.

———. 2003. "Different Paths: Lao Historiography in Historical Perspective." In *Contesting Visions of the Lao Past: Lao Historiography at the Crossroads,* ed. Christopher E. Goscha and Soren Ivarsson, 97–110. Copenhagen: Nordic Institute of Asian Studies.

Gabaude, Louis. 1979. *Les Cetiya de Sable au Laos et en Thaïlande: Les Textes.* Paris: EFEO.

Gay, Bernard. 2002. "Millenarian Movements in Laos, 1895–1936: Depictions by Modern Lao Historians." In *Breaking New Ground in Lao History: Essays on the Seventh to Twentieth Centuries*, ed. Mayoury Ngaosrivathana and Kennon Brezeale, 281–296. Chiang Mai: Silkworm Books.

Geertz, Clifford. 1971. *Islam Observed: Religious Developments in Morocco and Indonesia.* Chicago: University of Chicago Press.

———. 1981. *Negara: The Theater State in Nineteenth Century Bali.* Princeton, NJ: Princeton University Press.

Godakumbura, C. E. 1970. "Sinhalese Festivals: Their Symbolism, Origins and Proceedings." *Journal of the Royal Asiatic Society* (Ceylon Branch) (n.s.) 14:91–131.

Gombrich, Richard. 1971. *Precept and Practice: Traditional Buddhism in the Rural Highlands of Ceylon.* Oxford: The Clarendon Press.

———, and Margaret Cone. 1977. *The Perfect Generosity of Prince Vessantara.* Oxford: Oxford University Press.

———, and Gananath Obeyeskere. 1988. *Buddhism Transformed: Religious Change in Sri Lanka.* Princeton, NJ: Princeton University Press.

Goscha, Christopher. 2003. "Revolutionizing the Indochinese Past: Communist Vietnam's 'Special' Historiography on Laos." In *Contesting Visions of the Lao Past: Lao Historiography at the Crossroads*, ed. Christopher E. Goscha and Soren Ivarsson, 265–299. Copenhagen: Nordic Institute of Asian Studies.

Grabowsky, Volker. 1997. "Origins of Lao and Khmer National Identity: The Legacy of the Early Nineteenth Century." In *Nationalism and Cultural Revival in Southeast Asia: Perspectives from the Centre and the Region*, ed. Sri Kuhnt-Saptodewo, Volker Grabowsky, and M. Grossheim, 145–167. Wiesbaden: Harrassowitz Verlag.

Granet, Marcel. 1977. *The Religion of the Chinese People.* New York: Harper and Row. Originally published in 1922.

Gunn, Geoffrey C. 1982. "Theravadins and Commissars: The State and National Identity in Laos." In *Contemporary Laos: Studies in the Politics and Society of Lao People's Democratic Republic*, ed. Martin Stuart-Fox, 76–99. New York: St. Martin's Press.

———. 2003. *Rebellion in Laos: Peasant and Politics in a Colonial Backwater.* Revised edition. Bangkok: White Lotus Press.

Guthrie, Elizabeth. 2004. "A Study of the History and Cult of the Buddhist Earth Deity in Mainland Southeast." Ph.D. diss., University of Canterbury (Christchurch, NZ).

Guthrie, Stewart Elliott. 1993. *Faces in the Clouds: A New Theory of Religion.* New York: Oxford University Press.

Hansen, Anne. 2007. *How to Behave: Buddhism and Modernity in Colonial Cambodia.* Honolulu: University of Hawai'i Press.

Hardacre, Helen, and Alan Sponberg. 1988. *Maitreya: The Future Buddha.* New York: Cambridge University Press.

Harris, Ian. 2005. *Cambodian Buddhism: History and Practice.* Honolulu: University of Hawai'i Press.

Hayashi, Yukio. 2003. *Practical Buddhism among the Thai-Lao: A Regional Study of Religion in the Making.* Kyoto: Kyoto University Press.

Holt, John Clifford. 1981. *Discipline: The Canonical Buddhism of the Vinayapitaka.* Delhi: Motilal Banarsidass.

———. 1991a. *Buddha in the Crown: Avalokitesvara in the Religious Traditions of Sri Lanka.* New York: Oxford University Press.

———. 1991b. "Protestant Buddhism?" *Religious Studies Review* 17:307–312.

———. 1996. *The Religious World of Kirti Sri: Buddhism, Art and Politics in Late Medieval Sri Lanka.* New York: Oxford University Press.

———. 2004. *The Buddhist Visnu: Religious Transformation, Politics and Culture.* New York: Columbia University Press.

———, ed., and U. P. Meddegama, trans. 1993. *The Anagatavamsa Desana: The Sermon of the Chronicle-to-be.* Delhi: Motilal Banarsidass.

Iijima, Akiko. 2003. "The Nyuan in Xayabury and Cross-Border Links to Nan." In *Contesting Visions of the Lao Past: Lao Historiography at the Crossroads,* ed. Christopher E. Goscha and Soren Ivarsson. Copenhagen: Nordic Institute of Asian Studies.

Ivarsson, Soren. 2003. "Making Laos 'Our' Space: Thai Discourses on History and Race, 1900–1940." In *Contesting Visions of the Lao Past: Lao Historiography at the Crossroads,* ed. Christopher E. Goscha and Soren Ivarsson, 239–264. Copenhagen: Nordic Institute of Asian Studies.

Jackson, Peter A. 2003. *Buddhadasa: Theravada Buddhism and Modernist Reform in Thailand.* Chiang Mai: Silkworm Books.

Keomanichanh, Virachit. 1979. *India and Laos: A Study of Early Cultural Contacts.* New Delhi: Books Today.

Kettate, Boonyong. 2000. "The Ancestral Spirit Forest (*Dan Pu Tai*) and the Role Behavior of Elders (*Thao Cham*) in Northeast Thailand." *The Journal of the Siam Society* 88:96–110.

Keyes, Charles F. 1977. "Millennialism, Theravāda Buddhism and Thai Society." *Journal of Asian Studies* 36:283–302.

———. 2002. "National Heroine or Local Spirit? The Struggle over Memory in the Case of Thao Suranari of Nakhon Ratchasima." In *Cultural Crisis and Social Memory: Modernity and Identity in Thailand and Laos,* ed. Shigeharu Tanabe and Charles F. Keyes, 113–136. Honolulu: University of Hawai'i Press.

King, Winston. 1992. *Theravada Meditation: The Buddhist Transformation of Yoga.* New edition. Delhi: Motilal Banarsidass.

Kirsch, Thomas. 1977. "Complexity in the Thai Religious System: An Interpretation." *Journal of Asian Studies* 36 (1977):241–266.

Koret, Peter. 2003. "*Luep Phasun* (Extinguishing the Light of the Sun): Romance, Religion and the Politics of Interpretation in the Interpretation of a Traditional Lao Poem." In *Contesting Visions of the Lao Past: Lao Historiography at the Cross-*

roads, ed. Christopher E. Goscha and Soren Ivarsson, 181–208. Copenhagen: Nordic Institute of Asian Studies.

Kremmer, Christopher. 2003. *Bamboo Palace: Discovering the Lost Dynasty of Laos*. Sydney: HarperCollins Publishers.

Ladwig, Patrice. 2000. "Relics 'Representation' and Power: Some Remarks on Stupas Containing Relics of the Buddha in Laos." *Tai Culture* 5:70–84.

———. 2002. "The Mimetic Representation of the Dead and Social Space among the Buddhist Lao." *Tai Culture* 7:120–134.

Lafont, Pierre-Bernard. 1982. "Buddhism in Contemporary Laos." In *Contemporary Laos: Studies in the Politics and Society of the Lao's People Democratic Republic*, ed. Martin Stuart-Fox, 148–162. New York: St. Martin's Press.

Larcher-Goscha, Agathe. 2003. "On the Trail of an Itinerant Explorer: French Colonial Historiography on Auguste Pavie's Work in Laos." In *Contesting Visions of the Lao Past: Lao Historiography at the Crossroads*, ed. Christopher E. Goscha and Soren Ivarsson, 209–238. Copenhagen: Nordic Institute of Asian Studies.

Lefferts, Leedom. 1999. "Women's Power and Theravada Buddhism: A Paradox from Xieng Khouang." In *Laos, Culture and Society*, ed. Grant Evans, 215–225. Chiang Mai: Silkworm Books.

Levy, Paul. 1940. "Les traces de l'introduction du Bouddhisme a Luang Prabang." *Bulletin de l'Ecole Francaise d'Exteme Orient* 40:411–424.

Lockhart, Bruce. 2003. "Narrating 1945 in Lao Historigraphy." In *Contesting Visions of the Lao Past: Lao Historiography at the Crossroads*, ed. Christopher E. Goscha and Soren Ivarsson, 129–164. Copenhagen: Nordic Institute of Asian Studies.

Lorrillard, Michel. 2003. "The Earliest Lao Buddhist Monasteries According to Philological and Epigraphic Sources." In his *The Buddhist Monastery: A Cross-cultural Survey*, 139–148. Paris: Ecole Francaise d'Extreme Orient.

Mabbett, I. W., and D. P. Chandler. 1975. Introduction. In *India as Seen from the East: Indian and Indigenous Cults in Champa*, ed. I. W. Mabbett and D. P. Chandler. Monash: Monash University Centre for Southeast Asian Studies; Monash Papers on Southeast Asia, No. 3. Originally published as "Cultes indiens et indigenes au Champa." *Bulletin de l'Ecole Francaise d'Extreme Orient* 33 (1933):367–410.

The Mahavamsa. 1964. Wilhelm Geiger, ed. and trans. London: Luzac and Co. for the Pali Text Society.

Malalgoda, Kitsiri. 1976. *Buddhism in Sinhalese Society: 1750–1900*. Berkeley: University of California Press.

Malandra, Geri H. 1993. *Unfolding a Mandala: The Buddhist Caves at Ellora*. Albany: State University of New York Press.

Marston, John, and Elizabeth Guthrie, eds. 2004. *History, Buddhism and New Religious Movements in Cambodia*. Honolulu: University of Hawai'i Press.

McArthur, Meher. 2002. *Reading Buddhist Art: An Illustrated Guide to Buddhist Signs and Symbols*. New York: Thames & Hudson.

McCoy, Alfred W. 1970. "French Colonial Laos, 1893–1945." In *Laos: War and Revolu-*

tion, ed. Nina S. Adams and Alfred W. McCoy, 67–99. New York: Harper and Row.

———. 1991. *The Politics of Heroin in Southeast Asia: CIA Complicity in the Global Drug Trade.* Revised edition. Brooklyn, NY. Lawrence Hill.

McDaniel, Justin. 2002a. "The Curricular Canon in Northern Thailand and Laos." *Manusya: Journal of Thai Language and Literature Special Issue:* 20–59.

———. 2002b. "Transformative History: *Nihon Ryoiki* and *Jinakalamalipakaranam.*" *Journal of the International Association of Buddhist Studies* 25:151–207.

———. 2008. *Gathering Leaves and Lifting Words: Histories of Buddhist Monastic Education in Laos and Thailand.* Seattle: University of Washington Press.

McMullen, David. 1987. "Bureaucrats and Cosmology: The Ritual Code of T'ang China." In *Rituals of Royalty and Ceremonial Traditional Societies,* ed. David Cannadine and Simon Price, 181–236. Cambridge: Cambridge University Press.

Mendelson, E. Michael. 1975. *Sangha and State in Burma.* Ed. John P. Ferguson. Ithaca, NY: Cornell University Press.

Morev, Lev N. 2002. "Religion in Laos Today." *Religion, State and Society* 30:395–407.

Mus, Paul. 1935. *Barabudur.* Paris: Ecole Francaise d'Extreme-Orient.

———. 1975. *India Seen from the East: Indian and Indigenous Cults in Champa.* Trans. from the French by I. W. Mabbett, ed. I. W. Mabbett and D. P. Chandler. Monash: Monash University Centre of Southeast Asian Studies; Monash Papers on Southeast, No. 3. Originally published as "Cultes indiens et indigenes au Champa." *Bulletin d'Ecole Francaise d'Extreme Orient* 33 (1933):367–410.

Ngaosrivathana, Mayoury. 1990. "On the Edge of the Pagoda: Lao Women in Buddhism." Thai Studies Project, Canadian International Development Agency. Paper No. 5. York, Canada: York University.

———. 1995. "Buddhism, Merit Making and Gender: The Competition for Salvation in Laos." In *"Male" and "Female" in Developing Southeast Asia,* ed. Wazir Jahan Karim, 145–160. Washington, DC: Berg Publishers.

Nginn, Pierre S. 1959. "New Year Festivities (5th month Festival)." In *Kingdom of Laos: The Land of the Million Elephants and of the White Parasol,* ed. Rene de Berval. Saigon: *France-Asie.*

Owen, Taylor, and Ben Kiernan. "Bombs over Cambodia: New Light on US Air War." http://japanfocus.org/products/details/2420

Pholsena, Vatthana. 2006. *Post-War Laos: The Politics of Culture, History and Identity.* Ithaca, NY: Cornell University Press.

Phothisane, Souneth. 2002. "Evolution of the Chronicle of Luang Prabang: A Comparison of Sixteen Versions." In *Breaking New Ground in Lao History: Essays on the Seventh to Twentieth Centuries,* ed. Mayoury Ngaosrivathana and Kennon Brezeale, 73–94. Chiang Mai: Silkworm Books.

Pye, Lucien. 1985. *Asian Power and Politics: The Cultural Dimensions of Authority.* Cambridge, MA: Harvard University Press.

Rahula, Walpola. 1974. *The Heritage of a Bhikkhu.* New York: Grove Press.

Reynolds, Frank E. 1969. "Ritual and Social Hierarchy: Traditional Religion in Buddhist Laos." *History of Religions* 9:78–89.

———. 1994. "*Ramayana, Rama Jataka* and *Ramakien*: A Comparative Study of Hindu and Buddhist Traditions." In *Many Ramayanas: The Diversity of a Narrative Tradition in South Asia*, ed. Paula Richman, 50–63. Berkeley: University of California Press.

Rhys Davids, T. W., and C. A. F. Rhys Davids, eds. and trans. 1921. *Dialogues of the Buddha (Digha Nikaya)*. 3 vols. London: Pali Text Society.

Richman, Paula. 1991. *Many Ramayanas: The Diversity of a Narrative Tradition*. Berkeley: University of California Press.

Sahai, Sachchindanand, ed. and trans. 1996. *The Rama Jataka in Laos: A Study in the Phra Lak Phra Lam*. 2 vols. Delhi: B.R. Publishing Co.

Sarkisyanz, E. 1965. *Buddhist Backgrounds of the Burmese Revolution*. The Hague: Martinus Nijhoff.

Seneviratne, H. L. 1978. *Rituals of the Kandyan State*. Cambridge: Cambridge University Press.

———. 1999. *The Work of Kings: The New Buddhism of Sri Lanka*. Chicago: University of Chicago Press.

Sisouphanthong, Bounthavy, and Christian Taillard. 2000. *Atlas of Laos: Spatial Structures of the Economic and Social Development of the Lao People's Democratic Republic*. Copenhagen: Nordic Institute of Asian Studies.

Smith, Jonathan Z. 2005. "Introduction." In *The Myth of the Eternal Return,* by Mircea Eliade, ix–xxi. 2nd ed. Princeton, NJ: Princeton University Press.

Soontravanich, Chalong. 2003. "Sila Viravong's *Phonsawadan Lao*: A Reappraisal." In *Contesting Visions of the Lao Pas: Lao Historiography at the Crossroads*, ed. Christopher E. Goscha and Soren Ivarsson, 111–128. Copenhagen: Nordic Institute of Asian Studies.

Southwold, Martin. 1983. *Buddhism in Life: The Practice of Sinhalese Buddhism and the Anthropological Study of Religion*. Manchester: University of Manchester Press.

Spiro, Melford. 1967. *Burmese Supernaturalism*. Englewood Cliffs, NJ: Prentice-Hall.

Strong, John S. 1991. *The Legend and Cult of Upagupta: Sanskrit Buddhism in North India and Southeast Asia*. Princeton, NJ: Princeton University Press.

———. 2004. *The Relics of the Buddha*. Princeton, NJ: Princeton University Press.

Stuart-Fox, Martin. 1983. "Marxism and Theravada Buddhism: The Legitimation of Political Authority in Laos." *Pacific Affairs* 56:428–454.

———. 1996. *Buddhist Kingdom, Marxist State: The Making of Modern Laos*. Bangkok: White Lotus Press.

———. 1997. *A History of Laos*. Cambridge: Cambridge University Press.

———. 1998. *The Lao Kingdom of Lan Xang: Rise and Decline*. Bangkok: White Lotus Press.

———. 2002. "Historiography, Power and Identity: History and Political Legitimisation in Laos." In *Contesting Visions of the Lao Past: Lao Historiography at the*

Crossroads, ed. Christopher E. Goscha and Soren Ivarsson, 71–96. Copenhagen: Nordic Institute of Asian Studies.

———, and Rod S. Bucknell. 1982. "Politicization of the Buddhist Sangha in Laos." *Journal of Southeast Asian Studies* 13:60–80.

Swearer, Donald K. 2004. *Becoming the Buddha?* Princeton, NJ: Princeton University Press.

———, and Somai Premchit. 1995. *The Legend of Queen Camadevi.* Albany: State University of New York Press.

Tambiah, S. J. 1970. *Buddhism and the Spirit Cults of Northeast Thailand.* Cambridge: Cambridge University Press.

———. 1976. *World Conqueror, World Renouncer.* Cambridge: Cambridge University Press.

———. 1992. *Buddhism Betrayed?* Chicago: University of Chicago Press.

Tanabe, Shigeharu, and Charles Keyes, eds. 2002. *Cultural Crisis and Social Memory: Modernity and Identity in Thailand and Laos.* Honolulu: University of Hawai'i Press.

Tannenbaum, Nicola. 1987. "Tattoos: Invulnerability and Power in Shan Cosmology." *American Ethnologist* 14:693–711.

Terwiel, Baas J. 1978a. "The Origin and Meaning of the Tai City Pillar." *Journal of the Siam Society* 66:159–171.

———. 1978b. "The Tais and Their Belief in Khwans: Towards Establishing an Aspect of 'Proto-Tai' Culture." *The South East Asian Review* 3:1–16.

Tiyavanich, Kamala. 1997. *Forest Recollections: Wandering Monks in Twentieth-century Thailand.* Honolulu: University of Hawai'i Press.

Trankell, Ing-Britt. 1999. "Royal Relics: Ritual and Social Memory in Louang Prabang." In *Laos: Culture and Society,* ed. Grant Evans, 191–213. Chiang Mai: Silkworm Books.

UNESCO. 2004. *Impact: The Effects of Tourism on Culture and the Environment in Asia and the Pacific: Tourism and Heritage Site Management in Luang Prabang, Lao PDR.* Bangkok: Office of the Regional Advisor for Culture in Asia and the Pacific, UNESCO, Bangkok, and the School of Travel Industry Management, University of Hawai'i.

Valmiki. 1957–1962. *The Ramayana.* Trans. by Hari Prasad Shastri. 3 vols. London: Shanti Sadan.

———. 1984–1991. *The Ramayana of Valmiki.* Trans. by Robert Goldman. 5 vols. Princeton, NJ: Princeton University Press.

Veidlinger, Daniel M. 2007. *Spreading the Dhamma: Writing, Orality and Textual Transmission in Northern Thailand.* Honolulu: University of Hawai'i Press.

Vickery, Michael. 2003. "Two Historical Records of the Kingdom of Vientiane." In *Contesting Visions of the Lao Past: Lao Historiography at the Crossroads,* ed. Christopher E. Goscha and Soren Ivarsson. Copenhagen: Nordic Institute of Asian Studies.

Warner, Roger. 1996. *Shooting at the Moon: The Story of America's Clandestine War in Laos*. South Royalton, VT: Steerforth Press.

Wolters, O. W. 1982 and 1999. *History, Culture and Region in Southeast Asian Perspectives* Singapore: Institute of Southeast Asian Studies. Revised edition. Ithaca, NY: Southeast Asia Publications, Southeast Asia Program, Cornell University.

Zago, Marcello. 1972. *Rites et Ceremonies en Milieu Bouddhiste Lao*. Rome: Universita Gregoriana Editrice.

———. 1976. "Buddhism in Contemporary Laos." In *Buddhism in the Modern World*, ed. Heinrich Dumoulin and John C. Maraldo, 120–129. London: Collier Macmillan Publishers.

Zimmer, Heinrich. 1946. *Myth and Symbol in Indian Art and Civilization*. Princeton, NJ: Princeton University Press.

Index

Abhay, Thao Nhouy, 272–274
agriculture: Buddhist novice origins, 203–204; collectivization, 154–159, 165; Laos population engaged in, 8, 203; slash-and-burn, 8, 135, 179, 188, 276n9, 297n59; Sri Lanka, 14
Aijmer, Goran, 35, 36–38
Americans. *See* United States
anatta ("without self"), 13, 177
ancestors: creation by primordial, 38; "divine right" of kings descended from, 34, 36–37; veneration of, 4, 26, 31, 39, 44, 49, 51, 62, 251, 307n39
Angkor, 56, 60, 94, 281n29; *devaraja* cult, 48–49, 65; Fa Ngum/Lan Xang influences, 34, 41–42, 280n28, 282n36; kingship, 48–49, 280n25; mandala polity, 4, 29, **33** map, 39, 48–50; UNESCO World Heritage Site, 192; *Vessantara Jataka*, 312n28. *See also* Cambodia
animism. *See* spirit cults
Annam. *See* Vietnam
Anouvong, Chao, 72–75, 163, 166, 286n75; 287nn78, 79, 294n37, 296n51
Anuradhapura, 13–14, 192
Archaimbault, Charles, 37
architecture: French-Lao, 93, 188; *vat*, 67, 73
art: Anou's revolt, 286n75; "Cultural Survival in Luang Prabang," 190; Fa Ngum depictions, 169, 282n35; Lan Xang, 58, **58** photo, **59** photo, 69; *Ramayana*, 267–269, **268** photo; "socialist realism," **167** photo, 168; *Vessantara Jataka*, 58, **58** photo, **59** photo, 212. *See also*

architecture; Buddha images; statues; temples
Asoka, Emperor, 13, 39
Atlas of Laos (Sisouphanthong and Taillard), 8, 205
authenticity, 183, 184, 191, 192–193, 294n40
Avalokitesvara, 63, 283n52
axis mundi: *lak muang*, 29; Mount Meru, 48; *phi* shrine, 61; Phra Bang, 47
Ayutthaya, 45–46, 54, 68, 280n28; Fa Ngum/Lan Xang connections, 42, 55–56; Lan Na and, 66, 281n29; mandala polity, 29, 34, 70

ban. See villages
Bandaranaike, S.W.R.D., 102
Bangkok, 71, 288n6; Buddhism, 10, 93–94, 97; Chakri dynasty, 71, 72, 76, 81, 243; Lao of Isan, 243–244, 248; mandala polity, 71–75, 77–78, 86, 243; modernization, 76–77, 86, 93, 148, 178, 288n5; nation-state, 80, 243; Thai dialect, 10, 98; Thai monarchy, 100, 173. *See also* Siam; Thailand
Ban Phra Muan, 213–214, 220
basi ceremony, 235, 271–274, 312n32
beauty pageants, 221, 222. *See also* Miss Lao
Berval, Rene de, 105
bhikkhu monks, 13, 193–210, **197** photo, 219, 256, 308n7
bindabath, 197–198, **197** photo, 204, 209, 309nn11, 12
bodhisatta-prince, 40, 211
bodhi tree (*Ficus religiosus*), 51, 284n54

About the Author

John Clifford Holt is William R. Kenan, Jr., Professor of Humanities in Religion and Asian Studies at Bowdoin College in Brunswick, Maine. He has authored numerous books, among them *The Buddhist Visnu: Religious Transformation, Politics and Culture* (2004), *The Religious World of Kirti Sri: Buddhism, Art and Politics in Late Medieval Sri Lanka* (1996), and *Buddha in the Crown: Avalokitesvara in the Buddhist Traditions of Sri Lanka* (1991), for which he received an American Academy of Religion Book Award for Excellence. His research awards include fellowships from the National Endowment for the Humanities and the Fulbright Program. He has taught around the world, at the University of Peradeniya, Hong Kong University of Science and Technology, and the University of Calgary, and received numerous awards, including an honorary Doctor of Letters from the University of Peradeniya and Alumnus of the Year (2007) from the University of Chicago Divinity School. His next book, *Sri Lanka: History, Politics, and Culture* is scheduled for publication in 2010.